# THE AMERICAN SYMPHONY

# The American Symphony

Neil Butterworth

**Ashgate**

Aldershot • Brookfield USA • Singapore • Sydney

Published by
Ashgate Publishing Limited
Gower House
Croft Road
Aldershot
Hants GU11 3HR
England

Ashgate Publishing Company
Old Post Road
Brookfield
Vermont 05036–9704
USA


British Library Cataloguing-in-Publication data

Butterworth, Neil
    The American symphony
    1. Symphony – United States
    I. Title
    784.1'84'0973

Library of Congress Cataloging-in-Publication data

Butterworth, Neil, 1934–
    The American symphony / Neil Butterworth.
    Includes bibliographical references, discography, and index.
    1. Symphony – United States. I. Title.
ML 1255.B985    1998
784.2'184'0973—dc21          98–14764
                                    CIP
                                    MN


ISBN 1 85928 459 0

Printed on acid-free paper

Typeset in Sabon by Bournemouth Colour Press, Parkstone, Poole, Dorset and printed in Great Britain by Biddles.

# Contents

# List of plates

# Preface

My enthusiasm for American music began when I was a teenager, after acquiring those pioneering 78rpm recordings of Aaron Copland's *El Salón México* and Roy Harris's Third Symphony and Bruno Walter's performance of the First Symphony of Samuel Barber. A year as a student at London University enabled me to visit the United States Information Service Library to borrow records, scores and books on a wide range of American music that was almost totally unknown on this side of the Atlantic.

Since no book on the subject was published in Britain at that time, I decided to redress the balance. The result, my *Dictionary of American Composers*, occupied me for over 20 years, by which time Wilfred Mellers had written *Music in a New Found Land* and the recording companies had begun to issue orchestral works by American composers, in particular the valuable series conducted by Howard Hanson.

In my position as Head of Music at Napier College in Edinburgh, I was able to perform many works by American composers, including British premières of music by Barber, Bernstein, Copland, Cowell, Diamond, Hovhannes, Virgil Thomson and others. Today the situation has vastly improved with an abundance of compact discs available throughout the world. A glance at the discography at the end of this book will reveal the healthy state of the market as we approach the end of the twentieth century.

I hope that this study of the symphonies of American composers will draw further attention to the riches of a repertoire that deserves to be known to all lovers of serious music.

Neil Butterworth

# Acknowledgements

In compiling this book I am deeply indebted to the many composers who have provided information unobtainable from any other sources and for their advice in improving the text. Considerable assistance was also given generously by various musical organizations, notably the American Composers' Alliance, the American Society of Composers, Authors and Publishers and from music publishers.

Michael Keyton of Dallas, Texas supplied many dates of composers for the catalogue of symphonies. I shall be pleased to receive additional data for this section of the book.

I also wish to thank the following publishers for permission to include musical examples.

*Associated Music Publishers*

| | |
|---|---|
| Roy Harris | Symphony No.3 c. 1939 |
| | Symphony No.7 c. 1956 |
| Alan Hovhaness | Symphony No.2 c. 1958 |
| Charles Ives | Symphony No.3 c. 1991 |
| Walter Piston | Symphony No.4 c. 1953 |
| | Symphony No.6 c. 1957 |
| William Schuman | Symphony No.3 c. 1941 |
| | Symphony No.5 c. 1943 |
| | Symphony No.6 c. 1952 |

*Boosey and Hawkes*

| | |
|---|---|
| Leonard Bernstein | Jeremiah Symphony c. 1949 Estate of Leonard Bernstein and Leonard Bernstein Music Publishing Co. The Age of Anxiety c. 1950 Estate of Leonard Bernstein and Leonard Bernstein Music Publishing Co. |
| Aaron Copland | Dance Symphony c. 1931 The Aaron Copland Fund for Music Inc. |

First Symphony c. 1931 The Aaron Copland Fund for Music Inc.
Short Symphony c. 1955 The Aaron Copland Fund for Music Inc.
Third Symphony c. 1947 The Aaron Copland Fund for Music Inc.

*Carl Fischer Inc.*
Howard Hanson          Symphony No.1 c. 1932
                       Symphony No.2 c. 1945, 1955
Peter Mennin           Symphony No.7 c. 1967

*Alfred A. Kalmus Ltd* on behalf of *Theodore Presser Co.*
William Schuman        Symphony No.8 c. 1962
                       Symphony No.9 c. 1971

*G. Schirmer Inc.*
Samuel Barber          Symphony No.1 c. 1970
                       Symphony No.2 c. 1950

# Introduction

In this book I have attempted to bring together relevant material from diverse sources to create a clear and comprehensive progression of the symphony in America, from the earliest European influences to the present day. Where appropriate I have treated the works of major composers in some detail including analysis. To some degree this reflects personal preference but the results are intended to be objective and proportionate to the artistic standing and achievements of these figures.

The great Austro-German symphonic heritage which began in the eighteenth century with Haydn and Mozart, through Beethoven, Brahms and Bruckner, virtually died out with Mahler. In the twentieth century only Karl Amadeus Hartmann and Hans Werner Henze dedicated themselves to writing symphonies. Hindemith is a special case; two of his six symphonies are derived from operas, one is for symphonic wind band. The Symphony in E flat, the *Sinfonia Serena* and the Pittsburgh Symphony conform to traditional patterns.

Very few Frenchmen have kept the symphonic flag flying in their country. For the past 400 years, the Italians have been more concerned with opera. Gian Francesco Malipiero amassed an impressive 16 symphonies, but these need to be set in context beside over 35 operas he wrote. Even Respighi, who alone in Italy championed the orchestra during the first part of the twentieth century, wrote only one work with symphony in the title.: *Sinfonia Drammatica* (1913–14). Only in the Soviet Union, and to a lesser extent in Great Britain, have leading composers maintained a flow of symphonies, comparable to that of their American contemporaries.

Why, then, have American composers been so eager to contribute to the symphonic repertoire when their contemporaries in other countries have turned away from the form? Compared to that of the Old World, the musical tradition of the United States is not only relatively brief in time but also ineluctably heterogeneous. In terms of orchestral music, an identifiable 'American' style is less than a century old. Thus the strong desire to establish a national musical heritage to emulate that of Europe has been a powerful stimulus to many composers. Since the symphonies of Haydn, Mozart et al. are the backbone of European classical and romantic music, it is natural for composers in the United

1

States to follow their examples. The catalogue at the end of this book is evidence of the extent to which the symphony has been of such importance: Hanson produced a total of seven, Piston eight, Sessions nine, Schuman 10, Harris 15, Cowell 20 and Hovhaness at least 67.

In recent years a new phenomenon has appeared, the extended repertoire offered on compact discs. Works that are seldom if ever heard in our concert halls are now widely available in recordings. A prime example is the case of the English composer George Lloyd. In 1980 he was hardly a name even to professional musicians. A decade later his entire output of 12 symphonies had been issued on CD with sufficient sales to cover the entire cost of the recording sessions. In spite of this commercial success, the works themselves seldom feature on concert programmes.

Composers who have lost faith in live performance may in future look to the studios for the survival of their music. In the United States, David Diamond and Alan Hovhaness have benefited from this trend. Newly composed symphonies by Christopher Rouse, John Harbison and John Corigliano have found their way onto disc within months of the premières. This is an encouraging development that increasingly allows us to evaluate the significance of new music.

It is, however, notable that many American composers in this century have written one symphony early in their career. This might represent a rite of passage, a challenge to be faced to establish self-esteem. More likely they have been discouraged from composing more symphonies because of the lack of interest from conductors and orchestras, turning instead for economic rather than musical reasons to works more likely to achieve public performance. Perhaps the future now holds out more hope for them.

Many composers in the catalogue were born outside the United States. The definition of 'American' has been interpreted rather freely. Stravinsky has been omitted since he remained essentially Russian regardless of the citizenships he took and where he lived. Only his *Symphony in Three Movements* was composed wholly in the United States. Bohuslav Martinů, in exile from Czechoslovakia during the Second World War, wrote his first five symphonies (1942–46) in the United States but he cannot be considered American even by temporary adoption. The two symphonies by Kurt Weill (omitted) were written in Germany; three of the eight symphonies of Ernst Krenek (included) were composed after he had acquired American citizenship.

As far as possible this survey is arranged chronologically to trace the historical sequence of the symphony in America. Composers, however, do not conform to neatly arranged patterns so that consecutive chapters inevitably overlap in time. Gathering together like-minded figures is fraught with problems since they are individuals with their own personalities. Nevertheless I do detect stylistic trends which are indicated to some degree by the chapter headings.

Neil Butterworth

# 1 Early Years and Orchestral Beginnings

Music in North America got off to an unpromising start. The early settlers at the beginning of the seventeenth century, the Pilgrim Fathers, were not particularly sympathetic towards music. They accepted the singing of hymns and psalms in church but instrumental music, especially if associated with dancing, was forbidden as it was regarded as the work of the devil. For practical reasons, these emigrants could take with them only the basic essentials for survival in the New World: farming implements, animals, tools, seeds, firearms, food. Musical instruments were a very low priority. However, there are some inexplicable exceptions: inventories of two New Hampshire households in July 1633 include '15 recorders and hoeboys' in the Great House, Newitchwaniche, and '26 hoeboys and recorders and 1 drum' at Pascattaquack.

The British soldiers who were later sent out to protect the colonists were, for the most part, not Puritans. Naturally they enjoyed their own music-making, however primitive. Marches for pipes, trumpets and drums must have contrasted sharply with the solemn church music of the settlers, and often gave rise to complaints.

Thus during the seventeenth century when Europe was experiencing the birth of opera with Monteverdi, the lavish court entertainments of Louis XIV at Versailles and the masques and semi-operas for which Purcell provided the music in London, the North American continent could offer only hymns and marches. These two forms, one religious, the other secular, constitute the fundamental ingredients of American music up to the present day, from jazz to the symphonic repertoire.

By 1700 changes had occurred. Many of the more recent arrivals from Europe were not Puritans. They still held strong religious convictions but were not confined by the strictures of the original settlers, especially with regard to music. Also the British Isles were no longer the exclusive origin of the newcomers; other Europeans followed in ever-increasing numbers, bringing with them music and instruments to a musically-deprived continent. In 1716 the *Boston Newsletter* advertised:

> This is to give notice that there is lately come over from England a choice collection of instruments, consisting of Flageolets, Flutes, Hautboys, Reeds for Hautboys, books of instruction for all instruments, books of ruled paper. To be sold at the Dancing School of Mr Enstone in Sudbury Street, near the Orange Tree, Boston.

The first organ was constructed in Philadelphia in 1703. In the following year an English organ-builder, Dr Christopher Witt, arrived to supervise the building of more instruments in Philadelphia and Boston. Around 1732, Karl Theodore Pachelbel, son of Johann Pachelbel, organist and composer of the famous *Canon*, arrived in Boston from Germany.

The strongest stimulus to music making in eighteenth-century America was the establishment of the Moravian sect in Bethlehem, Pennsylvania in 1741. Although called the Moravians, many of their members came from Germany and Holland. Over the years these musical people brought with them instruments and the latest compositions including in particular the works of Joseph Haydn. Johann Friedrich Peter (1746–1813) made copies of Haydn's music in Vienna in 1767 and 1769, including a complete set of parts of Symphony No.17 in F. He took these with him to America in 1770 where he settled in the Moravian Pennsylvanian communities of Nazareth, Bethlehem and Lititz. There is no confirmation of when or where he may have performed these pieces.

The first performance in America of at least a part of Haydn's oratorio *The Creation* is believed to have taken place in one of these towns less than two years after the Vienna première in 1798. The Moravian composers concentrated on writing anthems for soloist, chorus and orchestra for the Sunday services. The Haydnesque style of the music contrasts sharply with the stark hymn tunes of the older settlers. No fewer than six players in Haydn's orchestra in London in 1791 settled in America, including James Hewitt (1770–1827), an exact contemporary of Beethoven who conducted concerts and opera in New York.

Evidence of perhaps the earliest public concert appeared in the *Boston Newsletter* of 16 and 23 December 1731:

> On Thursday, the 30th of this instant December, there will be performed a 'concert of Music' on Sundry instruments At Mr Pelham's great Room, being the house of the late Doctor Noyes near Sun Tavern. Tickets to be delivered at the place of Performance at 'Five Shillings' each. The concert to begin exactly at Six o'clock and no Tickets will be delivered after Five the day of Performance. N.B. There will be no admittance after Six.

Peter Pelham was an engraver who had emigrated from London in 1726. His son, also Peter, became an assistant to Karl Theodore Pachelbel and took part in the earliest recorded concert in New York in 1736.

The Moravians were also responsible for the first musical organization in America, Collegium Musicum, founded in Bethlehem in the 1740s and replaced in 1820 by the Philharmonic Society. With the increasing population, the Southern states were also flourishing musically. The St Cecilia Society of Charleston, South Carolina, established in 1762, had 120 members, each of them paying an annual fee of £25, quite a considerable sum for that time. When vacancies arose in the orchestra, advertisements were placed in the newspapers of major cities, offering contracts of two and three years. Throughout the season there were two concerts a month of music by contemporary European composers, including Abel, J.C. Bach, Haydn, the Earl of Kelly, Pichl, Carl Stamitz and Toeschi. Although the orchestra was small by present day standards, it was complete: 2 flutes, 2 oboes or clarinets, 2 bassoons, 2 horns, 4 first violins, 3 second violins, 2 violas, 2 cellos and harpsichord. The society survived for over 150 years.

By 1800 immigrants were flooding into America as refugees, more from political and economic than religious oppression. The French Revolution of 1789 produced an influx of Parisian aristocrats; for them music was the only useful training that they had received, so that an upper-class hobby became the sole means of earning a living. One such is the Chevalier Marie Robert de Leaumont (d. 1812), a violinist, who is reported to have directed an orchestra in Boston in 1790 and on 1 June 1796 he conducted symphonies by Haydn and Stamitz.

A significant figure who greatly improved the standard of orchestral playing in Boston was Gottlieb Graupner (1767–1836). The son of an oboist in a German army band, he was born in Hanover. In 1788 he went to London and played oboe in Salomon's orchestra during Haydn's first visit to England. He moved to America in the early 1790s, making his debut in Boston on 15 December 1794. In 1810 he founded the Philharmonic Society of Boston, an orchestra of professional and amateur musicians who played symphonies by Haydn and others for their own pleasure. It was dissolved in 1824. With two other musicians he established an organization to provide authentic performances of music by Handel and Haydn. This was later to become the Handel and Haydn Society of Boston, one of the oldest surviving musical institutions in America.

There is evidence that a symphony by J.C. Bach was heard in Boston on 17 May 1771 and Haydn's Symphony No.85 (*La Poule*) was played in Philadelphia on 29 December 1792. Until recently it was believed that the first performance in America of Beethoven's Symphony No.1 took place in Lexington, Kentucky on 12 November 1817 conducted by Anton Philipp Heinrich, although probably only one movement was given on that occasion. What was claimed to be the première of the complete symphony is credited to the Musical Fund of Philadelphia in a concert on 24 April 1821 directed by Benjamin Carr. It is now known that an unspecified symphony by Beethoven was played in the Moravian community of Nazareth on 13 June 1813.

In the first quarter of the nineteenth century orchestras were assembled to play for choral societies and opera companies. In 1800 Philadelphia was the largest city in the United States with a population of 70 000, enough to sustain increasingly ambitious musical events. New York was almost the same size with 60 000 inhabitants and growing by the day with new arrivals from Europe. By comparison Boston was more modest, population about 25 000, but musical life there was as enterprising as any place on the Eastern seaboard. Among the American premières were Handel's *Messiah* (Philadelphia 1801), Haydn's *The Creation* (complete) (Boston 1816), Rossini's *The Barber of Seville* (New York

1819), Mozart's *The Marriage of Figaro* (New York 1823), Weber's *Der Freischütz* (New York 1823) and Mozart's *Don Giovanni* (New York 1826).

The Musical Fund Society of Philadelphia was founded in 1821, whose leading lights were three musicians from Britain, Raynor Taylor (1747–1825), Benjamin Carr (1768–1831) and a Scotsman George Schetky (1776–1831). They had been inspired by the Royal Society of Musicians in London. At their first concert on 24 April 1821 no fewer than six conductors participated. The Music Fund Hall was completed in 1824; it was demolished in 1982 to make way for a residential building.

In Boston Lowell Mason (1792–1872) and George James Webb (1803–1887) established the Boston Academy of Music in 1833. Webb, born in England, took responsibility for instrumental tuition and founded an orchestra which performed seven of Beethoven's symphonies. In 1847 the orchestral work was transferred to the Musical Fund Society which Webb also conducted shortly before it became defunct in 1855.

In 1848, the Germania Orchestra in New York, consisting of 25 players – mostly from Berlin seeking refuge from the revolutions in Central Europe – became the first orchestra to rehearse regularly on a daily basis. The players moved to Boston in the following year and in spite of financial difficulties and personal rivalry, the orchestra stayed together for six years, after which the musicians scattered to seek employment in other cities. Although they had to pander to popular taste with programmes of light music, they included symphonies by Haydn, Mozart, Beethoven and Mendelssohn in their repertoire and gave the American premières of Mendelssohn's music for *A Midsummer Night's Dream* (1848) and Wagner's overtures to *Rienzi* (1853) and *Tannhäuser* (1855).

The brief visit to New York of the French conductor Jullien had an impact disproportionate to his status as a serious musician. Louis Antoine Jullien (1812–1860) gained a reputation for flamboyant behaviour on the platform, conducting Beethoven with white gloves and a jewelled baton; a white and gold throne was provided in which he rested between items.

After fifteen years in London, he arrived in New York in August 1853 for a series of Monster Concerts for the Masses in Castle Gardens and Metropolitan Hall. Jullien brought 29 musicians from Europe to whom he added 60 local musicians; the composer George Bristow and the conductor Theodore Thomas were two of them. The programmes combined complete symphonies instead of single movements, a rarity in America at the time, with popular music – quadrilles and opera selections. His famous novelty was *The Firemen's Quadrille* during which real firemen with real water extinguished real fires.

A more significant innovation was the inclusion of works by American composers including four symphonies by William Fry. Following the New York season, Jullien embarked on a six-month nationwide tour before returning for a number of farewell concerts in the summer of 1854. Critics were unimpressed by his exhibitionism; the *New York Courier and Enquirer* dismissed Jullien as 'A splendid, bold and dazzlingly successful humbug.' To his credit, however, by promoting popular concerts on a huge scale for an admission fee of only 50 cents, he proved that there was a demand for such events. Later Theodore Thomas adopted the practice without Jullien's gratuitous ostentation.


## Permanent professional orchestras

To New York goes the honour of establishing the first professional orchestra to have survived to the present day. In 1842 Ureli Corelli Hill (1802–1875), a violinist and pupil of Spohr in Germany, was appointed President of the Philharmonic Society of New York. In the inaugural concert on 7 December 1842 in which Beethoven's Fifth Symphony took pride of place, there were 53 players: 17 violins, 5 violas, 4 cellos, 5 double-basses, 3 flutes, 1 piccolo, 2 oboes, 2 clarinets, 3 bassoons, 4 horns, 2 trumpets, 4 trombones and 1 timpani. Hill conducted the first five seasons, returning to the orchestra in 1873 as a humble violinist. For the first 16 seasons, the orchestra gave four concerts a year. The repertoire was heavily weighted towards European, especially German, music. In 1846 the New York Philharmonic Orchestra gave the American premières of Beethoven's *Choral* Symphony, Chopin's First Piano Concerto and overtures by Berlioz. The first work by an American composer to appear in one of their programmes was George Bristow's *Concert Overture* in 1847, but it remained for years an isolated example of home-grown music.

The principal rivalry that faced the New York Philharmonic was the rise of the conductor Theodore Thomas (1835–1905). Born in Darmstadt, he was taken to the United States at the age of ten by which time he was already an accomplished violinist. After playing in various New York orchestras, he founded his own in 1862 for 'Symphony Soirées' in the Irving Hall, New York. His intention was to cultivate public taste for symphonic music by skilfully balancing popular works with the major German repertoire. A prodigious capacity for hard work enabled him to combine a winter season with a series of 100 summer concerts in Central Park. Between 1866 and 1875 he conducted 1227 concerts in the May to September season. In 1869 he undertook the first of his coast-to-coast tours, covering the whole of the United States from Maine to Georgia, across the continent to California with an excursion into Canada, thereby offering steady employment to his players. In later years he organized short seasons in Chicago and Boston.

In 1877 Thomas was appointed conductor of the New York Philharmonic Orchestra, which absorbed the leading members of his own orchestra. He held the post until 1891, with the exception of 1878 when he served as Director of the newly-opened College of Music in Cincinnati. Under Thomas's authoritarian regime, standards of orchestral playing in the United States were among the highest in the world. After a visit to the United States in 1872–73, the Russian pianist and composer Anton Rubinstein wrote:

I had no idea that such a new country had an orchestra like Theodore Thomas'. Never in my life, although I had given concerts in St Petersburg, Vienna, Berlin, Paris and London, had I found an orchestra that was as perfect as the organization Theodore Thomas had created and built up.

This one man was responsible for the extraordinary expansion of public interest in serious orchestral music. As a brilliant organizer, he brought the classics to almost every city in the country. Among his enterprising schemes were children's concerts and carefully planned programmes of 'pops' to recruit new audiences.

After leaving the New York Philharmonic, Thomas was encouraged to establish an orchestra in Chicago. In the fourteen seasons with the Chicago Symphony Orchestra (1891–1905), he conducted a total of 274 concerts including works by 170 composers, an indication of his broad musical taste. Pride of place went to Wagner with 164 performances of his works, with Beethoven in second place, a tally of 108 pieces. In his huge repertory, ranging from Bach to Wagner, were numerous American premières including symphonies by Berlioz (*Harold in Italy*), Brahms (Nos 2 and 3), Bruckner (4 and 7) Dvořák (7), Saint-Saëns (3), Schubert (8 and 9), Sibelius (2) and works by Wagner, Richard Strauss and Elgar. His services to American music were less impressive but he did give the first performance of pieces by George Bristow, Dudley Buck, George Chadwick, Frederick Converse and John Knowles Paine. His autobiography published posthumously in 1905 with reminiscences and appreciation by George Upton (reprinted Da Capo Press: New York 1964), presents a vivid account of the difficulties facing the performance of music in America in the second half of the nineteenth century.

The demand for concerts was such that New York acquired a third orchestra in 1878 when Leopold Damrosch (1832–1885) established the New York Symphony Orchestra. Like Thomas, Damrosch came from Europe; he was born in Poznan, now in Poland but at that time a part of Germany. Early in his conducting career in New York in December 1877, he gave the American première of Brahms' First Symphony. On his death he was succeeded by his son Walter (1862–1950) who continued to conduct the orchestra until its merger with the New York Philharmonic Orchestra in 1928.

Orchestral activity in Boston had begun with the Philharmonic Society in 1799 guided by Gottlieb Graupner. In the middle of the nineteenth century, the Boston Musical Fund Society and the orchestra of the Academy of Music served the people well. In addition there were the Boston Philharmonic Orchestra (1855–1863) and the Harvard Musical Association (1865–1882), providing a valuable concert life in the city. In light of the orchestral provision in New York, it was inevitable that Boston would need its own permanent professional orchestra. With the financial support of a prominent banker, Henry Lee Higginson, the Boston Symphony Orchestra was inaugurated in 1881. Most of the 68 players were of German origin, as was the first conductor, George Henschel (1850–1934). There were some initial misgivings as Henschel was better known as a singer and composer, with little conducting experience. The first season included a complete cycle of Beethoven's symphonies in chronological order which met with considerable acclaim and Henschel proved to be a conscientious and inspirational director for three seasons. Theodore Thomas was twice invited to become principal conductor but he preferred to remain in Chicago.

At the turn of the century, many other cities established their own professional symphony orchestras, with continued expansion in the next few decades.

| | |
|---|---|
| Cincinatti Symphony | 1895 |
| Oregon Symphony | 1896 |
| Philadelphia Orchestra | 1900 |
| San Diego Symphony | 1902 |
| Minneapolis (now Minnesota) Orchestra | 1903 |
| Seattle Symphony | 1903 |
| St Louis Symphony | 1907 |
| Dallas Symphony | 1911 |
| San Francisco Symphony | 1911 |
| Houston Symphony | 1913 |
| Baltimore Symphony | 1914 |
| Detroit Symphony | 1914 |
| Cleveland Orchestra | 1918 |
| Los Angeles Philharmonic | 1919 |
| Rochester Philharmonic | 1923 |
| Pittsburgh Symphony | 1926 |
| Indianapolis Symphony | 1930 |
| National Symphony Orchestra of Washington, DC | 1931 |

# 2　Pioneers

The honour of composing the first symphony on American soil probably goes to John Christopher Moller (1755–1803). Born in Germany, he settled in London from 1775 to 1785 where he established a music publishing business that issued some of his compositions. He moved to Philadelphia in 1785 and later to New York where he was a music publisher and concert promoter in addition to earning a living as organist and pianist. His Sinfonia was composed in Philadelphia in 1793. A modern edition prepared by W.T. Marrocco and H. Gleason was published in 1964 in *Music in America*: an Anthology from the Landing of the Pilgrims to the Close of the Civil War, 1620–1865 (W.W. Norton: New York).

Another early symphonist, William Cumming Peters (1805–1866), went to America from Devon, England around 1820. A composer of popular songs, he established a family music publishing firm in Pittsburgh with branches in Baltimore and Cincinnati. His two-movement Symphony in D was written in 1831 for the Harmony Society of Economy, near Pittsburgh.

Also dating from the 1830s is a four movement Symphony in E flat by Charles Hommann (c. 1800–c. 1862), written for the Bethlehem Philharmonic Society. The manuscript is preserved in the Archive of the Moravian Church, Bethlehem, PA.

These symphonies, historically significant, remained parochial, setting no example to follow and exerting no influence. Our first composer deserving serious consideration followed a life of almost legendary adventure, a pioneer in both his musical outlook and ascetic day-to-day existence.

**Anton Philipp Heinrich** (1781–1861), the son of a wealthy banker, was born on 11 March 1781 in Schönbüchel, in the German speaking part of Bohemia. In 1800 he inherited property and a thriving business from his uncle. After visiting America in 1805 he decided to settle there in 1810, living first in Philadelphia where he was a violinist, pianist and conductor. In the following year, as a result of the Napoleonic Wars and the financial crash in Austria, Heinrich lost his fortune and was forced to make a living through music. He moved to Lexington, Kentucky where he taught and played the violin. Even at this time he was striving to be accepted as an American musician. He thought that his work would revolutionize music in America, but almost all his persistent efforts towards having his pieces performed met with failure. His life seems to have been full of disappointments and misfortune, resulting from ill-health and the constant rejection of his compositions.

His orchestral works were all planned on a grand scale, often of great length with impressive, if pompous, titles: *Grand Symphony: The Ornithological Combat of Kings, or The Condor of the Andes and the Eagle of the Cordilleras* and *The Columbiad, a Grand American National Chivalrous Symphony* are two examples. American history was well commemorated and documented in such works as *The Treaty of William Penn with the Indians, a Concerto Grosso, an American National Dramatic Divertissement* for full orchestra 'successively in six different characteristic movements united into one'. Heinrich was possibly also the first composer to make use of the music of the American Indians as the basis for certain works. As early as 1831 he wrote *Pushmataha, a Venerable Chief of a Western Tribe of Indians* and in 1845, he composed *Manitou Mysteries or the Voice of the Great Spirits, a grand sinfonia misteriosa indiana*, both of which claim to be based on American Indian melodies.

After two further visits to Europe he settled in New York City in 1838. In 1842 he was chairman of the meeting which founded the New York Philharmonic Society and in the same year, at the Heinrich Grand National Festival in New York, seven of his works were heard to great acclaim from a large audience. A benefit concert of his music given in New York on 6 May 1846 was also well received. One critic commented:

> Much of the music is truly magnificent and grand; but in the midst of this sublimity and grandeur, we are sometimes startled by the quaintest and oddest passages we ever heard. There is certainly a wonderful deal of originality in all of Mr H's compositions, and the most fantastic parts are always artistically correct, and perfectly descriptive of their subject.

The music critic of *The Tribune*, 7 May 1846, observed that Heinrich's music

> could have been written by none but a man of the profoundest musical genius. Altogether, when we consider the variety of pieces and subjects introduced into this mammoth Concert, and remember that they are all the work of a single mind, we cannot but admit that that mind is a most extraordinary one.

The greatest moment of recognition came to 'Father Heinrich', as he was known, toward the end of his life. For years he had struggled to have his music performed, and on 21 April 1853, when he was 72, a Grand Valedictory Concert was given in Metropolitan Hall, New York, which included a number of his works. All the important musicians in the city took part, and judging from the programme, the concert must have lasted several hours, since at least four of his major orchestral pieces were played. An advance newspaper notice of the concert speaks of Heinrich in the following terms:

> He has gone on in his solitary attic, composing oratorios, operas, symphonies and songs, merely composing, not publishing till he had accumulated several large chests full

of original compositions. His only wealth. May the devoted old servant of St Cecilia be cheered by a full house, and may some of that inspiration which has sustained his long labours appear in his works and be felt by his audience.

Heinrich considered the Grand Symphony *The Ornithological Combat of Kings* to be his best work. The elaborate and colourful complete title may have its origin in his friendship with the naturalist and artist John James Audubon (1785–1851). In its first form the scoring of the symphony included voices with the orchestra. Ultimately the composer made seven versions, the last in 1850. As an inveterate reviser, Heinrich had much in common with that other original, Charles Ives.

The first movement of the symphony was performed in Graz on 10 June, 1836 by the Styrian Musik-Verein, not to the satisfaction of the composer who lamented the lack of sufficient string players in the orchestra. Since then it probably remained unheard until the recording issued in 1978 as part of the Recorded Anthology of American Music.

Although Heinrich provided descriptive titles to the four movements – the Conflict of the Condor in the Air: The Repose of the Condor: The Combat of the Condor on Land: Victory of the Condor – the music itself appears to contain no programmatic element as such. The only remarkable feature of the work is that it betrays no obvious European influence. We cannot be certain what music Heinrich knew before he went to America. During his five-year stay in London (1826–31), he doubtless became acquainted with the latest fashions, particularly Italian opera since he played in the orchestra of the Drury Lane Theatre. However, there is nothing of Rossini or Bellini in the *Combat* Symphony. His sympathies lie more closely with the early Germanic Romantic tradition of Weber, although he lacks that composer's sense of drama and rhythmic vitality. His melodic invention is undistinguished, with short-winded phrases treated discursively more in the manner of an overture than a symphony. Equally unremarkable is his handling of the orchestra, competent but without any particular flair. Only an extended passage in the slow movement where two solo violins add a decorative obbligato leaves any lasting impression.

In certain ways the hidden talents of Heinrich resemble the genius of Charles Ives, but the music of the former has few of the prophetic qualities of latter, and has no particularly notable features except quantity. After his brief success in New York, he visited Europe for the last time in 1857, where three concerts were given in his honour in Prague. He returned home in 1859, dying in poverty two years later.

Heinrich had endeavoured to establish himself as an American composer of integrity. For many of his works he had taken American themes of a national and patriotic nature. The descriptive music was in part influenced by the years he spent alone in the wilderness, living in a log cabin in Kentucky during the 1820s. Sadly his massive industry produced little impact on the development of music in his adopted country.

In *Our American Music*, John Tasker Howard paid tribute to him in the following terms:

We must respect him for what he tried to do, and never forget that he was the first to make the attempt. That he failed to accomplish his ends was unfortunate, in many ways tragic, but the important fact is that Heinrich was the first to attempt American nationalism in the larger forms of musical composition.

(J.T. Howard (1954) *Our American Music*, Thomas Crowell: New York, p. 238)

**William Henry Fry** (1813–1864) studied in Philadelphia with Leopold Meignen, a graduate of the Paris Conservatoire. By the age of 20 he had composed four overtures, but his overwhelming enthusiasm for the music of Bellini and Donizetti made him turn to writing operas. The first of these, *Aurelia the Virgin* (1841), was never performed. His next effort, *Leonora*, based on Bulwer Lytton's novel, was produced in Philadelphia in 1845. This represents probably the first grand opera to be staged in America by a native composer.

In spite of the success of *Leonora*, Fry turned to journalism as a profession, moving to Paris in 1846 as foreign correspondent for the *Philadelphia Public Ledger* and the *New York Tribune*. He was soon integrated into the European musical scene, although he failed in his attempt to persuade the Paris Opera to perform *Leonora*.

On his return to New York in 1852 he was appointed music editor of the *Tribune*, a position that empowered him to promote the cause of the American composer. Of particular, impact was the series of ten lectures entitled 'The Science and Art of Music' in the Metropolitan Hall, New York. At his own expense these lectures were illustrated with live performances from a group of Italian singers, a chorus of 100, a full orchestra and a military band. In the last of these lectures Fry lambasted American society:

> There is no taste for, or appreciation of true Art in this country. The public, as a public, know nothing about Art ... they have not a single enlightened or healthy idea on the subject. As a nation, we have totally neglected Art. We pay enormous sums to hear a single voice, or a single instrument, the beauties and excellencies of which (if it have any) we cannot discover. We will pay nothing to hear a sublime work of Art performed, because we do not know enough to appreciate it, and consequently such a performance bores us terribly.

Such a diatribe against the Philistines could have been delivered by a present day critic; times have not changed. Fry continued his polemic, directing remarks at composers of his own country:

> It is time we had a Declaration of Independence in Art, and laid the foundation of an American School of Painting, Sculpture and Music. Until this Declaration of Independence in Art shall be made – until American composers shall discard their foreign liveries and found an American School – and until the American public shall learn to support American artists, Art will not become indigenous to this country, but will only exist as a feeble exotic, and we shall continue to be provincial in Art. The American composer should not allow the name of Beethoven, or Handel or Mozart to prove an eternal bugbear to him, nor should he pay them reverence; he should only reverence his Art, and strike out manfully and independently into untrodden realms, just as his nature and inspirations may invite him, else he can never achieve lasting renown.

Fry's seven symphonies, dating from the early 1850s, all have descriptive titles which suggest programmatic content, perhaps influenced by Berlioz whom he met in Paris. Four of them, *Childe Harold*, *A Day in the Country*, *The Breaking Heart* and the *Santa Claus Symphony*, were performed during the 1853 New York season by the flamboyant French conductor Louis Antoine Jullien with his 98 strong orchestra.

Appropriately, *Santa Claus* was heard on Christmas Eve. An account of the piece in the *New York Tribune* describes it in naive inflated terms of a quasi-religious nature with reference to 'the songs of the stars, the fluttering ecstasies of hovering angels ... the change from starlight to sunlight'. The finale included a section for an orchestra of drums representing the rolling of the spheres, another idea doubtless taken from Berlioz. Much to the composer's annoyance, this lofty concept was not taken seriously by at least one critic. Writing in the *Musical Weekly*, Richard Storrs Willis (1819–1900) described the symphony as 'a kind of extravaganza which moves the audience to laughter, entertaining them seasonably with imitated snow-storms, trotting horses, sleighbells, cracking whips, etc.'

Fry was deeply hurt by these disparaging remarks. In a 25-page letter which was published by Willis, he complained:

> I think that the American who writes for the mere dignity of musical art, as I understand it, without recompense, deserves better treatment at the hands of his countrymen. This is more due from an American, as the Philharmonic Society of this city is an incubus on Art, never having asked for or performed a single American composition during the eleven years of its existence.

He added: 'Any work which begins in Heaven and then swings down to Hell, returns to Heaven and thence to earth to depict the family joys of a Christmas party is worthy of serious consideration.' He contended that *Santa Claus* was the longest unified instrumental composition that had ever been written on a single subject and was therefore entitled to an extended review. Pointing out the gap between earnest intention and artistic achievement Willis replied dismissively, 'The length of a piece of music is novel ground, certainly, upon which to base its musical excellence, or its requirement for a very long criticism.' In his *Journal of Music*, John S. Dwight (1813–1893) added his voice to the argument:

> Why is not friend Fry willing practically to submit the merit of the American symphonies to what he himself maintains to be the only true test? – namely to time and the world's impression. Of course the bulk of our public concerts and musical entertainments must consist of pieces of a guaranteed excellence, of works that the world *knows* to be good, sure to give pleasure, sure to inspire, and reward attention. If a work have genius in it, it will sooner or later make its mark upon the world. It is of no use to tell us why we ought to like *Santa Claus*, the thing is to make us like it.

Such an attitude towards new music prevails to this day where survival depends more upon public taste and market forces than intrinsic worth. In Fry's case there is the paradox of an American composer decrying the stifling force of European music while adopting its forms and language in his own works. The melodic and harmonic invention found in *Leonora* is indistinguishable from that of Bellini's *Norma*, and the character of the symphonies is closely derived from the orchestral music written in Germany during the first half of the nineteenth century.

Like Heinrich, Fry had endeavoured to produce works of symphonic structure that would establish American composers on an equal footing with their more famous European contemporaries. Unfortunately his talent was insufficient to make any significant impact at home that would provide an example for others to follow. Ultimately it was his strong support for native composers through lectures and journalism rather than his compositions that contributed to the cause.

In his activities to promote American music, Fry received the cooperation of **George F. Bristow** (1825–1898). The son of an English teacher, clarinettist and conductor who emigrated to America in 1824, Bristow received piano and organ lessons from Henry Timms and may have studied composition with Sir George Macfarren at the Royal Academy of Music in London. It was, however, as a violinist that he earned his living, joining the orchestra of the Olympic Theater in New York at the tender age of thirteen.

Bristow joined the New York Philharmonic Orchestra in 1843, remaining a player until 1880, except for a period in 1853 when he resigned in protest at the lack of American works in the repertoire. Ironically, of the three compositions by native composers performed during the first eleven years, one was an Overture by Bristow.

In addition to his violin playing, Bristow worked hard on behalf of American music, founding the American Musical Fund Society in 1852, the American Music Association in 1856 and the Metropolitan Music Association in 1859. He also conducted the Harmonic Society of New York from 1851 to 1862.

Bristow composed at least six symphonies although only five of them are currently extant. The first, in E flat, dating from 1845 is strongly influenced by Mendelssohn. In 1853 the famous French conductor Jullien conducted the Second Symphony in D minor, which later acquired the subtitle 'Jullien'. Symphony No.3 in F sharp minor, composed in 1858, displays more than mere competence, with an abundance of strong invention. It would be grossly unjust to dismiss the work as a derivative technical exercise. The lyrical slow movement entitled 'Nocturno' reveals Bristow's ability to spin a continuous flow of expressive melody. Mendelssohn is the obvious composer brought to mind in the Scherzo, given the quaint title 'The Butterfly's Frolic' The incidental music for *A Midsummer Night's Dream* is the origin of the delicate scoring of the opening section but thereafter the composer takes a more adventurous path of his own.

In spite of the minor key, there is to the whole symphony an appealing, carefree atmosphere, most notably in the breezy finale where Bristow is at his most confident in handling symphonic form. Such a work contradicts the impression conveyed by some writers that American composers of orchestral music in the second half of the nineteenth century were too closely imitating their

European contemporaries to produce anything of lasting interest of their own. Recent efforts by recording companies to bring to light large-scale compositions of the period have allowed us to form our own opinions.

His *Arcadian* Symphony was performed in New York by the Philharmonic Orchestra on 14 February 1874. Bristow designated his last work *Niagara* a symphony but the result is in effect an extended choral cantata. How appropriate it is that a man so eager to promote native American music should finally choose a national subject for his musical farewell.

**Louis Moreau Gottschalk** (1829–1869) showed remarkable musical talent as a child. In 1842 at the age of 13 he was sent to Paris to study the piano with Charles Hallé. He also impressed Berlioz who taught him composition, as did Liszt. Most of his works are for piano or piano duet, but he also wrote two so-called symphonies, although neither is precisely symphonic in form or stature. Symphony No.1, subtitled *La Nuit des Tropiques* (Night in the Tropics) was composed in 1859 on the island of Guadeloupe while Gottschalk was on a two-year concert tour of the West Indies.

Like his teacher Berlioz, Gottschalk enjoyed conducting huge orchestral forces in the musical extravaganzas he presented in foreign cities he visited. *Night in the Tropics* employs not only a full orchestra and a band but also an extra group of Afro-Cuban percussionists, making a total of over 150 musicians.

The opening *Andante*, first performed on its own in Havana in 1860, is rhapsodic in character with strikingly effective scoring for flute and strings at the outset in the touchingly simple melody that represents the first subject. Its development on a solo trumpet resembles a sentimental Stephen Foster ballad. The whole movement suggests a transcription of vocal music with echoes of Italian opera. It is, however, the second movement, marked *Allegro moderato*, that breaks new ground. With a battery of exotic Caribbean percussion instruments providing a sustained ostinato, Gottschalk produced an extended orchestral samba. Except for a brief central episode at a faster tempo reminiscent of Rossini, with an unexpected but totally integrated fugato, this is music of the American continent, quite unlike anything to be heard in Europe.

For the première of the entire Symphony in Havana in April 1861, Gottschalk employed native drummers from Santiago de Cuba. *Night in the Tropics* may not fulfil the criteria for a standard symphony, but it is an engaging work of considerable originality, adopting rhythmical elements and instrumental colours that were not to be heard again until well into the twentieth century in the music of Darius Milhaud and Villa Lobos.

Although termed a symphony by the composer, Symphony No.2, *A Montevideo*, is an orchestral fantasy or rhapsody in a single movement. Gottschalk composed it in Uruguay in the last year of his life, 1869, as one of his customary tributes to the country he was visiting. In the course of the piece, he quotes the Uruguayan National Anthem, *Hail Columbia* and *Yankee Doodle*, combining all three in the finale in a manner that would have impressed Charles Ives. This is a deft piece of craftsmanship but of only slight musical or historical significance beyond illustrating the composer's original approach to composition occasioned by his extensive travels throughout the Americas.

The acceptance of American literature on an international scale, due to writers of the calibre of Whitman, Emerson and Melville, was not yet paralleled by American composers of music. But although the music of Heinrich, Fry and Bristow made little impact in their time on an indifferent public, their determined advocacy of a national music movement forced critics and performers to treat the matter seriously.

# 3   John Knowles Paine
## (1839–1906)

Although several composers, including Heinrich, Fry and Bristow, had composed symphonies, the American musical establishment needed a work of stature to stand beside European models of which they could be proud. This appeared in 1876 from the pen of John Knowles Paine.

Paine had been born into a musical family. His grandfather, John K.H. Paine (1787–1835) was an organ builder in Portland whose three sons all became musicians. John Knowles studied in the United States under Hermann Kotzschmar (1829–1909), a German emigré. From 1858 to 1861 he attended the Hochschule in Berlin where he was a pupil of Karl August Haupt (1810–1891). While in Berlin, Paine began work on his Mass in D, a strongly Germanic setting owing much to Beethoven's *Missa Solemnis*. His first important musical achievement was the première of the Mass at the Singakademie in Berlin on 16 February 1867, when he was only 28 years old; part of the Mass was heard in Boston in the following year.

Paine's 43-year association with Harvard University began in 1862 with his appointment as an Instructor of Music, becoming Assistant Professor in 1873. In 1875 he was awarded the first chair in music to be established at a university in America when he was elected a full Professor at Harvard. Among his distinguished pupils were John Alden Carpenter, Frederick S. Converse, Arthur Foote, Edward Burlingame Hill and Daniel Gregory Mason.

His Symphony No.1 in C minor, Op.23, was composed between 1872 and 1875. The première in Boston on 26 January 1876 under the direction of Theodore Thomas confirmed the composer's position as a vital pillar of the musical society in New England. At last a native-born composer had produced a work that would be performed in Europe to much acclaim. The score was published by Breitkopf and Haertel in Leipzig two years after Paine's death.

Although Gunther Schuller has described the work as 'the best Beethoven Symphony that Beethoven didn't write himself', Paine's own personality is clearly evident in the music. Recalling the première after many years, George W. Chadwick commented:

To me it was a great event, not only on account of its intrinsic beauty, of which it had a great deal, because it proved we could have a great musician, and that he got a good hearing. To me there was something Godlike in the very name of Symphony. Besides, this symphony showed great skill and knowledge, especially in the Adagio, the theme of which I still remember.

The sonata-form first movement, *Allegro con brio*, alternates between the rhetoric of Beethoven and the lyricism of Schumann expressed through a delicacy of instrumentation that is Paine's own. Reliance on repeated short motifs, both rhythmical and melodic in the development section, in particular the figure [musical notation], inevitably acts as a reminder of Beethoven's Fifth Symphony in the same key.

The second movement, *Allegro vivace*, is a scherzo, Schumannesque in scoring with another reiterated Beethoven rhythm [musical notation] that permeates the first movement of his Seventh Symphony. In contrast the slower Trio is a gentle waltz.

At the heart of Paine's First Symphony is a poignant sonata-form *Adagio* marked by expansive melodic invention with no obvious European influence. In the more assertive central section the composer transcends the models which had shaped the rest of the symphony. There is an almost Elgarian swagger to the boisterous C major Finale marked *Allegro vivace*. Again the shadow of Schumann hovers over the orchestral texture but the material itself is notably original in character and handled with considerable expertise. It is not necessary to offer apologies for Paine's First Symphony. Here is a work rightly recognized at the time by the Boston critics as a landmark in the American musical heritage.

The Second Symphony in A, Op.34, completed in 1879, is a notable advance on its predecessor, showing a surer hand in the ambitious 50-minute span, less predictable in form and more chromatic in harmonic language. The subtitle *In Springtime* may have been chosen as a direct tribute to Schumann's *Spring* Symphony published as his First in 1841. A closer contemporary of Paine, the Swiss composer Joachim Raff (1822–1882) gave the title *Frühlingsklänge* (The Sound of Spring) to his Symphony No.8 in A dating from 1878. It is unlikely that Paine knew this work when he began his Second Symphony in the same key.

In 1889 the American writer Alfred J. Goodrich provided an analysis of the symphony adding headings to the movements, presumably with the composer's approval. These are too general and naive to offer much insight into a programmatic basis for the work.

I    Introduction: Adagio sostenuto. 'Departure of Winter' Allegro ma non troppe: 'Awakening of Nature'

II   Scherzo: Allegro. 'May-Night Fantasy'

III  Adagio: 'A Romance in Springtime'

IV   Allegro giocoso: 'The Glory of Nature'

The quiet opening of the first movement creates an atmosphere reminiscent of the symphonic poems of Liszt with echoes of Wagner in the imaginative orchestration. This introduction represents Winter with a strong theme in A minor on the cellos.

Ex. 1

Adagio

It is later contrasted with the Allegro (A major) depicting Spring, culminating in a coda that combines both ideas.

As with the First Symphony, the D minor Beethoven-like Scherzo enfolds a slower Waltz in the major key, as the Trio section. The lengthy Adagio in rondo form explores romantic depths in an increasingly intense expression of passionate emotion as the movement proceeds. The sonata-form finale refers back to the first movement and the Scherzo, transforming the material into an easy-going joyful celebration of Nature that reaches a climax in a noble tune, heard three times, which sets a stamp of assured optimism on the whole work.

Paine's Symphony No.2 achieved the remarkable distinction of two performances in Boston on consecutive days by different orchestras. The première on 10 March 1880, by the Boston Symphony Orchestra conducted by Bernard Listemann, was followed on the next afternoon by a second hearing by the Harvard Musical Association under the direction of Carl Zerrahn. Both occasions proved to be hugely successful with critics and audience. The *Gazette* reported that the Symphony was 'by far the finest work written on American soil by an American composer'. An eye witness at the première reported that the highly respected critic John S. Dwight 'stood on his seat frantically opening and shutting his umbrella as an expression of uncontrollable enthusiasm'. In the same year the full score was issued by Arthur P. Schmidt, the first symphony by an American to be published.

In *Contemporary American Composers* (1900, L.C. Page & Co.: Boston, p.146), Rupert Hughes commented, 'Before Mr Paine, there had never been an American music writer writing of serious consideration in the larger forms.' Today Wilfred Mellers considers Paine a composer of international stature, the writer of the first American symphony that should be in the repertoire of the world's leading orchestras.

Although neither of Paine's symphonies survived long in public performance into the twentieth century, they represent cornerstones of the American symphonic tradition. Together they provided the next generation of composers with the confidence to follow in Paine's footsteps. With recent recordings as evidence, the historical significance of both works can now be recognized.

# 4 Dvořák and the Search for National Identity

The desire to be uniquely American affected writers sooner than it did composers. There was no problem over language since English was the mother tongue. Literature is a more direct means than music for the expression of national pride.

James Fennimore Cooper's novel *The Last of the Mohicans* published in 1826 embodied for both an American and a European readership the essence of the American pioneering spirit. A generation later Henry Wadsworth Longfellow's epic poem *Hiawatha* (1855) created a sensation on both sides of the Atlantic. In 1837, the essayist Ralph Waldo Emerson expressed the need to be independent of foreign influence: 'We Americans must "walk on our own feet and speak our own minds".' Without deliberately adopting a non-European approach, the poetry of Walt Whitman, the novels of Herman Melville and the writings of Mark Twain proved that before the end of the nineteenth century, the United States had her own literary culture, in spirit and setting.

How could American composers achieve a similar national recognition? Heinrich had chosen American subjects for his grandiose orchestral works, but they remained stubbornly European in musical idiom. Others, including Paine, were content to follow the German symphonic tradition without striving to be American.

The arrival of Antonín Dvořák in New York in 1893 as Director of the National Conservatory of Music provided the catalyst to focus attention on the need for music in the United States to explore new paths. Mrs Jeanette Thurber, the patron of the Conservatory, held a visionary plan for the institution:

America has, so far, done nothing in a National way either to promote the musical education of its people or to develop any musical genius they possess, and that in this, she stands alone among the civilized nations of the world.

On 21 May 1893, the *New York Herald* published an interview with Dvořák in which he urged American composers to look to their own country for inspiration:

In the negro melodies of America, I discover all that is needed for a great and noble

21

school of music. They are pathetic, tender, passionate, melancholy, solemn, religious, bold, merry, gay or what you will. There is nothing in the whole range of composition that cannot be supplied with themes from this source.

Public reaction to these sentiments was immediate. Many musicians who had never considered such music of any value were shocked. Others were quick to explain that negro spirituals were derived from gospel hymns and did not therefore conform to the notion of folk music. One of the earliest collection of spirituals, 'The Story of the Jubilee Singers', published in London in 1875, prints them like conventional hymns with nineteenth-century harmonization and most of the now-familiar syncopations as smoothed out rhythms.

In an article 'Music in America' written in February 1895 for Harper's *New Monthly Magazine*, Dvořák answered his critics:

> The point has been urged that many of these touching songs, like those of [Stephen] Foster, have not been composed by the Negroes themselves, but are the work of white men, while others did not originate on the plantations, but were imported from Africa. It seems to me that this matters little. One might as well condemn the Hungarian Rhapsody because Liszt could not speak Hungarian. The important thing is that the inspiration for such music should come from the right source, and that the music itself should be a true expression of the people's real feelings.

The comparison between spirituals and Hungarian Rhapsodies is hardly valid since Liszt based his piano works on ostensible folk songs. One should remember that Dvořák, Bohemian by birth, felt a strong national pride in his country at a time when it was part of the Austro-Hungarian Empire. For him Czech nationalism was a political and cultural attitude he felt deeply which could be expressed through music. In declaring his admiration for these negro melodies, he was to some degree naive in his diagnosis, but was also misunderstood. In the *Harper Magazine* article he developed his views:

> Whether the original songs which may have inspired the composers came from Africa or originated in the plantations matters as little as whether Shakespeare invented his own plots or borrowed them from others. The thing to rejoice over is that such lovely songs exist and are sung at the present day. I, for one, am delighted by them. Just so it matters little whether the inspiration for the coming folk songs of America is derived from Negro melodies, the songs of the creoles, the red man's chant, or the plaintive ditties of the homesick German or Norwegian. Undoubtedly the germs for the best music lie hidden among the races that are comingled in this great country.

These observations may seem obvious to us today, but it required a distinguished visitor from Europe to draw the attention of musicians in America to the resources immediately on hand. In a letter to the *New York Herald*, dated 28 May 1893, he offered advice and foresight which would have direct results:

> There is no longer a reason why young Americans who have talent should go to Europe for their education. It is a waste of money and puts off the coming day when the Western world will be in music as in many others, independent of other lands.

In the same letter he presented an optimistic view of music in America, an inspiration not only to his own pupils, but also to the broad span of composers in America:

> The country is full of melody, original, sympathetic and varying in mood, colour and character to suit every phase of composition. It is a rich field. America can have great and noble music of her own, growing out of the very rich soil and partaking of its nature – the natural voice of a free and vigorous race.
>
> This proves to me that there is such a thing as nationality in music in the sense that it may take on the character of its locality. It now rests with the young musicians of this country and the patrons of music to say how soon the American school of music is to be developed.

Dvořák's declaration that 'The new American school must strike its roots deeply into its own soil' was vigorously supported by American composers. Arthur Farwell (1872–1952) who made an extensive study of American Indian music, endorsed Dvořák's assertions. In an article entitled 'An affirmation of American Music' published in the *The Musical World* Volume III, No.1 (1903) he wrote,

> The swiftly increasing group of American composers of the present generation has tasted of the regenerative sunlight flooding the wide stretches of our land, has caught glimpses of the wealth of poetic lore in the traditions of Negroes and Indians, and seen that justice must be done at last to the myriad sights and sounds of our own country. Europe will never respect America artistically, until she sees the results of this rebirth. And American composers are pressing to the mark. Every year sees them more numerous, fearless, energetic, prolific. Their compositions are sounding less German, less European, and more untrammelled and redolent of a new composite spirit, insistent, yet still undefined. And this we must bear in mind: that their shelves are already laden with an incredible number of completed manuscripts of all degrees of size and value; the very existence of which will not be generally known until their champions have a little longer 'nourished active rebellion'.

Dvořák put his principles into practice when he awarded first prize of $500 in a competition organized by the National Conservatory to Henry Schoenefeld (1857–1936) for a symphony subtitled *Rural*, which incorporated plantation songs into the score. Schoenefeld had studied in Leipzig, returning in 1879, settling first in Chicago before making his home in Los Angeles. His concert music drew heavily on American themes including an overture *The American Flag*, *American Caprice*, two *Indian Legends*, an overture *In the Sunny South*, two *American Rhapsodies*; and an opera *Atala* and a pantomime ballet *Wachicanta*, both based on American Indian subjects. He composed a Second Symphony entitled *Spring*.

Three of Dvořák's pupils, Henry T. Burleigh (1866–1949). Will Marion Cook (1869–1944) and Henry Rowe Shelley (1858–1947) made extensive use of negro spirituals in their instrumental and vocal music. Later many other composers followed their example: Henry Gilbert, Rubin Goldmark, Louis Gruenberg, Henry Hadley and Daniel Gregory Mason among them. John Powell's *Rhapsodie Nègre* (1918) for piano and orchestra enjoyed a huge vogue for several years until eclipsed by Gershwin's *Rhapsody in Blue*.

Although not directly advocated by Dvořák, American Indian music became the subject of serious research in the opening years of the twentieth century. Charles Wakefield Cadman, Frederick S. Converse, Victor Herbert, Arthur Nevin and Charles Sanford Skilton wrote operas on Indian stories. Similar themes inspired major works by Marion Bauer, Amy Beach, Ernest Bloch, John Alden Carpenter, Henry Gilbert, Rubin Goldmark, Charles Tomlinson Griffes and Frederick Jacobi.

In an article 'Folk-Music in Art-Music' written in 1917, a quarter of a century after Dvořák's arrival in America, Henry Gilbert could take a longer, more considered view:

> Our coming American music will perhaps not be built upon but will contain and reflect elements derived from all the folk-songs of various races – fused together by the new and all-powerful element that dominated American spirit; a mood of fundamental optimism and heroic valor: a will of accomplishments laughing at death. For America is surely the great adventure of humanity in modern times.

> ('A Discussion and Theory', *Music Quarterly*, Vol.3 No.4, October 1917: p. 601)

The First Symphony of Charles, Ives, written between 1897 and 1898 while he was at Yale under the supervision, maybe duress, of Horatio Parker, reflects the spirit of Dvořák, especially in the slow movement. Many years later in 1932, Ives expressed a contempt for the snobbish attitude of certain music lovers who accepted popular music only when heard through 'respectable' foreign composers.

> Since nice people, whenever they hear the words 'Gospel Hymn' or 'Stephen Foster' say 'Mercy me', and a little high-brow smile creeps over their brow – 'Can't you get something better than that in a symphony?' The same nice people, when they go to a properly dressed symphony concert under proper auspicies, led by a name with foreign hair, and hear Dvořák's *New World* Symphony, in which they are told this famous passage was from a negro spiritual, then they think it must be quite proper, even artistic, say 'How delightful.' But when someone proves to them that the Gospel Hymns are fundamentally responsible for the negro spirituals, they say 'Ain't it awful' – 'You don't really mean that.' 'Why, only to think!' 'Do tell,' – I tell you, you don't ever hear Gospel Hymns ever mentioned up there to the New England Conservatory!'

> (J. Kilpatrick (ed.) (1972) *Memos*, W.W. Norton: New York, p. 52)

In this explosion of spleen, the curmudgeonly old man was unwittingly acknowledging Dvořák's influence in bringing the American vernacular into the concert hall. Ives' own use of hymn tunes, vaudeville songs and folk melodies served a similar higher motive.

Dvořák's stylistic features are most strongly evident in the music of an American composer who had not been one of his pupils. George Chadwick had heard the Czech master's works when he was studying in Europe. His Second and Third Symphonies both contain a lightness of touch and a sense of humour akin to Dvořák. The closest comparison is found in Chadwick's *Symphonic Sketches* composed at about the same time as the Symphony *From The New World*. The opening of the movement entitled *Noel* with the string introduction to the main subject played on a cor anglais cannot but remind one of the Adagio of Dvořák's symphony.

Similarly, *A Northern Ballad* (1899), an orchestral work by Horatio Parker, then Professor of Music at Yale University, could be mistaken for a symphonic poem by Dvořák. One can find numerous other examples of music by American composers at the turn of the century pursuing a pastoral idiom with strong traces of folk material. The 'wide-open-spaces' music of early Hollywood westerns often looks back to a similar source but disguised by the inclusion of 'cowboy' songs that have an Anglo-Scottish-Irish origin. Dvořák spent only three years in the United States but the force of his personality on pupils and other active musicians was profound. Partly as a result of his influence, the German dominance of musical thought declined rapidly in America after 1900.

# 5  After Dvořák: The Romantics

The specific long-term effect of Dvořák's presence in America is difficult to quantify. His encouragement boosted self-esteem among musicians who had come into direct contact with him. Following the example set by Paine and Parker, composers gravitated towards universities and conservatories where, with their long tenure, they in turn exerted a profound influence upon generations of students. Chadwick at the New England Conservatory (1899–1931), Stillman Kelley at the Cincinnati Conservatory (1911–1934), D.G. Mason at Columbia University (1905–1942) and David Stanley Smith at Yale (1916–1946) passed on their principles and prejudices to their pupils.

Anti-German feeling aroused by the First World War diminished the dominance of European music throughout America. The works of German composers figured less prominently in programmes. Although a naturalized Swiss, Carl Muck, the conductor of the Boston Symphony Orchestra, was arrested in March 1918 and deported in August 1919 as an undesirable alien. Even Fritz Kreisler, an Austrian, was forced to cancel his North American tour in 1917. It should be noted that in 1920, 21 of the 101 players in the Boston Symphony Orchestra were German born.

For over three decades **George Whitefield Chadwick** (1854–1931) exerted a considerable influence over music in Boston, inheriting the mantle of John Knowles Paine as composer and mentor. He led the so-called 'Second New England School' or the 'Boston Classicists', a group of like-minded musicians which included Horatio Parker and Arthur Foote.

After attending the New England Conservatory in Boston, he studied in Germany, first in Leipzig under Carl Reinicke, later more profitably in Munich where he was a pupil of Josef Rheinberger. Following his return home he joined the faculty of the New England Conservatory in 1882, becoming its Director in 1897, a post he held until his death in 1931. It was his inspiration that turned the institution from a college training piano teachers into a leading conservatory.

Although his compositions show that he had absorbed European influences, especially from Dvořák, they are less Germanic than those of most of his

American contemporaries. He did not set out to establish an American idiom; this came about partly as a result of his New England ancestry. His own personality is clearly evident, with elements of humour, described by the Boston critic Philip Hale as 'a certain jaunty irreverence, a snapping of the fingers at Fate and the Universe'.

Chadwick's three symphonies belong to the early part of his career. Symphony No.1 in C, Op.5, was begun in 1878 and first performed by the Harvard Musical Association on 23 February 1882.

The Scherzo from his incomplete Second Symphony was played by the Boston Symphony Orchestra in March 1884 for which he received the princely sum of $13. It was so well received by the audience that an encore had to follow, something unheard of previously. The entire Symphony No.2 in B flat, Op. 21 was premièred on 10 December 1886, again to a rapturous response. Over the whole work lies the shadow of Dvořák, not only in the scoring, especially in the wind writing, but also in the simple folk-song character of the themes. A pentatonic horn call at the outset serves as a unifying motto for all four movements.

The slow introduction to the first movement has all the confidence of a mature composer with long sweeping melodies, leading to a powerful sonata Allegro. The gem of the Second Symphony is the delightful Scherzo that so appealed to the listeners in 1884. Chadwick's delicate instrumentation is worthy of Mendelssohn, although even he would not have been so bold as to relax the tempo for the Trio section in order to introduce such a cheerful new melody. The noble dignity of the slow movement is unexpectedly interrupted by a faster agitated middle section of dark moods otherwise avoided in the score. There is an out-of-doors feeling to the exuberant Finale, triumphant and joyful, devoid of any Teutonic gloom.

Symphony No.3 in F (1893–94) was awarded a prize of $300 in a competition sponsored by the National Conservatory of Music, New York where its principal, Dvořák was one of the judges. It was first performed in Boston on 19 October 1894 under the baton of Theodore Thomas to whom it is dedicated. With the exception of a playful Scherzo, the Third Symphony lacks the naive spontaneity of its predecessor. Chadwick the academic is more intrusive, which leads to some garrulous passages, particularly in the finale.

John Tasker Howard summed up the essence of this highly respected musician thus:

> Chadwick had the craftsmanship of Paine, and beyond that a genuine spark of inspiration; in his music one hears now a sly chuckle, now a voice of real emotional warmth. There were remarks in his music that only a Yankee could have made with impunity.
>
> (J.T. Howard (1941) *Our Contemporary Composers*, Thomas Y. Crowell: New York, p. 11)

As a greatly revered and influential teacher Chadwick laid the foundations of serious musical study at the New England Conservatory; his impact in this respect was widely felt through his many pupils who included Horatio Parker, Henry Hadley, Daniel Gregory Mason, Quincy Porter, Arthur Shepherd, William Grant Still and John Vincent.

Few symphonies written by Americans before 1900 forked much lightning. Mention should be made of a handful of composers who created some impression at the time and whose work may be due for some degree of revival.

**Mrs H.H.A. Beach** (Amy Marcy Cheney) (1867–1944), celebrated during her lifetime for numerous songs, choral works and solo piano compositions, completed her *Gaelic* Symphony in E minor in 1894. It was premiered in Boston on 31 October 1896 under the direction of Emil Paur and heard again several times in Germany before the First World War. Performances followed in New York, Buffalo, Kansas City and Chicago conducted by Theodore Thomas. The symphony is conceived on a grand scale, imitating European Romanticism for the principal themes with quasi-Irish folk tunes as secondary material. This 'Gaelic' element is evident in the second movement where the opening oboe melody could be an Irish traditional song, and the central section has some folk dance affinities, although transformed into symphonic proportions. A folk song flavour can also be detected in the solo violin obbligato in the slow movement.

In the *Gaelic* Symphony, Mrs Beach wished to express the trials and tribulations of the Irish people, although her own family traced its roots back to England. She shows an acute ear for instrumentation, remarkable for her only purely orchestral work, especially in the wind writing which includes an effective role for the bass clarinet. Her handling of symphonic form follows conventional lines without showing any serious weaknesses. The conductor Neemi Järvi revived it in 1991 for a recording with the Detroit Symphony Orchestra.

The long-lived **George Templeton Strong** (1856–1948) was a musical maverick who abandoned the United States in 1892, discouraged by the lack of recognition of American composers at home. He settled permanently in Vevey, Switzerland where he continued to compose copiously but with little success in gaining performances. For a while he gave up music to devote himself to watercolour painting.

His early works were influenced by the music of Liszt whom he had met in Weimar when he was a student. Later he fell under the spell of French composers, notably Debussy and Fauré. His three symphonies all have programmatic titles: No.1 in F, *In den Bergen* (In the Mountains) performed in New York on 24 November 1887; No.2 *Sintram*; No.3 *An der See* (By the Lake).

The *Sintram* Symphony (1895) was dedicated to his friend Edward MacDowell. It is based on a romance of that name by the German romantic writer Friedrich Heinrich Karl de la Motte Fouqué (1777–1843) and the famous Dürer print *Ritter: Tod und Teufel* (Horseman: Death and Devil). Strong treats the subject of Man's struggle against the Powers of Evil more as a symphonic poem than a formal symphony, taking both Liszt and Richard Strauss as models. While the two central movements are succinct and impressive, the outer movements suffer from unnecessary repetition and padding.

Had the composer returned to the United States and become integrated into the American musical scene he might have developed as a significant voice in his native country. Isolated in Switzerland, Strong remained in obscurity for most of his life.

Unlike the reclusive Strong, **Henry Kimball Hadley** (1871–1937) pursued a gregarious life-style, becoming a noted figure on the music scene of New York and the East Coast. He studied in Boston with Chadwick and later in Vienna under Mandyczewski. Back in the United States he devoted much of his time to conducting with the Seattle Symphony and the San Francisco Symphony Orchestras. In 1920 he was appointed assistant conductor of the New York Philharmonic and in 1929 he established the Manhattan Symphony Orchestra with the intention of including works by American composers in every programme. He founded the National Association of American Composers and Conductors and was an active member of the American Society of Composers, Authors and Publishers (ASCAP).

Amid his multifarious activities, he still found time to write a large quantity of music including five symphonies. The First, subtitled *Youth and Life*, dating from 1897 and performed in New York on 2 December 1897, depicts the struggles of a young man. The opening movement describes the conflict between good and evil on a metaphysical level, the second shows doubt and despair with a climactic death knell. A lighthearted dance-like scherzo provides a more optimistic preparation for the heroic finale.

Symphony No.2, *The Four Seasons*, was premièred on 20 December 1901 in New York and published in the following year. It is, in effect, a sequence of symphonic poems, beginning with Winter and ending with Autumn. It won the Paderewski Prize in 1902. Symphony No.3 in B minor, composed in 1907, received its première in Berlin in 1908 and was performed in Boston on 11 April that year.

Symphony No.4 in D minor (*North, East, South, West*) devotes a movement to each of the points of the compass. It was commissioned in 1911 for the Norfolk Festival where it was heard on 6 June, and later performed by the Boston Symphony Orchestra and in the Queen's Hall, London.

Symphony No.5 was commissioned for the Connecticut Tercentenary in 1935. The first movement, entitled *1635*, portrays the hardships of the early settlers and includes Indian melodies. The second movement, *1735*, depicts rural contentment and the finale, *1935*, represents everyday life at that time.

As a composer, Hadley enjoyed considerable success. Writing in 1915 Louis C. Elson claimed 'One may pay the sincerest tribute to Hadley's music in its freedom from morbidness and excessive dissonances.' (*The History of American Music* (1915): Macmillan: New York, p. 192.) In 1933 The *Musical Courier* described him as 'probably the most important composer in the contemporary American musical scene.' Even for the time, this was exaggerated flattery. After his death in 1937, Hadley's easy going, amiable music rapidly lost favour; its unchallenging romanticism could not survive in a modern age.

Yet another worthy figure highly regarded in his time as a composer and academic but forgotten today is **David Stanley Smith** (1877–1949). He was appointed to the Music Faculty of Yale in 1903 succeeding Horatio Parker as Professor and Director of the Department in 1920, retiring in 1946. He composed four symphonies: No.1 performed in 1912 by Frederick Stock and the Chicago Symphony Orchestra; No.2, commissioned for the 1918 Norfolk Festival; No.3 (1928); No.4 completed in 1937 and premièred by the Boston Symphony in 1939.

Alas, Smith is now simply a footnote in American history, a position shared by **Daniel Gregory Mason** (1873–1953) in his role as a composer. Mason is, however, remembered today as a writer on a wide range of subjects. His 18 books are a valuable contribution to the literature on music, offering a key insight into attitudes and opinions of musical America in the first half of this century. From 1910 he taught at Columbia University, becoming a professor in 1929; he retired in 1940.

Mason was born into a musical family; his grandfather was Lowell Mason (1792–1872), the composer of hymn tunes and a significant figure in music education during the nineteenth century. William Mason (1829–1908), his uncle, was an influential pianist and teacher.

In both his writing and compositions Mason was a reactionary, believing for example that Vincent D'Indy, whose pupil he had been, was of greater significance than Debussy or Ravel. He was, however, a strong supporter of American composers but insisted that 'for better or for worse American music is necessarily eclectic and cosmopolitan, and that the kind of distinctiveness to be looked for in it is individual rather than national.'

Mason's Symphony No.1 in C minor was performed by Stokowski and the Philadelphia Orchestra on 18 February 1916. It was revised in 1924 and given a new première by Koussevitzky and the Boston Symphony Orchestra in 1928. Subsequent performances followed in Detroit, New York and Chicago. Symphony No.2 in A was composed in 1929 and played in the following year by the Cincinnati Symphony Orchestra under Fritz Reiner.

Mason's *Lincoln* Symphony was introduced by the New York Philharmonic Symphony Orchestra in 1937 conducted by John Barbirolli. The first movement *The Candidate from Springfield* makes use of a tune from the 1860s 'Quoboag Quickstep'. *Massa Linkum*, the slow movement, is the lament of a slave for the dead president, in the form of a spiritual. In the finale *1865*, the quickstep is transformed into a funeral march.

The financial problems facing even successful composers in the 1930s is typified by Mason's Second Symphony. Although it was taken up by the Chicago Symphony Orchestra, Cincinnati Symphony Orchestra and the New York Philharmonic under Bruno Walter, the composer was ultimately out of pocket. Copying expenses of $395 were balanced against royalties of only $175, a net loss of $220.

As a crusty critic, Mason is still a figure to arouse interest, but with the exception of the Clarinet Sonata, most of his music has been forgotten.

The music of **Edgar Stillman Kelley** (1857–1944) has suffered a similar fate to that of D.G. Mason. Although he composed most of his works after he had been appointed to the Cincinnati Conservatory in 1910, Kelley belonged in spirit to the Boston School of Chadwick and Parker. His *New England Symphony* (1913, rev. 1922) became one of the most frequently performed American symphonies for over a decade, almost achieving repertoire status in the United States. Although it makes use of birdsong, Indian melodies and Puritan psalm tunes, the overall style of the work remains Germanic in origin.

Another symphony begun in 1914, subtitled *Gulliver*, remained unfinished for many years. At the age of 78 Kelley was encouraged to return to the score which he completed in 1935. The four movements depict in turn: Voyage and Shipwreck: Gulliver's Dream and Sleep: Lilliput: Hornpipe – Gulliver's Return. The first performance was given in a radio broadcast in April 1937 by the NBC Symphony Orchestra under Walter Damrosch. If only for curiosity value, this is one neglected work that might be deserving of revival.

Kelley viewed nationalism in a wide context:

> The American composer should apply the universal principles of his art to the local and special elements of the subject matter as they appeal to him, and then, consciously or unconsciously, manifest his individuality, which will involve the expression of mental traits and moral tendencies peculiar to his European ancestry, as we find them modified by the new American environs.

Lack of recordings, even in long-playing format, makes objective assessment of these figures from the first half of the twentieth century impossible. It would be unwise to assume that the 50 years of neglect is deserved. Any opportunity to hear a major work by Hadley, Smith or Mason would enlighten what is a dark period of musical history in the United States. Perhaps the revivalist movement which has espoused the cause of the European Baroque and Classical era will eventually explore American music written between the two world wars.

Another once-respected academic, **Frederick Converse** (1871–1940) was a pupil of Paine at Harvard. Following his graduation in 1893 he took composition lessons with Chadwick in Boston, before moving to Germany in 1896 where he studied with Rheinberger in Munich. His Symphony in D, Op.7 was performed in Munich on 14 July 1898 at his graduation from the Royal Academy of Music in that city. On his return to the United States in 1899 he taught at the New England Conservatory, joining the music faculty at Harvard in 1901. From 1920 to 1938 he taught composition at the New England Conservatory.

Converse acquired fame by becoming the first American composer to have an opera performed at the Metropolitan Opera in New York. *The Pipe of Desire*, a one-act tragic fairy tale, was staged there on 18 March 1910. Three other operas were later produced in Boston.

He withdrew the score of his D minor Symphony, giving the designation Symphony No.1 to another work in C minor composed in 1919, and performed on 30 January 1920 by Pierre Monteux and the Boston Symphony Orchestra.

The same forces gave the première of Converse's Second Symphony in E minor (1931) on 21 April 1922.

Symphony No.3 in F dates from 1934. On 7 November 1940 the Indianapolis Symphony Orchestra conducted by Fabian Sevitzky gave the first performance of a Symphony in F minor shortly after the composer's death. For some unknown reason the score for this work in the Edwin Fleisher Library in Philadelphia is labelled No.6, Op.107, but numerically it is his fourth symphony.

**Charles Wakefield Cadman** (1881–1946) was one of the first musicians after Anton Heinrich to take a serious interest in the music of American Indians. His arrangements of four American Indian songs *From the Land of Sky-Blue Water* published in 1909 became very popular, as did his song *At Dawning*. In 1918 the Metropolitan staged his opera *Shenewis* or *The Robin Woman* based on the life of Princess Redfeather who had assisted him in his numerous lecture recitals on native American music. Cadman was also one of the founders of the Hollywood Bowl and the composer of several film scores.

His Symphony No.1 in E minor (*Pennsylvania*) was composed in 1939 and performed in March 1940 by the Los Angeles Philharmonic Orchestra conducted by Albert Coates. It portrays aspects of Cadman's early life with melodies in the score marked 'Hymn Tune', 'Pioneer Theme' and 'River Theme'. Except for certain repeated rhythmic figures, the work contains nothing from his study of American Indian music. In spirit and musical language, the Symphony belongs to the late nineteenth century, broadly romantic with simple treatment of folk-like material. It bears some resemblance to the symphonic works of George Chadwick. The one novelty is the inclusion of a specially designed metal plate which is heard in the finale to simulate the sound of a steel foundry.

Following a period of study in Berlin (1890–95), **Howard Brockway** (1870–1951) settled in New York City as a teacher and pianist. From 1903 to 1910 he taught at the Peabody Institute in Baltimore, after which he spent the rest of his life in New York teaching at the Institute of Musical Art and the Mannes College of Music. In 1895 his Symphony in D was performed in Berlin by the Berlin Philharmonic Orchestra, quite an achievement for a 25-year old American composer. The symphony was heard again in 1907 when Karl Muck conducted a performance with the Boston Symphony Orchestra.

After graduating from Harvard where he had been a pupil of J.K. Paine, **Edward Burlingame Hill** (1872–1960) studied in Paris with Widor (1898) and in Boston with Chadwick. He followed a distinguished teaching career at Harvard (1908–1940); among his pupils were Leonard Bernstein, Elliott Carter, Ross Lee Finney, Randall Thompson and Virgil Thomson. The influence of French impressionism is apparent, particularly in his orchestral music. He composed three symphonies, all premièred by Koussevitzky and the Boston Symphony Orchestra: No.1 in B flat, Op.34 (1927) on 30 March 1928: Symphony No.2 in C, Op.41 (1930) on 27 February 1931: Symphony No.3 in G (1937) on 3 December 1937.

**Louis Gruenberg** (1884–1964) moved with his family from Russia to the

United States when he was 12 months old. He soon revealed a considerable talent as a pianist and in 1903 went to Berlin to become a pupil of Busoni. In 1919 he gave up a pianistic career to devote himself to composition.

Gruenberg made his name in the 1920s as a composer of symphonic jazz. In the next decade he turned to the stage, writing 11 operas, five operettas and a musical, but with little lasting success. The first of his five symphonies, a lengthy work lasting almost an hour, completed in 1919 and revised in 1928, won the Victor Recording Company Prize in 1930. The following four symphonies failed to find a place in the repertoire, in spite of the composer's later revisions to gain public appeal. He died an embittered man whose music had been largely neglected in the last 30 years of his life.

After following an active career as pianist and teacher, **Harl McDonald** (1899–1955) took up the post of manager of the Philadelphia Orchestra in 1939. He had previously enjoyed a close association with the orchestra which had given the première of his first four symphonies: No.1, *The Santa Fé Trail* (1934), No.2, *Rumba* (1935), No.3 *Tragic Cycle* for soprano, chorus and orchestra, based on Chinese poems (also subtitled *The Lament of Fu Hsuan* (1936)), No.4 (1938). A Fifth Symphony on Familiar Themes, composed for a children's concert, was performed in 1948.

As a composer McDonald was both prolific and successful in receiving performances of his music. *The Santa Fé Trail* commemorates the coming of Anglo-Saxon pioneers to the South West, early explorers, the Spanish settlers and the California goldrush. In using a rumba as the scherzo in his Symphony No.2 and a cakewalk in Symphony No.4, he was adept at creating works of instant appeal. *Rumba* was frequently heard on its own and a recording by Stokowski became a best seller.

During the 1940s and 1950s many of his shorter pieces including *The Legend of the Arkansas Traveler*, *Festival of the Workers*, *Bataan* and *Suite from Childhood* enjoyed considerable popularity.

**Bernard Wagenaar** (1894–1971), son of the Dutch composer Johan Wagenaar (1862–1941), studied violin and composition in Holland before moving to the United States in 1920 where he became an American citizen in 1927. From 1921 to 1923 he was a violinist in the New York Philharmonic Orchestra where he was encouraged by the conductor Willem Mengelberg, a fellow countrymen.

Wagenaar taught at the Institute of Musical Art in New York from 1925, remaining there when it became the Juilliard School, until his retirement in 1968. Among his many pupils were Norman Dello Joio, Jacob Druckman, Ned Rorem, William Schuman, Elie Siegmeister and Robert Ward. His music follows German and French traditions with neo-classical tendencies.

Willem Mengelberg conducted Wagenaar's First Symphony with the New York Philharmonic Orchestra on 7 October 1928. The success of this event led Toscanini to commission the Second Symphony which he conducted with the same orchestra on 10 November 1932. Writing in the *London Musical Standard*, Leigh Henry commented:

> In this Second Symphony, Wagenaar has contributed something vital to contemporary music and something to which it would be difficult to attach the label of this or that modern school in spite of its modernity in the best sense.

The composer and critic Virgil Thomson was impressed by Wagenaar's Third Symphony (1935). Writing in the *New York Herald Tribune* after the première on 23 January 1937 by the Juilliard School Orchestra conducted by the composer, he described it as 'Authoritative, cultured, worldly, incisive without profundity, brilliant without ostentation'. From the remarks of these two critics it can be assumed that Wagenaar's work aroused respect rather than warm enthusiasm. His compositions were the product of a capable teacher who showed craftsmanship without demonstrating a strong personal style of his own.

Symphony No.4 was premièred on 16 December 1949 by the Boston Symphony Orchestra under the composer's direction. In a programme note he wrote:

> The 'inspiration' for the composing of this piece was the desire to say what I wanted to say about shaping orchestral sounds into a, formally speaking, rather compact version of the compound musical construction known as a 'symphony'. The [five] movements are mostly short, therefore.

Although Wagenaar's symphonies earned a degree of recognition, even in his lifetime he fell out of fashion. His middle-of-the-road conservatism was viewed as an almost inevitable outcome of his European background and a long teaching career. The revival of at least one of these symphonies would allow the present generation to re-evaluate his position.

In recent years such attention has been extended to the music of **William Grant Still** (1895–1978) with the issue of recordings of his first three symphonies. Almost every work by Still is a reflection of life as a black American. Still studied at the Oberlin Conservatory and the New England Conservatory and with Varèse. His first important composition was the *Afro-American Symphony*, composed in 1930, which established his reputation and helped him earn a Guggenheim Fellowship in 1933, enabling him to work for a time in Europe.

The *Afro-American Symphony* was premièred in 1931 by the Rochester Philharmonic Orchestra, conducted by Howard Hanson, and later taken up by Stokowski. It was the first symphony by a black American composer to be performed by an American orchestra. Still insisted that 'The American colored man of today is, in so many instances, a totally new individual produced through the fusion of white, Indian and Negro blood'.

In present day terminology the symphony is a 'crossover' work that fuses elements of jazz and spirituals with classical forms. Unlike the novelties of Paul Whiteman's symphonic jazz, Still produced a substantial four-movement score lasting some 24 minutes, one of the few convincing pieces to straddle two separate musical traditions.

Symphony No.2 (*Song of a New Race*) is in essence an extension of the *Afro-American Symphony* to which it is closely related in thematic material. It was first performed under the direction of Leopold Stokowski in December 1937. Three other symphonies were composed in 1945, 1947 and 1958 but none of them achieved the success of the *Afro-American Symphony*.

Like William Grant Still, **Erich Korngold**'s reputation has undergone a major reassessment in the last decade, some 30 years after his death. Erich Wolfgang Korngold (1897–1957), the 'wunderkind' who composed a ballet at the age of eleven and his opera *Die tote Stadt* when he was 20, seemed destined to be remembered solely for a handful of Hollywood film scores dating from the late 1930s and 40s. Newly-released recordings of his brilliantly scored film music and the late-romantic operas have given Korngold a status in the twentieth century which sadly he did not enjoy in his lifetime.

Although his Violin Concerto and Cello Concerto sound at times like film music and include material from some movies, the Symphony in F# (1951/2) is in the tradition of the romantic symphonies of the nineteenth century. The angular melodic lines and chromatic harmonies of the rugged and assertive first movement are worlds away from the cinema. Here there is a complex structure with real thematic development conceived in long musical paragraphs. Behind the outward gaiety of the tarantella-like Scherzo and its ghostly Trio lies a sardonic and abrasive wit, thoroughly modern in idiom with occasional Walton-like touches. The hint of a funeral march in the extensive slow movement inevitably evokes memories of Bruckner and Mahler but the broad span of the passionate melodies belong to the twentieth century. Korngold is closer to his customary extrovert self in the playful Finale, in the manner of another incurable romantic from central Europe in exile in the United States, Dohnányi. References back to music from the other movements provide a semblance of cyclic form.

Although backward-looking historically, Korngold's symphony is a score of real integrity; its recent rediscovery is well deserved. Although the work received a number of radio performances in Germany, the public première did not take place until 27 November 1972, two decades after its completion and fifteen years after the composer's death. Rudolf Kempe conducted the Munich Philharmonic Orchestra who made a recording in the same year.

The death of Korngold in 1957 marked the end of the Romantic tradition in America which had originated in the early nineteenth century in Europe, long deemed obsolete by critical opinion. It is, however, ironical that within twenty-five years a new movement, neo-Romanticism, was beginning to emerge as a reaction against ultra-Modernism. This in turn has led to a reassessment of the immediate past and the restoration of composers, including Korngold, Howard Hanson, David Diamond and others whose reputations had suffered through changing fashions.

# 6   Charles Ives (1874–1954)

Charles Ives was a uniquely American phenomenon. His early musical upbringing under the guidance of his father George combined conventional tuition in piano, harmony and counterpoint with distinctly unorthodox aural experiments. Following service during the Civil War as a bandmaster in the Union Army, George Ives taught music in Danbury, Connecticut and conducted the local band.

His curiosity in all things acoustic led him to construct a device that could produce quarter tones, and on occasions he arranged his bandsmen into spaced groups, each playing simultaneously different pieces in different keys and tempi. Attempts to make his children identify quarter tones failed, but he did teach them to sing tunes in one key while he accompanied them in an other one. The young Charles was exposed to every prevailing influence: dance bands, church music and popular songs in addition to Bach, Handel and Beethoven. In later life he was able to combine and interchange these disparate elements with equanimity, ignoring the boundaries which, for most other people, exist between them.

The death of George Ives in November 1884, when Charles was ten years old, had a devastating effect upon his son. He admired his father above all other musicians, and there was now no-one to whom he could turn who understood his music.

At the age of fourteen, Charles Ives was appointed organist at the First Baptist Church in Danbury, the youngest salaried organist in the state. A Fugue in four keys for organ he wrote at this time was a natural consequence of the musical environment in which he had grown up. By the time he entered Yale University in 1894, Ives was a gifted pianist and organist with a number of compositions to his credit and a firm grasp of standard music theory which enabled him to follow the traditional academic course without affecting his independent spirit. His composition teacher, Horatio Parker, a pupil of the German organist Rheinberger, was a strict disciple of European traditions, remaining loyal to German harmonic and contrapuntal practices. He was totally incapable of appreciating the eccentricities of the young Ives, dismissing such oddities as the *Fugue in Four Keys* as a joke. Ives recalled 'He would look at a measure or two, hand it back with a smile or joke "hogging all the keys at one meal" and then talk about something else. After two or three weeks in Freshman year, I did not bother him with any of the experimental ideas that [my] Father had been willing for me to think about and try out.'

Ives began sketches for his First Symphony in D minor 1895 during his second year as a student, completing the scoring in May 1898. Since the second and fourth movements of the First Symphony were to be part of his composition thesis, Ives took the sensible step of setting aside his personal idiom and following conventional nineteenth-century lines, although his teacher was not always satisfied with the results. The opening was meant to be in D minor but the first subject passed through no fewer than eight different keys, so that Parker made him produce another first movement. Ives later maintained that the original was better. Similarly a replacement slow movement in F major was required for one in G flat that Ives had composed.

Although the First Symphony is uncharacteristic of the real Charles Ives, the work should not be dismissed simply as a student exercise. The score proves that he possessed a sound technique to produce a convincing if conventional symphony. No specific composer or work seems to have been the model. The naive simplicity of the woodwind writing in the development section of the opening *Allegro moderato* contains echoes of MacDowell. Ives' choice of a cor anglais accompanied by the strings for the slow movement, marked *Adagio molto*, inevitably invites comparison with the slow movement of Dvořák's Symphony No.9 (*From the New World*), written some two years earlier, but in character the music more closely resembles *Noel*, the second of George Chadwick's *Symphonic Sketches*, also dating from 1895 although not published until 1907 and therefore unknown to Ives at the time. The ghosts of Beethoven and Mendelssohn are spirited up in the compact *Scherzo* where the chatter of woodwind reveals Ives' skill as an orchestrator. In the discursive Finale (*Allegro molto*), answering scales between wind and strings and the grand coda owe something to Tchaikovsky.

Written under academic restrictions, the First Symphony lacks any distinct personality. The entire score is devoid of quotations from popular songs, hymns and marches that one would expect in 'genuine' Ives. There is nothing in the music to suggest that this is the work of an American, but in his twenties Ives could handle symphonic form with a high degree of competence.

In March 1910 Walter Damrosch conducted the last three movements of the First Symphony with his New York Symphony Orchestra at a Saturday morning rehearsal. He praised the workmanship but felt the music was too complex for the public and would require an excessive amount of rehearsal. The first performance of Symphony No.1 was eventually given on 20 April 1955 by the National Gallery Orchestra of Washington conducted by Richard Bales, over half a century after its completion.

The Second Symphony (1897–1904) was Ives' first large-scale composition after he left Yale. He began work on the score in 1897, gathering together separate pieces written over several years. Some passages were derived from short overtures, marches and other orchestral pieces that had been tried out privately by Frank Fichtl's Hyperion Theater orchestra in New Haven and the New Haven Brass Band.

The opening Andante moderato is based on an Organ Sonata Ives had played at the Center Church, New Haven and an overture, *Down East*, both of which are now lost. Another lost overture, *In These United States*, provided material for the second movement. An organ prelude composed in 1896 was scored in 1902 to constitute the central Adagio cantabile; the movement was slightly revised in 1909. The Lento maestoso is derived from another lost overture, *Town, Gown and State*, written in 1896. For the Finale Ives adapted an overture *American Woods* dating from 1889, which depicted a fiddle band of old farmers who play at a barn dance with jigs, galops and reels.

Ives, now settled firmly in New York and working in the insurance business, looked back with nostalgia in this symphony to the rural life of his birthplace Danbury, Massachusetts. The work represents a collage of his personal musical experiences, a transformation of vernacular elements from the world around him into symphonic form.

Throughout the score Ives inserted references to European composers. Beethoven's opening motto in the Fifth Symphony can be heard, quietly reiterated in the third movement. Other fragments from Brahms' First and Third Symphonies, Wagner's *Tristan and Isolde*, Dvořák's *New World Symphony*, Bach and Bruckner rub shoulders with *America the Beautiful*, *Columbia, Gem of the Ocean*, *The Campdown Races*, *Turkey in the Straw* and several hymn tunes, including *When I Survey the Wondrous Cross* and *Bringing in the Sheaves*. All these disparate ingredients produce a remarkably consistent whole, although it is burdened by some heavy-handed orchestration. Had the Second Symphony been performed shortly after its completion, it would have exerted a powerful influence upon the younger generation of American composers seeking a national style. In 1910 Ives sent the professionally copied score to the conductor Walter Damrosch who promised to look at it. Regrettably nothing came of the proposal and the score was not returned.

When Leonard Bernstein agreed to conduct the première of the Second Symphony in 1951, almost half a century after the piece was completed, the score could not be found. A laborious reconstruction was made from the composer's early pencil sketches. The première on 22 February 1951 caused a considerable stir, bringing the unique qualities of the composer to the attention of a wide audience, both in the concert hall and on radio, who were generally unaware of his music. In the context of the 1950s, Ives' dated work was a distinct curiosity. Nevertheless its appearance led to an avid exploration of his more experimental works, including the Fourth Symphony with its polytonal and polyrhythmic features which were closer to the post-serial world of Stockhausen, Boulez and Elliott Carter.

The unexpected dissonant final chord, a rude 'raspberry', has given rise to diverse explanations. It seems likely that Ives was simply recalling the practice of the high school dance bands of his youth which adopted such a measure to indicate that the evening's dancing was over. Although his wife attended the concert, Ives himself could not face being present in the concert hall – instead he listened at home on a radio provided by his maid.

Ives completed his Third Symphony, subtitled *The Camp Meeting*, in 1904. As with the previous symphony he based each movement on earlier works (now lost), in this case two preludes and a communion for organ dating from 1901. It is conceived on a relatively modest scale, lasting 17 minutes and scored for single woodwind, two horns, trombone, strings and, in the closing bars, bells. In contrast to the robust Symphony No.2, the Third is predominantly lyrical. The titles to the movements and the extensive quotations of hymn tunes are proof that Ives considered this as much a descriptive piece as a symphony. Indeed, the European symphonic model is seldom evident. In keeping with the atmosphere of a revivalist meeting, the simple contrapuntal treatment of the hymns stays close to the 'fuging tunes' of the eighteenth century.

The first movement, Andante, subtitled *Old Folks Gatherin*, makes use of three hymn tunes, 'O What a Friend We Have in Jesus', 'There is a Fountain Filled With Blood' and 'Take it to the Lord'. The abrupt harmonic changes in the chorale-like opening are characteristic of Ives' fluid sense of tonality:

Ex. 2

*Reproduced by permission of G. Schirmer Inc.*

Each chord is identifiably diatonic but the relationship to what has gone before and what follows creates harmonic ambiguities. Over 30 years later unrelated diatonic triad sequences form the stylistic basis of symphonies by Roy Harris and William Schuman. This is now recognized as a distinctly American characteristic which can be traced back to Charles Ives.

The dense orchestration, with the wind instruments often doubling the strings, emphasizes the heavy, ponderous and pedantic features of Ives' counterpoint.

Here the composer reminds the listener of the origin of the music in an organ prelude with all the stops out. Of more daring is the second subject marked *Adagio cantabile*, where enharmonic shifts produce constant modulations:

Ex. 3

*Reproduced by permission of G. Schirmer Inc.*

The central Allegro (*Children's Day*) in more lively mood, is a modified Scherzo and Trio that quotes the hymn 'There is a Happy Land'.

The Lento Finale (*Communion*) is derived from the hymn 'Just as I am Without One Plea', although the angular melodic contours are more instrumental than vocal in character. Contrapuntal development is highly chromatic with complex independent lines. According to Henry Cowell, the editor of the revised published edition, Ives was unsure about the bells in the closing bars. What he probably wanted was the sound of church bells offstage that need not coincide in pitch and rhythm with the orchestra.

In 1911 Gustav Mahler expressed an interest in conducting Ives' Third Symphony but Mahler's death later that year prevented a performance and the score was lost. For the première on 5 April 1946, the composer Lou Harrison deciphered Ives' pencil sketches to produce a new score and parts. The symphony was played by the New York Little Symphony Orchestra under his direction.

This was the first symphony by Charles Ives to be heard complete. Critical response was generally enthusiastic. The *New York Times* commented:

> It possessed a freshness of inspiration, a genuineness of feeling and an intense sincerity that lent it immediate appeal and manifested inborn talents of a high order. The music is close to the soil and deeply felt.

The symphony was repeated the following week, after which it received a special commendation from the Music Critics' Circle of New York. In May 1947 it was awarded the Pulitzer Prize for Music.

Ives worked on the score of his Fourth Symphony between 1910 and 1916. For a performance of the first two movements in January 1927, the composer wrote an extended essay on the motives behind the music.

The aesthetic program of the work is that of the searching questions of What? and Why? which the spirit of man asks of life. This is particularly the sense of the Prelude. The three succeeding movements are the diverse answers in which existence replies.

The 'replies' are represented as comic and chaotic (Allegretto), religious order (Andante Moderato) and universal transcendental religion (Largo Maestoso).

In assembling the thematic material for the symphony, Ives again drew upon his past, with hymn tunes at the heart of each movement and popular marches and songs jostling for a place in the Allegretto. In all four movements, Ives makes use of spatial effects, dividing the orchestra into several sections placed at varied distances from the audience. Often these separate groups play at different tempi simultaneously, a striking experiment that predates Stockhausen's *Gruppen* for three orchestras by nearly 40 years.

The short opening Prelude, *Maestoso*, derived from the fugue from the last movement of his First Violin Sonata (1906–8), is scored for trumpet, trombone, harp, piano, cymbal, bass drum and strings on stage, with an off-stage ensemble of flute, harp and strings. After a solo cello has quoted from 'The Sweet Bye and Bye', the off-stage players intone the hymn 'Bethany' at a tempo independent from the onstage instruments. Against the soothing unison chorus singing Lowell Mason's hymn 'Watchman, Tell us of the Night', the orchestra introduces a restless transformed version of 'Nearer My God To Thee'. In the context of the whole symphony, the Prelude sounds too short to balance the length and complexity of the ensuing Allegretto. In Ives' original plan, the two central movements had been reversed so that the Prelude directly preceded the Fugue.

The Allegretto is based partly on the 'Hawthorne' movement of the *Concord* Piano Sonata (1911). Ives took his inspiration from Hawthorne's satirical story *The Celestial Railroad* in which a group of modern men try to improve on John Bunyan's *The Pilgrim's Progress* by building a railroad to the Celestial City.

> The exciting, easy and worldly progress through life is contrasted with the trials of the Pilgrims in their journey through the swamps and rough country. The occasional slow episodes – Pilgrims' hymns – are constantly crowded out and overwhelmed by the former. The dream or fantasy ends with an interruption of reality – the 4th of July in Concord – brass bands, drum corps etc.

This movement represents Ives' most complex creation. As the separate elements are introduced on the various spaced groups, a texture of 14 independent lines is assembled. Through the orchestral mayhem, various tunes emerge: 'Red, White and Blue' (Fig.18), 'Columbia, Gem of the Ocean' (Fig.21), 'Beulah Land' (Fig.36). Less obvious are references to 'Turkey in the Straw' (Fig.13) and 'Long Time Ago' (Fig.28). Many of these melodic references had appeared in the Second Symphony. Ives devised a system of letters to highlight the more important lines, as Schoenberg and Berg had done in their scores.

At one point, the upper orchestral instruments increase in speed while the lower instruments remain at the same tempo until an eventual collapse occurs. A similar device can be found in Ives' *The Unanswered Question* (1908). The sudden cessation of the full orchestra *fff* before the pianissimo violin solo playing 'Beulah Land' was explained by Ives:

> In this and similar places, what is wanted in a way, is the suggestion of a feeling one may have when entering a church; and as the street noises are suddenly shut out, the organ is heard quietly playing an old church hymn which has ministered in the church for generations.

At the première of the complete symphony in 1965 the intricate mixture of different pulses and rhythms forced Stokowski to be assisted by two other conductors. Gunther Schuller has subsequently revised the polyrhythmic notation so that today a single conductor can cope. Part of the movement was transcribed in 1919 by the composer for piano solo with the title *The Celestial Railroad*.

The serene, slow Fugue that follows, based on the first movement of his String Quartet No.1 (1896), is in sharp contrast to the irreverent antics of the Allegretto. Here the modal harmony is decidedly conservative for Ives. The entries of the fugue subjects, the hymn tunes 'All Hail the Power' and Lowell Mason's 'From Greenland's Icy Mountains' follow textbook regularity, tonic-dominant-tonic-dominant. The movement can be viewed as an example of the composer's deep nostalgia for his earlier life in Danbury but stylistically it is at odds with the experimental, forward-looking language of the rest of the symphony.

Ives provided the following explanation of the finale:

> The last movement is an apotheosis of the preceding content in terms that have something to do with the reality of existence and its religious experience.

He further revealed his intention behind the music. One section is associated with

> a Communion Service, especially the memory of one, years ago in the old Redding Camp Meetings. In the middle there is something suggesting a slow out-of-doors march, which has for its theme, in part, the remembrance of the way the hymn *Nearer My God To Thee* sounds.

Throughout the movement a separate percussion ensemble quietly sustains its own independent ostinato. A second group of five violins and two harps acts as a distant choir. At the centre is a large orchestra including six trumpets. A wordless chorus enters in the closing pages, intoning the hymn tune 'Bethany'. In the slow, mysterious unfolding of the music beginning with 'Nearer My God To Thee' on the cellos as the outset, a sequence of tunes emerges: *Martyn* (Fig. 24) on trumpets, a Missionary Chant (Fig. 36) on wind and strings and the Westminster Chimes (Fig.65). Harmonically Ives was experimenting with atonality, quarter-tones and aleatoric devices, all of which he had discovered for himself. These were natural developments from his experiences as a child when his father had exposed him to polytonality as a normal element of his musical education.

On 29 January 1927 the first two movements of the Fourth Symphony were performed in the Town Hall, New York by an orchestra of 50 players drawn from the New York Philharmonic Orchestra conducted by Eugene Goossens. Some of the audience showed their disapproval but two leading critics provided favourable reviews that reflect well on their readiness to accept the totally new. Writing in the *New York Herald Tribune*, Lawrence Gilman observed:

> This music is as indubitably American in impulse and spiritual texture as the prose of Jonathan Edwards; and like the writing of that true artist and true mystic, it has an irresistable veracity and strength – an uncorrupted sincerity.

The equally respected Olin Downes reported in the *New York Times*:

> There are ineptitudes, incongruities. The thing is an hodgepodge, but something that lives and that vibrates with conviction is there. There is something in the music: real vitality, real *naïveté* and a superb self-respect. There is 'kick' in this piece. It rings truer, seems to have something genuine behind it.

In spite of the stir that this event aroused, little immediate reaction followed to further the cause of Ives' music. In 1929 Henry Cowell's *New Music* published the second movement and Bernard Herrmann conducted his own arrangement of the Fugue at concerts and on the radio during the 1930s. Not until the première of the complete Fourth Symphony on 26 April 1965, over ten years after the composer's death, was the work introduced to the public. Stokowski was the conductor with his American Symphony Orchestra in Carnegie Hall. The stereophonic recording issued shortly afterwards at last brought recognition to this American masterpiece.

Ives' last orchestral piece, the *Universe Symphony*, remained incomplete although he worked on it from 1911 until 1928. It was conceived on a massive and unrealizable scale. The idea for a huge spatial composition had occurred to him while on holiday in the Adirondacks. A number of choruses and orchestras would be placed around a valley, each having its own part to play before coming together in a single musical climax. This combination of Wagnerian megolomania and Hollywood spectacular remained only a visionary dream. Ives provided the following plan;

Section A:     Past – Formation of waters and mountains

Section B:     Present – Earth, evolution in nature and humanity

Section C:     Future – Heaven, the rise of all to the Spiritual

The lack of opportunities to hear his own music in performance, especially the symphonies, led Ives to explore an inner musical world where practical considerations became less and less important. As a result he rarely, if ever, attended concerts, even when his own works were being performed. The complexities of his scores in which numerous disparate activities take place simultaneously became abstract concepts that would not always be coherent in live performance. As he withdrew increasingly into his own private musical world, his vision transcended reality.

When his Second Symphony was to be given its first performance in 1951, he was unwilling to be present in the concert hall. He was afraid that mere mortal musicians would not be able to recreate the sounds that he had kept in his head for forty years. The illusions he had held about his own music were in danger of being shattered. His failure to complete the *Universe* Symphony may have arisen because he had come to realize that his musical conception was beyond the limit of human fulfilment. A performing version has been made by the composer Larry Austin.

The so-called *Holidays Symphony* is a compilation of four separate patriotic pieces: *Washington's Birthday* (1909), *Decoration Day* (1912), *The Fourth of July* (1911–13), and *Thanksgiving Day* (1912). In no way do these collectively constitute a symphony. The first performance by the Minneapolis Symphony Orchestra conducted by Antal Dorati took place on 9 April 1954, just over a month before the composer's death.

With the exception of the early and uncharacteristic First Symphony, the symphonies of Charles Ives occupy a vital historical place in the establishment of an American symphonic tradition. It is not merely the inclusion of hymns and popular tunes that makes his works the first truly national music of the United States. His idiosyncratic non-European approach to all aspects of composition confirm him as the supreme pioneer of American music.

# 7   Aaron Copland (1900–1990)

In the 1920s, the cultural centre of Europe was Paris. Here could be found the latest fashions in art, music, literature, poetry, theatre, dance and philosophy. In contrast to German orthodoxy, France offered the Bohemian life of an artist.

During the last half of the nineteenth century, Germany had been the destination for inspiring American musicians seeking to complete their musical training; now they looked to France. The establishment of the Guggenheim Memorial Fellowship in 1925 and the Fulbright-Hays Awards provided the necessary financial support in a country where the cost of living was relatively low.

The principal attraction was the quality of the teaching, especially that provided by the brilliantly gifted Nadia Boulanger. So many young Americans crossed the Atlantic to study with her that it would almost be easier to list those who were *not* taught by her. Except for her remarkable understanding of contemporary music, Boulanger was rather old fashioned in her methods, demanding high standards of technical skill. At the heart of her approach to music was the close analysis of masters of the past, many of whom, such as Monteverdi, were little known and seldom performed at the time. No longer a composer himself and free of dogma, Boulanger imposed no established style upon her protégés, encouraging them instead towards self-expression.

These young musicians formed an international fraternity around their inspirational leader. Aaron Copland was her first American pupil, soon to be followed by Virgil Thomson, Walter Piston, Roy Harris, David Diamond, Elliott Carter and a host of others. They experienced at first hand the cosmopolitan world of Picasso, Stravinsky, Gertrude Stein, Prokofiev, Ravel, Koussevitzky. Alan Howard Levy described the cultural milieu succinctly:

> For a generation of American composers, the Paris years were a type of university experience. Their intellects were probed, worked and broadened. In a competitive atmosphere they associated with others in their field from all parts of the world and with people in different but, as they discovered, related disciplines. They rose or floundered, in an atmosphere of freedom and ambivalence. Away from home they could see what had real meaning in their musical and cultural backgrounds.
>
> (A.H. Levy (1983) *Musical Nationalism: American Composers' Search for Identity*, Greenwood Press: Westport, Conn., p. 59)

In June 1921 the 20-year-old Aaron Copland set sail from New York for Europe to begin his musical studies in Paris as a private pupil of Nadia Boulanger. Under the guidance of Boulanger he composed a one-act ballet, *Grohg*, inspired by his seeing a German horror film *Nosferatu*, which is closely related to *The Cabinet of Dr Caligari*. To a scenario by Harold Clurman, *Grohg* concerns a vampire that sucks blood from dead bodies and possesses the magic power to revive the dead and make them dance. The ballet lasts 38 minutes and was completed in 1925 but it has remained unstaged. From the original score Copland arranged three sections to form the *Dance Symphony* which he entered for the RCA Victor Company Prize in 1929 as he had not completed his *Symphonic Ode*, the work he had intended to submit. He won a fifth of the prize money, which was shared with Louis Gruenberg and Ernest Bloch who each received $5000 and Robert Russell Bennett, who was awarded $10 000 for two works.

Although the Symphony for Organ and Orchestra was the first of Copland's orchestral works to be performed, the *Dance Symphony* should be considered his first in order of composition as the music was written between 1922 and 1925. The *Dance Symphony* employs a large orchestra, including triple woodwind, piano and two harps. The addition of two cornets to the brass section reflects the French influence, where composers from Berlioz to Debussy used these otherwise neglected orchestral instruments. The extensive array of percussion has a distinct American flavour.

There is little in the music of the *Dance Symphony* that specifically betrays its origin in a ballet. The strong rhythmic figures that abound in the first movement are derived from the thematic material itself and the separate movements are in no way the episodic or 'mood' music which one might have expected from a score originally composed to accompany dance. The structure of the three linked movements is somewhat unusual, although these follow a fast-slow-fast pattern. In the ballet the slow introduction depicted the domain of the necromancer Grohg. A number of musical fragments and motifs that reappear throughout the *Dance Symphony* provide a melodic unity for the thematic material of all three movements. In the opening bars (Ex. 4) the progression of triads on three muted trumpets repeats the interval of a third, usually a minor third, which can be traced in the harmonic and melodic material throughout the work.

Ex. 4

Reproduced by permission of Boosey and Hawkes Ltd

In the ensuing *Allegro*, 'Dance of the Adolescents', the fast tempo is not relaxed until the closing bars, *Adagio molto*, which lead into the second movement, a slow waltz originally entitled 'Dance of the Girl Who Moves as if in a Dream'. The viola solo that links the slow movement to the finale makes use of quarter-tones, a daring experiment for the early 1920s.

The last movement, 'Dance of Mockery', opens with a brilliant sprung rhythm in irregular metrical patterns (Ex. 5). This constituted the finale of the ballet where Grohg taunted his victims and servants. New material at Fig. 29 maintains regular time signatures but irregular accents. Copland's own essay on notation of irregular rhythms throws light on this problem and explains why he often altered bar lines in revised works for ease of reading (Aaron Copland (1961) *On Music*: Andre Deutsch: London, p. 273ff).

Ex. 5

*Reproduced by permission of Boosey and Hawkes Ltd*

At Fig. 38 the cross-rhythms between melody and accompaniment caused the composer to add an extra stave at the top of the score to indicate what the conductor should beat, a feature that is probably unique (Ex. 6). This is a curious and rather disturbing novelty as one assumes that the conductor beats according to bar-lines and time signature, not with the syncopations.

Ex. 6

*Reproduced by permission of Boosey and Hawkes Ltd*

The final orchestral *tutti* is an example of Copland's early mastery in combining four separate musical ideas that have appeared earlier in the movement into a coherent mix of contrapuntal intricacy (Ex. 7a). The last chord with its semitone dissonance in the bass (Ex. 7b) became in later orchestral pieces a characteristic 'trade mark' of the composer in ending his works.

Ex. 7a

Ex. 7b

*Reproduced by permission of Boosey and Hawkes Ltd*

Despite the balletic origins of the *Dance Symphony*, it would be wrong to regard it as a ballet suite. The development of melodic and harmonic material both within each movement and throughout the work produces a composition that in form and content is symphonic. The orchestration, especially in the finale, is functional rather than subtle. The rhythmic drive in the fast movements is distinctly American but the music remains cosmopolitan with no recognizable national flavour.

Shortly before Copland returned to the United States in June 1924, Nadia Boulanger was invited there by Walter Damrosch and Koussevitzky to appear as solo organist with the New York Symphony Orchestra and the Boston Symphony Orchestra respectively. Her confidence in the young American prompted her to ask him to write a work for her to play. Copland accepted the commission,

> despite the fact that I had written only one work in extended form before then, that I had only a passing acquaintance with the organ as an instrument, and that I had never heard a note of my own orchestration.
>
> (Aaron Copland (1941) *The New Music 1900–60*, McGraw-Hill: New York, rev. 1968 Macdonald: London, p. 156)

Copland began composing his Symphony for Organ and Orchestra in the Summer of 1923 while staying at Milford, Pennsylvania, where he was earning a living playing the piano in a hotel trio. It is surprising that he was able to complete the whole score by the Autumn of the same year. As with the *Dance Symphony* Copland uses a large orchestra: triple woodwind, full brass (but no cornets) and a percussion section requiring six players in addition to the timpanist.

The Symphony is in three movements, although the opening Prelude is merely an introduction to the second movement, a Scherzo, which takes on more significance than in most symphonies, acting as the powerful centre of the work. The principal theme of the Prelude heard on the solo flute in the first bars (Ex. 8) introduces the interval of a third, providing a reminder of the *Dance Symphony*, where the same interval is an integral feature of the whole work. The motif on the strings accompanying the entry of the organ also relies on a minor third. Copland's economical use of material allows him to derive all the thematic development from the opening flute melody.

Ex. 8

*Reproduced by permission of Boosey and Hawkes Ltd*

The Scherzo maintains a strong rhythmic impetus from beginning to end with one brief interruption of slower music. There is no clear 'theme' as such; all the melodic material derives from the pervading ostinato set at the beginning of the movement. Many of these passages are built up from irregular groupings of notes with uneven accents which disregard bar-lines.

The climax before the central Trio and its return at the end of the movement with the full force of brass and percussion is Copland at his most ferocious. It is little wonder that the New York audience at the première was overwhelmed by the work. The finale is more restrained emotionally; in a way that must have pleased Mlle Boulanger, the movement is a passacaglia in form but with only the first three notes being present at each repetition. The separate variations are usually based not directly on the theme itself but on the previous derivation of it. Bars 5–8 of the theme are a variant of bars 1–4 with certain intervals widened but the overall shape of the phrases is maintained (Ex. 9).

Ex. 9

*Reproduced by permission of Boosey and Hawkes Ltd*

In the succeeding 13 sections, the theme undergoes the customary contrapuntal treatment, in canon, diminution and augmentation with varied counterfigures. Copland's invention makes this no mere technical exercise; the development of the music is compact, avoiding episodic fragmentation. The result is a powerful expression of Copland in what he termed his 'European' voice. The role of the organist is partly that of soloist, partly a member of the orchestra; the passages where the organ is unaccompanied are brief. At other times it blends into the orchestral texture, but very little of the organ part doubles the instruments. Nevertheless the work is a symphony, not a concerto.

As promised, on 11 January 1925 Nadia Boulanger played the Symphony with the New York Symphony Orchestra under Walter Damrosch in Aeolian Hall, New York City. After the performance, the conductor turned to remark to the audience: 'If a young man at the age of 23 can write a symphony like that, in five years he will be ready to commit murder.' One critic described the Symphony as a 'new and seething crater'. A second performance, in Boston on 20 February of the same year, was the beginning of a valuable friendship between the composer and Sergei Koussevitzky. Copland began to write music to suit the characteristics of the Boston Symphony Orchestra, with their particular 'sound' in mind.

Virgil Thomson described the impact of the work upon him:

> When [Nadia Boulanger] asked me how I liked it, I replied that I had wept. 'But the important thing', she said, 'is why you wept'. 'Because I had not written it myself', I answered. And I meant that. The piece was exactly the Boulanger piece and exactly the American piece several of us would have given anything to write and that I was overjoyed someone had written.

> (V. Thomson (1966) *Virgil Thomson on Virgil Thomson*, Alfred A. Knopf: New York; Weidenfeld & Nicolson: London, p. 71)

In 1928 he made a version of the Organ Symphony which replaced the part for organ with additional orchestration. While retaining the original instruments, he added alto saxophone, four more horns, two trumpets, piano, tom-tom and glockenspiel. The organ part was allocated to the woodwind in lyrical passages and to the piano in the orchestral *tutti*. Otherwise the distribution of music among the orchestra remains substantially unchanged. The additional brass comes into its own, replacing the massive organ chords in the closing bars of the Finale. For some inexplicable reason there is a change of rehearsal letters in the second version. To distinguish the two works, Copland called the original 'Symphony for Organ and Orchestra', and the later one 'First Symphony'.

The First Symphony was completed in 1928 and premièred by the Berlin Symphony Orchestra under Ernest Ansermet in Berlin in December 1931. The Scherzo in this version had been heard on 4 November 1927 in Carnegie Hall, New York with the Philadelphia Orchestra conducted by Fritz Reiner. Looking back after many years, Copland wrote:

> For a while I thought of the Organ Symphony as being too European in derivation and

in the works that followed – in *Music for the Theatre* of 1925 and the Piano Concerto of 1926 I felt I had come closer to a specifically American idiom. In retrospect, however, I saw that the jazzy scherzo, for instance, points to the works that were to follow, and also that the Symphony generally was closer to my natural expressive idiom than I had realised.

(Sleeve note to the CBS recording of the Organ Symphony MS 7058)

The *Short Symphony* was completed in 1933 and first performed in Mexico City on 23 November 1934 under Carlos Chávez to whom it is dedicated. Although it was scheduled for performance in the United States on several occasions, it was found rhythmically too complex for the players. Not until 1944 was it heard in America, in a radio broadcast by the NBC Symphony Orchestra conducted by Stokowski. Even as late as 1962 it was to have been performed in London by the composer and the London Symphony Orchestra, but was withdrawn before the concert through insufficient time to prepare it adequately.

The problem of performance led the composer to make an arrangement of it in 1937 as a Sextet for clarinet, piano and string quartet and in this form it has been heard more often. Although the original music remains unchanged, except for the removal of the last two chords, certain bar-lines and time signatures are altered in an attempt to simplify the notation of complicated rhythms.

The scoring of the *Short Symphony* is for a medium-sized orchestra without timpani, percussion and trombones but including the almost obsolete heckelphone which doubles with the cor anglais and can be replaced by that instrument if necessary. The *Short Symphony* is cast in three movements: an opening *Allegro vivace* – for the first time in Copland an important movement, not merely an extended introduction; an elegiac *Lento*, notably simple in comparison to the outer movements; and a fast finale.

Initially there seems to be little in common between this Symphony and the previous two symphonies. The lyricism has been replaced by a brittle toccata-like quality with scant evidence of melodic interest. A careful examination reveals that most of Copland's compositional characteristics are still present although on the surface the style is different. A notable feature of the first movement is that the opening 82 bars are entirely in unison except for the punctuating chords and a brief passage of two-part counterpoint near the beginning. The germ of this movement lies in the first two bars. All the melodic figures that appear in the rest of the movement are derived from this short figure (Ex. 10). The sequence of notes is 'serial' in character, comprising a nine-note row.

This opening melody consists of five and six-note phrases, separated each time by interruptions on other instruments. As in Copland's previous works, the rhythmic impulse is produced by the pattern of quavers in irregular groups of two and three. Two characteristics of Copland's melodic writing are evident in almost every bar: the use of arpeggios and wide leaps, often of two octaves.

As with the *Dance Symphony*, the first movement is joined to the second by a short bridge passage. The nervous rhythmical energy gives way to a continuous flow of tranquil melody; the rush of irregular quavers is transformed into a

Ex. 10

sequence of slow minims. At one point in the middle of the movement, the slow, inevitable unfolding of melody over an ostinato bass has an affinity with Stravinsky's *Symphony of Psalms*, which was composed a few years earlier for the 50th anniversary of the Boston Symphony Orchestra.

The finale is similar in essence to the first movement. The dancing rhythms look forward to his later works especially *El Salón México* and the three popular ballets, *Billy the Kid, Rodeo* and *Appalachian Spring*. The melodic figures are based on wide intervals and arpeggios. Without relaxing the tempo, Copland introduces a contrasting passages (Ex. 11), based on the opening notes of the work but also recalling the mood of the slow movement.

Ex. 11

In this way, the musical ideas of all three movements are related. In a letter to the composer dated 1 December 1934, Chávez wrote:

> The dialectic of this music, that is to say, its movement, the way each and every note comes out from the other as the *only* natural and logical possible one, is simply unprecedented in the whole history of music. The work as a whole, I mean to say in its entirety, is an organism, a body in which every piece works by itself 100% but whose mutual selection is such, that no one part can possibly work or exist without the other. There has been much talk about music in which everything is essential, nothing superfluous, but as far as I know, *the talk* about such music exists; yes, but not the music itself. The 'Little Symphony' [*sic*] is the first realization of this I know of, and yet

the human content, the inner expression is purely emotional. It is precisely that tremendous human impulse which made possible such realization.

Let me tell you what I thought when I got the Little Symphony – well there is the real thing, here is our music, here is my music, the music of my time, of my taste, of my culture, here it is, a simple and natural fact to myself, as everything belonging to oneself is simple and natural.

(Reprinted in *Letters of Composers*, ed. Gertrude Norman and Miriam Lubell Shrifte (1979) Greenwood Press: Westport, Connecticut, pp. 393–4)

It is interesting to note that the complex rhythms of the *Short Symphony* which baffled American players appeared 'simple and natural' to the Mexican Carlos Chávez whose own works often explore irregular rhythmic ideas. Although the *Short Symphony* may never achieve the popularity of Copland's other music, its craftsmanship and logic produce increasing admiration on repeated hearings. As an abstract composition, it is a masterpiece of compact invention. The economy of material and relevance of all the melodic and rhythmical development typify the composer's thought processes.

After the completion of *Appalachian Spring* in 1944, Copland began work on his most extended composition, the Third Symphony. In the previous year he had received a commission from the Koussevitzky Music Foundation, and in July 1944 in Tepozlan, Mexico he began the initial sketches. He continued on the Symphony in several different locations from October 1944 to September 1946: New York; Bernardsville, New Jersey; New York; Ridgefield, Connecticut; New York; the MacDowell Colony, Peterborough, New Hampshire; Tanglewood, Massachusetts and Richmond, Massachusetts. The final bars were completed on 29 September, less than a month before the première in Boston under Koussevitzky. The haste in finishing the score is indicated by the revision (on the advice of Leonard Bernstein) of the closing pages, where two short sections were omitted in later performances (Fig. 129 to Fig. 130; Fig. 130 bars 5 and 6). Dedicated 'to the memory of my dear friend Natalie Koussevitzky', the Third Symphony gained the New York Music Critics' Circle Award for the best orchestral work of the 1946–47 concert season.

The excursion into folk music for some of his most recent compositions, especially the three ballets, inevitably left traces of a new style on the Symphony in spite of Copland's own assertion that 'It contains no folk or popular material. Any reference to jazz or folk material in this work is purely unconscious.' There is clearly no direct quotation of folk-song, but the idiom of folk-music and dance is often present in all four movements. In Copland's programme notes for the première he wrote of the first movement, *Molto moderato*:

The opening movement, which is broad and expressive in character, opens and closes in the key of E major. (Formally it bears no relation to the sonata-allegro with which symphonies usually begin.) The themes, three in number, are plainly stated: the first is on the strings at the very start without introduction; the second in related mood in violas and oboes; the third, of a bolder nature, in the trombones and horns. The general form is that of an arch, in which the central portion is more animated; and the final section is an extended coda, presenting a broadened version of the opening material.

Both the first and third themes are referred to again in later movements of the Symphony.

The first movement, like those of so many American symphonies acts as an introduction and is not a weighty sonata-form movement in the classical mould. The finale is the musical kernel of the work. The opening of the Third Symphony (Ex. 12) resembles the beginning of Copland's ballet *Appalachian Spring* in its self-effacing manner of embarking on a large-scale work, with simple melodic material quietly ushered in.

Ex. 12

*Reproduced by permission of Boosey and Hawkes Ltd*

The continuous unfolding of melody in crotchet note-values gives rise to the second subject (Ex. 13), basically the same in character as the first, but with a different outline.

Ex. 13

*Reproduced by permission of Boosey and Hawkes Ltd*

A feature of the first three pages of the score common to several earlier works, most notably the *Short Symphony*, is that much of the music is in unison, with only brief passages of chordal counterpoint and two-part writing between the strings and brass. After an intricate development of both themes, the movement gathers momentum with a gradual increase in tempo. Although the music is clearly diatonic, the tonal bass is constantly modulating from bar to bar. The third theme (Ex. 14) is related to the preceding music, but more determined in character.

As this theme is itself modulating, each repetition moves the music into new keys; thus in the canonical passage that follows, consecutive bars are unequivocally in the keys of C minor, B flat major, A flat major, G major, F major, and so on. The first three notes of this theme are later compressed into a figure (Fig. 15) which serves as the germ for the first subject of the following movement and plays a prominent part in the Fanfare which precedes the Finale.

Ex. 14

Più mosso

Trombone

*Reproduced by permission of Boosey and Hawkes Ltd*

Ex. 15

Horns

*Reproduced by permission of Boosey and Hawkes Ltd*

As with all Copland's extended symphonic movements, there is no simple recapitulation of the opening, but a reworking of earlier material to form the conclusion.

Of the Scherzo, Copland writes:

*Allegro molto*: the form of this movement stays closer to the normal symphonic procedure. It is the usual scherzo, with first part, trio and return. A brass introduction leads to the main theme, which is stated three times in Part I: at first on horns and violas with continuation in clarinets, then in unison strings and finally in augmentation in the lower brass. The three statements of the theme are separated by the usual episodes. After the climax is reached, the trio follows without a pause. Solo woodwinds sing the new trio melody in lyrical and canonical style. The recapitulation of Part I is not literal. The principal theme of the scherzo returns in a somewhat disguised form in the solo piano, leading through previous episodic material to a full restatement in the *tutti* orchestra. This is climaxed by a return to the lyrical trio, this time sung in canon and in *fortissimo* by the entire orchestra.

The Scherzo opens with a fanfare-like introduction of 22 bars, initiated by the horns and continued for the most part by the brass.

Ex. 16

Allegro molto

*Reproduced by permission of Boosey and Hawkes Ltd*

Before the theme itself is heard for the first time (on horns and violas), the fanfare is followed by nine bars of a new idea (Ex. 17) which is used later for the episodes. Copland's observance of the customary scherzo form in this movement even extends to maintaining F major as the key for each statement of the theme.

Ex. 17

The Trio is in complete contrast to the high spirits of the Scherzo. The lyrical oboe solo (Ex. 18) over sustained notes on clarinets, is further evidence of Copland's folk idiom in this work. The theme itself is not a folk-song but would not be out of place in the middle of *Rodeo* or *Appalachian Spring*, as it has all the qualities associated with American folk music.

Ex. 18

A new section adding to this theme continues the lyrical mood of the Trio (Ex. 19), until the gradual return to the Scherzo begins with the 'disguised form' of the theme on the piano, and the movement ends with a massive statement of the opening fanfare now scored for the full orchestra reinforced by a barrage of percussion.

Ex. 19

Of the slow movement, *Andante quasi allegretto*, Copland writes that it

is freest of all in formal structure. Although it is built up sectionally, the various sections are intended to emerge one from the other in continuous flow, somewhat in the manner of a close-knit series of variations. The opening section, however, plays no role other than that of introducing the main body of the movement. High up in the unaccompanied first violins is heard a rhythmically transformed version of the third (trombone) theme of the first movement of the Symphony. It is briefly developed in contrapuntal style, and comes to a full close, once again in the key of E major.

A new and more tonal theme is introduced in the solo flute. This is the melody that supplies thematic substance for the sectional metamorphoses that follows: at first with quiet singing nostalgia; then faster and heavier – almost dance-like; then more child-like and naive, and finally vigorous and forthright.

Imperceptibly the whole movement drifts off into the higher regions of the strings, out of which floats the single line of the beginning, sung by a solo violin and piccolo, accompanied this time by harps and celeste. The third movement calls for no brass, with the exception of a single horn and trumpet.

The slow movement opens with the first violins in their high register, playing a transformed version of the trombone theme of the first movement. A contrapuntal development of this theme prepares the way for the principal subject, a simple tune for flute (Ex. 20) that seems at first more like an accompanying melody than a significant theme in its own right, which later provides the material for almost the entire movement.

Ex. 20

*Reproduced by permission of Boosey and Hawkes Ltd*

From this point the tempo becomes progressively faster; this central section brings to mind the lively dances of *Appalachian Spring*. A new rhythmic and melodic figure inspired by the onward drive of the music appears first on the trumpet. In characteristic manner, Copland extends and adapts this theme. At the climax the principal subject is treated in close canon with one of the few passages of polytonality, so often heard in earlier works but seldom apparent in the Third Symphony. Other typical features of the composer's style evident here are the parallel movement of parts in sevenths and the rhythms of the melodic lines which fail to coincide with bar lines. The movement ends almost exactly as it began, with the high melody now on a solo violin playing harmonics against a quiet sustained chord.

Copland describes the last movement, *Allegro deliberato* (Fanfare) – Allegro risoluto, as follows:

> The final movement follows without a pause. It is the largest movement of the Symphony, and closest in structure to the customary sonata-allegro form. The opening fanfare is based on *Fanfare for the Common Man*, which I composed in 1942 at the invitation of Eugene Goossens for a series of wartime fanfares introduced under his direction by the Cincinnati Symphony. In the present version it is played first pianissimo by flutes and clarinets, and then suddenly given out by brass and percussion. The fanfare serves as a preparation for the movement which follows. The components of the

usual form are there: a first theme in animated sixteenth-note (semiquaver) motion; a second theme – broader and more song-like in character; a full-blown movement, leading to a peroration. One curious feature of the movement consists of the fact that the second theme is to be found embedded in the development section instead of being in its customary place. The development, as such, concerns itself with the fanfare and first theme fragments. A shrill 'tutti' chord, with flutter-tongued brass and piccolos, brings the development to a close.

What follows is not a recapitulation in the ordinary sense. Instead a delicate interweaving of the first theme in the higher solo woodwinds is combined with a quiet version of the fanfare on two bassoons. Combined with this, the opening of the first movement is quoted, first in the violins, and later in the solo trombone. Near the end a full-voiced chanting of the second song-like theme is heard in horns and trombones. The Symphony concludes on a restatement of the opening phrase with which the entire work began.

The Finale opens in the key of A flat with a *pianissimo* version of the fanfare on flutes and clarinets. At the entry of the fanfare itself at the thirteenth bar, there is an abrupt change into C major:

Ex. 21

*Reproduced by permission of Boosey and Hawkes Ltd*

The fanfare for brass and percussion is then played in its complete 1942 version. Between the fanfare and the *allegro*, Copland inserts a five-bar transition passage (Ex. 22) in which lower strings, clarinets and bassoon quietly ruminate on the first phrases of the fanfare.

Over this a solo oboe hints at the *allegro* theme, tentatively repeating the first note. In this way Copland provides a compatible relationship, even at this early stage, between two strongly contrasted elements, the fanfare and the *allegro* theme. The hints on the oboe in the above extract become the *allegro* theme itself as the music settles firmly into D major.

The ensuing *fugato* as each of the woodwind takes up derivatives of this figure is one of Copland's most delicate and delightful creations. With the entry of strings and later horns, the orchestra provides a highly-charged impetus. Considerable technical demands are made upon the players – the violinists in particular have to possess light-fingered virtuosity. At the climax (Fig. 101) Copland brings back the fanfare theme in the woodwind and trumpets and in augmentation on trombones, a piece of craftsmanship that is a natural synthesis of musical material, and no mere academic device.

Ex. 22

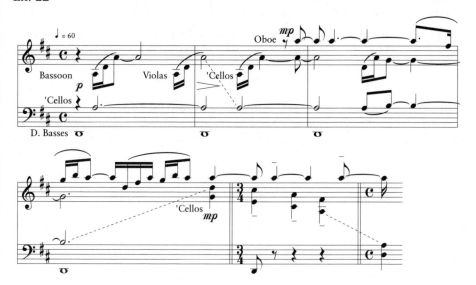

*Reproduced by permission of Boosey and Hawkes Ltd*

Ex. 23

Doppio mov. (Allegro risoluto)

*Reproduced by permission of Boosey and Hawkes Ltd*

A *pianissimo* statement of the fanfare combined with the principal theme provide a background for the introduction of the second theme, as Copland states, curiously appearing at this late stage in the development. An unusual feature of the new subject is the time-signature of regular 3/8 + 2/4 bars; this adds a new rhythmical interest, while the violins continue their chatter of semiquavers.

The recapitulation, following a *fff* chord, is 'far from literal' a characteristic of all his works in symphonic form, but certain figures and treatments of themes already heard make reappearances sufficiently consistent to indicate that the development has formally come to an end, and the recapitulation has begun, although now in D flat, a semitone lower than the exposition.

In the coda, Copland combines the fanfare theme, at times inverted, the opening theme of the first movement and both themes of the *allegro* of the finale. The majestic ending is an apotheosis of these thematic ideas now so consummately integrated. Of his previous orchestral works only the *Symphonic Ode* in its concluding pages possesses a similar declamatory grandeur.

Darius Milhaud recognized an emotional quality in the Third Symphony which might not be noticed by an American writer:

> His recent symphony has more grandeur and a deeper lyricism, but the melancholy simplicity of its themes are a direct expression of his own delicate sadness and sensitive heart.

(*Darius Milhaud* (1952) *Notes Without Music*, Dennis Dobson: London, p. 254)

The Third Symphony was first performed in Boston on 18 October 1946 by the Boston Symphony Orchestra conducted by Sergei Koussevitzky. It soon became one of the pillars of American symphonic music, a position it deservedly retains.

# 8 Elder Statesmen

Unlike their European colleagues, who confined themselves to teaching, most leading composers in America took up senior academic and administrative posts in institutions: Howard Hanson at the Eastman School, Randall Thompson and Walter Piston at Harvard, Peter Mennin at the Juilliard School and William Schuman at Juilliard and the Lincoln Center. Henry Cowell joined the music faculty at Stanford University in 1928 and thereafter taught at various universities and colleges before retiring from Columbia University in 1960. Only Copland and Barber declined a permanent post at a university or conservatory. Virgil Thomson sought financial security in journalism.

Randall Thompson, Walter Piston and Howard Hanson represented the academic élite in American music for more than 30 years, exerting an influence far beyond their institutions and their pupils. In addition to his activities as a composer and teacher, Henry Cowell's efforts as a supporter of American composers was of immense significance. He contributed numerous essays and articles to various journals, promoted concerts and in 1927 single-handedly established *New Music* in which were published works by contemporary composers including Ives, Schoenberg, Webern and Varèse.

In his position as music critic for the *New York Herald Tribune* from 1940 to 1954, **Virgil Thomson** (1896–1989) was the most influential writer on music in the United States. Reputations of composers and performers were made or destroyed by his trenchant comments. He set standards of impartiality and objectivity unequalled since his death.

Much of Virgil Thomson's music is a fusion of the American vernacular: hymn tunes, popular songs, ragtime, bands, much as had influenced Charles Ives – and an anarchic disregard for convention acquired during his time in Paris in the 1920s and 30s, perhaps influenced by the unorthodox French composer Erik Satie.

The *Symphony on a Hymn Tune* was composed in Europe between 1926 and 1928. In spite of the title, it is not a religious work beyond a thematic basis in two hymns: an old Scottish pentatonic tune 'How Firm a Foundation' and 'Yes, Jesus Loves Me'. Thomson sought to evoke the spirit of early nineteenth century rural life in America by weaving these revivalist hymns into the texture. The critic

Paul Rosenfeld likened the piece to a Currier and Ives print. Part of the finale was later used in the score for the Pare Lorentz film *The River* (1937) and the simple folk idiom is close to the music Thomson wrote for other films set in American landscapes.

The composer provided a brief description of the Symphony:

> It is a set of variations on the hymn 'How Firm a Foundation'; each movement consists of a further set of variations tightened up in various ways, the first in the manner of a sonata, the second as a Bach chorale prelude, the third a passacaglia. The fourth is twice tightened up, once as a fugato, once as a rondo.

In the opening movement, the hymn tunes appear in a distorted form, out of focus and harmonized at times bitonally, leading to grotesque cadenzas for trombone, cello and violin. The hesitant nature of the music with its sparse orchestration and frequent silences hardly suggests a symphonic movement.

The song-like *Andante Cantabile* is reflective and modest is pretentions. Following the passacaglia, based on a repeated four-bar phrase on the cellos, the finale introduces a new theme 'For He's a Jolly Good Fellow', not widely considered a hymn tune. Material heard in the earlier movements is reprised, culminating in a brass fugato. Basic diatonic chords are juxtaposed with polytonal phrases as the bass line wanders off, quite independent of the melodies above.

If the *Symphony on a Hymn Tune* was intended as an exercise of iconoclastic revolution, the composer failed to rouse the masses. It is essentially too soft-centred to create any serious impact. In 1928 Koussevitzky showed some enthusiasm on seeing the score, suggesting revisions to the finale. Thomson had to wait 17 years until he heard the work, when he conducted the New York Philharmonic Orchestra on 22 February 1945.

Symphony No.2 (1931) is an orchestration of Thomson's First Piano Sonata of 1929 with some revisions. At the end of the finale some 60 bars of the original are replaced by nine new ones. In 1941, after hearing part of the Symphony rehearsed in Newark, New Jersey, Thomson wholly rescored the work which was performed on 14 November 1941 by the Seattle Symphony Orchestra conducted by Sir Thomas Beecham.

The composer provided a short analysis:

> My Second Symphony is cyclic in thematic content and asymmetrical in form. Its opening measures are the motif, the germ from which the whole is developed. Its forward progress is continuous, moreover, no section and almost no phrase being repeated exactly. Its structure is that of an open curve.
>
> The first and third movements are squarely in C major, the second in A flat. The tunes are all diatonic, and so is the harmony. Tonalities are sharply juxtaposed, rather than superimposed. Instrumentation 'by threes' has facilitated the scoring of unrelated chords in contrasting colors. The expressive character of this symphony is predominantly lyrical. Dancing and jollity, however, are rarely absent from its thought; and the military suggestions of horn and trumpet, of marching and of drums, are a constant recurring presence both as background and as foreground.

Each movement is defined by a different musical interval; the *Allegro con brio* by a fourth, the *Andante* by a third, the *Allegro* finale by a second. The first movement is hardly what one expects of a symphony. It is exuberantly lighthearted, incorporating a jolly trumpet tune with jaunty accompaniments and hints of bitonality. Here is the essence of Parisian frivolity of the Twenties, simple diatonic tunes characteristic of 'Les Six', set in the manner of Stravinsky, dance music with its origin in night clubs and vaudeville. The large orchestra is used sparingly, in neo-classical, chamber music fashion.

The *Andante* is a curious amalgam of hymn tune and slow waltz with abruptly shifting tonality. There are vestiges of a waltz in the constantly interrupted finale where fragments of hymns and folk song are exchanged in lopsided phrase lengths, harmonized both tonally and bitonally, a Thomson characteristic Wilfred Mellers calls 'deliberately disrupting musical grammar and the logic of connection' (W. Mellers (1964) *Music in a New Found Land*, Barrie and Rockliff: London, p. 206).

Virgil Thomson was an inveterate recycler of material. Symphony No.3 has its origin in his Second String Quartet (1932) which in turn had been orchestrated to become ballet music in Act 3 of his third opera *Lord Byron* performed in 1972. It was subsequently dropped from the production. As Symphony No.3 it was premièred in New York on 26 December 1972 by the American Symphony Orchestra conducted by Kazuyoshi Akiyama.

In reality the Symphony belongs to the Paris years and in the quartet version follows chronologically on from the Second Symphony. It is much less adventurous than either of its predecessors, neo-classical in manner with dance elements a strong feature. There is an easy-going, unchallenging air to the whole work, especially in the two short middle movements, a waltz and a relatively sombre tango. That the score sounds like a *bone fide* orchestral piece is credit to the composer's skill in instrumentation.

Like his contemporary Roger Sessions, **Randall Thompson** (1899–1984) studied at Harvard before taking private composition lessons with Ernest Bloch. Similarly he spent a lifetime in teaching at several establishments including the University of California, Berkeley (1937–39), the Curtis Institute (1939–41), University of Virginia (1941–46), Princeton (1946–48) and finally at Harvard (1948–65), where his pupils included Samuel Adler, Leonard Bernstein and Lukas Foss.

Thompson was primarily a composer of choral music including the widely popular *Alleluia*, *The Peaceable Kingdom* and *The Last Words of David*. He has only seven orchestral works to his credit, three of them symphonies.

The First Symphony completed in 1929 was originally conceived as a choral piece. In its final form it was performed by the Eastman Rochester Symphony Orchestra conducted by Howard Hanson on 20 February 1930.

Symphony No.2 in E minor was commissioned by the Alice M. Ditson Fund of Columbia University and written in Gstaad, Switzerland where the composer was staying on a Guggenheim Fellowship. He dedicated the score to his wife.

Following the première by the Eastman Rochester Symphony Orchestra under Howard Hanson at an American Composers' Concert on 24 March 1932, it was heard in New York on 3 November 1933 under the baton of Bruno Walter. Its success was such that it entered the standard repertoire of American orchestras, receiving over 500 performances. Thompson explained his intentions behind the music:

> It is based on no program either literary or spiritual. It is not cyclical. I wanted to write four contrasting movements, separate and distinct, which together should convey a sense of balance and completeness.

The opening brass fanfare heralds a movement of abundant optimism and boundless energy, the get-up-and-go spirit of the age. In the elegiac slow movement there is a hint of folk-song in the lyrical interpolations on the woodwind into the flow of string melody. The jazzy *Scherzo* is followed by a finale of pure Americana. Framed by a slow introduction and epilogue, its high spirits are guaranteed to rouse instant enthusiasm from both players and audience.

Writing in the *New York Times*, Olin Downes stated:

> The important point about this symphony is that he [Thompson] has really succeeded in keeping the music simple, unforced, unaffected. He has made use of popular idioms, melodic and rhythmic, and his manipulation of these is civilized and craftsmanlike.

Lawrence Gilman in the *New York Herald Tribune* (3 November 1933) was equally perceptive without being patronizing:

> He has not hesitated at times to be obvious: he has not strained, he has not constricted his fancy and his feeling; he has not been afraid to sound quite different from Schoenberg. His music has humor, and warmth and pleasantness; many will find it agreeable and solacing.

Although later fashion has allowed Thompson's Second Symphony to fall out of favour, it stands as the archetypal American symphony of the 1930s and 40s, expertly crafted and deeply national in character without superficial jingoism. The complete antithesis of Sessions' symphonic philosophy, this work became for three decades the model for what an American composer could create adapting the European traditions.

Symphony No.3 in A minor (1947–49) failed to achieve the acclaim of its predecessor. First performed in New York at the Fifth Annual Festival of Contemporary Music at Columbia University on 15 May 1949 by the CBS Symphony Orchestra conducted by Thor Johnson, it was taken up by the Cleveland Orchestra, the Boston Symphony and other orchestras throughout the United States. The Third Symphony is darker hued than No.2 with powerful and dissonant climaxes in the opening *Largo elegiaco*. This movement is conceived as a single massive contrapuntal flow, expressively romantic to the point of emotional strain. An explosive beginning to the *Scherzo* marks the most aggressive music that Thompson ever wrote. Here is a composer of strong personality, more dynamic and assertive than at any other point in his symphonies. Although the movement ends in a quiet subdued mood, a feeling of menace prevails. The ensuing slow movement is sad without indulging in melancholy; a string chorale provides evidence of Thompson's considerable skill in writing for voices as the stepwise melodic lines suggest word setting.

The tragic elements of the first three movements are swept aside by the cheerful finale, dance-like in its rhythmic vitality that casts care aside. Although not of such immediate appeal as the Second Symphony, the Third is a more individual work that never resorts to the predictable. Its neglect is greatly undeserved; perhaps the future will accord it full recognition.

**Henry Cowell** (1897–1965) first made his mark with a series of experimental piano pieces using unusual techniques including chord-clusters (a term he invented), strumming the strings and hitting them with a mallet, exploiting the instrument for its percussive possibilities. Yet few of these innovations found their way into the symphonies, where the influences are predominantly folk music, both American and oriental, and early hymnody. His first musical impressions were the fiddle-playing of his Irish father and the folk-songs sung by his mother. Later he became familiar with the Chinese and Japanese cultures around the San Francisco Bay area.

Cowell's first formal training was at the University of California, Berkeley from 1914 to 1917, where he was a pupil of Charles Seeger who introduced him to a wider spectrum of folk music. A Guggenheim Fellowship in 1931 allowed him to study non-European music at Berlin University with Erich von Hornbostel. In most other aspects of composition he remained self-taught. Later in his career after visits to the Far East, Lebanon, Iran, India and Iceland, Cowell made use of oriental instruments and exotic folk music in works whose titles often indicate the country of origin.

All but the first of Cowell's 20 symphonies were written after 1935 by which time he had abandoned his experiments, returning to tonality and simplifying the complex rhythmic patterns which had been a significant feature of previous works. Except for No.13 subtitled *Madras*, which is scored for Indian instruments, and the inclusion of Indonesian instruments in Symphony No.19 (1964), his symphonies are relatively orthodox in form and content, a fusion of folk music, hymnody and standard symphonic form.

The Fourth Symphony is a typical example of Cowell's wish to express his folk music heritage in orchestral terms. Subtitled 'Short', it was composed in 1946 and first performed on 24 October 1947 by the Boston Symphony Orchestra conducted by Richard Burgin. The first movement is based on three contrasting hymn-like tunes. The first is a chorale with variations, followed by a more lyrical melody and a stricter modal hymn tune in the shape-note tradition. *Ballad*, the slow movement 'suggestive of a backwoods landscape' in the composer's words, is typical wide-open-spaces Americana, naive and appealing in its warm simplicity.

Cowell's Irish descent is reflected in the *Scherzo*, a lively jig recalling the square dance popular among the logging community throughout the United States. For the Finale Cowell turned to the 'fuguing tune' of eighteenth-century American hymnody. After an introduction, the fugue is fully developed, the relentlessly busy modal counterpoint more workmanlike than inspired.

For the Ninth and Tenth Symphonies Cowell transcribed three of his set of 18 Hymns and Fuging Tunes. Symphony No.15 (*Thesis*), dating from 1960, is based on his Second and Third String Quartets written over 25 years earlier. Only Symphony No.11 subtitled *Seven Rituals of Music* betrays evidence of his radical pioneering endeavours. Each movement is in a different style, a compendium of his entire *oeuvre*, including tone clusters alongside more traditional idioms.

Today Cowell's symphonies have disappeared from the repertoire, not even represented in current recordings. In their time they embodied the true American spirit but today the lack of individual personality beyond mere craftsmanship has relegated the entire set to past history.

# 9    Walter Piston (1894–1976)

On his father's side, Walter Piston was of Italian descent; his grandfather Antonio Pistone, a Genoese sea captain, sailed to Maine in his own schooner. After graduating from Harvard in 1924, Piston travelled to Paris on a John Knowles Paine Fellowship where he became a pupil of Nadia Boulanger. He also received composition lessons from Paul Dukas at the Ecole Normale de Musique. On returning to the United States in 1926 he joined the music faculty at Harvard, becoming a Professor in 1944, later succeeding E.B. Hill as Chairman of the Music Department. He retired in 1960.

Almost all his compositions are in the instrumental and orchestral field, with no operas or songs and only two choral pieces. The eight symphonies (1937–65) represent the backbone of his total output.

Through his lifelong commitment to teaching and as the author of four seminal books, *Principles of Harmonic Analysis* (1933), *Harmony* (1944), *Counterpoint* (1947) and *Orchestration* (1955), some critics have dubbed Piston's music 'academic' as a pejorative term. Such a ridiculous contention that a thorough technical command of harmony and counterpoint inevitably produces sterile music is refuted by an examination of Piston's symphonic output. Writing in 1941, Copland provided a strong defence:

> Piston's music, if considered only from a technical viewpoint, constitutes a challenge to every other American composer. It sets a level of craftsmanship that is absolutely first-rate in itself and provides a standard of reference by which every other American's work may be judged.

> (Aaron Copland (1968) *The New Music: 1900–1960*, MacDonald: London, p. 131)

A breadth and warmth of melodic invention in both slow and fast movements is evident in all eight symphonies. Head and heart are present in equal measures. In his masterful use of the orchestra, Piston explained his approach to instrumentation:

> I have always composed music from the point of view of the performers. I love instruments, and I value the cooperation of the performers. I believe in the contribution of the players to the music as written.

Piston's basic harmonic language is tonal although some of the earlier works have dodecaphonic implications and the music of his last decade, including the eighth Symphony, makes use of increased dissonance with, at times, chords of all 12 semitones.

Sergei Koussevitzky conducted the première of Piston's first orchestral work *Symphonic Poem* in 1928 with the Boston Symphony Orchestra. Some time later the following terse conversation took place:

*Koussevitzky*: Why you no write symphony?

*Piston*: But who would play it?

*Koussevitzky*: You write. I play.

It was not until 1937 that Piston felt confident enough to accept Koussevitzky's challenge in response to a commission from the League of Composers. The première of the First Symphony on 8 April 1938 was given by Koussevitzky's orchestra, the Boston Symphony, but under the direction of the composer.

In this First Symphony all the Piston characteristics are in place, in particular a strong formal structure and an abundance of counterpoint, often dissonant, with complex fugal writing that recalls Hindemith, another so-called 'academic'. As appropriate for one who later wrote the standard book on orchestration, his handling of instruments shows a mature, masterly hand.

The unassuming opening to the first movement, a simple bassoon solo accompanied by pizzicato strings, starts with a small cell which builds up to a complete symphonic exercise. In the central *Adagio*, he enters an atmospheric world not often encountered in his music. Perhaps this exploration of Bartokian 'night' music is a distant recall of his Paris days.

In a manner which was to become a feature of all the symphonies, the energetic finale of unflagging rhythmic drive represents a synthesis of European tradition and American optimism. It should be remembered that Piston was already in his forties when he wrote the First Symphony. It is a highly professional achievement but one notices a certain lack of individual personality which would mark it out to the listener as characteristic of the composer.

Symphony No.2 was commissioned in 1943 by the Alice M. Ditson Fund of Columbia University. The première on 5 March 1944 took place in Washington, DC with the National Symphony Orchestra conducted by Hans Kindler. It won the New York Critics' Circle Award for 1944–45 and was soon taken up by the Boston Symphony Orchestra, the New York Philharmonic and other leading orchestras in America.

Piston provided the following succinct analysis of the Second Symphony:

The first movement (*Moderato*) is based on two themes, one given out at the opening of the movement by violas and cellos, legato and flowing, the other first played by the oboe, accompanied by clarinets and bassoons, staccato and rhythmic. The first of these themes receives the principal development, and the movement ends with a canonic statement of the melody by the brass choir, *pianissimo*.

The second movement (*Adagio*) is a quiet lyrical development of the motive announced at the beginning by the bassoon and the melody played by the clarinet, accompanied by muted strings. The movement is continuous rather than sectional in form.

The Finale (*Allegro*) is compounded of three themes: the first vigorous and rhythmic, played by cellos and horns; the second march-like, by clarinets and bassoons; and the third, of more songful character, first heard on English horn and clarinet.

The three movements are interrelated, producing an organic whole of a deeply expressive nature. None of the other symphonies contain such a wealth of overt emotion.

Writing in the *New York Times* after the première of the Second Symphony, Noel Strauss commented:

> In this Symphony he is again the master craftsman, while at the same time he has managed to invest the content with a wealth of mood and meaning. There is character and strength in the score. It is closely knit and eloquent in each of its three movements. Moreover, in this opus there is no display of counterpoint for its own sake, and the simplification of means results in a new fund of genuine expression.

Piston summed up his own approach to composition:

> It is not one of my aims to write music that will be called modern, nor do I set out to compose according to any particular style or system. I believe my music is music of today in both manner and expression, since I am inevitably influenced by the art, thought and daily life of the present.
>
> The self-conscious striving for nationalism gets in the way of the establishment of a strong American school of composition and even of significant individual expression. If composers will increasingly strive to project themselves in the art of music and will follow only those paths of expression which seem to them the true way, the matter of a national school will take care of itself.
>
> The composer cannot afford the wild-goose chase of trying to be more American than he is.

> (David Ewen (1982) *American Composers*, Robert Hale: London, pp. 513–514)

Symphony No.3, completed in Woodstock, Vermont in the summer of 1947, was commissioned by the Koussevitzky Music Foundation and dedicated to the memory of Natalie Koussevitzky. Sergei Koussevitzky conducted the Boston Symphony Orchestra in the première on 9 January 1948, in which year it was awarded the Pulitzer Prize.

For the first performance the composer provided the following programme note:

> I *Allegro* 5/4 – based on three thematic elements: the first heard as a melody for the oboe; the second, more sombre in character, played on the bassoon, clarinets and English horn; the third, soft chords for brass. These ideas are developed singly and in combinations to form a prelude-like movement. Tonality C.

> II *Allegro* 2/4 – a scherzo in three-part form. The theme, stated by violas and bassoons, is treated in contrapuntal imitative fashion. The middle part is marked by a melody for flute, accompanied by clarinets and harps. Tonality F.

> III *Adagio* 4/4 – the movement has four large and closely connected sections, or rather 'phrases' of musical development. The first of these is the statement of strings of the

theme, which is in three parts (part one by violins, part two by violas, part three by all except basses). The second section is a variation of the theme, with woodwinds and harps predominating. The third section, starting with basses and celli, builds up to the climax of the movement, and the final section returns to the original form of the theme, played by solo viola, the closing cadence recalling the variation by clarinet and bassoon. Tonality G.

IV *Allegro* 4/4 – a three-part form similar to that of a sonata form movement. There are two themes, the first being developed fugily in the middle section. The second theme is march-like, first heard in oboes and bassoons, over a staccato bass, and later played by full brass at the climax of the movement. Tonality C.

Symphony No.4 was commissioned in 1950 by the University of Minnesota for its centenary celebrations of the following year. It was first performed on 30 March 1951 by the Minneapolis Symphony Orchestra conducted by Antal Dorati. Later in 1951 it was taken up by the Boston Symphony Orchestra and most other major American orchestras included it in their programmes. Piston considered his Fourth Symphony to be 'melodic and expressive and perhaps nearer than my other works to the solution of the problem of balance between expression and formal design'.

The first movement (*Piacevole*) opens in wistful mood with a characteristic Piston long-flowing melody on the violins ranging over two octaves, which provides most of the material for the entire movement.

Ex. 24

Reproduced by permission of G. Schirmer Inc.

There is a strong unifying logic that develops the music in an arch, beginning quietly, reaching two powerful climaxes before returning to the tranquillity of the opening.

The Scherzo, marked *Ballando* (dancing) is based on three separate, contrasted dances (Ex. 25a), a lively theme with spiky rhythms of irregular meters (Ex. 25b), an elegant waltz in 6/8 time and Ex. 25c, an outbreak of country fiddle music which link up to form an ABACABA form.

Ex. 25a

Ex. 25b

Ex. 25c

*Reproduced by permission of G. Schirmer Inc.*

The introspective clarinet theme which opens the slow movement (*Contemplativo*) has a hint of atonality, including 11 of the 12 chromatic semitones in its first three bars, although the melodic line retains tonal harmonic features.

Ex. 26

*Reproduced by permission of G. Schirmer Inc.*

It sets the dark mood of the slowly unfolding argument that leads to a dissonant and anguished climax. In a manner similar to the first movement, the music winds down to a peaceful close with a highly chromatic violin line with atonal implications.

The vigorous sonata-form Finale (*Energico*) possesses a passionate fervour reminiscent of Samuel Barber, in particular the Scherzo section of his First Symphony and the tempestuous orchestral outburst towards the end of his choral work *Prayers of Kierkegaard*. A more lyrical second subject (Ex. 27) introduced by the oboe and taken up on the strings restores Piston's customary *bonhomie*, but a restless mood permeates most of the movement, dispelled only in the rousing coda.

Ex. 27

*Reproduced by permission of G. Schirmer Inc.*

About this symphony Piston wrote:

> My music is becoming more relaxed, I think, more flowing, less angular and nervous. I feel a greater sense of ease in the Fourth Symphony than I have ever felt before. About that first long melody (in the opening movement), I felt strongly that I was following it wherever it was going, instead of pushing it along.

Symphony No.5 was commissioned for the 50th anniversary of the Juilliard School of Music in New York in 1955 but the première, conducted by Jean Morel, was delayed until 24 February 1956.

The first movement, in orthodox sonata form, opens with a reflective Lento introduction, melodically chromatic but tonal, which returns in a modified form after the *Allegro con spirito*, the body of the movement. Here Piston is at his most dissonant to date with frequent changes of tempo. In the central *Adagio*, he uses a 12-note theme, related to the material of the first movement, for a series of continuous variations. Most traditional of the three movements is the finale, a forthright *Allegro lieto* of unremitting driving rhythms.

Symphony No.6 was commissioned in 1955 for the 75th anniversary of the Boston Symphony Orchestra who premièred it on 25 November of that year, under the direction of Charles Munch. The score is dedicated to the memory of Sergei and Natalie Koussevitzky. It became the most widely performed of the set, played throughout the United States and recorded by RCA. The Boston Symphony took it on their 1956 tour of Europe and the USSR.

Piston commented:

> While writing my sixth Symphony, I came to realize that this was a rather special situation in that I was writing for one designated orchestra, one that I had grown up with, and that I knew intimately. Each note set down sounded in the mind with extraordinary clarity, as though played immediately by those who were to perform the work. On several occasions it seemed as though the melodies were being written by the instruments themselves as I followed along. I refrained from playing even a single note of this symphony on the piano.

As usual the composer provided a brief, unrevealing analysis of the symphony:

> The first movement is flowing and expressive, in sonata form; the second a scherzo, light and fast; the third a serene adagio, theme one played by solo 'cello, theme two by the flute; and the fourth an energetic finale with two contrasting themes. The symphony was composed with no intent other than to make music to be played and listened to.

From the opening bar of the first movement (*Fluendo espressivo*) we are in familiar territory, the unison theme on the strings, in this case not wide ranging but hovering round certain fixed notes, initially C.

Ex. 28

Fluendo espressivo

At the end of the slow movement we shall see retrospectively that this first subject above is based on a scrambled version of the famous BACH motif (Bb, A, C, B natural), though its relevance here remains a secret of composer. The frequent use of melodic and harmonic intervals of fourths and fifths creates a modal feeling that looks back to the rugged opening of Roy Harris's pioneering Third Symphony.

Descending figures on the two harps prepare for the second subject (Ex. 29) introduced by the flute and later shared among the woodwind.

Ex. 29

The tightly constructed development keeps to the first subject, worrying the phrases chromatically around certain fixed points.

For most of the agile *Scherzo*, the strings are muted in their rapid figuration, against a *sotto voce* percussion ostinato as if a veil has been drawn over the activities. For the first 66 bars the only dynamic is *pianissimo*; the first *mf* sign does not appear until bar 121. Knowing many of the Boston Symphony players personally enabled Piston to provide them with a technical challenge to show off their collective virtuosity. This movement is a spectacular display of orchestral technique confined to the most delicate textures at breakneck speed.

The eloquent cello solo that opens the slow movement possesses the late-romantic warmth of Samuel Barber where a deceptive tranquillity masks a troubled soul, although in Piston's case, the *angst* is in the music not the man. The composer's favourite instrument, the flute, announces the second subject, as it did in the opening movement. This in turn is handed over to the English horn with echoes from the bassoon.

Ex. 30

*Reproduced by permission of G. Schirmer Inc.*

Like the first movement, the melodic development moves around a limited number of notes with a narrow range. Piston's mastery of counterpoint is extensively exploited in the numerous independent instrumental lines woven into the score, remaining always clearly audible. These must be greatly satisfying to the performers. In the closing bars the solo cello returns to the opening theme of the symphony, now adapted to reveal the BACH motif.

Ex. 31

*Reproduced by permission of G. Schirmer Inc.*

The bustling Finale, set in motion by cross rhythms to produce a powerful momentum, is a festive celebration for the players. Without loss of pace, the woodwind turn to a song-like tune of ingratiating charm. After this is taken up by the whole orchestra, space is made for a cheerful fugue, based on the first subject, given a jazzy twist that parallels Hindemith's fugue in the second movement of his light-hearted *Metamorphoses on Theme of Carl Maria von Weber*. Throughout this movement Piston is in great good humour for the orchestra to mark its anniversary in a rousing manner. Here is American music at its most ebullient, a monument of patriotic fervour without recourse to any specific national material.

In composing his Symphony No.7, Piston had in mind both the acoustics of the Academy of Music in which the Philadelphia Orchestra performs and the rich string sound of the orchestra who commissioned it and gave the first performance on 10 February 1961 conducted by Eugene Ormandy.

The symphony follows a three-movement form – *Con moto: Adagio Pastorale:*

*Allegro Festevole*. Although it was awarded the Pulitzer Prize in 1961, the melodic material lacks memorability and the whole work goes through the symphonic motions without generating anything new. Only the dark brooding slow movement with its despairing climax explores depths of emotion not encountered in the earlier symphonies. In the third movement which combines scherzo and finale, the rapid string scales hark back to the scherzo of the Sixth Symphony but there is a lack of striking invention and subtlety.

Here and in the Eighth Symphony, Piston's approach is too formulaic, relying on strategy adopted before but now with little more than a repetition of ideas that had been more effective first time around.

Symphony No.8, commissioned by the Boston Symphony Orchestra, was premièred under Erich Leinsdorf on 5 March 1965. In structure it resembles the Seventh Symphony, except that the opening *Moderato Mosso* is more of an extended introduction, never reaching the expected sonata allegro. The slowly unfolding *Adagio*, one of Piston's longest movements, builds to a heavily scored dissonant climax in the manner of Shostakovich. At times there is a funereal tread to the music, hinting at atonality with the chromatic twisting of melodic lines. The customary energetic third movement, combining scherzo and finale, follows well-trodden paths.

With some justification, Copland believed that Piston was 'not adventurous enough'. His conservatism was such that in spite of the intrinsic value of each symphony, there is no overall development of character or scope from first to last. As Peter Jona Korn observed:

> Walter Piston has never been the subject of heated controversy, and never will be. He has established a reputation as a good, solid craftsman who turns out one splendid work after another. He has no passionate detractors nor adulating disciples. There is, in other words, nothing extraordinary about him – except, perhaps, the strong possibility that his symphonies may well turn out to be the most durable written in America today.

> (Robert Simpson (ed.) (1967) *The Symphony* Vol. 2, Penguin Books: Harmondsworth, p. 256)

Wilfrid Mellers provided a tribute that sums up the composer's qualities:

> Piston is a composer to be grateful for, since his beautifully written music is always delightful to play and agreeable to listen to and his professionalism marks the beginning of a truly American – as opposed to the old-fashioned Teutonicized – academic tradition.

> (Mellers, W. (1964) *Music in a New Found Land*, Barrie and Rockliff: London, p. 55)

# 10 Howard Hanson (1896–1981)

Howard Hanson was born of Swedish parents into the Swedish community of Wahoo, Nebraska. His first piano teacher, Albin Petersen, fired the imagination of his young pupil to celebrate his Scandinavian roots: 'What Grieg has done for Norway, you must do for Sweden.' As a student in his mid-teens at the Institute of Musical Arts in New York – now the Juilliard School – he produced a symphony for his teacher Percy Goetschius. As this work remained unperformed and unpublished, we can only surmise as to its character.

Hanson's Symphony No.1 in E minor Op.21, subtitled *Nordic*, was composed in 1922 in Rome where the composer was studying on a Prix de Rome scholarship. He conducted the première there on 30 May, 1923 with the Augusteo Orchestra. In the following year he returned to the United States to take up the post of Director of the newly established Eastman School of Music at the University of Rochester, NY. On 19 March 1924 he conducted the first American performance of the *Nordic* Symphony with the Rochester Philharmonic Orchestra.

In the *Nordic* Symphony, Hanson sought to combine Lutheran religious fervour with the spirit of Scandinavian pioneers. At the head of the manuscript but not in the printed score, Hanson provided a Biblical quotation: 'to him that overcometh will I give to eat of the tree of life, which is in the midst of Paradise' (*Revelations* 11.7).

On the first of its three movements, Hanson commented that the music 'sings of the solemnity, austerity and grandeur of the North, of its restless surging and strife, of its sombreness and melancholy'. From the dark opening for unaccompanied cellos to the joyous outbursts for full orchestra, the rhapsodic ebb and flow suggest a symphonic poem rather than an orthodox sonata form of the first movement of a symphony.

The warm romantic melodic lines and richly scored accompaniments extend throughout the symphony, notably in the central slow movement. Although beginning in pastoral tranquility, the *Andante teneramente* builds up to a passionate climax more Slav than Nordic in nature. Into the finale Hanson introduces as the second subject a genuine folk song of Swedish origin which is treated canonically with bass drum and timpani ostinato that suggests a funeral march. The closing section reintroduces the principal theme of the first movement to emphasize the cyclic form that recurs in all the later symphonies.

Much has been made of the influence of Sibelius upon Hanson's entire output. In the First Symphony the occasional writing for the woodwind in thirds in the slow movement and the use of long harmony pedal points suggest the Finnish master, although such influence appears to be of only superficial significance.

With the *Nordic* Symphony, Hanson established a symphonic style that underwent little change throughout his long career. The harmonic language is traditionally tonal, with modal elements, passionately emotional and lavishly scored for full orchestra. Like Sibelius he liberates the woodwind and brass for passages on their own. Except for an important role for timpani, percussion is generally limited to side drum, bass drum and cymbals, an example of self-restraint for an American composer. In his own recording of the *Nordic* Symphony, Hanson makes a cut in the finale – from letter P to letter Q.

Symphony No.2, Op.30 possesses the title *Romantic*, an adjective that could have been applied to any of the set. It was commissioned in 1930 by the Boston Symphony Orchestra for their 50th anniversary. Hanson was in distinguished company; other symphonies commissioned for the occasion were Honegger's First, Prokofiev's Fourth, Roussel's Third and Stravinsky's *Symphony of Psalms*. Copland composed his *Symphonic Ode* for the anniversary.

The *Adagio* introduction is dominated by three rising notes (Ex. 32a), later balanced by a mirror image of three descending notes which form the basis of the principal theme of the ensuing *Allegro* (Ex. 32b).

Ex. 32a

Ex. 32b

*Reproduced by permission of Carl Fischer Inc.*

A comparison might be made with the first movement of Sibelius' Second Symphony which is thematically unified by a rising figure of three notes.

The tonal ambiguity of the three-note motif creates an ever-changing key basis from bar to bar, a feature prevalent throughout the symphonies of both Roy

Harris and William Schuman a decade later. Hanson also produces passages of distinct bitonality that these two composers also adopted.

Ex. 33

Molto meno mosso (Largamente)

*Reproduced by permission of Carl Fischer Inc.*

The falling arpeggio of fourths, a device for effecting ease of modulation, became a recognizable characteristic of many American composers, notably Copland and Harris.

The loose structure of this first movement involving frequent changes of tempo, creates an episodic sequence that does not constitute a satisfactory symphonic movement. A further disconcerting feature is the constant building of tension which seems to be leading to significant goals that are seldom reached. Too often the drama engendered simply fades away into a period of calm instead of an uplifting resolution.

The lush atmosphere of the slow movement – thickly scored woodwind against a hymn-like melody in the strings over sustained chords – has been subsequently stolen by Hollywood composers to depict wide open spaces in western movies. Modal harmony on four horns represents the epitome of pastoral optimism. In the central section the three-note motto appears on the brass as the strings take over the opening theme originally heard on the woodwind.

Themes from both the previous movements are recalled in the *Allegro con brio* finale. The horn figure from the first movement (Ex. 33) bursts in at the opening, later combined with the principal theme of the slow movement transformed into a fanfare on three trumpets. By recalling material from earlier in the symphony, Hanson has produced a musically logical fusion of themes in cyclic form. The shadow of Sibelius is less evident but can be recognized in the finale in the woodwind ostinato (Fig. F), pizzicato strings over a 20-bar pedal C (Fig.G–I) and woodwind and brass in thirds for much of the movement.

Once again film composers of later generations have adopted Hanson's affirmative codas, blazing brass and soaring strings in their big screen spectaculars. As a student in Rome, Hanson had been a pupil of Respighi, the inspiration behind the first generation of Hollywood composers, Max Steiner, Erich Korngold and Miklós Rózsa. Hanson's more American home-spun language has suited well the likes of John Williams and Jerry Goldsmith some 40 years later.

Knowing that the *Romantic* Symphony would emerge into a world hostile to its message, Hanson issued an artistic *apologia*.

> The symphony represents for me my escape from the rather bitter type of modern musical realism which occupies so large a place in contemporary thought. Much contemporary music seems to me to be showing a tendency to become entirely too cerebral. I do not believe that music is primarily a matter of intellect, but rather a manifestation of the emotions. I have, therefore, aimed in this symphony to create a work that was young in spirit, lyrical and romantic in temperament, and simple and direct in expression.

Hanson's Third Symphony was commissioned in 1936 by the Columbia Broadcasting System to commemorate the 300th anniversary of the first Swedish settlement on the shores of Delaware in 1638.

Having completed three movements, the composer found problems in writing the finale. Like William Walton who had faced a similar crisis with his Symphony No.1, Hanson performed the three movements as they stood in a radio broadcast on 9 September 1937. Six months later on 26 March 1938 the complete symphony was given under the composer's direction by the NBC Symphony Orchestra. The first concert performance also under Hanson's baton took place on 3 November 1939 by the Boston Symphony Orchestra.

Writing about the work, Hanson stated that

> Temperamentally the Third Symphony is closely related to my First Symphony, *Nordic*. The Third Symphony springs definitely from the North and has its genesis in the composer's reverence for the spiritual contribution that has been made to America by the sturdy race of northern pioneers who as early as 1638 founded the first Swedish settlement on the Delaware and who were in later centuries to constitute such a mighty force in the conquering of the West.

Of all Hanson's symphonies the Third is the most Sibelian in character. The first movement (*Andante lamentando*) opens with a dark, brooding theme on cellos, double-basses and bassoons set against the blinding light of violins and high woodwind. Scalic figures that tail off into silence inhabit a similar mystic world to late Sibelius. Out of the gloom emerges a more hopeful chorale on trombones which becomes the *leitmotif* for the whole symphony. A contrasting central scherzo is later combined with the chorale to resolve the movement in an atmosphere of tranquillity.

Hanson's expansive lyrical invention is well illustrated in the second movement (*Andante tranquillo*) that opens with a gentle horn theme against a rocking accompaniment that grows in emotional intensity. Sibelius is again brought to mind in the scherzo where the solo timpani cross rhythms recalls the equivalent movement in Sibelius' First Symphony. The *Scherzo* of Dvořák's Symphony 'From the New World' is also a close relation.

Using the cyclic form of the previous two symphonies, in the finale of the Third Symphony Hanson reintroduces material from earlier movements, the dark opening, the main theme of the *Andante* culminating in the chorale from the first movement to bring the work to a blazing conclusion of jubilant exultation.

Symphony No.4, subtitled *Requiem*, the composer's favourite, is a work of deep personal significance inspired by the death of his father. Each movement is headed by a section of the Requiem Mass: *Kyrie, Requiescat, Dies Irae, Lux Aeterna*. The considerable use of imitative counterpoint is in keeping with an overtly religious work.

The restless opening of the *Kyrie* leads to Hanson's customary unifying motto theme (Ex. 34) which is later combined with the inevitable chorale that reaches an ultimate resolution in the close of the *Lux Aeterna*. This modal melody suggests both Swedish folk-song and liturgical chant.

Ex. 34

*Reproduced by permission of Carl Fischer Inc.*

Sibelius is again called to mind, the second movement of his Second Symphony, in Hanson's slow movement *Requiescat* as a solo bassoon unfolds a rising stepwise melody over pizzicato cellos and double-basses. This period of tranquillity is shattered by the bitter, angry *Scherzo* dominated, as in the Third Symphony, by the solo timpani.

In the finale *Lux Aeterna*, Hanson recalls material from the previous movements, ending in quiet bell-tolling chords on divided strings. The Fourth Symphony was first performed by the Boston Symphony Orchestra on 3 December 1943, conducted by the composer. In the following year it was awarded the first Pulitzer Prize for music.

A more specifically religious motive lies at the heart of Symphony No.5, Op.43, subtitled *Sinfonia Sacra*. It was inspired by the account of Christ's resurrection as described in the Gospel of St John. Hanson explained that his intension was 'to evoke some of the atmosphere of tragedy and triumph, mysticism and affirmation of the story which is the essential symbol of the Christian faith'. Unlike any of its predecessors, *Sinfonia Sacra* is cast in a single movement, after the form of Sibelius's Seventh Symphony, with three distinct sections. As so often before, it is the shadow of Sibelius that hangs over the opening bars for brass and lower strings. The principal theme, a plainsong-like melody, is developed into a characteristic brass chorale that concludes this compact 15-minute work. Eugene Ormandy conducted the première with the Philadelphia Orchestra on 18 February 1955.

Symphony No.6 was commissioned by the New York Philharmonic Orchestra in 1967 for their 125th anniversary. It was premièred under the composer's baton on 29 February 1968. Like the *Sinfonia Sacra*, the Sixth Symphony is a one-movement work comprising six linked sections. In his programme note, the composer wrote:

> Most of my symphonies are essentially cyclic in construction. The Sixth, in contrast, is held together by a very simple three-note 'motto', which, I think, unifies the entire structure.
>
> The first movement asks the question. The second and fourth movements are rather sardonic *scherzi*, surrounding the third movement which is quiet and contemplative. Since the fifth movement, a kind of improvisatory *parlando*, leads without a pause into the dynamic finale, the slow movement becomes a kind of keystone of the architectonic 'arch' of the six movements – a small, intimate soul surviving in the framework of cynicism and strife.

Hanson was aged 81 when he composed his Seventh and final symphony. It was written to mark the 50th anniversary of the National Music Camp at Interlochen, at summer school near Traverse City, Michigan. He conducted the student choir and orchestra in the première on 7 August 1977. Although entitled *A Sea Symphony*, it is simply a choral work in three movements setting three short texts by Walt Whitman. Comparison is inevitable with Vaughan Williams's *Sea Symphony*; indeed Hanson uses some of the same lines that appear in the finale of the English composer's score. This is vintage Hanson, with ecstatic choral climaxes, modal melodies and vivid sea effects in the orchestra but the results are hardly symphonic in concept.

Hanson was an unashamed romantic at a time when such a compositional style had become outdated. Within ten years of his death the pendulum had swung back in his favour. His own apologia has no sense of regret; in the prediction below his faith has proved justified.

> I recognize, of course, that romanticism is at the present time the poor stepchild without the social standing of her elder stepsister, neo-classicism. Nevertheless, I embrace her all the more fervently, believing as I do that romanticism will find in this country rich soil for a new, young and vigorous growth.

# 11 Roy Harris (1898–1979)

Harris is a child of nature with a child's love for his native hills and a childlike belief in the moral purpose of music. His music reflects these things faithfully – it owes nothing to city influences, but seems always full-blooded and spiritually pure. His melodies and, even more particularly, his harmonies are in no way revolutionary, yet they have a strange personal flavor.*

So wrote Aaron Copland prophetically in 1926 before Harris had composed any of his extant works.

Roy Harris, the quintessential 'pioneer', was born in Oklahoma on Lincoln's birthday in 1898 in a log cabin built by his father. Both his grandfathers had been stagecoach drivers so that he could claim an almost legendary background for himself. After receiving composition lessons in 1924–5 from Arthur Farwell in California, Harris moved to the East Coast where he met Aaron Copland. It was on his recommendation that he went to France to study with Nadia Boulanger. Under her guidance he composed his First Symphony entitled *American Portrait* in 1929.** Having heard it played privately by the Philadelphia Orchestra under Stokowski, he withdrew the score.

In 1933 Copland introduced Harris to Sergei Koussevitzky who invited him to write a 'a big symphony from the west'. He responded with Symphony *1933* which he originally considered his Second but later designated it the First. In a programme note for the première by the Boston Symphony Orchestra on 26 January 1934 under the baton of Koussevitzky, Harris wrote:

In the first movement I have tried to capture the mood of adventure and physical exuberance; in the second, of the pathos which seems to underlie all human existence; in the third the mood of a positive will to power and action.

In the First Symphony are to be found all the Harris idiosyncrasies that typify symphonic writing throughout his career: raw rugged textures, short modal motifs, powerful forward movement through reiterated rhythms and an overall sureness of purpose.

---

\* Aaron Copland (1961) *Copland on Music*, Andre Deutsch: London, p. 148. Originally in *Modern Music* Vol. III No.3, March–April 1926: Copyright League of Composers.

\*\* An *Andante* for orchestra dating from 1926 was intended for an unfinished symphony.

After the Boston première, Koussevitzky took the First Symphony to New York where it was recorded, becoming the first symphony by an American to be issued in a commercial recording. Unfamiliar with the techniques of recording a live concert, the engineers missed the first note on the timpani and lost several bars in the second movement in changing from side 3 to 4 in the 78rpm discs. In a studio session held after the performance part of the second movement was re-recorded and dubbed into the CD transfer, although the earlier missing bars were never replaced. The original Columbia 78s were later transferred to a long-playing disc that remains an historic record. As the first of the canon of 15 surviving symphonies, it is a remarkably confident work, one of the earliest symphonies by an American with a truly distinctive voice.

Harris' musical language is strongly personal, based on modality with polytonal implications. In his harmony he employs sudden juxtapositions of major and minor triads that step from key to key but preserve a tonal structure. The frequent use of fugato is derived not from academic European sources but from the 'fuging tunes' of early American hymnody.

Writing in 1932, Arthur Mendel had already identified the new compositional path that Harris was pursuing:

> Roy Harris, instead of basing his work on novelty in the sensuous materials of the art, focusses his attention on the structure of the music. [He] is trying to work out an idiom in which the structure shall be based on the self-determined growth of the melodic material, not on any superimposed form. In theory, he is attempting to do in music what was done long ago in poetry – to free it from the limitations corresponding to rhythm, meter and conventional forms. He feels that the composer of the future must free himself of these shackles. His music must be just as cogent and logical and structurally perfect as he can make it. But its form must be determined by its content. It must grow as a plant or an animal grows, along lines dictated by its own inner necessity, not imposed on it from above.

> (A Change in Structure, in *The Nation*, 6 January 1932)

Critical response to the First Symphony was enthusiastic. Leonard Leibling of *Musical Courier* declared:

> Brethren, make no mistake, this is important music by a writer with sound training, serious utterance and an individual mentality and temperament. The whole structure rests on solid form, trestled and riveted with well-ordered, recognizable counterpoint. At no time is the ear puzzled by the nature of sound. The entire composition enjoyed my fancy and held me in absorbed response.

The respected H.T. Parker of the *Boston Evening Transcript* called the performance:

> An event in the course of American music. Mr Harris' eagerness for rhythms, fertility with them, reliance upon them, are natural again to these times; but throughout the mature First Symphony they are distinctively his own and distinctively American.

Koussevitzky was also responsible for giving the première of Harris' Second Symphony (1934) in Boston on 28 February 1936.

Symphony No.3 has established itself as the most widely performed and recorded of all American symphonies. Once again it was Koussevitzky who offered the commission and gave the first performance in Boston on 24 February 1939 and recorded it for RCA Victor, which brought Roy Harris to the attention of the world. The composer himself regarded this version as the finest interpretation. At 16 minutes 40 seconds in duration it is almost two minutes faster than the recording by Leonard Bernstein and the New York Philharmonic Orchestra. The live performance by Toscanini on 16 March 1940 (now available on the Dell'Arte label) equals Koussevitzky's timing but includes the two passages cut by the composer. Harris attended the performance and does not appear to have objected. Curiously the NBC Symphony brass omit their entry in one bar (Fig. 50, bar 4); equally inexplicable is the cymbal stroke on the final bar of the recording by Howard Hanson. When asked about this by the author, Mr Hanson could not offer an explanation.

The impact of the Third Symphony on young musicians in the United States was immediate. Here at last was a voice offering a totally new symphonic concept which would prove an inspiration for a wide circle of composers. Writing in 1980 on the work, William Schuman stated:

> For me the sounds were like no others I had ever heard – his whole 'autogeneric' concept of form, the free and strong orchestration, the extraordinary beauty and sweep of the melodic material. He was a new voice, and between that time and now, that voice, as it matured, underwent enormous change and growth yet all discernably evolving from the youthful kernel.

Some commentators have compared its single-movement form with that of the Seventh Symphony of Sibelius, but it is fanciful speculation to believe that any direct outside influence had an impact on its composition. Plainsong, Renaissance polyphony, hymnody and Anglo-American folk song are the origins of his melodic invention. The only recognizable similarity between Sibelius and Harris is the frequent use of the orchestral forces in 'choirs' – where strings, woodwind and brass are often self-sufficient units, with long passages on their own or co-existing with their own exclusive material. He also shares with Sibelius the use of notation in large note values, although this may have derived more from his admiration for Renaissance polyphony.

In the Third Symphony, Harris clarified his approach to melody and harmony. He wrote, 'Harmony should reflect what is in the melody, without being overshadowed by the tonality in which the melody lies.' The form is determined by melodic evolution, a gradual organic growth. Here the overtone series of perfect fourths and fifths exert a powerful effect, what the composer termed his 'organum', the frequent use of parallel root position chords.

Harris believed that harmony serves three specific functions:

1   in the architecture of tonalities
2   for the delineation of melodies
3   for dynamic resonance.

Harris was also acutely aware of the significance of rhythm to American composers:

> Our rhythmic impulses are fundamentally different from the rhythmic impulses of Europeans; and from this unique rhythmic sense are generated different melodic and form values. Our sense of rhythm is less symmetrical than the European rhythmic sense. European musicians are trained to think of rhythm in its largest common denominator, while we are born with a feeling for its smallest units. That is why the jazz boys, chained to an unimaginative commercial routine which serves only crystallized symmetrical dance rhythms, are continually breaking out into superimposed rhythmic variations which were not written in the music. This assymetrical balancing of rhythmic phrases is in our blood; it is not in the European blood.
>
> We do not employ unconventional rhythms as a sophistical gesture; we cannot avoid them. The rhythms come to us first as musical phraseology, and then we struggle to define them on paper. Our struggle is not to invent new rhythms and melodies and forms; our problem is to put down into translatable symbols and rhythms and consequent melodies and form those that assert themselves within us.
>
> There is nothing strange about this American rhythmic talent. Children skip and walk that way – our conversation would be strained and monotonous without such rhythmic nuances, much like a child's first attempts at reading: nature abounds in these freer rhythms.
>
> (Henry Cowell (ed.) (1933) *American Composers on American Music*, Stanford University Press: Stanford)

Although the Third Symphony is in one movement, the composer acknowledged that there are five sections which he termed Tragic; Lyrical; Pastoral; Fugue Dramatic; and Dramatic Tragic. In spite of the Harris's description, 'tragic' is not the mood most likely to be evoked in the listener. Beginning with an unaccompanied cello line (Ex. 35) the music sets out in an intense lyrical vein; the latent energy suggests a positive feeling of life awakening, not about to end.

Ex. 35

Con moto

*Reproduced by permission of G. Schirmer Inc.*

The modal tonality effortlessly takes the melody from one key to another. G. major/minor is one tonal centre that recurs throughout the symphony. Block chord harmonies emphasize the intervals of bare fourths and fifths.

Ex. 36

Con moto

Violas
'Cellos **ƒ**

*Reproduced by permission of G. Schirmer Inc.*

Above the overlapping contrapuntal phrases, Harris introduces chorale-like unison themes which return at strategic points in the work.

Ex. 37

Con moto

*mf* sonore < > < > *mf* <    > >
Woodwind

*Reproduced by permission of G. Schirmer Inc.*

Harris's term 'Lyrical' for the second section (beginning at Fig. 14) is no more illuminating than 'Tragic' since the word could apply to much of the Third Symphony. Here the tonality is in G minor. A short arpeggio figure (Ex. 38) first heard on the horns assumes increasing significance in the antiphonal exchanges between strings and wind.

Ex. 38

*Reproduced by permission of G. Schirmer Inc.*

A network of overlapping arpeggios on the woodwind is transferred to the strings for the third section 'Pastoral', a sequence of fragmentary tunes on solo woodwind, none of them the same, over a harmonic cushion created by the muted strings. After the first performance, Harris made two cuts in this section. Fig. 27 bar 4 to Fig. 30 bar 1; Fig. 30 bar 8 to Fig. 31 bar 6, a total of 37 bars in all. These are observed in all current recordings except those of Toscanini and Neemi Järvi.

Tension is gradually built up to prepare for the climactic fourth section 'Fugue Dramatic'. This is not a fugue as such, the six-bar theme (Ex. 39) being treated in fugato and canon, principally by the brass.

Ex. 39

*Reproduced by permission of G. Schirmer Inc.*

Like the finale of Sibelius's Second Symphony, for Harris this is a point of arrival after a tortuous and at times agonizing musical journey. A long processional transition, where the exchanges between the brass are accompanied by unison chorales in canon between the wind and strings, leads to the final section 'Dramatic Tragic'. This epilogue in the form of a funeral march marked by a relentless drum beat reintroduces the chorales of the second section 'Lyrical'.

The Third Symphony continues to hold its place in the repertoire as the archetypal American symphony – rugged, abrasive, with the true pioneering spirit, a work of recognized originality and integrity. Nothing he wrote later can equal its artistic standing.

In its first form Symphony No.4, *Folksong Symphony* for chorus and orchestra, was performed at the American Spring Festival in Rochester NY on 26 April 1940 conducted by Howard Hanson. To allow the singers some respite, Harris added two interludes and in this version it was premièred on 26 December 1940 by the Cleveland Orchestra under the direction of Rudolph Ringwall. Harris made further revisions for the final version which was heard on New Year's Eve 1942, played by the New York Philharmonic Orchestra conducted by Dimitri Mitropoulos.

Harris stated that he wrote the *Folksong Symphony* in 1940 'when our nation was deeply committed in World War II and I conceived a form that reflected the feelings of the time'. This hardly accords with history since the United States did not enter the War until December 1941.

Harris continued:

The work opens with the song 'The Girl I Left Behind Me' and ends with 'When Johnny Comes Marching Home Again', both famous Civil War Tunes. To express the nostalgia of loneliness, I chose two of America's best loved lonesome songs, 'Bury Me Not On the Lone Prairie' and 'He's Gone Away'. For the Negros – who so admirably represent our nation both in war and music – I chose that wonderful spiritual 'De Trumpet Sounds It In my Soul'. I wrote the choral parts for the range of good high school choruses, with the thought that such choruses might have a work to prepare with the symphony orchestras of our cities.

Harris also provided an informative programme note of the individual movements:

*First Movement*: The Girl I Left Behind Me. This is a Civil War song which is sung in the spirit of bravado to keep up the courage of both the young men and the young women whom war had parted. It should be sung in the gayest of moods.

*Second Movement*: Western Cowboy. The movement uses three well-known Western folk songs: 'O Bury Me not on the Lone Prairie', 'Old Chisholm Trail' and 'Laredo'. These three songs characterize the lonesomeness, hilarity and tragedy which the early Western cowboys live with every day.

*Third Movement*: First Interlude for String Orchestra and Percussion. This is a dance for fiddles and is naturally made from a combination of many fiddle tunes of the early pioneer days.

*Fourth Movement*: Mountaineer Love Song. A love song from the life of the mountain folk of the South, based on the tune 'He's Gone Away', possessing both the pathos and the strange wildness which characterizes these passionate people.

*Fifth Movement*: The Second Interlude for Orchestra: A gay work using the folk song 'Jump Up My Lady', and a dance tune which is a composite of many fiddle tunes.

*Sixth Movement*: Negro Fantasy. Two Negro Spirituals, 'Little Boy Named David' and 'De Trumpet Sounds It In My Soul', from the deep South of longstanding tradition, are used in this movement.

*Seventh Movement*: When Johnny Comes Marching Home: This is, of course, the famous song that came out of the Civil War. In it I hoped to capture the spirit of exhilaration and joy which our people would feel when the men came home from war.

This last movement is adapted from Harris's own orchestral piece *American Overture: When Johnny Comes Marching Home* dating from 1934. He had also made an arrangement of the song for unaccompanied mixed voices in 1937. A choral version of *He's Gone Away* was completed at around this time.

These folk songs are given the Roy Harris treatment – modal, mildly dissonant accompaniments and linking passages, abrupt modulations, incidental polytonality and languid scoring for the sad sentimental tunes. What he avoids is an over-sophisticated gloss that would have conflicted with the simplicity of the original songs.

Symphony No.5 was composed in 1943 and inspired by the struggle of the Russian people against the Nazis. The first performance by the Boston Symphony Orchestra and Koussevitzky on 26 February 1943 was simultaneously broadcast to the Soviet Union. Harris himself conducted the work in Moscow on 15 October 1958, becoming the first American composer to conduct his own music in the USSR. During the notorious MacCarthy witch-hunt in the early 1950s, Harris suffered political persecution for what were seen as his communist sympathies expressed in the Fifth Symphony.

As with the Third Symphony, Harris later made two short omissions in the opening movement, the first of eight bars (Fig.1 bar 6 to Fig.2 bar 3 and the second of nine bars, Fig.5 bar 4 to Fig.6 bar 2). The Fifth Symphony contains little not already encountered in the Third Symphony and lacks the spontaneity and concision of the earlier work. With its over-reliance on one-bar phrases and the repeated rhythmic figure ♩. ♫ ♩. ♫ the first movement is naive and turgid.

The pounding funeral drum at the beginning of the central movement is a reminder of the ending of the Third Symphony. Harris gradually increases the tempo to a point where the music is travelling at four times the speed of the opening bars. A concluding chorale with phrases exchanged between the brass and strings is the most convincing part of the symphony. Like the first movement, the finale is weakened by repetition often leading to empty bombast. The Third Symphony explored similar territory but in a more effective and cogent manner.

The same feeling of having heard it all before is engendered by Symphony No.6 *Gettysburg* (1944). It was inspired by Lincoln's Gettysburg Address but the piece is purely orchestral with no direct reference to Lincoln's words. The score is dedicated to 'the Armed Forces of Our Nation' and was first performed in Boston under the direction of Koussevitzky on 14 April 1944. Here Harris has degenerated into mannerisms and gestures, serving up features encountered in earlier orchestral works but without much that is either new or memorable.

Symphony No.7 restores one's faith in Roy Harris as a symphonist. Cast as a single movement, the new work inevitably invites comparison with the Third Symphony. Here again we have the separate sections of the orchestra acting as independent units; indeed the symphony seems to be composed primarily for the sonorous string textures, with brass interpolations. The woodwind operate almost exclusively as a group, doubling the strings and brass without any solos, each part shadowed by at least one other instrument.

Rhythmically and technically Harris makes intense demands upon his players. The first violin line is frequently pitched high above the stave, in texture much more opaque than in any of his previous scores. The very tight structure of the Seventh Symphony is emphasized in Harris' own analysis which, it is to be noted, treats the music in totally abstract terms:

> The work was conceived as a dynamic form with an uninterrupted time span of 20 minutes. In one sense it is a dance symphony; in another sense it is a study in harmonic and melodic rhythmic variation. The first half is a passacaglia with five variations. The second half is divided into three sections – contrapuntal variations in asymmetrical rhythms; contrapuntal variations in symmetrical meter; and further statement and development of the preceding two sections, wherein the original passacaglia theme is restated in large augmentation and orchestration, while ornamentation develops the melodic and rhythmic materials of the second section. A final variation of the rhythmic materials of the work serves as the coda.

The Seventh Symphony is in effect cyclic in form with the passacaglia theme unifying every development, so that its reappearance as a slow stately theme in the coda is inevitable. In typical Harris style, the symphony opens with the weary tread of a solemn procession (another funeral march?) over which the passacaglia theme slowly passes from the first violins to the violas, back to the violins (Ex. 40).

Each subsequent variation emerges imperceptibly one from another. The first (Fig.5 bar 5) is in block strings chords, the second (Fig.9 bar 6) unison strings with brass echoes, the third (Fig.11 bar 9) at an increased tempo in 9/4 time, strings again with woodwind and trumpet counter-melodies, the fourth (Fig.16 bar 5) in 6/4 more agitated and rhythmically wild leading to the fifth (Fig.25 bar 5) in 2/2, still string-dominated rising in tension to the second half of the symphony. Only at this point does the dance element arise at Fig.31 with

Ex. 40

*Reproduced by permission of G. Schirmer Inc.*

alternating passages in 11/8 and 5/8 metre where the strings and brass in assymetrical exchanges recall the so-called 'Fugal Dramatic' section of the Third Symphony. A new lively theme is introduced on the woodwind and taken up by the violins (Ex. 41).

Ex. 41

*Reproduced by permission of G. Schirmer Inc.*

Contrapuntal variations in symmetrical meter are established with the more regular time signature 2/2 but cross-rhythms still predominate. At the end of this section Harris has a surprise in store – an ecstatic climax where harmonic stability replaces counterpoint. The impassioned outburst from unison violins over solid chords marks an uplifting moment that surpasses even the finest passages in the Third Symphony. Once more the coda is in Harris's stately march form, as the unison strings present the passacaglia as a dignified chorale.

Although not as direct as its impact as the Third Symphony, Symphony No.7 is its equal in all other respects. A much needed new recording would provide the opportunity to assess its value. The first performance was given in Chicago on 20 November 1952 by the Chicago Symphony Orchestra and Rafael Kubelik. The revised version was heard in Copenhagen on 15 September 1955 conducted by Eugene Ormandy.

The single-movement Symphony No.8, *San Francisco*, was commissioned for the 50th anniversary of the San Francisco Symphony Orchestra. The symphony evokes five episodes in the life of St Francis, the patron saint of the city. The première took place on 17 January 1962.

Symphony No.9, *1963*, was commissioned by the Philadelphia Orchestra who performed it on 18 January 1963 under the baton of Eugene Ormandy. Although a purely orchestral work, it was inspired by the preamble to the American Constitution and Walt Whitman, whose inscriptions are the titles to the three movements: Of life, Immense in Passion, Pulse and Power; Cheerful for Freest Action Formed; The Modern Man I Sing.

To commemorate the assassination of Abraham Lincoln, Harris composed his Tenth Symphony. Scored for speaker, women's chorus, men's chorus, mixed chorus, brass and two amplified pianos, the five movements set words by Lincoln and the composer. The première took place in Long Beach, California on 14 April 1965.

Symphony No.11 in one movement was commissioned in 1967 to mark the 125th anniversary of the New York Philharmonic Orchestra who gave the première on 8 February 1968 under the direction of Leonard Bernstein. Regarding war and peace, the subject matter which inspired it, Harris wrote:

> My theme is the conflict facing the entire world. We are about to decide whether or not civilization can save itself, whether problems can be solved through silence. [The symphony] begins in a mood of nervous agitation, dips downward and ends in an expansive affirmation and optimism.

Symphony No.12 (*Pere Marquette*) was written in response to a request from the Father Marquette Tercentenial to mark the 300th anniversary of the voyages of Father Jacques Marquette, the first white man to see the confluence of the Mississippi and Wisconsin Rivers. It is scored for speaker, tenor and orchestra, and uses texts from the Ordinary of the Mass and the Bible. The première took place in Milwaukee on 8 November 1968.

Symphony No.13, completed in 1969, has yet to be performed and published. Only a recording of the complete cycle of Harris's Symphonies will bring it to light.

Symphony No.14 was composed in 1974 to commemorate the American Bicentennial. Scored for speaker, chorus and orchestra, it sets passages from the United States Constitution and words by Abraham Lincoln and the composer. The première was given by the National Symphony Orchestra conducted by Antal Dorati in Washington DC on 10 February 1976.

Symphony No.15 dates from 1978. Through lack of performances, these later symphonies remain an unknown factor in Harris's development. Publication and recordings of the scores would greatly assist a more comprehensive overview of the entire set.

In 1958 a fellow composer, William Flanagan, acknowledged Harris's status:

> To many Roy Harris, the 'composer from the West', was the first assertion of the purely

'American' national genius. Harris, far from being sophisticated, has never quite been tamed by formal training and was, for that matter, a primitive of sorts. He remains, nevertheless, one of the most extraordinarily original talents the United States has ever produced.

(Gilbert Chase (ed.) (1966) *The American Composer Speaks*, Louisiana State University Press: Baton Rouge, p. 260)

# 12 Serialism and Beyond

The leading figures of the Second Viennese School made little immediate impact on composers outside Germany and Austria. Among the numerous Americans who visited Europe in the early years of the twentieth century, only Wallingford Riegger and Roger Sessions adopted serialism. The post-Second World War revival of interest in the 12-note system which swept Europe again had only a marginal effect in the United States.

In certain academic circles, serialism became the fashion, taking Schoenberg rather than Webern as the model. Composers adapted the system to suit their own individual concepts. Thus we find atonality forced into neo-classical moulds or transformed into extreme chromaticism with late-romantic associations. This trend satisfied some aesthetic and intellectual needs, in part a desire to move away from nationalism to a universal language that could become the vernacular throughout the world. Ultimately in most respects, it proved to be a fruitless exercise since that language was understood only by composers. Audiences and many performers – then and today – feel little or no compunction to become acquainted with the 12-tone system, viewing it as the musical equivalent of Esperanto, a concocted means of communication, not one that has evolved naturally.

With regard to those composers who remained loyal to serialism, current popular taste indicates that their time has come and gone. Maybe future generations will look upon them with more sympathy.

**Wallingford Riegger** (1885–1961) studied at Cornell University and the Institute of Musical Art in New York (now the Juilliard School). In 1907 he went to Berlin where he was a pupil of Robert Haussman for cello and Max Bruch and Edgar Stillman Kelley for composition. Being partly of German descent may have influenced Riegger in his choice of Berlin for his studies.

On his return to the United States he became principal cello with the St Paul Symphony Orchestra. Hoping to follow a career in conducting, Riegger went back to Germany in 1911. He was appointed to posts at opera houses in Würzburg and Königsburg but the First World War forced him home in 1917. Riegger taught at Drake University, Des Moines Iowa (1918–22) and briefly at other institutions before finally settling in New York in 1929.

The time spent in Germany influenced his entire musical outlook. He was one of the first composers in America to adopt serialism. In the 1920s and 30s he was considered an ultra-modernist, associating with other avant-garde musicians including Henry Cowell and Edgard Varèse in promoting concerts of contemporary music. In addition Riegger worked with several dance companies where advanced idioms were more acceptable than in the concert hall. Ballet scores were commissioned from Dorothy Humphrey, Martha Graham and Hanya Holm which allowed the composer freedom to experiment.

Riegger's First Symphony Op.37, completed in 1944 was performed in New York on 3 April 1949 but subsequently withdrawn. A similar fate befell the Second Symphony Op.41, written for school orchestras, dating from 1945.

Symphony No.3 Op.42 (1946–47) was commissioned by the Alice M. Ditson Fund of Columbia University and dedicated to the musicologist and administrator Oliver Daniel. It was premièred at the Fourth Annual Festival of Contemporary Music held in the McMillin Academic Theater of Columbia University on 16 May 1948 by the CBS Symphony Orchestra conducted by Dean Dixon. Subsequently the symphony was taken up by several conductors including Leopold Stokowski and Hermann Scherchen and heard throughout the United States and Europe.

In his free use of serialism, Riegger has much in common with Roger Sessions; his affinity is closer to European than American models. The first movement of the Third Symphony is in truncated sonata form, the thematic material based on a tone row presented at the outset as a lyrical oboe melody. Fugal treatment of the material abounds in an assertive, often aggressive, cogent argument. The slow movement is derived from a dance score *With My Red Fires* written in 1936 for Dorothy Humphrey. Fugal writing also dominates the Scherzo which gathers momentum and cohesion with a gradual increase of tempo. The finale, a passacaglia and fugue, is marked by rhythmic vitality and colourful fiery orchestration.

Riegger twice revised the score before it reached its final form in 1962. In the 1952 *Bulletin of the American Composers' Alliance*, Elliott Carter wrote:

> Riegger has followed the dictates of his own philosophy and musical instinct unobtrusively for years, without caring whether he was or was not in step with the fashions of the time, or apparently, whether he would become known or his music performed.

Riegger's retiring nature and reluctance to promote his own music is partly to blame for the late recognition of his works.

Symphony No.4 Op.63 was commissioned by the Fromm Music Foundation of Chicago and first performed at the Festival of Contemporary Arts in Urbana on 12 April 1957 by the Illinois University Orchestra conducted by Bernard Goodman. Here the musical language is almost entirely tonal and key-centred with only marginal serial applications. The modal implications of the first movement make this a decidedly American work. The Boston critic Cyrus Durgin commented:

This is a symphony which has both head and heart appeal and whose texture ranges from free flowing melody to grinding dissonances, with a good amount of mild and tonal harmony in between.

As with the Third Symphony, Riegger used part of a dance score for the slow movement; it is based on *Chronicle*, written in 1936 for Martha Graham. The ballet describes the suffering of the Spanish people during the Civil War. It is, however, the last movement which suggests dance, with repeated figures in the final scherzo section, a turbulent movement of stormy dramatic contrasts.

With this blend of the tonal and serial, it is tonality that ultimately prevails. In a programme note for a performance in Cleveland, Klauss G. Roy wrote:

> One may feel the work almost as a series of searching questions, the exposition of fascinating problems, rather than a confident declaration or the offering of decisive solutions.

Following the publication of the full score, Riegger continued to make revisions, including extensive cuts. In the last years of his life he began a Fifth Symphony but too little was completed for performance.

In 1910 at the age of 14 **Roger Sessions** (1896–1985) became the youngest student ever to enter the Music Department of Harvard University. On graduating in 1915 he transferred to Yale where he became a pupil of Horatio Parker. Of greater influence were the private composition lessons he received from Ernest Bloch in New York and time spent in Europe from 1927 to 1933, firstly in Florence, later in Berlin and Rome. On his permanent return to the United States in 1933 he devoted his life to teaching at Boston University (1933–35), Princeton (1935–44), the University of California, Berkeley (1944–53) and Princeton again (1944–53). On his official retirement he continued to teach at Harvard and the Juilliard School in New York almost until his death.

Throughout his career as a composer he adopted a universal, non-nationalistic language that owed more to German-Austrian models, especially Mahler and Schoenberg.

> I don't believe in it [American national consciousness] and I don't believe it can be done like that – you create music and if it's genuine and spontaneous music written by an American, why then it's American music. These things have to grow naturally. For me nationalism is the wrong approach.

> (Vivian Perlis and Aaron Copland (1984) in *Copland 1900 Through 1942*, Faber:
> London, p.149)

> A consciously 'national' style, in any field, inevitably becomes a picturesque mannerism, a kind of trademark, devoid of significant human content, irredeemably outmoded the moment the novelty has worn off.

> (Roger Sessions (1940) 'On the American Future', *Modern Music* XVII/2,
> January/February, p.73)

As his one-time colleague Aaron Copland has said of Sessions:

There still remains that attribute of his work that the French would call 'rebarbatif' – a certain stern, grim, dour aspect, as if the pieces themselves dared you to like them.

(Aaron Copland (1968) *The New Music 1900–1960*, MacDonald & Co.: London, p.130)

In the introduction to his book *Harmonic Practice* (1950), Sessions acknowledged his debt to Schoenberg:

It becomes always clearer that the influence of this truly remarkable man is not limited to his most immediate or obvious followers, but has had a far-reaching effect on friend and foe alike.

Sessions's music still makes great demands on performers and listeners, taking no account of the limitations of either. The intense concentrated complexities of harmony and melodic invention continue to distance him from a wide musical public. A particular problem with the symphonies is his avoidance of conventional symphonic form. Instead of sonata allegro opening movements, he employs a scheme of continuous variations, so that the listener is not able easily to recognize the structural argument.

Copland, a sympathetic admirer, could identify reasons for the inaccessibility of his works:

Sessions creates without the aid of surface mannerisms a music profoundly his own: music of an ineffable pessemism – resigned, unprotesting, inexpressibly sad, and of a deeply human and non-romantic quality.

(Aaron Copland (1968) *The New Music 1900–1960*, MacDonald & Co.: London, p.128)

Now that all but the Eighth Symphony* have been issued on compact disc, it will be possible to become better acquainted with these isolated works. To his admirers, especially former pupils, Sessions is held in high regard. Among them Andrew Imbrie and John Harbison have expressed great support, acknowledging the considerable impact of his teaching. John Harbison has written:

His [Sessions'] music reveals a cultivated but far from elitist personality, one able to resolve the intricate conflicts into challenging, direct communication.

(*Grove's Dictionary of American Music* (1986) Vol. IV, Macmillan: London and New York, p.194)

Some have placed Sessions with his nine symphonies on a par with composers of the past who achieved a similar tally: Beethoven, Schubert, Bruckner, Dvořák, Mahler and so on. Although at present musical opinion at large would not support such a claim, future generations may come to terms with these works and grant them an enhanced status.

A Symphony in D, written in 1917, was withdrawn by the composer. Another symphony dating from 1934–35 suffered a similar fate and the manuscript is now lost.

---

* Symphony No.8 was issued on a long-playing disc ARGO ZRG 702 in 1973.

Sessions completed his Symphony No.1 in E minor in 1927 while he was living in Italy. He returned to Boston for the première on 22 April 1927 by the Boston Symphony Orchestra conducted by Sergei Koussevitzky. It was heard again at the ISCM (International Society for Contemporary Music) Festival in Geneva on 6 April 1929, the only American work performed at the event.

Although the First Symphony betrays a certain Stravinskyan neo-classical austerity, the polytonality is closer to central European influences. The angular melodic lines, dense orchestral textures and ever-changing moods that typify Sessions' later music are abundantly evident in the 30-year-old composer. There are hints of jazz in the syncopated motor rhythms of the opening marked *Giusto*. The lyrical slow movement is more French in atmosphere, evoking Honegger in its comparative simplicity; similarly the exuberant noisy finale has little to suggest an American composer.

Nearly two decades elapsed between the First and Second Symphonies. Sessions was not prolific during this period of his life, devoting much time to teaching. Only three large-scale pieces were completed in these years: the Violin Concerto (1930–35), Quartet No.1 (1936) and the First Piano Sonata (1927–30).

Symphony No.2, commissioned by the Alice M. Ditson Fund of Columbia University, was first performed on 9 January 1947 by the San Francisco Symphony Orchestra conducted by Pierre Monteux. Sessions described the symphony as:

> A kind of milestone in my work, a point towards which I had been moving in a number of my previous works, and one which forms, as it were, a point of departure for the music I have written since.

While there are still vestiges of tonality (including key signatures), Sessions had moved closer to Schoenberg and the second Viennese School. The first movement alternates two quite different tempi: *molto agitato* and *tranquillo e misterioso*, which can be likened to first and second subjects, thereafter treated in the manner of a development and recapitulation, although not with any observance of traditional key relationships. The music twists and turns melodically and harmonically in a restless struggle of considerable strength. After a sardonic Scherzo, less than two minutes in length, the slow movement, dominated by muted strings, is an exercise in agonized dissonance. It is dedicated to the memory of Franklin D. Roosevelt who died while the composer was working on the symphony. The relatively optimistic finale marked *Allegramente* maintains a constant motion without significantly getting anywhere. Symphony No.2 was performed at the ISCM Festival in Amsterdam in 1948 and won the New York Music Critics' Circle Award in 1950, but public reaction remained unenthusiastic.

Symphony No.3 was commissioned by the Koussevitzky Foundation to mark the 75th anniversary of the Boston Symphony Orchestra who premièred it on 6 December 1957 under the baton of Charles Munch. Sessions commented:

> My Third Symphony is larger in conception and scale than the First and does not

contain the sharp and even violent contrasts of the Second.

By this time Sessions had adopted serialism, more as a natural absorption of the system than a sudden conversion. This application of the 12-note system is heard in the shaping of the melodic material, while Sessions' compositional methods remain basically unchanged. His initial reluctance to follow the Schoenberg line is explained by his pupil Andrew Imbrie:

> His preoccupation with continuity and linear direction seemed at first incompatible with a method which took as its point of departure a modular unit of twelve pitches, and the crystalline forms that such a unit could assume. To Sessions at the time, such a way of composing seemed mosaic-like, and laid undue emphasis on the arrangement of units and cells, at the expense of the larger melodic gesture, for whose explicit realization he saw no provision within the method.
>
> ('The Symphonies of Roger Sessions', *Tempo*, Vol.103, 1972: pp.25–32)

Sessions defined his own reconciliation of the conflict in a letter of 1958 to the *The Score and I.M.A. Magazine*:

> The series will determine the composer's vocabulary; but once the vocabulary has been so determined, the larger questions of tonal organization remain. My own strong feeling is that, while these questions must certainly be answered in terms not alien to the series, it is not serialism as such that can ever be made to account for them.

In the Third Symphony, it is the lack of any tonal implications that makes the argument in the turbulant first movement difficult to follow. As with the previous symphony, a volatile, spiky scherzo precedes the relaxed deeply expressive slow movement. The more extrovert finale has touches of humour in its jazzy irregular rhythms.

Symphony No.4 (1958) was commissioned for the centennial of the State of Minnesota and first performed on 2 January 1960 by the Minneapolis Symphony Orchestra conducted by Antal Dorati. Sessions conceived the work as a set of three character pieces of diverse moods: *Burlesque*, *Elegy* (in memory of his brother who died in 1948), and *Pastorale*, a tranquil finale that ultimately fades into silence.

Beginning with the Fifth Symphony in 1964, Sessions composed four symphonies in the space of just four years. Symphony No.5 was commissioned by Eugene Ormandy and the Philadelphia Orchestra who introduced it on 7 February 1964. It is a highly concentrated score of three movements played without a pause, thematically related by a single figure heard at the opening.

Although totally abstract pieces, the next three symphonies are associated with the Vietnam War. The composer stated:

> They form in my mind a kind of series connected with the events of the time. The Sixth Symphony becomes grim at the end and the Seventh is grim all the way through.

Symphony No.6 was commissioned jointly by the New Jersey Symphony Orchestra and the State of New Jersey for the 300th anniversary of the founding of the state. The score was begun in South America in 1965 and completed at

Tanglewood in the summer of the following year. The première took place in Newark on 19 November 1966 conducted by Kenneth Schermerhorn, although the first movement had been performed on 19 January 1966.

Symphony No.7 was commissioned for the Centennial of the University of Michigan in 1967. It is dedicated to Jean Martinon who conducted the Chicago Symphony Orchestra in the première in Ann Arbor on 1 October 1967. This was Sessions' own favourite symphony although he admitted that the finale was 'a most brutal movement' before the slow epilogue of deep pessimism.

Symphony No.8 was one of 18 works commissioned from various composers for the 125th anniversary of the New York Philharmonic Orchestra. It was first performed under the direction of William Steinberg on 2 May 1968. The score is dedicated to the composer's daughter Elizabeth. Cast in two movements, it is at 14 minutes the shortest of the set and the most accessible. Sessions uses a large orchestra with an expanded percussion section that includes vibraphone, xylophone, marimba and glockenspiel.

Symphony No.9 was commissioned in 1978 by the Syracuse Symphony Orchestra and its then conductor Frederik Prausnitz. The première was given by the orchestra conducted by Christopher Keane on 17 January 1990. The composer knew that it posed problems for both performers and audience: 'I'm afraid it will not be easy to play, but it has to be what it has to be.' More expansive than the Eighth Symphony, it has as its basis a portrayal of evil. Images of the lion and the lamb in William Blake's poem *The Tyger* were the initial inspiration, the conflict between brutality and gentleness: 'I set myself a rather special task in this work and it involves both agony and joy in the making of it.'

In a review of recordings of Sessions' Symphonies 6, 7 and 9, the distinguished writer Wilfred Mellers identified shortcomings that prove an obstacle to easy acceptance of this music. In his view they are:

> singularly deficient in melody, not because they lack Tchaikovsky-like tunes – but because their lines, stabbing, thrusting, spurting or whizzing, don't grow 'organically' and so can't sing, even on the rare occasions when they want to. For all his compositional care and craft, his grudging music does not stay memorable, and is, today, not easy to love.

*(Musical Times, April 1996: p.20)*

Throughout his life **John J. Becker** (1886–1961) was an ardent champion of modern music in the Midwest. He was an active supporter of the ultra-modernists and closely associated with Charles Ives, Roger Sessions, Henry Cowell and Wallingford Riegger, known to some as the 'American Five'. His own compositions, underestimated in his lifetime, have not received the attention they deserve since his death.

Becker's early music shows the strong influence of German late Romanticism but in the 1920s his style abruptly changed to include an increased dissonance and polytonality. His admiration for sixteenth-century contrapuntalists is evident in his compositions, although the harmonic language is modern. He wrote seven symphonies, none of them published.

Symphony No.1 *Etude Primitive*, was composed between 1912 and 1915 but not performed until 1936. Originally written for organ, Symphony No.2 *Fantasia Tragica*, dating from 1920 was heard at the ISCM Festival in Frankfurt in 1927. After the music was lost, the score was reconstructed by the composer in 1937.

Symphony No.3 *Sinfonia Brevis*, the only one of Becker's works to be heard with any frequency, was written between 1929 and 1931 but did not receive its première until 1958 in New York under the direction of Leonard Bernstein. It is an abrasive piece, foreshadowing the symphonies of Roger Sessions. This intensely serious music is very certain in its purpose but betrays no intrinsic American characteristic. The uncompromising nature of the composer can be discerned in the titles of the two movements: No.1 A Scherzo in the Spirit of Mockery; No.2 Memories of War – Sorrow – Struggle – A Protest.

Symphony No.4 *Dramatic Episodes* (1940) for speaking chorus and orchestra was adapted from a theatre piece *Stagework No.3 A Marriage with Space*, dating from 1935. Symphony No.5, subtitled 'Homage to Mozart' was composed in 1942. Symphony No.6 (1942) is a choral symphony *Out of Bondage* for soprano, chorus and orchestra setting words by Abraham Lincoln. From the score Becker extracted a movement of patriotic topicality, *Victory March*. Symphony No.7, *Sermon on the Mount*, is also a choral work for speaking chorus, female voices and orchestra. It was composed between 1947 and 1954 but left incomplete at the composer's death.

Describing his method of orchestration, Becker stated that he used 'the juxtaposition of contrasting instruments, that is, instruments which have no relationship to each other as far as their orchestral color is concerned'. In the Third Symphony he adopted a feature whereby 'the top line of dissonant counterpoint or chordal movement in the orchestra is doubled by the piano played with a percussive stroke'.

Lack of publication, performance and recordings of Becker's music has made him a shadowy figure. We are left to assess his position in American music by just one work, the Third Symphony.

**Harrison Kerr** (1897–1978) studied in the United States before becoming a pupil of Nadia Boulanger at the Fontainebleau Conservatory where he was a fellow student with Aaron Copland. In 1937 he interrupted a teaching career to take up various posts in music publishing and as secretary of the American Composer's Alliance. He joined the music faculty of the University of Oklahoma in 1949, retiring in 1968.

Kerr's very strong self-criticism prevented his becoming a prolific composer, and except for a few songs he withdrew all his compositions written before 1929. His early works were conservative in idiom, but gradually he adopted a more chromatic language which eventually embraced a use of 12-note techniques in a Romantic manner.

His earliest work of significance is the single-movement Symphony No.1 in C minor, composed in 1928–29, revised in 1938 and first performed by the Rochester Symphony Orchestra in 1945. A Second Symphony, completed in

1939, was withdrawn and replaced by another in E minor, written between 1943 and 1945, performed by the Oklahoma City Symphony Orchestra in 1951. Symphony No.3 in D minor followed in 1953; it was premièred in Oklahoma City in 1971. A Fourth Symphony remained unfinished at his death.

After attending the University of Minnesota and Carleton College, Northfield, Minnesota, **Ross Lee Finney** (1906–1997) travelled to Paris to study with Nadia Boulanger (1927–28). He later spent a year at Harvard (1928–29) before returning to Europe where he was a pupil of Alban Berg (1931–32). Subsequently he also received composition lessons from Roger Sessions.

During the late 1940s, as a delayed result of his work with Berg, Finney felt the need for greater chromatic integration in his music. Though he never abandoned the concept of tonal orientation (pitch polarity) in the larger forms of his work, the small details were determined by a serial technique. He called this process a 'system of complementarity'. His adoption of the 12-note system was certainly not the product of sterile academic dogmatism. He wrote:

> I have always wanted my music to 'sing' whatever devices or systems I might use in composing it. Beneath the surface, however, is a complexity of memories and functions and abstractions that give depth to the musical experience but only if the music flows and 'sings' without interruption from beginning to end.

Finney wrote four symphonies. Symphony No.1, subtitled *Communique 1943*, completed in that year, was not performed until 8 December 1964 by the Louisville Orchestra conducted by Robert Whitney. It was composed in the aftermath of Pearl Harbor. Finney explains: 'No literal folk song has been used since that would injure the work, but it does reflect my imagining American folksongs.'

Symphony No.2 was commissioned by the Koussevitzky Foundation in 1959 and first performed by the Philadelphia Orchestra under Eugene Ormandy on 13 November 1959, and subsequently heard throughout the United States and in Europe. It uses a 12-note row and four variants to determine both pitch and rhythm. Explaining his outlook, Finney noted:

> It is hard to realize that in this symphony I was *not* reacting against tonality. I just don't find a serial organization an opposition to a strong tonal process.

In the following year Finney completed his Third Symphony while he was composer-in-residence at the American Academy in Rome. In this piece he adopted a more lyrical approach with less rigid adherence to serialism. The whole work is based on a tone row and four variants. Finney explained:

> The work that best shows my thinking in composing, the Third Symphony, is a short chamber orchestra work *Landscape Remember*. The work is based on symmetrical Hexachords that are the circle of fifths starting on F. This work uses folk song and a serialism (that) comes from the Hexachord.

In the *New York Times*, Harold Schonberg commented:

> Finney has manipulated the line and intervals of those variants for minimum

dissonance. The chances are that few would recognize it as a serial composition without the musical examples printed in the program notes before one's eyes.

Once again the première was given, on 6 March 1964, by Ormandy and the Philadelphia Orchestra who took it on tour to several American cities.

Symphony No.4 (1972) was premièred on 9 May 1973 by Sergio Comissiona and the Baltimore Symphony Orchestra who had commissioned it. In this piece Finney makes use to a certain degree of indeterminate notation. Finney explained his method of composition:

> No work that I have ever written has sprung from logic; music springs, I am sure, from musical ideas and gestures. The real problem, therefore, and one that concerns me more and more, is to find a lyrical expression within the bounds of organization that seem to me important.

For **Elliott Carter** (b. 1908) the symphony has not represented an important place in his orchestral works. An early exercise in the form composed in 1937 was withdrawn. His Symphony No.1 was written in New Mexico in 1942 and first performed on 27 April 1944 by the Eastman Rochester Symphony Orchestra conducted by Howard Hanson. Like the ballet *Pocahontas* (1936) and *Holiday Overture* (1944), it belongs to the brief period in Carter's career when his music was overtly American. Although the score was revised in 1961, he turned away from any intension to be nationalistic. 'I soon began to realize that whatever American character my music had would be the character of myself making music.'

*Symphony of Three Orchestras* (1976) continued the sequence of complex virtuosic orchestral works begun with *Variations for Orchestra* (1954–55) and *Concerto for Orchestra* (1968–69). Commissioned by the New York Philharmonic Orchestra it was premièred on 17 February 1977 under the baton of Pierre Boulez. The standard symphony orchestra is divided into three separate groups:

Orchestra I:    brass, strings, timpani
Orchestra II:   clarinets, piano, vibraphone, chimes, marimba, solo violins and basses, and a group of cellos
Orchestra III:  flutes, oboes, bassoons, horns, violins, violas, basses and non-pitched percussion

The symphony was inspired by the opening lines of Hart Crane's poem *The Bridge*, the subject of an oratorio which Carter began in 1937 but left unfinished.

> How many dawns, chill from his rippling rest
> The seagull's wings shall dip and pivot him,
> Shedding white rings of tumult, building high
> Over the chained bay waters Liberty –
> Then, with inviolate curve, forsake our eyes
> As apparitional as sails that cross
> Some page of figures, to be filed away:
> – Till elevators drop us from our day...

The composer provided the following note:

> The opening music starts in the highest registers of the three orchestras and slowly descends as the trumpet announces one of the themes heard at various times in Orchestra I; it ends in a series of rapidly plunging passages.
>
> The opening descent immediately leads to a *giocoso* theme played by bassoons, the central idea of the first movement of Orchestra III that begins the main section of the score. From here to the coda, twelve differently characterized movements are heard, each with its own related themes, four played by each Orchestra. The four movements of each Orchestra, while differing in expression and speed are related, of course, not only by spatial location and instrumental color but also by characteristic harmonies and rhythms. While no Orchestra plays two of its movements at a time, each of the twelve is introduced while another movement of another Orchestra is being played, briefly surfaces to be heard alone, and then becomes the background for another entrance of another movement. Thus there is a continual overlapping and changing flow of music. The listener, of course, is not meant, on first hearing, to identify the details of this continually shifting web of sound any more than he is to identify the modulations in *Tristan und Isolde*, but rather to hear and grasp the character of the kaleidoscope of musical themes as they are presented in varying contexts.
>
> The main section is brought to a stop by a series of repeated short, loud chords for the full orchestra that shatter the previous flow. The score ends in a coda that recalls fragments of the previous music, alternating repetitive passages and expression bursts, and finally sinks to the lowest registers of the three Orchestras as the beginning is remembered. Although not in any sense an attempt to express *The Bridge* in music, many of the musical ideas were suggested by it and others of Hart Crane's works.

To appreciate the structure of the *Symphony of Three Orchestras* it is vital to *see* a live performance to identify the spatial and multilayered aspects of the music distributed laterally between the three orchestras. The instrumental scoring contains a mass of detail in a relatively short time span, the glittering melodic fragments creating an ever-changing aural kaleidoscope.

In 1997, Carter completed his most recent orchestral work, Symphonia. Oliver Knussen conducted the première with the BBC Symphony Orchestra in Manchester on 26 March 1998.

**Ben Weber** (1916–1979) was one of the first American composers to adopt Schoenberg's serial principles from 1938. Largely self-taught, he concentrated on instrumental music. His best known work, *Symphony on Poems by William Blake* Op.33 (1950) for baritone and chamber orchestra treats the voice more as an instrument within the ensemble than a soloist. In his choice of instrumentation – wind, percussion, cello, celeste and harp – Weber avoided the use of strings to create a less veiled texture which would allow the utmost clarity for the voice.

A single tone row suffices for all four movements. In the dramatic setting of four poems, the intricate Bergian counterpoint suits the elliptical concentrated multi-meaning verse of Blake. Except for Roger Sessions, Weber stands almost alone in the United States as a successful follower of Schoenberg's twelve-note system.

**Andrew Imbrie** (b. 1921) studied composition with Roger Sessions at Princeton and Berkeley where he joined the faculty in 1947. Except for two spells at the American Academy in Rome, he remained at Berkeley where he was appointed Professor of Music in 1960. In 1970 he also became Chairman of the composition department at the San Francisco Conservatory.

His First Symphony was commissioned by the San Francisco Symphony Orchestra in 1965. A Chamber Symphony followed in 1968 and a Second Symphony was performed by the San Francisco Symphony Orchestra in 1970. Also in that year the Hallé Orchestra in Manchester gave the première of Imbrie's Third Symphony.

Of his own compositions Imbrie has written:

> My music does not strive to be American like my nationality, nor Scottish like my ancestry. It is neither experimental nor conventional. I always start at the beginning and let the ideas shape themselves as they must; the direction they will pursue and the changes in character they will undergo become increasingly clear as I go on. I find that an initial musical statement, once made, raises obligations that the composer must have the wit to recognize and to fulfill.
>
> (Sleeve note for recording of Symphony No.3, CRI SD 308)

In this respect he follows the precepts of Sessions. His compositional approach is predominantly contrapuntal creating complex textures and dissonant harmony.

In addition to his early Symphony for Brass and Percussion, **Gunther Schuller** (b. 1925) has composed a Symphony for orchestra. It was commissioned by the Fine Arts Department of the Dallas Public Library for the Dallas Symphony Orchestra who performed it under Donald Johanos on 8 February 1965.

In a programme note the composer wrote:

> In this work I have attempted to evolve certain contemporary analogies to the eighteenth- and nineteenth-century forms which have been generally considered obsolete and unusable in orthodox twelve-tone writing.
>
> These principles afforded me the opportunity to write a four-movement symphony which, though employing very advanced compositional techniques, allows for the return to formal procedures used by Bach, Beethoven and others *without* being aesthetically in discrepancy with them. This is not to say that the music will sound like Bach or Beethoven, but that the underlying formal structures will at least provide a known and previously experienced point of reference.
>
> Each movement employs different aspects or variants of the basic twelve-note row, creating thereby a movement-to-movement progression of 'Key relationships' analogous to those in a Beethoven symphony, let us say (the key being not a diatonic tone center, but the tonal chromatic pitch content ordered in a singular way by the composer specifically for this work). Thus the first and fourth movement use the primary 'tonic' twelve-note row, the other movements variously derived rows (or sets) – derived in a manner analogous to that in which a minor key is derived from its relative major.

The first and last movements act as a frame to the two central movements. In the slow movement Schuller acknowledges a debt to both Bach and Webern, although the listener is likely to be more aware of the latter in the contrapuntal textures. Here the composer follows a six-part fugue with a four-part double canon. The fragmenting of the melodic lines between different instruments produces what Schoenberg called *Klangfarbenmelodie* (tone-colour-melody).

What Schuller calls 'a full-blown Scherzo' has a Trio which introduces more romantic solos for clarinet and horn. To emphasize the importance of symmetry, the B section is in two parts, the second an exact reverse of the first. One is conscious throughout the Symphony of a highly structured approach in which every development is related to the overall organization of the whole work in its adherence to 12-note procedures.

# 13  Samuel Barber (1910–1981)

Barber composed his First Symphony in Rome during 1936 towards the end of his first year at the American Academy as winner of the Prix de Rome. At the time he had only two previous orchestral works to his credit, the glitteringly brilliant overture *The School for Scandal* and the subdued brooding *Music for a Scene from Shelley*, both scores written mainly while the composer was on holiday in Switzerland and Italy.

Symphony No.1 is the first by an American composer to be cast in a single movement; it follows Sibelius's monumental Seventh of 1924 and predates the Third Symphony of Roy Harris by two years. Although the Symphony is a continuous work, the changes of tempo between sections reveal a traditional four-movement pattern. The unity of thematic material and single-mindedness of purpose justify the one-movement appelation.

Barber provided his own concise analysis:

> The form is a synthetic treatment of the four-movement classical symphony. It is based on three themes of the initial *Allegro non troppo*, which retain throughout the work their fundamental character. The *Allegro* opens with the usual exposition of a main theme. After a brief development of the three themes, instead of the customary recapitulation, the first theme, in diminution, forms the basis of the scherzo section (*Vivace*). The second theme (oboe over muted strings) then appears in augmentation, in an extended *Andante tranquilo*. An intense crescendo introduces the finale, which is a short *passacaglia* based on the first theme (introduced by the violoncelli and contrabass), over which, together with figures from other themes, the closing theme is woven, thus serving as a recapitulation for the entire symphony.

Over a pedal E, the strings in unison introduce the first and most important theme characterized by an octave leap in the first phrase and an arpeggio of a falling seventh in the second (Ex. 42). These two melodic figures reiterated in the opening bars establish easily identifiable motifs.

The second subject, a flowing melody on violas and cor anglais contrasts in its smooth contours with the angularity of the first subject. The third bar of this theme is derived from the second phrase of the first subject (Ex. 43).

Repeated rising scales based on this second theme provide the link to the third subject, introduced at the same tempo as the opening of the Symphony.

106

Ex. 42

Allegro ma non troppo

*ff espr.*          *molto largamente*          *a tempo*

*Reproduced by permission of G. Schirmer Inc.*

Ex. 43

Violas     *p espr.*

*Reproduced by permission of G. Schirmer Inc.*

Ex. 44

*ff*

*Reproduced by permission of G. Schirmer Inc.*

The development melodically exploits the first subject, at times in inversion (Ex. 45a) or extended by sequences. (Ex. 45b).

Ex. 45a

Più animato

*mf*

Ex. 45b

*mf*     *espr.*          *cresc.*          *f*

*Reproduced by permission of G. Schirmer Inc.*

Through the texture a trombone intones, in the manner of a *cantus firmus*, a derivation of the first subject which later becomes the passacaglia theme of the final section of the Symphony (Ex. 46) This is the only passage in the entire work that appears to echo the Seventh Symphony of Sibelius where the same solo instrument crowns the climax in a similar way.

Ex. 46

*Reproduced by permission of G. Schrimer Inc.*

The ensuing *scherzo* is based on the first subject, with the octave a clear means of identification.

Ex. 47

*Reproduced by permission of G. Schirmer Inc.*

In the second part of this section, Barber employs the wind instruments in pairs or threes, moving in parallel intervals, a feature of Sibelius in his scoring where he rarely allows a flute, oboe or clarinet to be heard on its own. The strings in particular leap around like scalded cats in a headlong rush, that ultimately becomes locked on a repeated rhythmic figure (Ex. 48), which leads to a powerful utterance of the opening of the first subject, presented sequentially in descending phrases on the brass.

Ex. 48

*Reproduced by permission of G. Schirmer Inc.*

A brief coda to the *scherzo* for clarinets, bassoon and timpani passes without a break to the elegiac slow movement. Over a broken-chord accompaniment for muted strings, Barber produces one of his characteristic passionate oboe melodies that he saves up for the emotional core of his works. This feature appeared in the Overture *The School for Scandal* and was to recur later, most notably in the Violin Concerto. This slow movement theme (Ex. 49) is based on the second subject (Ex. 43), now extended to 26 bars.

Ex. 49

Reproduced by permission of G. Schirmer Inc.

The finale combines the first subject as a passacaglia in the bass with a version of the second theme on woodwind.

Ex. 50

Reproduced by permission of G. Schirmer Inc.

As the contrapuntal invention unfolds, all three themes of the opening of the Symphony reappear in varied but clearly recognizable forms. Such economical and logical use of material would probably have earned the admiration of Brahms, the finale of whose Fourth Symphony, also a passacaglia, preserves a similar seamless flow over the recurring regularity of the ground bass.

Barber's first excursion into the daunting field of symphonic composition reveals a rigorous self-discipline and confidence remarkable for a man still in his mid-twenties with no previous large-scale orchestral work behind him. Following the première in Rome on 13 December 1936 conducted by Bernardino Molinari, Barber returned to the United States for the American première on 21 January 1937. This should have been conducted by Artur Rodzinski but through illness his place was taken by Rudolph Ringwall directing the Cleveland Orchestra. A further performance with the same orchestra under Rodzinski followed in New York on 24 March and Rodzinski introduced it at the Salzburg Festival in July of that year, the first American work to be heard in that Festival.

In 1942 Barber revised the Symphony replacing the original *Scherzo* with a more extended section, and tightening the structure of the *Andante* and *Passacaglia*. This version was premièred in 1944 under the baton of Bruno Walter who recorded the work for Columbia Records.

In April 1943, Barber was conscripted into the US Army where he was given clerical duties as he was deemed medically unfit for combat. After a few months he was transferred to the Air Force where he was able to devote much of his time to composition. The US Army Air Forces commissioned him to write a symphony and the enlightened authorities even allowed him to work at home for some of the time.

Although the Second Symphony is contemporary with international conflict that increasingly affected the American people at home, it would be misleading to associate the dissonant harmonies and stormy nature of the outer movements with the realities of war. As with Stravinsky's *Symphony in Three Movements*, written a year later than Barber's work, only in a general way can it be regarded as a reflection of World War II. Except for the deliberate incorporation of the sound of a homing-beacon in the slow movement, the Second Symphony should be considered primarily as an abstract work. The composer's melancholy introspection is at the heart of this emotionally volatile work.

The first movement of the Second Symphony is in sonata form; the principal feature of the first theme is the interval of a major second, both harmonically and melodically.

Ex. 51

*Reproduced by permission of G. Schirmer Inc.*

Comparison could be made with the opening of the Fourth Symphony of Vaughan Williams whom Barber had met at Bryn Mawr College in 1932. Vaughan Williams uses a minor second to create a similar atmosphere of unresolved conflict.

Barber's jagged rhythms and angularity of line produce a dark aggressive mood that dominates the movement; the wartime background to the Symphony's composition could be attributed in part to such unease, but the composer denied that was an influence. A secondary figure emerges in the bass line, which later becomes the theme of the finale. As with so many of Barber's melodic figures, it is made up of reiterated thirds.

The agitated opening, with its sudden explosive outbursts, gives way to a more tranquil, flowing second subject, introduced by Barber's favourite solo wind instrument for lyrical melodies, the oboe (Ex. 53). The accompanying strings

Ex. 52

*Reproduced by permission of G. Schirmer Inc.*

provide a throbbing which maintains in the background the restless nature of the earlier part of the movement.

Ex. 53

*Reproduced by permission of G. Schirmer Inc.*

The development, marked *Delicato e misterioso*, is based initially on the first subject, but in characteristic manner, Barber combines the first and second subjects.

Ex. 54

*Reproduced by permission of G. Schirmer Inc.*

Also, rising and falling arpeggios of thirds, treated in canon, frequently appear.

Ex. 55

*Reproduced by permission of G. Schirmer Inc.*

A frenetic barrage of timpani and woodblocks leads directly into the recapitulation where much of the music is an almost exact replica of the exposition. The peaceful close of the movement on a high C sharp in the violins creates a certain tonal ambiguity for a movement that began in F sharp minor.

The slow movement, unequivocally in A minor, is in the ABA form usual for Barber in large-scale works. Sombre orchestral colours prevail throughout, established at the beginning by an eight-bar introduction on muted divided cellos and double basses in six parts. The main theme is given to the cor anglais.

Ex. 56

*Reproduced by permission of G. Schirmer Inc.*

The 5/4 meter prevents the flow of phrases from becoming predictable. A more intense central section, based on the introduction, provides the strings with wide leaps, a link with the opening of the first movement.

Ex. 57

*Reproduced by permission of G. Schirmer Inc.*

The introductory music returns on the full strings. Against it, the E flat clarinet intones an A, the radio beam signal to guide an aircraft at night. This is the only specific reference Barber allows to his wartime experience that lies behind the Second Symphony.

The finale opens boldly with an unbarred unison cadenza for violins and violas, the second part being an almost exact inversion of the first (Ex. 58).

This is combined with a horn call derived from the second figure of the first movement (Ex. 59).

These two thematic ideas recur throughout the movement. There follows a chain of continuous variations based on a simple two-phrase theme on the cellos. The descending first four notes are clearly recognized as a harmonic bass line, while the second phrase is developed melodically.

If the opening cadenza reminds one of the finale of Hindemith's *Mathis der Maler* Symphony, the culminating fugue of this movement will also suggest the

Ex. 58

Presto senza battuta

Ex. 59

Ex. 60

Allegro risoluto

craftsmanship and character of the German master. Falling thirds, Barber's stylistic trade mark, appear as a counter-melody. The climax of the fugue, a loud chord of C major on the full orchestra, leads to a partial recapitulation of earlier material. The tranquil close before the coda brings to mind Béla Bartók, whose canonical counterpoint for strings is reincarnated here (Ex. 60).

Ex. 61

Tranquillo

The coda restores the *allegro* and the combination of the two elements of the first theme with repetition of previous music. The final chord of F sharp minor reinforces the implied tonality of the whole work.

In the mid-1960s, Barber withdrew the Second Symphony in a melodramatic way. Hans W. Heinshelmer, his editor at G. Schirmer, gave a first-hand account of the circumstances.

> Why is it that all your concert works are successful, that is they all seem to stay alive, no matter how old they are... all with the exception of your Second Symphony? This one we just can't get off the ground.' There was, again, no hesitation. 'The reason is very simple', Barber said. 'It is not a good work.' While such an admission was unusual enough, what followed was even more startling. 'Let's go back to the office and destroy it', he said. And that is what we did. We went back, got all the music from the library... and Samuel Barber, with a gusto that increased our admiration for him from one torn page to the next, tore up all those beautifully and expensively copied materials with his own hands.

('The Composing Composer: Samuel Barber', *ASCAP Today*, Autumn 1968: pp.4–7)

Why did Barber annihilate this Symphony many years after its completion? Was his destruction of the scores and parts at his publisher's warehouse an act of pique or revenge on an ungrateful music profession which had largely ignored his compositions? His own comment that it was 'not a good work' cannot be accepted.

The outer movements reveal the composer in uncompromisingly aggressive mood, more dissonant and tonally ambiguous than in any earlier works. One might have expected the critics to see this advance as a progression in the right direction for an almost incurable Romantic. Perhaps Barber despaired of ever gaining critical acceptance; he was certainly deeply hurt by attacks on his music.

The central movement he retained is the most conservative of the three but the only one able to exist on its own. This he reissued under the title *Night Flight*, with a quotation from Antoine de Saint-Exupéry at the head of the score. Barber had been flown from one air base to another so that he would have been familiar at first hand with night flying. Saint-Exupéry (1900–44), the French aviator and novelist, made use of his own experiences in his book *Night Flight* (1931) which describes the perils faced by pilots in overcoming the fear of flying at night.

For *Night Flight* Barber made only slight changes to the original scoring. He added two and a half bars of suspended cymbal roll, and altered the rhythm of the radio beacon signal to give a closer resemblance to Morse Code.

Public performances of *Night Flight* have been no more numerous than when it was part of the Second Symphony. The withdrawal of the score and parts of the Second Symphony did not extend to a ban on the sale of the composer's recording which was reissued on the Everest label in the 1960s and has been in and out of the catalogue periodically since. With the passing of time, regret at Barber's impulsive action has increased since there is much to admire in the lost outer movements. In the late 1980s a new recording of the Second Symphony by the New Zealand Symphony Orchestra conducted by Andrew Schenk was issued. This has subsequently led to three further recordings, including one of the Koussevitzky première with the Boston Symphony Orchestra on 3 March 1944.

Ex. 62

*Reproduced by permission of G. Schirmer Inc.*

Together the two symphonies by Barber occupy a significant place in the development of the symphony in the United States. While neither betrays any specific 'American' musical features, no folk songs or jazz, they are both reflections of the American psyche. The neuroses and violence, particularly in the Second, reflect urban life as experienced by a sensitive artist. Within the generation of composers who emerged after the Second World War, notably William Schuman and Peter Mennin, the symphony was often the means of expressing feelings similar to those in Barber's symphonies, but in a less overtly Romantic language.

# 14 William Schuman (1910–1992)

After hearing Roy Harris's *Symphony '1933'*, the young William Schuman enrolled at the Juilliard School in New York for the summer of 1936 so that he could study with Harris. He continued privately with him until 1938.

Schuman began his First Symphony in Paris in 1935, scoring it for an ensemble of 18 instruments. The submission of the work for the Bearns Prize offered by Columbia University proved unsuccessful. One of the judges, the ultra-conservative Daniel Gregory Mason, was unsympathetic towards its uncompromising, advanced harmonic idiom, but even Harris considered the score 'long on thematic material, short on development'. Although the composer was downcast at the verdict, Schuman's First Symphony did receive one performance on 21 October 1936 by the Gotham Symphony Orchestra conducted by Jules Werner at a Composers' Forum Laboratory sponsored by the Works Progress Administration.

The Second Symphony, even more radical than its predecessor, is cast in a single movement and based on the note C which is sounded or implied throughout. It was completed in 1937 and successfully entered for a competition organized by the Musicians' Committee of the North American Committee to Aid Spanish Democracy. The judges were Bernard Wagenaar, Roger Sessions, Aaron Copland and Roy Harris. Unfortunately lack of funds prevented the performance, publication and recording which had been promised but again the Works Progress Administration came to the rescue. The première took place on 25 May 1938 by the Greenwich Village Orchestra conducted by Edgar Schenkman. A repeat performance followed on radio by the CBS Symphony Orchestra conducted by Howard Barlow, after which one listener wrote to the composer 'Your symphony made one lose faith in the power of the aspirin tablet.'

The attention of Sergei Koussevitzky was drawn to Schuman's Second Symphony by Aaron Copland, which led to its Boston première in February 1939. However, the support of the great conductor did not lessen the hostile reception, accompanied by hissing, given to the new work by both critics and audience. Only Moses Smith in the *Boston Transcript* proffered any praise. This adverse public reaction may have been the reason that Schuman withdrew the Second Symphony as he had done the First. In the study of his music published in 1954,* both works are described as 'withdrawn pending revision' but neither was reissued.

Of principal benefit for Schuman at this time was his first meeting with Aaron Copland who wrote 'Schuman is, as far as I am concerned, the musical find of the year.'**

Symphony No.3, completed in 1941, was the turning point in Schuman's career, transforming him instantly in the eyes of the musical public from a minor pariah into a much lauded composer. Little wonder that the new work received the first award to be made by the New York Music Critics' Circle in 1942. Today it has lost nothing of the stunning impact it made upon the listeners at the première on 17 October 1941 by the Boston Symphony Orchestra under the baton of Sergei Koussevitzky. Not even Roy Harris's Third Symphony had created such a strong impression at a first hearing.

The Third Symphony is cast in two movements, each subdivided into two linked sections: Passacaglia and Fugue; Chorale and Toccata. These titles alone suggest baroque forms in modern guise. The Passacaglia theme, stated at the outset on unaccompanied violas, comprises wide intervals that can be easily recognized in subsequent thematic material in the ensuing variations and developed in the other parts of the symphony.

Ex. 63

*Reproduced by permission of G. Schirmer Inc.*

The theme is taken up in strict canon first by the strings – 2nd violins, cellos, 1st violins, double basses (with lower wind), and later by horns, upper woodwind, building into a characteristic sonorous Schuman texture of sturdy activity. Although Walter Piston is usually acknowledged to be the leading contrapuntalist among twentieth-century American composers, Schuman is equally a master in this field. The shadow of Roy Harris lies over this slow unfolding of material, the raw open string sound familiar to the opening of Harris's Third Symphony.

*Variation 1* (bar 50): Against the passacaglia theme on trumpets and trombones, the strings develop the theme in triplets with the significant intervals of octaves and fourths in particular providing the basis:

---

\*    Flora Rheta Schreiber and Vincent Persichetti (1954) *William Schuman*, Schirmer, New York.
\*\* *Modern Music*, May/June 1938.

Ex. 64

*Variation 2*: (bar 74). The strings and lower wind are locked on an A major/ C major chord as the upper woodwind continue the triplet figuration:

Ex. 65

A transition prepares for the quieter *Variation 3* (bar 87) with the violins in octaves presenting a version of the theme where the intervals are compressed. Underneath cellos sustain a continuous murmur of rapid *sotto voce* scales.

Tension increases as the strings adopt ever shorter note values, leading to the dotted rhythm of *Variation 4* (bar 121), against which the trombones play the Passacaglia theme in four-part harmony (Ex. 66). The string ostinato and the stark block triadic trombone harmonies again recall Roy Harris.

Ex. 66

The Fugue follows without a break; its principal subject (Ex. 67) is based on the Passacaglia theme now transformed into jagged phrases.

Ex. 67

Fugue: Vigoroso

The chromatically rising fugal entries (on Bb, B♮, C, Db, D) reflect those of the Passacaglia (E, F, F#, G). A spectacular canonic compression of the subject on four trumpets (bar 195) leads to a tranquil variation (bar 220) where the English born embellishes the fugue theme (Ex. 68) later taken up by the other woodwind, in a similar way to Harris's wind solos over string arpeggios in the second section of his Third Symphony.

Ex. 68

Solo timpani ushers in the second variation (bar 273) and final section as the strings pursue a headlong drive culminating in the final appearance of the fugue subject on trombones against a massive brass chorale (bar 354).

Ex. 69

Within a span of just 13½ minutes Schuman has packed an extraordinary amount of material, closely argued development entirely derived from the Passacaglia theme by means of extensive transformation. This is no abstract intellectual exercise but an expression of changing moods and emotions, generating excitement and ecstasy at the climactic points.

The Chorale and Fugue are guided by the same compositional discipline exerted in the first movement. The two-part writing for violas and cellos at the beginning of the Chorale in preparation for the Chorale theme itself is again derived from Harris's, modal 'wide-open-spaces' music. Over parallel root-position chords on lower strings, a solo trumpet intones the Chorale, whose melodic shape is derived from the Passacaglia, the first bar preserving the original intervals; octaves and fourths again predominate.

Ex. 70

Chorale: Andantino

Reproduced by permission of G. Schirmer Inc.

The influence of Harris is strong with occasional hints of Copland's 'folk' idiom, (bars 48–50) and even a passage for strings that could have been taken directly from Vaughan Williams' *Fantasia on a Theme of Thomas Tallis* (bars 54–64).

A powerful setting of the Chorale theme for wind and strings marks the climax of this section. This is characteristic Schuman polytonality; the bass line is pitched one whole tone higher than the block triads in the upper parts.

Ex. 71

Reproduced by permission of G. Schirmer Inc.

Without a break, a solo side drum taps out the rhythm of the Toccata subject in advance of its appearance on the bass clarinet, another derivative of the Passacaglia theme.

Ex. 72

Toccata

Bass Clar.

*Reproduced by permission of G. Schirmer Inc.*

The ensuing virtuoso display on the woodwind leads to a hymn-like augmention of the Toccata theme.

Ex. 73

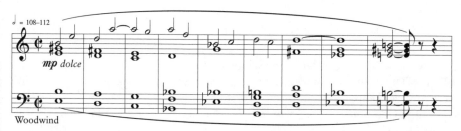

Woodwind

*Reproduced by permission of G. Schirmer Inc.*

Two cadenzas, the first for divisi cellos, the second for violins, are in effect variations on the Chorale. The final section (bar 312) brings together material from the whole symphony. The strings set up an ostinato on fragmented versions of the Chorale and Toccata themes.

In the increasing frenzy similar to the ending of the first movement, the Toccata theme returns in augmentation on the lower wind and brass, culminating in the reintroduction of the pounding chords of the first variation of the Passacaglia in the final bars.

Schuman's Third Symphony is a remarkable achievement, a totally American work of considerable integrity. It owes some debt to his teacher Roy Harris, particularly in the modal harmonic and melodic idiom and significant features of orchestration, especially the use of instruments in their separate self-sufficient

Ex. 74

*Reproduced by permission of G. Schirmer Inc.*

groupings. The formal structure and rhythmic vitality are, however, Schuman's own and the Harris influences have been absorbed into his style.

After the New York performance, the *New York Times* critic Olin Downes wrote:

> This symphony is full of talent and vitality, from first to last, and done with exuberance and conviction on the part of the composer that carry straight over the footlights.

Lazare Saminsky, a trenchant and often severe critic of music by his fellow American composers, provided enthusiastic support:

> Schuman's Third Symphony is an example of remarkable tonal building attained through outer and physical roads – play of sonorities, thematic extension, working the episode and grotesque – not through the inner biological blossoming of works of supreme art. But even so, this work is a significant attainment in American art, a mark of its triumph and high achievement of craft.

> (Lazare Saminsky *Living Music of the Americas* (1949) Howell, Soskin and Crown Publishers: New York, p.74)

Like William Walton, in later life Schuman faced competition with his younger self. The Third Symphony received such acclaim that his subsequent major works were always compared to it, often with adverse results.

Schuman completed his Symphony No.4 on 17 August 1941 exactly two months before the première of the Third Symphony. It was commissioned by the Cleveland Orchestra and performed by them on 22 January 1942 conducted by Artur Rodzinski.

To follow up the ground-breaking Third Symphony so soon with a new symphony was a considerable challenge. (Beethoven had faced the same problem after the *Eroica*.) The Fourth Symphony has several features in common with its predecessor, the Harris-like non-functional triadic harmony, the frequent segregation of the separate orchestral groups, and the long non-repetitive cantilenas symptomatic of Schuman's freedom in melodic manipulation. What is missing is the single-minded unity of form and material that is the strength of the Third Symphony. The vital sense of inevitability is absent where thematic development is diffuse with little feeling of spontaneity. For example, the fugue for strings in the middle of the finale is contrived, more an academic exercise than natural symphonic argument. Too often the composer relies on his own formulae when inspiration flags. Nevertheless there are some fine passages, the curious opening wind dialogue over a walking bass, the lush sonorities of the chorale in the slow movement and the bold writing for brass throughout the symphony.

Schuman preferred to call his Fifth Symphony *Symphony for Strings*, perhaps to avoid comparison or competition with Beethoven. With this, the most compact of the set at 17 minutes, he had completed three symphonies in as many years. It was commissioned by the Koussevitzky Foundation and finished in New Rochelle, NY on 31 July 1943. Following the première in Boston on 12 November of that year conducted by Koussevitzky, it was widely performed and represented the USA at the 1946 ISCM Festival in London. Critical response was enthusiastic; only the *New York Times* correspondent was unimpressed, dismissing it as 'dry and not particularly communicative'.

The whole work is a virtuoso display for all sections of the string orchestra. A powerful opening unison theme for the violins on the G string, marked *Molto agitato ed energico*, provides material for all three movements. Between repeated note patterns, four 'motifs' are the essential cells for development later in the movement.

Ex. 75

Molto agitato ed energico

Reproduced by permission of G. Schirmer Inc.

Schuman alternates melodic fragmentation with polyphonic invention and homophonic points of cohesion. The second subject, derived from motif b (Ex. 75) beginning on violas, is treated in strict canon leading to a passage of polytonal chords, which are subjected to intricate rhythmic disintegration to create the climax. Throughout the movement there is hardly a single let-up in the frenetic forward drive. Open fifths abound to colour the sonorous string textures.

Dual tonalities widely spaced are a feature of the slow movement (Ex. 76).

A long, slowly unfolding second subject on the first violins, the beginning of a canon, continues this duality between the melody and accompaniment (Ex. 77).

Shorter note values increase the emotional intensity of the music, in the manner of Pachelbel's famous *Canon*. The coda restores the peaceful chords of the opening.

The Presto Finale is a free rondo where the nervous muttering theme is varied at each repetition (Ex. 78).

The pizzicato first episode criss-crosses back and forth over the ensemble, like the Scherzo of Tchaikovsky's Fourth Symphony. In contrast the second episode

Ex. 76

Larghissimo

*Reproduced by permission of G. Schirmer Inc.*

Ex. 77

Larghissimo, tenderly

*Reproduced by permission of G. Schirmer Inc.*

Ex. 78

Presto Leggiero

*Reproduced by permission of G. Schirmer Inc.*

introduces arching phrases of smooth flowing canonic counterpoint. Like the first movement, the impetus is seldom relaxed, culminating in a solid D major conclusion.

Commissioned by the Dallas Symphonic League, Symphony No.6 in one movement was completed in 1948 and first performed in February of the following year by Antal Dorati and the Dallas Symphony Orchestra. Probably the finest of the cycle of symphonies, it contains dark brooding music with aggressively vigorous passages of rhythmical energy. Although it earned warm approval, the Sixth Symphony never achieved wide popularity, probably on account of its overriding pessimism. The composer responded laconically by asking why, if it was so good a work, the symphony was seldom heard in his lifetime. To date it still awaits a modern recording to replace the Columbia disc by the Philadelphia Orchestra and Eugene Ormandy of the 1950s.

Initially Schuman conceived the Sixth Symphony as a Divertimento in several movements before transforming it into a symphony. Although in a single movement, the form betrays six contrasting sections: Moderato con moto – Leggieramente – Adagio – Allegro risoluto – Presto – Larghissimo.

A deceptively quiet three-bar brass chorale contains latent menace, a snarl that will later fuel the more violent outbursts. Muted violins introduce a typical Schuman extended, mostly stepwise, melody that wanders freely like a lost soul above the sustained wind harmonies.

Ex. 79

Largo

*Reproduced by permission of G. Schirmer Inc.*

The more insistent theme in the bass initiates the *Moderato con moto* where a counter-melody (horns and cellos) sets off an elaborate canon, a contrapuntal *tour-de-force* which increases the tension. Two extraordinary passages for the entire woodwind exemplify Schuman's complex unison rhythms.

Ex. 80

*Reproduced by permission of G. Schirmer Inc.*

Aaron Copland had drawn attention to this particular feature: 'Curiously Schumanesque rhythms, so skittish, so personal, so utterly free and inventive; there is nothing quite like these rhythms in American music, or any music for that matter' (*The Musical Quarterly*: July 1951).

Schuman treats the separate sections of the orchestra as self-contained units, each with its own distinctive material violently locked in battle. This marks some of the most radical music that Schuman wrote. A phrase used by Lazare

Saminsky with regard to the *Symphony for Strings*' 'planned polyphonic turmoil' goes some way to describe the wild frenzy that has overwhelmed the music, seemingly beyond human control.

Cessation of hostilities is brought about by an unaccompanied solo timpani passage that links the *Moderato con moto* to the second section marked *Leggieramente*, a scintillating scherzo, mostly pianissimo, that barely touches the ground. Beginning on the strings, the irregular rhythmic patterns are tossed back and forth across the orchestra, with unexpected sudden dynamic surges from *pp* to *ff* to catch the unwary. Once these exchanges are over, the second part of the scherzo loses some sense of direction, caught in a playful contrapuntal merry-go-round for woodwind and strings.

Muted strings dominate the central *Adagio*, the emotional heart of the symphony. The violin solo which emerges above the packed harmonic texture (bar 455) is a pre-echo of a passage from the first movement of Schuman's Violin Concerto of 1950, where in similar fashion, a clarinet adds a complementary obbligato to the violin.

Ex. 81

*Reproduced by permission of G. Schirmer Inc.*

The deeply poignant effect of the intertwining instruments reveals Schuman as a closet Romantic, allowing real passion to be expressed. Peace is soon shattered in a second pitched battle, percussion providing the artillery, supported by reiterated brass chords. Here in the *Allegro risoluto*, the conflict is if anything more bitter than before, more co-ordinated, less mayhem.

The ensuing *Presto* is related melodically and contrapuntally to the *Leggieramente*, characterized by rising scale patterns, now more heavily scored. One finale cathartic climax marks the beginning of the coda *Larghissimo*, a chorale for the strings based on the opening subject of the symphony, set against *fff* repeated brass chords in irregular rhythmic patterns. In the closing bars, a typical Schuman chord based on E – minor in the lower register, major at the top – is eventually resolved on the minor tonality, deep in the violas, cellos and doublebasses.

In its compact single movement form, the Sixth Symphony covers a vast gamut of moods, from dark despair to wild exertion, similar in some features to the symphonies of one of Schuman's contemporaries, Shostakovich, but achieved with totally different musical means. The gloomy pessimism and sheer ferocity of utterance that characterize the music have mitigated against its popular acceptance. Live performance would have both a disturbing and invigorating effect upon players and audience; the Sixth is not a comfortable or comforting work. It is, however, because of, not in spite of, the uncompromising language that Schuman's Sixth Symphony occupies a major position in the symphonic output of American composers this century.

Twelve years elapsed before Schuman wrote his next symphony. He remarked 'My own general feeling is that my Seventh, Eighth and Ninth Symphonies are somehow connected in my mind, perhaps because they represent the efforts of more or less a single decade.' Symphony No.7 was commissioned by the Koussevitzky Music Foundation to celebrate the 75th anniversary of the Boston Symphony Orchestra who performed it under Charles Munch on 21 October 1960. Of the complete symphonic canon it is the most conventional, lacking few truly memorable moments; the composer's characteristics have become mannerisms.

Music from a documentary film score *The Earth is Born* (1959) was incorporated into the symphony and the third movement is an expanded version of the second of Schuman's *Three Piano Moods* (1958). The first of its four linked movements is a dark brooding introduction of dense polytonal chords. There is a debilitating overuse of thick scoring of multiple parallel triads in a very slow tempo that inevitably leads to a monotonous tonal texture. The melodic interval of a rising seventh, sometimes with an intervening third, is the motivic germ which unites all the movements.

A curious cadenza for bass clarinet, later joined by a clarinet, leads to the scherzo, marked *Vigoroso*. The trumpet and trombone unison fanfare, based on the rising seventh motif, lifts the gloom, but heavy orchestration and lack of melodic development never allow the music to generate momentum or excitement. The third movement, *Cantabile intensamente*, is the only part of the Seventh Symphony with any distinct personality. Scored for strings only, it begins quietly and builds up in an arch to an outpouring of emotional strength, before returning to tranquillity. Although the endless melodic flow based on the first three notes of the movement is highly chromatic, tonal implications are never lost.

Wind and percussion return for the Finale but like the scherzo, nagging irregular rhythms never escape the treadmill repetition, again seriously weighed down by hefty orchestration. The mind-numbing impact of the full forces, including an unrelenting percussion section, merely serves to underline the lack of significant development of the initial material.

Symphony No.8 (1961–62), scored for large orchestra, was commissioned by the New York Philharmonic Orchestra for the opening of Philharmonic Hall (now Avery Fisher Hall) at the Lincoln Center, New York on 4 October 1962 conducted by Leonard Bernstein. In a letter to Edward Downes, annotator for the New York Philharmonic programmes, Schuman expressed a wish *not* to have his Symphony No.8 analysed too closely:

> Frankly, over the years I have become increasingly resistant about issuing play-by-play accounts of my own music. Perhaps I'm making a minor protest against the elaborate essays which these days so often accompany the launching of new works. Complicated polemics for particular aesthetic creeds of compositional procedures may be of value to scholars, but they confuse the layman. This is not to say that it is not desirable to help an active listener to hear more in his first exposure to a new work (passive listeners are not receptive to help, since their particular joy is sound-bathing). In time, the music will be judged by its inherent worth.

The Eighth Symphony is close in character to the Sixth Symphony, with extremes of mood from dark sombre static chords in the first movement to the fiery explosive brass in the finale, more violent than anything else he wrote. The second and third movements are orchestral reworkings of the last two movements of his String Quartet No.4 (1950). At the risk of incurring the wrath of the composer's ghost, some commentary on the score is required.

As with many American symphonies, the first movement acts as an extended introduction, beginning with heavy major/minor bell-like chords which return at various points in the work to restore calm. Against these repeated chords, Schuman weaves one of his customary long polytonal melodies, first the horn, passing it on to the oboe and later to violins, reaching a massive climax with the weight of full forces. In the central section exultant brass break free in spectacular virtuosity in the *Vigoroso* (bar 123), which recalls the Sixth Symphony. This forward drive is brought to a halt by solo timpani in a widely spaced cannonade.

The slow movement, *Largo*, follows without a break, beginning on the strings (like the third movement of Symphony No.7). Here the intensely chromatic texture is devoid of counterpoint. Against more bell chords on harps, piano and glockenspiel, a typical Schuman hymn-like theme is introduced by the violas, taken over by the woodwind, culminating in a powerful oration from the trombones and tuba against a fiery accompaniment of repeated irregular rhythms on the other brass. The original tempo is transformed into a Scherzo marked triple forte, abruptly interrupted by the bell chords to restore peace in the coda.

It is the Rondo finale, Presto, which carries the principal emphasis of the Eighth Symphony (Ex. 82).

With a relentless pace and persistent nervous energy, the fleeting exchanges of melodic fragments and brass outbursts tax the skill of both conductor and players to the limits. The frenzy of the closing pages marks Schuman's most brilliant writing, frightening in its menace and intense ferocity.

Writing in *High Fidelity*, Alfred Frankenstein described the Eighth Symphony as

Ex. 82

Presto

*Reproduced by permission of Alfred Kalmus Ltd*

one of the most sombre, profound, monumental and moving symphonies in recent years. Following none of the academicisms of contemporary music, this work is, like most of Schuman's music, ingeniously complex, altogether original in form, and wonderfully orchestrated.

Symphony No.9 was first performed by the Philadelphia Orchestra conducted by Eugene Ormandy on 10 January 1969. It is dedicated to the memory of Alexander Hilsberg (1900–1961), concert master of the orchestra from 1926 to 1953, whose friends had commissioned the work. Subtitled *La Fosse Ardeatine*, the symphony was inspired by the composer's visit to a cave near Rome where the Germans had murdered 335 Italian civilians in May 1944 in retaliation for resistance activities. In spite of a reluctance to analyse his music, Schuman provided a substantial programme note explaining the background to the Ninth Symphony.

> The mood of my symphony, especially in its opening and closing sections, is directly related to emotions engendered by this visit. But the entire middle section, too, with its various moods of fast music, much of it far from somber, stems from fantasies I had of the variety, promise and aborted lives of the martyrs. Candidly, however, there is no compelling musical reason for my adding to the title Symphony No.9. The work does not attempt to depict the events realistically. And its effect on the emotional climate of the work could have remained a private matter. My reason for using the title is not then musical but philosophical. One must come to terms with the past in order to build a future.

Although the composer refers to three sections: Anteludium, Offertorium, Postludium, these titles do not appear in the score itself. Indeed of the three symphonies deemed to be in a one-movement form, it is the Ninth which most has the feeling of a single unbroken span.

The opening Anteludium begins slowly and quietly with a typical Schuman theme, an extended free-roaming melody in octaves on first violins and cellos (Ex. 83).

Characterized by wide leaps, particularly 7ths, it is revealed to be a fugue subject with the entry of 2nd violins and violas in bar 12. From the entry of the woodwind (bar 34) treating the subject in augmentation, there is a gradual increase in rhythmic activity. The arrival of the brass (bar 67) transforms the fugue subject into a chorale, against which unison strings fiercely add an obbligato derived from the earlier woodwind figuration.

Ex. 83

*Reproduced by permission of Alfred Kalmus Ltd*

The Offertorium which forms the major portion of the symphony follows without a pause (bar 110) at a much faster tempo. Schuman provided a simple description:

> The moods are varied and range from the playful to the dramatic. The music is fast with the exception of several short contrasting interludes which always return to the fast tempo. The climax of the Offertorium is reached with an even faster tempo and a sonorous climax for full orchestra, with three pairs of struck cymbals employed in rhythmic patterns.

Here Schuman makes use of long passages for selected sections of the orchestra to the total exclusion of other instruments: woodwind (bars 183–231), strings and piano (bars 232–247), muted strings, horns and trombones (bars 318–340), strings and woodwind (bars 344–373). This specific stratification of the orchestra has been noted in earlier symphonies, but never before has it been employed with such rigidity.

Of the final section, Schuman wrote:

> The music of the Postludium at first echoes, in slow tempo, some elements of the climax just heard. Finally the opening theme of the symphony is again stated, but in an even slower tempo than at first. The setting is different and the melody, although again played by the strings, is harmonized in the trombones and tuba. New figurations are introduced and reference is made to the music of the Offertorium. The symphony draws to a close with a long freely-composed quiet ending characterized by an emotional climate which sums up the work and eventually leads to a final concluding outburst.

Although Schuman disclaimed any realistic representation of the Second World War atrocity at the Ardeatine Cave, two passages of the Postludium stand out in graphic detail. The *sotto voce* exchanges of short percussion figures (called 'flams' by the players) between side drum, tenor drum, bass drum and timpani inevitably possess military associations. In bar 600, a sudden triple forte stroke on timpani and bass drum shatters the calm, followed by a piercing chord on four trumpets. Is this not a depiction of the execution of the Italian civilians and the subsequent blowing up of the cave by the Germans?

At a first hearing, Symphony No.9 may not create as strong an impact as earlier works, but further study will reveal strikingly new features amidst much that is familiar.

Symphony No. 10 (*American Muse*) was commissioned to celebrate the American Bicentennial by the National Symphony Orchestra of Washington who performed it under Antal Dorati in April 1976. The opening movement is based on a *Prelude for a Great Occasion* dating from 1974. Slabs of sound, unrelentingly heavily scored dissonant chords with multiple doublings soon prove wearisome to both listeners and players. The ear longs for some dynamic variation and a little contrapuntal relief amid the indigestible textures. Even the central *Larghissimo*, beginning on muted strings, is anchored to the ground by repeated triadic chords covering the whole orchestral range. A wistful violin theme marked 'cantabile dolce, quasi parlando' is supported by Schuman's customary non-diatonic parallel triads. Again the composer avoids polyphony, content to have simply a single melodic line and harmonic accompaniment.

As with Symphony No.8, the Finale, a modified rondo, is the most substantial of the three movements. After the unison pizzicato string opening, the first episode at a slower tempo is scored for an array of tuned percussion, a fine example of Schuman's imaginative use of the orchestra. The debt he owed to his teacher Roy Harris is evident in the chorale-like treatment of the rondo theme which precedes the Presto coda.

The Tenth Symphony represents a summing up of Schuman's symphonic style, introducing little that has not been heard before, but reprocessed in a new guise. In using a very large orchestra – quadruple woodwind, 6 horns, 4 trumpets, 4 trombones, tuba and extensive percussion in addition to the strings – its grandiose utterances reflect the 'American Muse'. Without ever resorting to folksong or jazz, Schuman is the epitome of an American composer. The boldness of gesture, a willingness to take risks and the elaborate rhythmical complexities owe nothing to European influences. His eight surviving symphonies are a cornerstone of mid-twentieth century symphonic achievement.

# 15 The American Spirit

Living abroad often sharpens the sense of nationality. George Antheil spent the 1920s and 30s in France and Germany, exploiting the novelty of jazz to establish his American credentials. A generation later another American, David Diamond, settled in Italy for sixteen years without deviating stylistically from his intrinsic American pastoral, lyrical language.

Moving in the opposite direction, the German-born Lukas Foss immediately shed the dust of Europe when he arrived in the United States in his teens and adopted all the trappings of American culture. While still reflecting his Italian ancestry, Paul Creston indulged in a particular fancy for syncopated rhythms derived from popular dance music. Without in any way creating a 'school', each of these composers represented the essence of America in their work.

**George Antheil** (1900–1959) gave his autobiography published in 1945 the title *Bad Boy of Music*. During the 1920s when he lived in Europe he acquired the reputation of an *enfant terrible* with a series of iconoclastic works including the notorious *Ballet Mechanique* performed in Paris in 1926. This 'succès de scandale' had been written three years earlier to accompany an abstract film by the artist Fernand Léger. It is scored for a group of normal instruments and a collection of noise-making machines: anvils, an aeroplane engine, electric bells, two octaves of motor horns, pieces of tin and steel, a player piano and up to ten pianos.

The first three of Antheil's symphonies date from this period of wild exhibitionism. The exact identification of these and later works has given rise to much confusion, mostly attributable to the composer's habit of revising scores and transferring the original numbering.

Symphony No.1 *Zingareska*, completed in 1921 was begun when Antheil was a pupil of Ernest Bloch. It was first performed in 1922 by no lesser a body, then the Berlin Philharmonic conducted by Schutz von Dornberg, formerly a famous German fighter pilot in World War I. Like the Jazz Symphony for chamber orchestra (1925) and Symphony in F (1926) (at one time called Symphony No.1), it makes use of jazz. The Jazz Symphony is based on the finale of *Zingareska*.

Symphony No.2 (1931–38) was performed with some success in Paris. Symphony No.3 (*American*) (1936–39) was also mostly written in Europe. This neo-romantic work was premièred by the National Symphony Orchestra of Washington conducted by Hans Kindler.

After dividing his time between Europe and America, Antheil settled in the United States before the outbreak of the Second World War. Although he remained prolific in his output, writing music for the theatre and films, Antheil the rebel had been tamed. As his fortunes declined, he earned a living undertaking various bizarre activities, for example as a lonely-hearts columnist, writing non-musical articles for *Esquire* and even, it is reported, inventing a radio-controlled torpedo in collaboration with the film star Hedy Lemarr.

With the Fourth Symphony (1942), Antheil temporarily recovered ground as a composer. Inspired by the war, he deliberately imitated Shostakovich's symphonic style. The opening unison theme on brass echoes Shostakovich's *Leningrad* Symphony although he could not have heard the piece at this time. Militaristic and defiant with trumpet calls and cannonading drums, it is a convincing clone of a Soviet-style symphony. Even the extended passages of stirring music for strings are Russian in tone. Antheil's experience as a film composer proved useful in this respect.

The main theme of the first movement reappears in the second. Prokofiev is a model here. Even the scoring of the Scherzo with its high clarinet and xylophone solos over repeated ostinati is replica Shostakovich. In contrast the trio is American in its 'schmaltzy' sentimentality. All the military paraphernalia return in the finale; a mournful bassoon melody accompanied by tambourine is yet another East European device. The bombastic ending reaches heights of banality barely acceptable, even as a reaction to events in wartime. Only an excess of national feeling can account for the success of the Fourth Symphony at its première on radio in 13 February 1944 by the NBC Symphony Orchestra conducted by Stokowski. *Time* magazine described it as 'the loudest and liveliest symphonic composition to turn up in years'. Virgil Thomson's verdict was 'bright, hard, noisy, bumptious, efficient and incredibly real'.

In *Bad Boy of Music*, Antheil writes of his Symphony No.5, *Tragic*, composed in 1945–46 as a requiem for those who died in World War II (including his younger brother Henry). Later a quite different Fifth Symphony subtitled *Joyous* appeared, composed between 1947 and 1948. Taking the same basic precepts of Symphony No.4, Antheil used American themes as the material. It was first performed in Philadelphia under Eugene Ormandy on 31 December 1948.

Writing of the Fifth Symphony, Virgil Thomson commented:

> Although it is a well written, vigorous and thoroughly viable work, it represents an observation of some kind, the ceremony of writing a symphony. Perhaps, more than a direct statement about anything beyond its reference to the history of symphonic expression.

> (*Music Right and Left* (1951) Henry Holt and Co., New York: p.109)

The first movement of Symphony No.6 (*After Delacroix*) completed in 1948 was inspired by the French artist's famous painting 'Liberty Leading the People'. The symphony was first performed in San Francisco conducted by Pierre Monteux on 10 February 1949.

Antheil's turbulent early life burnt itself out leaving an empty shell. Of his huge output only the novelty value of the Jazz Symphony remains.

**Paul Creston** (1906–1985) was born in New York of Sicilian parents. He was christened Guiseppe Guttivergi, later changed to Guttoveggio; on his marriage he adopted the name Paul Creston. Although he learnt to play the piano as a child, it was not until he reached the age of 26 the Creston decided to devote himself to composition, remaining self-taught as a composer.

The impact of the dance on his music is evident from the titles of the pieces he wrote; ten of them include the word 'dance' in the title (his wife was a professional dancer.) His preoccupation with rhythm led to his writing a text book *Principles of Rhythm*, published in 1964. He was also much influenced by Gregorian chant, particularly in the Third Symphony.

Creston's First Symphony Op.20 was composed in 1940 and performed on 22 February 1941 under the baton of Fritz Mahler. Later it was taken up by Eugene Ormandy and the Philadelphia Orchestra, winning the New York Music Critics' Circle Award for 1941 in a season which included new works by Copland, Harris and William Schuman. In the *New York Times*, Olin Downes wrote:

> The symphony is characterized by clear-cut, straightforward musical thinking, by a balance of lyrical, rhythmical and contrapuntal elements, by the general skillfulness and sound-worthiness of the instrumentation and by a style that did not ride to death some technical theory, form or formula.

Creston described his Second Symphony Op.35 (1944) as 'an apotheosis of the two foundations of all music, song and dance'. Like Schuman's Symphony No.3 it comprises two movements, each subdivided into two sections:

1  Introduction and Song
2  Interlude and Dance

The slow fugal opening on strings recalls the beginning of Roy Harris's Third Symphony; the subsequent development is not contrapuntal but a lush flow of impressionistic harmonies, rare for an American composer in the 1940s, reminiscent of *The Pleasure Dome of Kubla Khan* (1916) by Charles Griffes. Like Griffes, Creston includes an important part for piano amidst the scoring for full orchestra. The restless syncopated rhythms of the Dance section of the second movement with its percussion ostinato has a distinctly Latin American flavour.

The critic and composer Lazare Saminsky detected a definite origin for Creston's mixed style.

> I believe the clue to the duality in Creston's creative self lies to some extent in his racial antecedents. The inbred Italian taste for descriptive and operatic power and for massed

colour is, of course, greatly involved and not always easily traced in Creston's *mode de penser*. But there is a harsh kind of dramatic coloring in his music, that flowing from Puccini rather than Bellini.

(*Living Music of the Americas* (1949) Howell, Soskin & Crown Publishers: New York, p.129)

Regarding musical motivation, Creston saw himself in a different light:

In the use of the materials of composition, I strive to incorporate all that is good from the earliest times to the present day. If modality serves the purposes of expression, I utilize it; and if atonality is called for, I utilize it with an equally clear conscience. I make no special effort to be American: I conscientiously work to be my true self, which is Italian by parentage, American by birth and cosmopolitan by choice.

Creston's growing reputation was greatly enhanced after the première of the Second Symphony on 15 February 1945 by the New York Philharmonic Orchestra conducted by Artur Rodzinski.

Commissioned in 1950 by the Worcester Music Festival, Massachusetts, Symphony No.3 *Three Mysteries* (Op.48) reflects the composer's strong religious convictions. In each of the three movements, entitled 'The Nativity' 'The Crucifixion' and 'The Resurrection', Creston exploits the natural, irregular rhythms of plainsong which constitutes the thematic material. The composer provided the following explanation:

Though it derives its inspiration from these Biblical events, historic and mystic, the work is a musical parallel of inherent emotional reactions rather than a narrative or painting, these emotions being sometimes of the spectators of the first enactment of the drama and sometimes of the spectators of the annual re-enactment. The programmatic content, such as there may be, also justifies the utilization of Gregorian Chant in a non-liturgical aspect.

The first performance on 27 October 1950 by Eugene Ormandy and the Philadelphia Orchestra was greeted with universal critical acclaim.

Recordings of Creston's Second and Third Symphonies made by the National Orchestra of Washington under Howard Mitchell led directly to the première of Creston's Fourth Symphony Op.52 (1951) on 30 January 1952. For the same orchestra's 25th anniversary, he composed his Fifth Symphony Op.64 in 1955, performed on 4 April 1956. Creston succinctly summed up the essence of the Fifth Symphony:

The keynote of the emotional basis of this symphony is its intensity, and the feeling is generally one of spiritual conflicts which are not resolved until the final movement.

The first movement is explosive and agitated in a way not encountered in the earlier symphonies. However the turbulence is vigorous and discursive, lacking the desperation of Peter Mennin and the single-mindedness of William Schuman. The *Largo* is in Creston's warm romantic vein, with impassioned melodic outbursts and surges of harmonic lushness. An energetic finale brings the symphony to a positive conclusion.

More than 25 years elapsed before Creston produced his Sixth and final symphony, scored for organ and orchestra and completed in 1981. Creston wrote:

> My philosophical approach to composition is abstract. I am preoccupied with matters of melodic progression, not with imitation of nature, or narrations of fairy tales or propoundings of sociological ideologies.

The early death of **Irving Fine** (1914–1962) on 23 August 1962 at the age of 47 robbed America of a remarkable composer at the peak of his achievement. On 23 March of that year the Boston Symphony Orchestra under the baton of Charles Munch had given the première of Fine's last work, a Symphony.

Fine's early works are neo-classical, much influenced by Stravinsky. After 1952 he turned to the 12-note system, following a lyrical romantic course modelled on Schoenberg and Berg. This Symphony, conceived on a larger scale than any of his other works, represents a synthesis of these two conflicting styles to produce a definitively personal language. It is scored for full orchestra with an expanded percussion section.

Although possessing no programme as such, the composer suggested that the first movement *Intrada* (originally entitled *Eclogue*) 'is a kind of choreographic action in which characters enter, depart and reappear altered and in different groupings... all of this serving as background for a lyrical or at times pastoral narrative'. There is a strong rhythmic nervous energy in the music which conjures up the image of dance, with a dramatic force that recalls the ballets of Stravinsky.

The central *Capriccio* is a scherzo comprising a sequence of related episodes. It is the finale, *Ode*, a slow processional that most clearly relates to Stravinsky, the inexorable bell-like passacaglia evoking memories of the coda of the *Symphony of Psalms*. Fine provided the following description of the Ode in a programme note for the première:

> The last movement, *Grave*, is essentially a dithyrambic fantasia with a concluding recessional or epilogue. In the fantasia, much of the material employed in the Symphony recurs highly metamorphosed in fragmentary statements or outbursts, in brief dramatic canons, or in static ruminating passages with florid figuration. The prevailing mood is darker than in the first movements.

Especially in the composer's own recording with the Boston Symphony Orchestra at Tanglewood eleven days before his death, Fine's Symphony comes over as a work of fierce integrity. In the exploration of larger forms, it represents a departure into new territory which he was prevented from exploring further. As it is we must be satisfied with this single masterpiece.

**David Diamond** (b. 1915) studied music from an early age, learning the violin and composing over 100 works by the time he was eighteen. Later at the Eastman School he was a composition pupil of Bernard Rogers before attending the Dalcroze Institute in New York where he received tuition for Roger Sessions. In 1938 he travelled to Paris to continue studies with Nadia Boulanger, remaining there until the threat of war in the following year drove his home. He returned to Europe in 1949, settling in Italy in 1951, dividing his time between Rome and

Florence. Not until 1965 did he live permanently in the United States. Although his early compositions received public performances, Diamond withdrew most of them including two symphonies (1933, 1937) and a chamber symphony (1936).

The first four published symphonies speak a modal language, having a kinship with Roy Harris but maintaining a closer contact to traditional forms. Symphony No.1 (1940–41) was written soon after his return from Paris. As an exercise in economy and rigorous control of material, it would certainly have pleased his teacher, Nadia Boulanger. The symphony was begun at the Yaddo Artists' Colony near Saratoga, and is dedicated to the writer Kathleen Anne Porter who was also working there at the time. This is the music of a young man, full of muscular energy with heavy scoring for the orchestra. Diamond adopts a thematic cyclic form, basing each of the three movements on a rising figure of three notes: B, D, E. The première in Carnegie Hall with Dimitri Mitropoulos and the New York Philharmonic Orchestra on 21 December 1941 marked the composer's first public success in his own country. A report in the journal of the Institute for Studies in American Music praised Diamond's music: 'It speaks a language familiar to most audiences and does so with imaginative new inflections – such sumptuously long-breathed themes, such rhythmic vitality and such crystalline orchestration.'

The Second Symphony (1942–43) reflects the unsettled times of the Second World War. As with Symphony No.1 there are thematic relations between the movements. Here also is a strong emotional energy with contrasting passages of pastoral calm: a ferocious scherzo balanced by a tranquil Andante espressivo. The optimistic end of the exciting Rondo finale expresses triumph over adversity. Sergei Koussevitzky and the Boston Symphony Orchestra gave the first performance on 22 October 1944.

The first three linked movements of Symphony No.3 (1945) contain many of the elements found in the previous two symphonies: the unflagging energy of the Allegro, a lyrical slow movement and a violent Scherzo. What is new in concept is the elegiac finale, devoid of any disturbing elements. In spite of the public acclaim of the Second Symphony, the composer experienced difficulty in finding an orchestra to perform the Third. Plans for its première by Artur Rodzinski and the Chicago Symphony and George Szell and the Cleveland came to nothing. Eventually Charles Munch, whom Diamond had met in Paris in 1937, took an interest and the Symphony was first heard on 3 November 1950, played by the Boston Symphony Orchestra under Munch.

By this time Diamond had composed his Fourth Symphony which was also premièred by the Boston Symphony on 23 January 1948 conducted by Leonard Bernstein. The subsequent recording by Bernstein brought Diamond's name to a wide audience. The Symphony had been commissioned by the Koussevitzky Foundation and the score is dedicated to the memory of Natalie Koussevitzky. It is scored for a large orchestra, including quadruple woodwind, six horns and four trumpets. Diamond's handling of symphonic form is more compact in the Fourth, the three movements lasting no more than 17 minutes. There is also a greater assurance in the ceaseless propulsion of the opening Allegro and the lush string writing of the Adagio, reminiscent of the modal harmonies and the multi-part counterpoint of Vaughan Williams.

There is a marked stylistic change in the Fifth Symphony. The language is less tonal, more chromatic melodically and in shorter phrases although his lyrical characteristics still appear in the opening of the second of its two movements. Each of these movements is subdivided into different tempi. The first is marked Adagio: allegro energico; the second Andante; Fuga; Allegro; Adagio. Both the opening and close of the symphony are quiet, elegiac in mood, more introspective than anything Diamond had written before. The delay in finding a performance for the Fifth Symphony was even greater than for the Third. By the time it reached the concert hall, the Fifth Symphony had undergone revision and Diamond had completed three more symphonies, all performed before No.5. It is dedicated to his friend Leonard Bernstein who conducted the première with the New York Philharmonic Orchestra on 26 April 1966.

In the intervening years Diamond had composed Symphony No.6 (1951–54), performed by Charles Munch and the Boston Symphony Orchestra on 8 March 1957, Symphony No.7 (1959), performed by Eugene Ormandy and the Philadelphia Orchestra on 26 January 1962, and Symphony No.8 (1958–60), written as a tribute to Aaron Copland on his 60th birthday. It was premièred by the New York Philharmonic Orchestra under Leonard Bernstein on 27 October 1961. In this work Diamond's approach is more chromatic and rhythmically flexible, even adopting a 12-note row but treating it lyrically with tonal implications.

The un-numbered Choral Symphony *To Music* for tenor, baritone, chorus and orchestra sets poems by John Masefield and Longfellow. It was commissioned in 1969 for the dedication of a new auditorium at the Manhattan School of Music where Diamond had taught from 1965 to 1967. The composer conducted the première there on 31 January 1970.

Perhaps to avoid comparison with Beethoven, Diamond did not give his Choral Symphony the number 9. That is reserved for what is in effect a song cycle to texts by Michelangelo Buonarroti for baritone and orchestra. It was first performed on 17 November 1985 by the American Composers' Orchestra conducted by Leonard Bernstein.

During the early 1990s Diamond worked simultaneously on his next two symphonies. No.10 was composed for Gerard Schwartz and the Seattle Symphony in recognition of the conductor's ten-year tenure with the orchestra; it was performed in 1994. Symphony No.11 was commissioned for the 150th anniversary of the New York Philharmonic Orchestra and performed by them under Kurt Masur in December 1992. It is conceived on a broad scale, lasting some 50 minutes and calling for a large orchestra including extended percussion and two sets of timpani placed apart on the platform.

For several decades Diamond's music was ignored by the majority of critics and performers since it failed to recognize changes in critical taste. He was seen as a reactionary unwilling to take on board the innovations there were developing around him. The current revival of interest in his symphonic works is a tribute to his spirit of survival. He has commented, 'It is my strong feeling that a romantically inspired contemporary music is the way out of the present period of creative chaos. To me the romantic spirit in music is important as it is timeless.'

**Lukas Foss** (b. 1922) began writing music at the age of seven and had his first published work issued when he was only fifteen. In 1933 the rise of Hitler forced his family to leave Berlin where he had been born to live in Paris. After studying at the Paris Conservatoire with Lazare Lévy (piano) and Noel Gallon (composition), he went with his parents to the United States in 1937. At the Curtis Institute in Philadelphia his teachers included Rosario Scalero and Randall Thompson for composition, Isabelle Vengerova for piano and Fritz Reiner for conducting. In addition he was a pupil of Paul Hindemith at Yale from 1940 to 1941.

With a remarkable command of compositional technique, Foss was soon able to adapt to American idioms. It was with the cantata *The Prairie* (1942–44) to words by Carl Sandburg that he first came to public attention. In this work with its distinctly American character, Foss expressed love for his new country. It received the New York Music Critics' Circle Award for 1944.

Fifty years separate his First and Fourth Symphonies. Foss himself conducted the première of Symphony No.1 in G (1944) with the Pittsburgh Symphony Orchestra on 4 February 1945. Composed at the MacDowell Colony, it is a spirited youthful score full of the vigour of its 22-year old composer.

*Symphony of Chorales* (No.2) was commissioned by the Koussevitzky Music Foundation on the recommendation of the Boston friends of Dr Albert Schweitzer. In this work Foss employs chorales by J.S. Bach as the basic material. William Steinberg conducted the first performance with the Pittsburgh Symphony Orchestra on 24 October 1958.

In 1957 Foss effected a radical change in musical direction with the founding of the Improvisation Chamber Ensemble of clarinet, cello, piano and percussion. In this development of controlled improvisation, he turned from tonality towards a form of serialism combined with indeterminacy and graphic notation. For the next two decades his music explored this avant-garde world of experimentation.

From the late 1980s Foss returned to more conservative media. Symphony No.3, *Symphony of Sorrows*, was written in 1991–92.

Symphony No.4, *Window to the Past*, was commissioned in 1994 by the City College of New York to honour the memory of Harold Newman, the publisher who had greatly encouraged the young Lukas Foss. As a mark of conformity, the first movement is entitled 'Sonata'. The second movement, which is prefaced by the symphony's subtitle, is autobiographical. Foss explained 'Moments from my early pieces published by Newman came back "like ghosts" to haunt the new music.'

A lively scherzo follows, with two trios, the second an inversion of the first. The finale 'Fireworks' is, as the composer says, 'a series of cheerful explosions'. Foss conducted the première in 1995 with the Boston University Symphony Orchestra in the Tsai Performing Center, Boston.

# 16 Traditionalists in the Shadows

Inevitably with public attention concentrated upon leading figures, composers of the second rank, neglected in their lifetime, are often forgotten after their death. As live performances become infrequent or non-existent, reliance on reissues of archive recordings are the only means of hearing such lost music.

We are greatly indebted to pioneering conductors and enterprising companies who are recording 'unfashionable' music of the recent past. In their time these composers contributed to the American symphonic tradition; although their music may not have broken new ground, such works have much to offer.

**John Vincent** (1902–1977) was a pupil of Chadwick and Converse at the New England Conservatory, before studying at Harvard with Piston and in Paris with Nadia Boulanger. Later he received private lessons from Roy Harris. With such an illustrious pedigree, it is not surprising that Vincent followed an academic career himself, succeeding Schoenberg as Professor of composition at the University of California in Los Angeles (1946–1969).

His only work to achieve any wide reputation is the Symphony in D, subtitled *A Festive Piece in one movement*. It was commissioned by the Louisville Orchestra who premièred the work in 1955. The composer made some minor revisions in 1957.

Unlike many single movement symphonies, such as Barber's First and Harris's No.3 which adopt a basic linked four-movement pattern, Vincent's symphony is a large-scale sonata Allegro with an integrated slow introduction that presents the two 'seed ideas' of the whole work. The Symphony in D is an entrovert celebratory piece, tuneful, rhythmically exuberant and of instant appeal. Vincent was the author of a text book *The Diatonic Modes in Modern Music* published in 1951, whose precepts he follows in the symphony. In the romantic manner of Howard Hanson, he breaks no new ground but has produced a popular concert work which is the epitome of the twentieth-century symphony that could have been written only by an American.

Vincent's close contemporary, Russian-born **Nikolai Lopatnikoff** (1903–1976) settled in Germany in 1920 where his Symphony No.1 (1929) won a German

Radio Composition Prize in 1930. It was well received by the critics and taken up by Bruno Walter and the Berlin Philharmonic Orchestra. The symphony was also played on tour by the Philadelphia Orchestra in 1930, bringing his name to the United States.

With the rise of the Nazi Party, he left Berlin in 1933 to live for the next six years in London. In 1939 he moved to the United States where he became an influential teacher in Pittsburgh. Symphony No.2 was first performed by the Boston Symphony Orchestra on 22 December 1939 under the baton of Sergei Koussevitzky. Symphony No.3 (1954) and Symphony No.4 (1972) were both premièred by the Pittsburgh Symphony Orchestra under William Steinberg.

Lopatnikoff acknowledged the influence of Stravinsky and Hindemith on the neo-baroque and neo-classical features of his music.

**Marc Blitzstein** (1905–1964) was a man of the theatre, the creator of a controversial left-wing musical *The Cradle Will Rock*, much influenced by the Weill-Brecht *Die Dreigroschen Oper*, and a full blooded romantic opera *Regina*, first performed in 1949 and produced widely in the United States and Europe.

His so-called symphony *The Airborne* (1943–44) is in effect a choral work, a patriotic documentary composed during the Second World War while Blitzstein was serving in the US Eighth Air Force in London. It is a distinctly occasional piece of its time, hardly performable today except as an historical curiosity. Blitzstein wrote his own text which is set for narrator, tenor, baritone, men's chorus and orchestra. The twelve sections arranged into three 'movements' describe the history of flight from Greek mythology via the Wright brothers to modern aerial warfare. The lyrics, mostly blank verse, are direct and he treats them in an expressionist manner, at times hectoring and affected, but less artificial than similar works for narrator and orchestra that may have been highly emotive at the time but now appear unctious and embarrassing. The rapidly-changing conditions of the war following D-Day delayed the intended première and the score was for a time lost. On the advice of Leonard Bernstein, Blitzstein reconstructed the music in 1945 but the missing score came to light in Boston. Of the two versions, the composer preferred the new one which was performed on 1 April 1946 under the direction of Bernstein. The theatre critic Harold Clurman wrote:

> The talent is theatrical, showman-like, even Broadway, and has a new sophistication – that of the youthful urban intelligentsia nurtured in the Thirties. Even what is 'corny' and pretentious in *The Airborne* is part of the American consciousness trying to find itself amidst the ubiquitous commercialism in which the ambitious artist must perforce live.

**Elie Siegmeister** (1909–1991) became widely known for his research into early American music and as a collector and arranger of folk-songs. He was also a founder of the American Composers' Alliance in 1938 and served on numerous committees promoting American music. Like Blitzstein, he espoused left-wing politics, a dangerous position to take during the 1950s in the McCarthy years.

His early works are a modern dissonant style with a certain input from jazz. A second phase makes more use of American idioms strongly influenced by his own discoveries in folk music. With his First Symphony of 1947 he broadened his vision to adopt a more personal approach to composition. This symphony was commissioned by Stokowski and performed under his direction by the New York Philharmonic Orchestra on 30 October 1947. Adopting classical forms, he used original thematic material with strong American characteristics.

Symphony No.2 (1950) was premièred in New York on 25 February 1952. Siegmeister intended it to represent 'One man's thoughts, the search for love, the struggle against violence, and the belief in the human.' In the *New York Herald Tribune*, Virgil Thomson wrote: 'Its tone is serious and its emotional content is all the more real.'

The one-movement Symphony No.3 (1957), first performed in Oklahoma City on 8 February 1959, is cast in variation form. Symphony No.4, performed by Lorin Maazel and the Cleveland Orchestra on 6 December 1973, introduces ragtime and children's songs into the slow movement with polyrhythms and polytonality in the dissonant finale. The neo-impressionist Symphony No.5 (*Visions of Time*) was written in 1971 for the Baltimore Symphony Orchestra who performed it under Sergio Comissiona in Washington DC on 2 May 1977. In the last decade of his life Siegmeister completed three further symphonies.

All the music of **Don Gillis** (1912–1978) is unashamedly in a popular American style as the titles suggest. American history and pastoral life provided the inspiration for his large-scale works.

Seven of his ten numbered symphonies have subtitles: No.1 (*American*) (1941); No.2 (*Symphony of Faith*) (1940); No.3 (*Symphony of Free Men*) (1940–41); No.6 (*Midcentury U.S.A.*) (1947); No.7 (*Saga of a Prairie School*) (1948) No.8 (*Dance Symphony*) (1949); No.10 (*Big D*) (1967). In addition there are two unnumbered symphonies; *Star Spangled Symphony* and his best known work Symphony No.5½ (*Symphony for Fun*) (1947), a jazz-inspired symphonic spoof, first performed in April 1947 by Arthur Fiedler and the Boston Pops Orchestra.

Taking a more intellectual, less nationalistic stance is **Roger Goeb** (1914–1997) who studied in Paris with Nadia Boulanger and with Otto Luening in New York. Although he has a notable *corpus* of compositions to his credit, including six symphonies, he suffered from the one-work syndrome.

His Third Symphony, premièred by Leopold Stokowski and the CBS Symphony Orchestra in April 1952, enjoyed a limited success at the time, particularly through a recording Stokowski made of the piece. The three movements have a character and confidence which make one regret that none of Goeb's other music has come to public attention. In this one work, there is an individual voice, more European than American, with a sure sense of purpose and expert orchestration.

Following the example set by Piston, Hanson and Randall Thompson, **Vincent Persichetti** (1915–1987) devoted himself to a lifetime of teaching, principally at the Juilliard School in New York from 1947, becoming chairman of the composition department in 1963. He produced a large quantity of music in almost every medium. His considerable technical skill has been compared to that of Hindemith. His early compositions reveal an allegiance to neo-classicism but he later developed a more personal language akin to that of William Schuman.

Persichetti composed nine symphonies. Symphony No.1 (1942) was performed by the Rochester Symphony Orchestra conducted by Howard Hanson on 21 October 1947. Like the Second Symphony of 1943, it remained unpublished. Eugene Ormandy and the Philadelphia Orchestra premièred Symphony No.3 (1946) on November 21 1947, and Symphony No.4 (1951) on 17 December 1954.

The Louisville Orchestra commissioned Symphony No.5 in one movement for string orchestra, Persichetti's most widely-known work. Robert Whitney conducted the first performance on 28 August 1954. Among Persichetti's thirteen works for concert band is Symphony No.6 premièred in St Louis, Missouri on 16 April 1956. It has become a standard band repertoire item.

To mark their 80th anniversary, the St Louis Symphony Orchestra commissioned Symphony No.7 in 1959. Subtitled *Liturgic*, it is based on Persichetti's own *Hymns and Responses for the Church Year* of 1955. Eduard van Remoortel conducted the first performance in St Louis on 24 October 1959. Symphony No.8 was written in 1967 for the Baldwin Wallace Conservatory, Berea, Ohio.

The one-movement Symphony No.9 (*Janiculum*) written in 1970 was commissioned in memory of Alexander Hilsberg, concert master and associate of the Philadelphia Orchestra who died in 1961. Persichetti composed the score in Rome on a Guggenheim Fellowship. While he worked on the music, he could hear the bells of the local church, whose sounds he incorporated into the beginning and end of the symphony. The Janiculum Hill in Rome is named after the Roman god Janus who has two faces, symbolizing opposites in life: comedy and tragedy, good and evil. Eugene Ormandy conducted the Philadelphia Orchestra in the première on 5 March 1971.

**Gordon Binkerd** (b. 1916) studied at the South Dakota Wesleyan University (1933–37) at the Eastman School (1940–41) under Bernard Rogers and at Harvard (1946–49) where he was a pupil of Walter Piston and Irving Fine. From 1949 to 1971 he was Professor of Composition at the University of Illinois.

Binkerd was a latecomer to composition, writing his first surviving works after the age of thirty one. Symphony No.1, completed in 1954 at the MacDowell Colony, Peterborough, NH, is dedicated to Mrs Edward MacDowell. Each of the three movements is scored for a different instrumental ensemble and based on a tritone: the opening *Allegretto* on E flat – A, the *Adagio* on D – G# and the finale, a double fugue, on B flat – E. As the composer explains, the symphony marks his abandonment of the 12-note system:

> From the beginning the serial technique worked for me like a charm. But between the second and third movements I suddenly experienced an intense revulsion away from the system. I gave it up and have returned to it only briefly, and in a sense casually.

The second movement's emphasis on minor thirds is derived from the song of the Alder Flycatcher bird which the composer heard in the woods at the MacDowell Colony.

Binkerd's preoccupation with counterpoint, doubtless derived from his studies with Piston, is extensively exploited in Symphony No.2, commissioned in 1956 by the Fromm Foundation and the University of Illinois; it was premièred in the following year by the University of Illinois Symphony Orchestra under Bernard Goodman. The Symphony is in two movements, a highly propulsive *Allegro* of great tension and excitement, reminiscent of Hindemith, and a long rhapsodic *Largo*. The music is highly chromatic but basically tonal lying around the key of E flat.

Symphony No.3 (1959) comprises a highly concentrated single movement lasting only 13 minutes; it is dedicated to Walter Piston. Symphony No.4, commissioned by the St Louis Symphony Orchestra in 1963 was later revised and retitled *Movement for Orchestra*.

**Robert Ward** (b. 1917) studied at the Eastman School from 1935 to 1939 in that golden era before World War II. A pupil of Bernard Rogers and Howard Hanson, he is a typical product of the Hanson regime, relatively conservative in style and strongly influenced by American folk-song and jazz. His opera *The Crucible* (1961) based on the play by Arthur Miller brought his name to a wide musical public.

The first of Ward's symphonies dates from his student days at the Juilliard School where it was performed under his direction on 10 May 1941. As with his next three symphonies, he adopted a three-movement form: Sonata allegro; theme and variations; scherzo finale. Symphony No.1 was well received by the critics: the *Washington Herald* commented: 'It is concise, logical in development, significant in ideas, virile in mood and exciting in its several climaxes.'

Symphony No.2 was premièred by the National Symphony Orchestra of Washington under Hans Kindler on 25 January 1948. Here Ward combined classical models with elements of jazz. The composer provided a brief description, 'The first movement includes both a traditional sonata form and a fugue; the slow movement is more akin to an aria of the baroque period. The finale is a rondo of dance tunes with variations. 'In essence the slow movement is a 'symphonic' blues.

Symphony No.3 for chamber orchestra was commissioned for the Dumbarton Oaks Orchestra who first performed in under the composer's baton on 31 March 1950. Encouraged by its reception, Ward restored it for full orchestra; it was premièred in this version in 1953 by Jean Morel and the Juilliard Orchestra.

Completed in 1958, the Fourth Symphony had to wait until 3 August 1968 to be heard. Ward subsequently withdrew the score for revision. The new version was first performed in Albany NY on 3 May 1980. Meanwhile to celebrate the American Bicentennial in 1976, Ward set texts by Walt Whitman and Longfellow for his Fifth Symphony subtitled *Canticles of America*. Scored for narrator, soprano, baritone, choir and orchestra, the work traces the development of the American spirit through two centuries.

'In the melodies of the symphony', the composer wrote, 'the listener will, I suspect, be aware of the influence of the music I came to know in my youth as a boy soprano in every kind of church and school performance and later as a band leader during World War II.' The *Charlotte Observer* described the Fifth Symphony 'as American as apple pie'.

Symphony No.6 was completed in 1988. As with all his music, the symphonies of Robert Ward represent the epitome of the American symphonic tradition of the mid-twentieth century, rooted deeply in folk-song; up-to-date in idiom but breaking little new ground.

More radical than Robert Ward and covering a wider stylistic spectrum are the eleven symphonies of **Irwin Bazelon** (1922–1995). Bazelon studied with Darius Milhaud at Mills College (1946–48) and briefly with Paul Hindemith at Yale and Ernest Bloch at the University of California, Berkeley. From the earliest works, his music was impulsive with boundless energy which, according to his acquaintances, reflected his personality. Bazelon completed ten symphonies, Symphony No.1 (1960–62) was premièred by the Kansas City Philharmonic Orchestra on 29 November 1963.

His most successful composition, the Second Symphony subtitled *Short Symphony: Testament to a Big City* dates from 1962. Bazelon conducted the first performance with the National Symphony Orchestra of Washington on 4 December 1962. Subsequently it was taken up by other conductors in the United States. Scored for an orchestra with a large battery of percussion, it possesses an explosive force which the composer described as 'the rebellious mutterings, cross rhythms, nervous tension and energy of the city'.

In his orchestral scores, Bazelon had a preference for brass and percussion. The Third Symphony, scored for brass, percussion, piano and string sextet was composed in the following year. Symphony No.4 (1964–65) was first performed on 21 February 1966 in Seattle. Izler Solomon and the Indianapolis Symphony Orchestra gave the première of the Fifth Symphony on 9 May 1970. Symphony No.6 (1969–70) is based on music Bazelon wrote for a documentary film of the Israeli Six-Day War, entitled *Survival 1967*. It was heard in Kansas City on 17 November 1970.

Symphony No.7 (*Ballet for Orchestra*) was composed in 1980 but not performed until it was recorded in July 1995, two months before the composer's death. Although not noticeably balletic in character, the symphony is wild and dramatic, uncompromising, unpredictable in its direction and often ear-splittingly ferocious. His use of the orchestra is strikingly virtuosic. It was followed by Symphony No.8 for strings orchestra in 1986 and the curiously numbered Symphony No.8½ of 1988, presumably given this appelation since, in the composer's estimation, it did not measure up to the reputation accorded other ninth symphonies. The single-movement Ninth Symphony (1992) is an orchestration of a piano piece *Sunday Silence*, dedicated to a celebrated racehorse of that name which won the 1989 Kentucky Derby and declared the Horse of the Year. Bazelon was a lifelong enthusiast of horse-racing. As the composer explained, the symphony is a totally abstract work, 'not descriptive, but rather evocative'. A solo piano and cello are given concertante passages to balance the almost relentless battery of brass and percussion.

At the time of his death Bazelon was working on a Tenth Symphony, one movement of which, entitled *The Prelude to Hart Crane's The Bridge*, was performed in 1993.

**Ned Rorem** (b. 1923) is a prolific composer noted especially for his songs and choral music. Among his orchestral works are three symphonies. The First Symphony, completed in 1950, was premièred in the following year by the Vienna Symphony Orchestra conducted by Jonathan Steinberg. Symphony No.2 was commissioned by Nikolai Sokoloff for the Musical Arts Society of La Jolla, California who performed it on 5 August 1956.

Rorem completed his Third Symphony in New York in April 1958, shortly after returning to the United States from France where he had lived for eight years. Cast in five movements, it is very much the archetypal American piece of the 1950s, lyrical and modal in the slow sections, racy with jazz influences of Copland and Bernstein in the fast movements. Leonard Bernstein conducted the première with the New York Philharmonic Orchestra on 16 April 1959. Rorem has written two unnumbered symphonies, *Sinfonia* for wind and percussion (1957), performed in Pittsburgh by the American Woodwind Ensemble, and Symphony for Strings premièred by the Atlanta Symphony Orchestra under Robert Shaw on 31 October 1985.

# 17 Eastern Influences

While many composers were consciously seeking a national identity through folk-song or jazz, others looked beyond America for self-expression, not to Europe but further East.

Although born in the United States, Alan Hovhaness and Richard Yardumian remained loyal to their Armenian ancestry, especially in the extensive use of modal chant from the Armenian Church at the centre of their work. Lou Harrison's interests were more widely spread, a result in part of his travels to Japan and the Far East. Nevertheless, all three composers produced music in Western forms; some ingredients are foreign, but the finished articles are essentially American.

**Alan Hovhaness** (b. 1911) was born in Somerville, Massachusetts of an Armenian father and a Scottish mother. He began to play the piano and to compose at a very early age. Later he studied with Frederick Converse at the New England Conservatory in Boston and in 1942 was a pupil of Martinŭ at Tanglewood.

His earliest enthusiasm was for music of the Renaissance; he was attracted by its modal harmony and melodic lines. This influence has been evident in the contrapuntal writing throughout his life, emphasized by his preference for using large note values. His classical music training is also reflected in the rigorous use of fugue.

> Fugue form I use strictly. I apply it to the modes. I like to develop those principles because I feel they're universal. I've always been a great admirer of Bach and Handel.

A symphony, subsequently withdrawn, was performed at the New England Conservatory in 1933 and awarded a prize. Other music written at this time is believed to have taken Sibelius as a model. Hovhaness's earliest surviving symphony subtitled *Exile* dating from 1936 was performed in London on 26 May 1939 by the BBC Symphony Orchestra by Leslie Heward.

In 1936 Hovhaness heard for the first time music of the East when a group of musicians from North India performed in Boston. Their non-Western scales (*ragas*) and elaborate rhythms (*tala*) were to have a strong impact on his later compositions. During the 1940s he undertook a deep study of Armenian religious music, inspired by the Armenian composer-priest Gomidas Vartabed who died in 1936. From 1940 to 1947 Hovhaness played the organ at the Armenian Church in Watertown, near Boston, where he had the opportunity to study closely Armenian religious music.

With this new dimension to his compositions, Hovhaness destroyed over 100 of his earlier works including seven symphonies. Nevertheless he continued to compose prolifically; his opus numbers passed the 400 mark in the 1980s, including 67 symphonies to date. Hereafter his music became a fusion of Western and Eastern idioms. Symphony No.8 *Arjuna* (1947), based on Armenian folk song patterns was performed in Madras, India in 1960. Symphony No.9 *St Vartan* (1950) depicts the life of an Armenian folk hero martyred in AD 451. It was premièred by the New York Philharmonic Orchestra under the composer's direction on 11 March 1951. In this work Hovhaness experimented with polymodal canons producing richly resonant effects.

The first work to bring Hovhaness to wider public attention was Symphony No.2, *Mysterious Mountain*, commissioned by the Houston Symphony Orchestra who gave the première on 31 October 1955 conducted by Leopold Stokowski. It is the first of six symphonies which have the word 'mountain' in the title. The composer explained:

> Mountains represent symbols, like pyramids, of man's attempt to know God. Mountains are symbolic meeting places between the mundane and spiritual worlds. To some *Mysterious Mountain* may be the phantom peak, unmeasured, thought to be higher than Everest, as seen from a great distance by fliers in Tibet. To some it may be the solitary mountain, the tower of strength over a countryside.
>
> I love mountains very much, and I used to climb them a great deal. So I titled this symphony *Mysterious Mountain*. I named it for that mysterious feeling that one has in the mountains – not for any special mountain, but for the whole *idea* of mountains. This could be about any mountain that one loves.

A mysterious, deeply personal meditative quality pervades the whole symphony as it does with most of his music. Long before Henryk Górecki and Arvo Pärt were writing their minimalist religious works, Hovhaness had explored the inner spiritual world of ritual repetition and rapt serenity.

*Mysterious Mountain* is typical of Hovhaness's 'Armenian' style before the impact of Far Eastern culture had affected him. The block-chord chorale on divisi strings which opens and closes the first movement will remind many of the *Fantasia on a Theme of Thomas Tallis* by Vaughan Williams. Only the independent pizzicato walking double-bass line with its polytonal implications confirms that this is not a work by an English pastoral composer (Ex. 84).

The free-flowing woodwind melodies (Ex. 85) which follow have the timeless quality of Armenian monody, made more exotic by the gentle dissonances of the bitonal accompaniment, and the impressionistic wash provided by celeste and harp whose figuration and tonality are at odds with the basic diatonic harmonic structure.

1   Samuel Barber

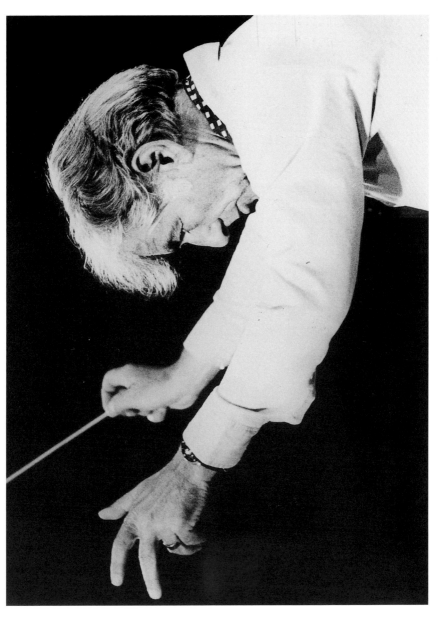

2　Leonard Bernstein

3   William Bolcom

4    Aaron Copland

5   Howard Hanson

6   John Harbison

7   Lou Harrison

8   Alan Hovhaness

9　Serge Koussevitzky

10    Peter Mennin

11   Walter Piston

12    George Rochberg

13   Christopher Rouse

14   William Schuman

15   Ellen Taaffe Zwilich

Ex. 84

Andante con moto

Strings *p*

*mp* D. Bass pizz.

*Reproduced by permission of G. Schirmer Inc.*

Ex. 85

*Reproduced by permission of G. Schirmer Inc.*

The central movement is entitled Double Fugue; more correctly it should be defined as two separate fugues, both predominately for strings. The first at a moderate tempo in Hovhaness's typical hymn-like modal vein written in long note values, reflects music of the Renaissance. The second, at a very fast tempo, exploits scales and other baroque figuration, executed at breakneck virtuosic speed. At the climax of the second fugue, the subject of the first fugue is superimposed as a unison chorale, firstly on horns, then trumpets and finally by the whole orchestra.

The finale restores the meditative mood of the first movement, a ritornello chorale with two contrasting episodes, the first marked *con moto* set in motion by the harp, with the gradual addition of the strings, the second a new chorale for the woodwind, decorated by harp and celeste. The opening chorale, fully scored, serves as the coda.

Like Roy Harris, Hovhaness treats the sections of the orchestra as separate entities, with a preponderance of the music devoted to the strings. Woodwind perform either as a complete unit or as single instruments providing improvisatory cantelenas. *Mysterious Mountain* is a remarkably original symphonic concept, strikingly unusual for its time and still a novel experience for anyone unfamiliar with his unique language.

In later works Hovhaness introduces passages at different speeds across the orchestra without co-ordination. In certain respects these are aleatoric but precisely notated. The composer calls them 'rhythmless' but it is more accurate to say they lack a common pulse. Usually subject to changing dynamics, they often begin as a gentle murmur, rising to a massive roar before subsiding into silence.

In 1959 Hovhaness was awarded a Fulbright Fellowship to explore the traditional music of India and Japan. In Madras he studied Karnatic music and composed a work for South Indian instruments. This experience had an instant effect upon his own music which began to adopt certain oriental melodic features, and develop rhythmic patterns related to Indian music.

A Rockefeller grant in 1962 took him to Japan where he made a detailed investigation of *Gagaku*, the ancient court music of the country. He took the opportunity to visit neighbouring countries, making a study of *ah-ak*, the court music of Korea. Symphony No.16 (1962), scored for an orchestra of Korean instruments was performed in Seoul on 26 January 1963. Hovhaness explained that it was inspired by 'the beauty of Korean mountains – the sublimity of Korean traditional music, the wisdom and nobility of Korean people'. Symphony No.35 (1978) for full orchestra and ancient *ah-ak* instruments was commissioned to open the Seoul Art Center on 9 January 1978.

In the music of Hovhaness there is an implied religious content. The tranquillity, mystery, sublimity and ecstacy have a parallel with the works of Messiaen, but for Hovhaness it is unspecific, neither Christian nor Eastern, maybe pantheistic or pagan in its reverence for the natural world.

Typical of the Eastern influence is Symphony No.15, *Silver Pilgrimage* (1963), named after a novel by the Indian writer M. Anantanarayan. The first movement 'Mount Ravana' suggests the wrath and mystery of a mountain prophet. 'Marava Princess', the second movement, is a dance using just six notes, like an Indian *raga*. The third movement 'River of Meditation', a long flute solo without metrical indications, evokes the spirit of a sage meditating as he sits by a river. In the finale 'Heroic Gate of Peace', Hovhaness combines ancient Chinese melodies and Western Renaissance counterpoint in a spiritual hymn that resolves the conflict between heaven and earth. This is an expression of universal wisdom and grace that transcends any one religion. The symphony was first performed in New York in December 1963 by the Orchestra of the Americas conducted by Stokowski.

'Symphony' is a term Hovhaness uses for almost any large-scale composition. Six are scored for wind band, two include chorus, three have important parts for solo singers and five are in effect solo instrumental concertos: No.29 for baritone horn, No.34 bass trombone, No.36 flute, No.39 guitar and No.51 trumpet.

On the morning of 18 May 1980 in Hovhaness's home state of Washington, Mount St Helens erupted violently, causing massive destruction as the side of the mountain was blown away. This cataclysmic event prompted Hovhaness to devote a symphony to describing his impressions. In his programme note for Symphony No.50 *Mount St Helens* completed in 1983, the composer is explicit in relating the music to the landscape and the eruption:

The first movement is in the form of a Prelude and Fugue, suggesting the grandeur of the mountain before the destruction of May 18. The opening theme rising in the horns is followed by lyrical extensions and elaborations in long melodic lines, leading to the grand fugue in praise of Mount of Helens.

*Spirit Lake* attempts to capture the beauty of the lake before its violent destruction. Gently vibrating, liquid-sounding bells in the style of 'Jhala Taranea', or waves of water, lead the expressive melodies of the English horn and other solo winds. A lyrical duet for flutes dissolves into vibrating bells.This watery sound expresses the memories of Paradise Lake, forever lost.

*Volcano* is the morning of May 18. A dawn-like hymn is heard in the horns over mysterious, murmuring, plucked basses, followed by a rising passage for solo flute. This is interrupted by a violent explosion in the drums. Eruption music is heard in the brass – the power of molten forces beneath the mountain. Chaos is sounded by stormy strings and violent trombone glissandi, then a strict, blazing triple canon in 20 voices of winds, brass and strings, followed by percussion. After the music of violence and destruction, the dawn hymn returns in triumph. A rapid fugue on the dawn hymn motif becomes a hymn of praise to the youthful power and grandeur of the Cascades, the volcanic energy renewing the vitality of our beautiful planet, the living earth – to the life-giving power that builds mountains, rising majestically, piercing the clouds of heaven.

Here we see the composer's naive poetic vision is coupled with an objective analysis of the techniques involved in creating the music. Like any imaginative artist, Hovhaness maintains a tight control of the form of his work while sustaining a sense of freedom of invention. Symphony No.50 with its precise programme represents one of the most approachable works by this enigmatic composer.

Except for the deliberate occasional inclusion of Eastern influences, there is little stylistic change between the early symphonies of the 1940s and those of recent composition. The melodies remain essentially diatonic with the incidental alterred note to provide an oriental flavour; harmonies are for the most part consonant and modal with an occasional clash from notes outside the key and brief passages of polytonality.

With music of such simplicity and limitation of resources a feeling of repetition from one work to another is inevitable. It could be said that there is insufficient variety of invention for each of the 60 or more symphonies to betray unique qualities. Writing in 1964, Wilfred Mellers expressed some misgivings:

Although fluency is a joy in a creatively constipated society, one cannot help suspecting that Hovhaness' music is too easy to write and too easy to listen to. To pretend that one is an Ancient Armenian may be part of the American Dream.

(Mellers, W. (1964) *Music in a New Found Land*, Barrie and Rockliff: London, p.154)

Hovhaness's approach to each work is basically the same, subjecting the material to a consistent system: chorales of static chordal repetition, step-wise melodic incantation over slow-moving harmonies, polymodal and polytonal lines independent of the prevailing harmonic movement. He has created his own very personal restricted idiom which is applied to all his works so that each new composition bears a close resemblance to its predecessor. To appreciate his world, it is necessary to shed most of one's preconceived ideas of twentieth-century music and accept him on his own mystical terms.

Throughout his life, **Lou Harrison** (b. 1917) has been an eclectic composer. Each new musical experience he encountered became a part of his style. From his first teacher Henry Cowell he absorbed both experimental and traditional elements. After studying with Arnold Schoenberg in Los Angeles in 1943, he adopted atonal practices which survive from time to time until the present day.

After working with John Cage on percussion, Harrison began to build and adapt instruments, most notably the tack-piano, an upright with drawing pins in the hammer heads, producing a sound similar to a dry harpsichord. In 1953 he met Harry Partch in California who encouraged him to further his instrumental experiments.

Another potent influence was a visit to Japan, Taiwan and Korea in 1961 which opened up a whole new world of oriental music involving different scales, pitch relationships and microtones. The experience of the Far East also led to his interest, as a composer, performer and constructor, in Gamelan music and instruments.

With this intense absorption in non-Western music, it might seem strange that Harrison should ever enter the classical world of the symphony. By its very instrumentation, his *Simfony in Free Style* for 17 flutes, trombones, 5 harps, bells, drums, celeste, vibraphone and 8 viols is not a part of his symphonic *corpus*.

The four orchestral symphonies reflect Harrison's multi-cultural outlook, while maintaining certain features of the classical norm. The *Symphony on G* occupied him from 1947 until 1964. The composer explained:

> The title itself (*on* G not *in* G) refers to the fact that the whole work, though serially composed with twelve tones, is nonetheless tonally centred on the note G. In the first three movements the technique is classical 12-tone procedure, but in the Finale I have ignored the forbiddance concerning octave-conjunction, and written freely in the 'grand manner'.

The nervous, lyrical character of the opening Allegro is indebted to the teaching of Schoenberg, although the textures are less opulent, often simple monody or two-part counterpoint. It is early late-romantic Schoenberg who dominates the long slow movement.

Harrison's unconventional approach is evident in the Scherzo; it is a sequence of four independent dances in totally unrelated styles. A Bergian set of Waltzes for strings is followed by a jazzy Polka featuring a clarinet solo *à la* Benny Goodman, accompanied by tack-piano, an Air for strings and harp, French Impressionistic in mood, and a Rondeau for piano, tack-piano and harp. How these disparate pieces fit into a symphony remains the composer's secret.

After the première in 1964, Harrison replaced the Finale with a new movement, a pulsating energetic Allegro for full orchestra, based on a recurring three-note motif. More tonal than the first movement, it is the most obviously

American part of the symphony, optimistic and exuberant with a confident swagger. The first performance took place at the Cabrillo Music Festival, Apros, California in August 1964. For a revival on 8 February, 1966 by the Oakland Symphony Orchestra, Harrison provided the new Finale.

The period of gestation of Harrison's Second Symphony was even greater than that of the Symphony on G. The first sketches are dated 11 October 1942, the score completed in 1975. The music is prefaced by two quotations: the first is from Horace: 'Bitter sorrows will grow milder with music.' The second is taken from Epicurus: 'Where Death is, we are not; where we are, Death is not; therefore, Death is nothing to us.'

Harrison gave his Second Symphony the subtitle Elegiac and provided the following guide:

> The angel of music, Israfel ('whose heartstrings are a lute' – Edgar Allan Poe), stands with his feet in the earth and his head in the sun. He will blow the last trumpet. Six times daily he looks down into hell and is so convulsed with grief that his tears would inundate the earth if Allah did not stop their flow. For three years he ministered to Mohammed before Gabriel took this office, although Israfel is nowhere mentioned in the Koran.

Although the composer designated this piece a symphony, it is in effect a five-movement suite with little evidence of symphonic implications. Movements 1 and 3 are both entitled 'Tears of the Angel Israfel'. The first combines Cowell-like modal string passages of long melismas over pedal points with repeated figuration on the tack-piano against a drone representing an oriental lute. This element recalls the mystical world of Alan Hovhaness. As canonical entries of new melodies accumulate to build up a passionate climax, the imitative counterpoint is still predominantly Western in character.

The second 'Tears' movement is also modal with pentatonic themes on cello, horn and two solo double-basses, this last a tribute to Sergei Koussevitzky to whose memory the work is dedicated. There is a indefinable air of oriental antiquity in this part of the symphony.

Between these two movements, Harrison interpolates a short Allegro rondo of intricate cross-rhythms and explosive outbursts on full orchestra. The fourth movement 'Praises for Michael the Archangel' is celebrated by brass and bells – vibraphone, celeste, glockenspiel, piano, harp, tubular bells. At times the music is very dissonant with turgid *tuttis* hampered by lumbering brass.

For the Finale, 'The Sweetness of Epicurus', the longest movement, Harrison reverts to the elegiac mood of the opening; here the tonal, modal expansive themes have a decidedly American flavour in the manner of Roy Harris bringing the symphony to a consolatory close.

The *Elegiac* Symphony was commissioned by the Koussevitzky Foundation and is dedicated to the memory of Sergei and Natalie Koussevitzky. It was first performed in Oakland, California on 7 December 1975 by the Oakland Symphony Youth Orchestra conducted by Denis de Coteau. Some revisions of the score were made by the composer in 1988.

Symphony No.3 was commissioned for the Cabrillo Music Festival in 1982. Like its two predecessors, it does not at first sight conform to the usual symphonic pattern. Closer examination reveals that the first movement follows basic sonata form with an almost literal recapitulation. The next three short movements collectively make up the scherzo, as is the case with the Symphony on G, and the remaining sections constitute a slow movement and Allegro finale.

The first movement, Allegro Moderato, has the feel of improvisation, independent modal lines free to expand at will, in the manner of Alan Hovhaness but without his oriental inflections. The long melismas have a Copland-like diatonicism, related to folk music.

*A Reel in Honor of Henry Cowell* begins like an Irish dance for violin and percussion but soon departs from its Celtic origins into a more surreal world of polytonality. *A Waltz for Evelyn Hinrichsen* (his publisher) in slow tempo is rather sad in a Gallic way. To restore a more genial mood *An Estampie for Susan Summerfield* with its irregular rhythms and spicy scoring for oboe and percussion recreates the world of the Middle Ages in Europe.

A single unbroken melodic line on the violins against repeated accompaniment chords is sustained throughout the Largo Ostinato. Harrison's delight in bell sounds is given its head in the joyous finale, the energetic activity often recalling the ostinato of a Gamelan orchestra.

*Last Symphony* (Symphony No.4) was completed in 1990 but subjected to revisions in 1991, 1993 and 1995. It was commissioned by the Brooklyn Academy of Music and the Brooklyn Philharmonic Orchestra who gave the première on 20 November 1990 conducted by Dennis Russell Davies. It is scored for large orchestra with a baritone soloist in the last of the four movements. The finale sets three texts, two Amerindian tales and one with words by Daniel-Harry Steward.

Harrison has always been an independent spirit, whose eclectic approach to composition is reflected in the four symphonies. External influences are strong, especially folk music from East and West and the examples set by his teachers, Cowell and Schoenberg, but the finished product can belong only to him.

**Richard Yardumian** (1917–1985) was born in Philadelphia of Armenian parents. Largely self-taught in composition, he was greatly influenced by religious subjects. He developed a highly organized 12-note system based on sequences of thirds, which produced an implied diatonic language. Later studies of medieval and renaissance music and Armenian chant brought new dimensions to his works.

His First Symphony, begun in 1950 and completed in 1961, is based on the life of Noah. The opening movement, *Legend*, a theme and ten variations, closely follows the story of the Flood. *Aria*, the central movement, makes use of the American hymn 'O Wondrous Love'. The finale, *March*, recalls music of the first movement in depicting the departure of the animals from the Ark and Noah's later life. The symphony was first performed on 1 December 1961 by Eugene Ormandy and the Philadelphia Orchestra with whom Yardumian enjoyed a close association from 1949 to 1964.

The first movement of Symphony No.2 was written in 1947 and the whole work finished in 1964. Inspired by Armenian church music, it is a setting for mezzo-soprano or baritone of Psalms. The première was given by the singer Lili Chookasian and the Philadelphia Orchestra on 13 November 1964. A Third Symphony dates from 1981.

One of the many unusual figures in American music is **Vazgen Muradian**. Born in Armenia in 1921, he showed an early aptitude for music but poverty prevented his receiving tuition until his teens. His career was interrupted by the Second World War when he was drafted into the Soviet army. As a refugee in post-war Europe, he eked out a living as an orchestral musician.

In 1950 Muradian emigrated to the United States where he became a viola player in various orchestras. After settling in New York he turned from performing to composition. Among his large output of orchestral works are over 60 concertos, many for neglected instruments such as the viola d'amore and Armenian folk instruments: dudek, tar, kamancha and kanon.

To date he has completed 36 symphonies, to which number he is still adding. Muradian considers his music to be neo-classical in character but a more accurate description would be pseudo 'classical' since he composes in a late-eighteenth- – early nineteenth-century style using forms, textures, melodies and harmony that would not have seemed out of place in any European city around the year 1800.

With remarkable single-mindedness and industry worthy of a German *kapellmeister*, Muradian continues to write well crafted 'classical' scores, oblivious of the outside musical world that prefers the genuine article to replicas, however expertly crafted.

# 18 Peter Mennin and George Rochberg

Peter Mennin and George Rochberg defy simple classification. Both dedicated themselves to abstract works in classical forms with symphonies at the core of their output.

Peter Mennin (1923–1983) completed his First Symphony in 1941 at the age of 18 while he was a student of Normand Lockwood at the Oberlin Conservatory, Ohio. He later withdrew the score. On 27 March 1945, one movement of a Second Symphony, entitled *Symphonic Allegro*, was performed by Leonard Bernstein and the New York Philharmonic Orchestra in Rochester, NY on 27 March 1945, when the composer was studying at the Eastman School. It was awarded the George Gershwin Prize and the complete symphony received the Joseph H. Bearns Prize of Columbia University in 1945.

It was, however, Mennin's Third Symphony that caused the greatest stir. Completed in May on his 23rd birthday, it was first performed by the New York Philharmonic Orchestra under Walter Hendl on 27 February 1947 and recorded by Dmitri Mitropoulos as a result of a Naumburg Foundation grant. Here, with little warning, was a fully-fledged symphonic composer in his early twenties.

In the *New York Herald Tribune*, Virgil Thomson described the Third Symphony as 'an accomplished work, in a sense that its shape holds together and that its instrumentation is professional. Its expressive content is eclectic, ranging from a Sibelian-like sadness to a syncopated animation suggestive of William Schuman.' At a greater distance of time it is now possible to hear more clearly the influences of Vaughan Williams and, in the fast movements, William Walton, particularly in the mercurial scoring for the woodwind.

The Third Symphony aroused much comment and it was performed throughout the United States. Today, regrettably, the work has fallen from the repertoire; the new recording issued in 1997 offers the opportunity reassess its merits in the context of other symphonies by American composers of the same period.

Symphony No.4 (1948), subtitled *The Cycle*, is a setting of three short philosophical texts by the composer for chorus and orchestra. It was

156

commissioned by the Collegiate Chorale and first performed by them and members of the New York Philharmonic Orchestra under the baton of Robert Shaw on 18 March 1949.

Virgil Thomson in the *New York Herald Tribune* was again enthusiastic:

> 'I don't think I've heard a choral symphony in which the vocal and instrumental forces are so well equilibrated in the whole expressive achievement.'

The essence of the poem lies in the first two lines of the last movement:

> Time passing, waters flowing,
> The great cycle begins once more,
> Washing stains away.

The orchestral part is so complete in itself that the choral contribution, mostly homophonic, sounds more an addition to the texture grafted on than an independent element. This impression is confirmed by the instrumental character of the vocal lines often doubled by the orchestra. As with the Third Symphony, the shadow of Walton lies heavily over the driving rhythms of the fast movement.

Symphony No.5 (1949) was commissioned by the Dallas Symphony Orchestra who premièred it on 2 April 1950 conducted by Walter Hendl. Performances followed in Boston, New York, San Francisco and in Europe and South America under such distinguished conductors as Charles Munch and Pierre Monteux. Like its predecessors, the three-movement symphony is direct and assertive. The energetic finale has the strong sense of purpose and headlong forward propulsion encountered in all his major orchestral works.

Symphony No.6 was a Louisville Orchestra commission performed on 17 November 1953 under the baton of Robert Whitney. The critic of the *Louisville Courier Journal* praised the work for its emphatic affirmation: 'The new symphony compels attention from the portentous introduction through to the triumphant finale.'

By the age of 30, Mennin had six substantial symphonies to his credit. In 1958 he was appointed Director of the Peabody Conservatory in Baltimore, succeeding William Schuman in 1962 as President of the Juilliard School where he remained until his death in 1983.

With so much of his energy devoted to administration, Mennin found less time for composition. More than a decade elapsed before the Seventh Symphony appeared. It was composed in 1962 and first performed by George Szell and the Cleveland Orchestra on 23 January 1962. Mennin's style had undergone much change since the earlier symphonies. Gone are the mannerisms, motor rhythms for pages at a time and over-repetition of figures. The harmonic language is now less tonal with more complex contrapuntal writing.

The structure of the symphony is also radically different. Subtitled *Variation Symphony*, it is cast in a single movement that is divided into five linked sections. The composer explained 'It has little relationship to the consecutive variation principle, but instead uses techniques of variation resulting from the overall structural and dramatic concept.'

The Seventh Symphony is planned on a substantial scale where the five sections correspond to a certain degree to customary symphonic form: the fifth movement an extensive Allegro epilogue to sum up the discourse. The theme itself embraces the 12 chromatic semitones but the 'row' is arranged in such a way as to imply tonal centres (Ex. 86).

Ex. 86

*Reproduced by permission of Carl Fischer Inc.*

The more advanced and complex treatment of this material reminds one of William Schuman. There is an increased dissonance and less predictable thematic development as the direction of the music is constantly changing. Like Schuman, Mennin often separates the orchestra into self-contained, self-sufficient sections where strings, woodwind and brass have their own independent and distinctive material. The ferocious interjections of syncopated fragments on the brass is another borrowing from Schuman, as are the richly romantic textures of the writing for strings alone, deeply passionate in the dramatic climaxes of the slow passages. The wide-ranging, extensive lyrical melodies might be traced to the same source. In spite of the Schuman influence, Mennin's Seventh Symphony represents the peak of his symphonic achievement, a closely argued work of massive integrity. It can rank among the finest of the American symphonic tradition this century.

From 1970 to his death in 1983, Mennin composed only five works. Writing of his later compositions, the critic Walter Simmons commented:

> These and subsequent works reveal a bold vision of abstract forces in ceaseless, violent conflict, escalating in intensity towards cataclysmic explosions of almost manic brutality.

(Sleeve note; Mennin Symphonies No.8 & 9 New World, NW 371.2)

Symphony No.8 was performed on 21 November 1974 by Daniel Barenboim and the New York Philharmonic Orchestra. The composer offered no explanation for the Biblical title given to each of the four movements and it is impossible to divine anything specific in the music itself: In principio; Dies Irae; De profundis clamavi; Laudate Dominum. The language is uncompromisingly harsh, at times dense in texture and often very dramatic. The *Dies Irae* movement is intensely wild with scintillating scoring, frighteningly fierce in impact. Only in the slow movement

*De profundis clamavi* is there any sustained calm, achieved by stark sombre counterpoint. Even the finale *Laudate Dominum* lacks a feeling of optimism, usual in most settings of Psalm 150. This frenzied, menacing *moto perpetuo* concludes a work of disturbing violence which makes huge technical demands on the orchestra.

With hindsight, Symphony No.9 (*Sinfonia capricciosa*) might be viewed as a valedictory offering but it was completed in 1981 before the onset of the composer's final illness. It had been commissioned by the National Symphony Orchestra of Washington. Mennin provided an explanation for the subtitle:

> As the title implies, *Sinfonia capricciosa* has many capricious moments, many sharp changes, and more contrasting sections than the usual symphony.

Nevertheless the three movements conform to customary symphonic patterns. The first movement begins like the Seventh Symphony in mysterious mood with the opening theme on cellos. Gradually a power and momentum are built up in a manner similar to the fast passages of the previous two symphonies.

The emotional heart of the Ninth Symphony lies in the dignified, elegiac central Adagio. Mennin places the emphasis on the strings for a passionate outpouring of grief, ending the movement with the tolling of a bell. The bell image is continued in the frenetic finale marked *Presto tumultuoso*. Outbursts on the brass and percussion plunge the music on a headlong stampede to the resolute but dark conclusion.

The last three of Mennin's nine symphonies represent a total contrast with the earlier ones of the set. Gone is the exhilarating *bonhomie* and academic professional correctness to be replaced by an resolute determination to express the darker side of life.

**George Rochberg**, born in 1918 the son of Russian immigrants, began to compose at the age of ten. As a school boy he was already writing popular songs and playing in a jazz band.

He had no formal training in composition until he was 21 when he studied for a year at the Mannes School of Music in New York City with Hans Weisse and George Szell. When the United States entered World War II, he was drafted into the army, serving as a Second Lieutenant in the infantry and was wounded in action. After the war, at the age of 27, he moved to Philadelphia, where he studied counterpoint at the Curtis Institute of Music with Rosario Scalero, the teacher of Samuel Barber and Gian Carlo Menotti.

By 1950 Rochberg had begun to explore atonality and the 12-note method. This involvement with serialism lasted until 1965 when he abandoned the system in favour of a freer use of tonality. His wartime experience required a more penetrating musical language with which to express the darker, painful sides of human existence. When in the mid-60s he decided to re-embrace the old tonal world, it was because, as he said, he wanted to 'find a way to marry the tonal with the atonal. What I wanted to do was treat the idea of tonality as an enlarged stable language which could be combined with the unstable elements of atonality.'

In his later compositions, Rochberg has closely identified himself with Mahler in an endeavour to integrate his experiences with musical expression. 'It is true that there was a time in my life when I was superconscious of Mahler. He had a profound influence upon me, musically, emotionally and so on.'

At the heart of Rochberg's output of major works are the six symphonies covering his entire post-war composing career. His First Symphony, written in 1948–49, was originally a work in five movements of which his *Night Music* was the second movement. For reasons which he later regretted, he reduced the work to three movements, removing *Night Music* and another movement, *Capriccio*. It was this version which Eugene Ormandy introduced with the Philadelphia Orchestra on 29 March 1958. Rochberg restored the work to its original form with some revisions and reworkings by 1977. The First Symphony shows the influence of three composers he greatly admired, Hindemith, Stravinsky and Bartók.

His Second Symphony, composed in 1956, crystallized his very personal use of serialism which had taken on a new dimension the previous year in the large-scale *Sonata-Fantasia* for piano solo. This was to be followed a few years later by his Second String Quartet (with voice) which explored simultaneity of different tempi and speeds while giving voice emotionally to the powerful pantheism reflected in Rilke's 'Elegy' which he used as text. His former teacher George Szell conducted the première of the Second Symphony with the Cleveland Orchestra on 26 February 1959.

The Third Symphony of 1966–69, for four soloists, double chorus, chamber chorus and an enlarged orchestra, was the only completed part of a vast project Rochberg originally intended to be a 'Passion According to the Twentieth Century' in which he wanted to show the beastliness of human beings out of control. In the symphony he brings the past into collision with the present, simultaneously commenting on the present with the greater wisdom of the past. He accomplishes this by juxtaposing music by Heinrich Schütz, J.S. Bach, Beethoven (the *Eroica* Symphony) with Mahler and Charles Ives in the context of his own music. As Rochberg has said, 'using other peoples' music in this way makes theirs mine in exactly the same spirit as Keats thought that "All poetry is written by one mind"'. The Third Symphony was commissioned by the Juilliard School whose orchestra and chorus with the Collegiate Chorale gave the first performance on 24 November 1970 under the direction of Abraham Kaplan.

The Fourth Symphony was written in 1976 for the Seattle Youth Orchestra which performed it under Vilem Sokol on 15 November 1976. Rochberg described it as

> hardly a small work, with less performance and interpretive problems because it was first played by youngsters. In fact it is large scale and combines a highly emotional, romantic first movement with a dance-parody second movement based on a [tone] row and ends by tipping its hat very broadly in Haydn's direction.

Symphony No.5 was commissioned in 1984 by the Chicago Symphony Orchestra to mark the 150th anniversary of the founding of the city of Chicago. Lasting 25 minutes, the Fifth Symphony is cast in a single movement with seven distinctive sections. Rochberg describes the form as a 'constantly evolving and spiraling funnel, which gathers up ideas already stated to create a finale where everything is brought together and unified'.

The symphony is a neo-romantic outpouring of passionate emotion, of abruptly changing moods. The turbulent spirit is balanced by passages of richly expressive melodic invention that constantly boil up to renewed violence. This uncompromising potent work is very much of our times, a virtuoso display piece for the Chicago players. Georg Solti conducted the première on 30 January 1986.

Rochberg believes very strongly that wherever possible, music should be written for specific performers and musical organizations. The Sixth Symphony was commissioned by the Pittsburgh Symphony Orchestra for whom he had composed his Violin Concerto in 1974 with Isaac Stern as soloist.

Symphony No.6, written in 1986, is intended as the second part of trilogy, starting with the Fifth Symphony, to be completed by a seventh in the next few years. Whereas the one-movement Fifth Symphony is compact and emotionally intensive, the Sixth is structurally freer, comprising two expansive movements. For the première, conducted by Lorin Maazel in the Heinz Hall for the Performing Arts in Pittsburgh on 16 October 1987, the composer provided the following programme note.

The Sixth Symphony is in two parts, designed as *Fantasia* and *Marcia*, respectively. Central to the *Fantasia* are various kinds of fanfares, evoking not only the ancient association with what we know to be the false glories of war, but also the hidden, underlying tragic implications of mankind's perennial passion for making war and its inability to rid itself of the sophisticated barbarism reationalized as the military side of national defence. I find nothing glorious in death and destruction regardless of the rhetorics overtly or covertly advanced in their cause. These fanfares come in unexpected places during the course of the *Fantasia*, emerging out of or interrupting or taking over other kinds of musical ideas. The core of this ensemble of other ideas is a lento which goes below the surface of things into dark and probing regions and provides the basis for deriving different yet related motives and melodic ideas.

Part Two is comprised of a series of three different marches, of which the first is the overall frame for the second and third. In the old classical tradition of character pieces such as the scherzo, march and dance forms, contrasting parts were called 'trios'. In that sense, each of these other two marches can be thought of as an extended 'trio'. Fanfares again occur in these 'trios' – some of them variants of the fanfares from the *Fantasia*, others brand new. The main tune of the third march – all three marches have clearly defined tunes of different character and attitude – was the principal tune of a parade march that I wrote in 1943 or 1944 for the 65th Infantry Division Band when I was briefly attached as a Special Service officer to one of the companies of that division while I was training in Camp Shelby, Mississippi. The march itself is 'lost' – i.e. I possess no copy of it; but the tune I use in this work haunted me during all the ensuing time after World War II, and I knew someday I would make use of it. The figures in the woodwind accompanying this tune are drawn from the material of the second march, thus making a kind of polyphonic joining of the two. What perhaps can be called the 'Epilogue' – really an extended coda – of Part Two pulls the marches back into the world of the *Fantasia*.

# 19 Leonard Bernstein (1918–1990)

Not one of Bernstein's three symphonies is a purely abstract orchestral work. The finale of the *Jeremiah* Symphony is a setting for mezzo-soprano of verses from the book of Lamentations; the Second, subtitled *The Age of Anxiety*, includes an important concertante part for piano; No.3 *Kaddish* is a choral work for speaker mezzo-soprano, boys' chorus, mixed chorus and orchestra.

The *Jeremiah* Symphony was composed for a competition sponsored by the New England Conservatory. It was completed on 31 December 1942, a day before the deadline for submission. Although Bernstein did not win,* he later played through the piece to Koussevitzky who had been chairman of the jury but the conductor was unimpressed. Fritz Reiner, who had taught Bernstein conducting at the Curtis Institute, was eager to have the work performed by his Pittsburgh Symphony Orchestra. As a result, the composer directed the première on 28 January 1944 with Jennie Tourel as soloist.

Reiner had urged Bernstein to add a fourth movement, deeming the Lamentation ending too depressing for the audience. Naturally he refused to comply. The symphony was received with great acclaim and Bernstein conducted four performances with the New York Philharmonic Orchestra in the following March and April, after which it was heard throughout the United States that year including a nationwide broadcast by the NBC Symphony Orchestra directed by Frank Black.

The *Jeremiah* Symphony won the New York Music Critics' Circle Award for the most outstanding new orchestral work of the season. Later Guido Cantelli conducted the Italian première and a recording by Leonard Bernstein and the St Louis Symphony Orchestra was issued by RCA.

In the published score, the composer provided the following comments:

In the summer of 1939 I made a sketch for a 'Lamentation' for soprano and orchestra. This sketch lay forgotten for two years, until in the spring of 1942 I began a first

---

*    The first prize was awarded to Gardner Read for his Symphony No.2 in E flat minor.

movement of a symphony. I then realized that this new movement, and the scherzo that I planned to follow it, made logical concomitants with the 'Lamentation'. Thus the symphony came into being, with the 'Lamentation' greatly changed, and the soprano supplanted by a mezzo-soprano. The work was finished on 31 December 1942 and is dedicated to my father.

The symphony does not make use to any great extent of actual Hebrew thematic material. The first theme of the scherzo is paraphrased from a traditional Hebrew chant, and the opening phrase of the vocal part in the 'Lamentation' is based on a liturgical cadence still sung today in commemoration of the destruction of Jerusalem by Babylon. Other remembrances of Hebrew liturgical music are a matter of emotional quality, rather than of the notes themselves.

As for programmatic meanings, the intention is again not one of literalness, but of emotional quality. Thus the first movement (Prophecy) aims only to parallel in feeling the intensity of the prophet's pleas with his people; and the scherzo (Profanation) to give a general sense of the destruction and chaos brought on by the pagan corruption within the priesthood and the people. The third movement (Lamentation), being a setting of poetic text, is naturally a more literary conception. It is the cry of Jeremiah, as he mourns his beloved Jerusalem, ruined, pillaged and dishonored after his desperate efforts to save it. The text is from the book of Lamentations.

In this, his first orchestral work, Bernstein shows remarkable assurance. Even at this point in his career, reticence was not part of his character. One would expect with any young composer that certain role models would be evident, but only in the asymmetrical 'additive' rhythms of the scherzo is there evidence of the influence of Aaron Copland. The outer movements sound like no-one but Bernstein himself.

The first subject of the opening movement *Prophecy* heard at the outset on first horn is derived from the final phrase of the liturgical *Amidah* from the High Holy Day Service.

Ex. 87

Largamente

*Reproduced by permission of Boosey and Hawkes Ltd*

Bernstein's treatment of this theme is richly romantic, passionately rhapsodic and in the climaxes highly dissonant. Samuel Barber is the composer brought to mind in the dark, tense outpouring of grief. The more lyrical second subject marked *Molto calmo* is based on the second half of *K'rovoh*, part of the 18 Blessings.

Ex. 88

*Reproduced by permission of Boosey and Hawkes Ltd*

The quiet ending owes a little to Copland's characteristic simplicity that resolves the conflict in a number of his scores, e.g. *Billy the Kid*.

It is Copland who is evoked in the Scherzo (*Profanation*) with its irregular metre. Some writers have called this jazzy but these complex dancing rhythms have little to do with jazz; the mood is grim, not joyous. The melodic contours have their origin in *Ashkenazic** cantilena.

Ex. 89

*Reproduced by permission of Boosey and Hawkes Ltd*

Although at the same tempo as the Scherzo, the brief trio section, based on a brass motif from the first movement (Fig.7), is more relaxed. In the melodic invention there is a hint of later Bernstein, the dance episodes from the musicals *On the Town* and *West Side Story* (Ex. 90).

At the wild heights of the return of the Scherzo, horns blast out the Prophecy motif from the first movement. This is tough, uncompromising music, hard-hitting, single-minded and very American in style.

As the composer noted, the opening phrase of the vocal line in the Lamentation is based on a liturgical cadence from the dirges chanted on *Tisha B' Av* (the ninth day of the month of Ab); there are also references to the Ashkenazic prayer *S'lichoth* (service of Forgiveness).

---

\*    German-Polish Jewish.

Ex. 90

*Reproduced by permission of Boosey and Hawkes Ltd*

Ex. 91

*Reproduced by permission of Boosey and Hawkes Ltd*

The instrumentation that accompanies the voice is sparse, comprising mainly static chords, allowing the singer freedom of rhythmic articulation although the notation is very precise. Only at one point does the mezzo-soprano have to contend with the brass, but even their indication of 'forte' is modified by the additional instruction 'dolce'. One passage of scoring reveals how Bernstein had absorbed the music of other composers he admired. A woodwind phrase at Fig. 9 is highly reminiscent of Copland in his outdoor pastoral vein. Its transformation onto muted string quartet in the closing bars is pure Bernstein, a little sentimental, but deeply affecting and intended to produce a tear (Ex. 92).

By any standards, the *Jeremiah* Symphony is a major achievement for Bernstein. However it was soon overshadowed by the huge popular success of the ballet *Fancy Free* and the musical *On the Town*, both staged in 1944, the year of the première of the symphony. Today at a distance of more than half a century, we are in a better position to assess it as more than simply the product of youthful talent. It is a serious and significant contribution to the establishment of the American Symphony in the mid-twentieth century.

We should also examine the historical context in which this lament for the destruction of Jerusalem was written. Before the première of the symphony, Bernstein said to his friend David Diamond, 'I am going to show these Nazis!' In

Ex. 92

Più lento

*Reproduced by permission of Boosey and Hawkes Ltd*

1942 the year of its completion, the German armies in Europe appeared to be unstoppable. By 1944 when the symphony was performed, the Second World War was beginning to turn in favour of the Allies. Jeremiah's words have a particular tragic significance for the Jewish people in the 1940s and Bernstein expressed their anguish in this deeply moving music.

Bernstein's Second Symphony *The Age of Anxiety* was commissioned by the Koussevitzky Music Foundation. It was written in various locations during his busy international conducting schedule, sometimes in hotels and on aeroplanes. The score, dedicated to Koussevitzky, was completed on 20 March 1949 less than three weeks before the première in Boston on 8 April. In 1950 Bernstein gave ten performances in Israel, directing from the keyboard.

The inspiration behind the music was a then recently published poem *The Age of Anxiety* by W.H. Auden, described as a 'baroque eclogue', which won a Pulitzer Prize in 1948. In his programme note for the première, Bernstein provided an explanation for the important role given to the solo piano.

> The pianist provides an almost autobiographical protagonist set against an orchestral mirror in which he sees himself, analytically, in the modern ambience.

This explanation is supported by the fact that the composer played the solo part in the concert.

Bernstein divides Auden's poem into six sections grouped into two parts, each of three sections, which are played without a break. He supplied a detailed description of the work.

**Part One:**

(a) *The Prologue* finds four lonely characters, a girl and three men, in a Third Avenue bar, all of them insecure and through drink, trying to detach themselves from their conflicts or, at best, to resolve them. They are drawn together by this common urge and begin a kind of symposium on the state of man. Musically, *The Prologue* is a very short section consisting of a lonely improvisation by two clarinets, echotone, and followed by a long descending scale which acts as a bridge into the realm of the unconscious, where most of the poem takes place.

(b) *The Seven Ages.* The life of man is reviewed from the four personal points of view. This is a series of variations which differ from conventional variations in that they do not vary any one common theme. Each variation seizes upon some feature of the preceding one and develops it, introducing, in the course of the development, some counter-feature upon which the next variation seizes. It is a kind of musical fission, which corresponds to the reasonableness and almost didactic quality of the four-fold discussion.

(c) *The Seven Stages.* The variation form continues for another set of seven in which the characters go on an inner and highly symbolic journey according to a geographical plan leading to a point of comfort and security. The four try every means, going singly and in pairs, exchanging partners, and always missing the objective. When they awaken from this dream-odyssey, they are closely united through a common experience (and through alcohol), and begin to function as one organism. This set of variations begins to show activity and drive and leads to a hectic, though indecisive, close.

Part Two:

(a) *The Dirge* is sung by the four as they sit in a cab en route to the girl's apartment for a nightcap. They mourn the loss of the 'colossal Dad', the great leader who can always give the right orders, find the right solution, shoulder the mass responsibility, and satisfy the universal need for a father-symbol. This section employs, in a harmonic way, a 12-tone row out of which the main theme evolves. There is a contrasting middle section of almost Brahmsian romanticism, in which can be felt the self-indulgent or negative, aspect of this strangely pompous lamentation.

(b) *The Masque* finds the group in the girl's apartment, weary, guilty, determined to have a party, each one afraid of spoiling the others' fun by admitting that he should be home in bed. This is a scherzo for piano and percussion alone (including harp, celesta, glockenspiel and xylophone) in which a kind of fantastic piano-jazz is employed, by turns nervous, sentimental, self-satisfied, vociferous. The party ends in anti-climax and the dispersal of the actors; in the music the piano-protagonist is traumatized by the intervention of the orchestra for four bars of hectic jazz. When the orchestra stops, as abruptly as it began, a pianino in the orchestra continues *The Masque*, repetitiously and with waning energy, as *The Epilogue* begins. Thus a kind of separation of the self from the guilt of escaping living has been effected, and the protagonist is free again to examine what is left beneath the emptiness.

(c) *The Epilogue.* What is left, it turns out, is faith. The trumpet intrudes its statement of 'something pure' upon the dying pianino: the strings answer in a melancholy reminiscent of *The Prologue*: again and again the winds reiterate 'something pure' against the mounting tension of the strings' loneliness. All at once the strings accept the situation, in a sudden radiant *pianissio*, and begin to build, with the rest of the orchestra, to a positive statement of the newly-recognized faith.

Although the composer might not have agreed, there is no direct need to know or follow the poem to appreciate the music since it has an abstract logic of its own. It is sufficient to recognize the mood of the the situation representing the nervous and hectic life in a modern city.

*The Age of Anxiety* has not been held in much esteem, being regarded as an eclectic work, composed in haste with little more status than a film score. After the première Olin Downes in the *New York Times* described it as 'wholly exterior in style, ingeniously constructed, effectively orchestrated and a triumph of superficiality'. Bernstein's craftsmanship is not in question. The piano writing, however derivative, is especially well laid out, at times of barn-storming virtuosity, rhythmically intricate and carefully co-ordinated with the orchestra.

The short Prologue for two unaccompanied clarinets introduces the theme for the 14 variations of the next two sections (Ex. 93). This passage was adapted from a duet for violin and cello written in 1939 as part of the incidental music for a production of Aristophanes' play *The Birds*, produced at Harvard. Bernstein has described this as 'the loneliest music I know'. He may have recalled subconsciously the solo trumpet in Copland's *Quiet City*, also originally incidental music for a play dealing with the isolation of the individual in a busy city.

Ex. 93

Lento moderato

*Reproduced by permission of Boosey and Hawkes Ltd*

The descending scale which acts as a bridge between the variations is also included in the thematic development. It happens to contain all twelve chromatic semitones:

Ex. 94

Poco più andante

*Reproduced by permission of Boosey and Hawkes Ltd*

The entry of the piano in Variation I closely resembles the chorale from Bartók's Third Piano Concerto, a work only three years old when Bernstein composed this music (Ex. 95).

The more flamboyant piano writing in Variation II takes Brahms and Rachmaninov as models. Variations III and VIII, the latter a passacaglia, may be an implied tribute to his friend Benjamin Britten. Bernstein had conducted the American première of *Peter Grimes* at Tanglewood in the summer of 1946. The

Ex. 95

(L'istesso tempo)

*Reproduced by permission of Boosey and Hawkes Ltd*

opera includes a passacaglia of similar character to the above variation. Variation VI is a piano solo which bears some resemblance to Schoenberg and the Second Viennese School. Elsewhere the brilliant, laconic piano writing echoes Shostakovich and Prokofiev with an occasional nod towards Stravinsky.

The first three sections of *The Age of Anxiety* which constitute Part One are in effect more like a concerto than a symphony in the relative significance of the solo role of the pianist. In spite of two cadenzas, Part Two is more symphonic. *Dirge* is the slow movement, solemn and forceful in the dissonant climaxes. Bernstein again resurrected an earlier unpublished composition for some of the material; in this instance he took the theme from a sonata for violin and piano written in 1939.

*The Masque* is the scherzo, a scintillating display of jazz piano virtuosity, aided by harp, celesta, tuned and untuned percussion and double-bass. Bernstein included references to a song 'Aint Got No Tears Left' which he had omitted from the score of *On The Town*.

In the original 1949 version of *Epilogue*, Bernstein omitted the piano except for a single chord on the final page, described by him as 'one eager chord of confirmation'. Perhaps the necessity to finish the work in time for the première was the prime reason for excluding the piano. In 1965 he recast the movement, transferring some of the orchestra onto the piano and adding a cadenza.

The Adagio reprises the chorale of Variation I now on the strings, developing through a passage of Coplandesque folkiness to a grandiose affirmation of optimism (not in the Auden poem) also suggesting Copland whose Third Symphony concludes in a similar massive expression of hope.

Bernstein has confessed: 'I have a deep suspicion that every work I write for whatever medium is really theater music in some way.' This certainly applies to *The Age of Anxiety*, whose score proved an apt vehicle for dance. In 1950 with choreography by Jerome Robbins, it was staged at the City Center, New York. Although critical opinion was mixed, the ballet proved a great public success and has been revived elsewhere in the United States and Europe.

Symphony No.3 (*Kaddish*) was commissioned in 1953 by the Koussevitzky Music Foundation to celebrate the 75th anniversary of the Boston Symphony Orchestra. Pressure of conducting engagements and other musical commitments prevented Bernstein from beginning work until the summer of 1961. The short score was completed on 19 August 1963 and the orchestration finished in the following November. John Kennedy's assassination at the end of that month caused the composer to dedicate his new piece to the president's memory. The Third Symphony is scored for speaker, soprano solo, boys' choir, mixed chorus and large orchestra employing a huge percussion section. The Boston Symphony Orchestra generously ceded the première to the Israel Philharmonic Orchestra who gave the first performance in the Frederick Mann Auditorium in Tel Aviv on 10 December 1965 under Bernstein's direction. The soloists were Hannah Rovina of the Habimah Theatre as the speaker, and the soprano Jennie Tourel.

Only in a loose sense is this a symphony. Each of the three 'movements' includes a different setting of 'Kaddish', the Jewish prayer for the dead chanted at the graveside or in the synagogue. Interpolated between these are texts written by Bernstein himself. He had consulted Robert Lowell and Frederick Seidel but decided to write his own words. It was this aspect which led critics to have serious misgivings about the whole work.

The speaker attempts to define man's relationship with God, addressing the Deity in familiar terms at times in anger, at times in naive sentimental claptrap. Some anxiety was felt in advance of the Tel Aviv première that Bernstein would be accused of blasphemy but in the event strict orthodox Jews stayed away, deeming concert halls to be dens of iniquity. Only in the United States were religious objections raised.

Taste is a very personal matter and difficult to judge objectively, but even the composer admitted that the spoken text contained 'too much talk'. In 1976 he made cuts and revisions to the original wording. What many critics had objected to was the over-theatrical, often hysterical rendition of the speaker's part by his wife, the actress Felicia Montealegre. Taking the stylized roles of Joan in Honegger's *Jeanne d'Arc au Bucher* and the narrator in Debussy's *Le Martyre de St Sébastien* as models, her pseudo-ecstatic exaggerated interpretation aroused acute embarrassment. This was so 'over the top' that it was difficult to appreciate the rest of the music.

In the revised version, Bernstein rewrote several passages, not only altering the text but also providing chorus humming and instrumental accompaniment to support the speaker and generally tightening the structure. He also permitted the speaker to be a male; the later 1978 recording with Michael Wager avoids many of the excesses of the original but to some listeners this spoken part still presents an obstacle.

The direct confrontation with God can be seen as a general questioning of authority, especially that of father and son. At a dinner to celebrate his father's 75th birthday in 1962 Bernstein had said:

> What is a father in the eyes of a child? The child feels: My father is first of all my Authority, with power to dispense approval or punishment. He is secondly my Protector; thirdly my Provider; beyond that he is Healer, Comforter, Law-Giver, because he caused me to exist.... And as the child grows up he retains all his life, in some deep

part of him, the stamp of that father-image whenever he thinks of God, of good and evil, of retribution.

(Quoted in Humphrey Burton (1994) *Leonard Bernstein*, Faber & Faber: London, pp. 326–27)

At the ultimate challenge to the Almighty, the speaker reacts violently to the words given to God.

> For lo, I do set my bow in the cloud..
> And I will look upon it, that I
> May remember my everlasting covenant.'
> our covenant! Your bargain with Man!
> Tin god! Your bargain is tin!
> It crumples in my hand!
> And where is faith now – yours or mine?

This may seem an extreme response, but it is in the Jewish tradition to challenge God. A parallel arises in Bernstein's *Mass* at the point where the Celebrant dashes the cross from the altar.

In assessing the *Kaddish* Symphony it is necessary to look beyond the purely religious aspect of the spoken text since the work is deeply autobiographical to a greater degree than either of the previous symphonies. In no other work had Bernstein explored atonality to such an extent which is used to denote conflict. In simple terms tonality represents peace and reconciliation; thus the symphony can be seen as a journey from darkness to light, from dissonance to consonance.

The first part *Invocation* opens with the speaker addressing a prayer to God in preparation for Kaddish I in Aramaic with some Hebrew sung by the chorus. Beginning with deceptive quiet, the music suddenly bursts into a vigorous and troubled expression of anguish; the intention is to stun. The chorus is required not only to sing but also shout, stamp their feet in unison and clap jazzy counter-rhythms. Bernstein's favourite 7/8 rhythm creates constantly shifting metre fluctuations, similar to the Scherzo of the *Jeremiah* Symphony, but with fiercer brass and percussion adding to the aural onslaught.

The second movement *Din-Torah* presents the speaker's challenge to God supported by timpani, untuned percussion and humming chorus. There follows a violent outburst for the full orchestra, first on the strings, later reinforced by wind, brass and percussion in an atonal expressionist frenzy of colossal force, culminating in shouts of 'Amen' and a passage of choral aleatoric overlapping phrases. Once the tumult has passed, the speaker's apology to God leads to a setting of the *Kaddish* as 5/8 lullaby for soprano and boys' chorus.

In the third movement, *Scherzo*, the speaker's words are accompanied by ghostly Schoenbergian orchestration, that bursts into life to produce the first hint of hope and reconciliation in a warm diatonic theme that will re-emerge after the boys' singing of *Kaddish* III, a simple exuberant canonic setting in five parts which is reminiscent of Britten's writing for treble voices and looks ahead to similar passages in Bernstein's Mass.

The Finale which follows without a break opens with the dark tones of lower strings before the full orchestra ushers in an exultant choral section, again in 7/8 time that resembles the first of the *Chichester Psalms* Bernstein composed two years later.

*Kaddish* will remain a problem piece, as the infrequency of performances has proved. There are magnificent moments both in the choral and orchestral writing but one must concede that it is a flawed work.

# 20 The Present Generation

In all areas of daily life it is customary to lament that the present generation cannot compare with the past. Where are the heroes of today to equal those of the past? In music who can compare with Gershwin, the songwriter; Copland the universally recognized musical ambassador; Bernstein, the multi-talented, multi-media magician?

Within an eight-year span, 1938 to 1946, there lie at least nine major symphonies by American composers: Barber No.1 and No.2, Copland No.3, Bernstein *Jeremiah*, Hanson No.4, Harris No.3, Mennin No.3, Piston No.2, Schuman No.3. What have we to offer today?

The achievements of the composers in the following chapter presage a similar 'Golden Age'. It is too soon to assess with objectivity the significance of the last decade; even at this proximity, I believe these composers have already contributed a powerful body of work which is still expanding and which posterity will acknowledge as a massive hope for the future.

**Easley Blackwood** (b. 1933) studied with Olivier Messiaen at Tanglewood and with Bernard Heiden at Indianapolis University. The primary influences upon him were his time at Yale (1950–54) where he was a pupil of Hindemith and the years in Paris (1954–57) with Nadia Boulanger. He was appointed to the music faculty of the University of Chicago in 1958 where he has spent his entire career.

In Paris in December 1955 he completed his First Symphony, the work which established his name in the United States. The first performance took place in Boston on 30 March 1958, three days before his 25th birthday, by the Boston Symphony Orchestra conducted by Richard Burgin. For such a young composer he was fortunate that the symphony was accepted for publication and recorded by the Boston Symphony Orchestra under Charles Munch.

The ruthless non-romantic nature of the music owes much to the discipline acquired from his teacher Hindemith in its expert craftsmanship and, via Boulanger, a post-Roussel Gallic exuberance. Musical cross references between the four movements are another marked characteristic of French symphonic composers. Writing in *High Fidelity* about the First Symphony, Alfred Frankenstein commented: 'What captivated us about this symphony was its freshness, its vitality, its dramatic epical qualities and the sense of a lively, uncompromising talent at work'.

Symphony No.2 was composed in 1960 to mark the centenary of his publisher G. Schirmer Inc. It was introduced by the Cleveland Orchestra conducted by George Szell on 5 January 1961. In essence it resembles the First Symphony but with more dissonant harmonies as Blackwood began to adopt certain aspects of serialism.

Symphony No.3 (1964) for chamber orchestra was premièred on 7 March 1965 by the Chicago Symphony Orchestra conducted by Jean Martinon.

Blackwood devoted six years to writing his most ambitious work, Symphony No.4. It was commissioned in 1968 to celebrate the Illinois sesquicentennial and completed in 1973. Georg Solti conducted the première with the Chicago Symphony Orchestra on 22 November 1978. After 1980 Blackwood turned away from serial techniques towards a more traditional tonal language.

Symphony No.5, composed in 1990, would not have been out of place in the 1930s. The composer wrote:

> I originally conceived the work as the kind of symphony Sibelius might have written had he experimented with the modernist techniques that attracted composers like Casella and Szymanowski.

The sonata-form first movement has a youthful exhilaration abounding in lyrical melody and touches of modal harmony. A warm romanticism in the central *Adagio molto* contrasts radically with Blackwood's earlier symphonies. Mysterious references to the *Dies Irae* plainsong look back to the late nineteenth century. Critics might be disconcerted by the uninhibited finale which combines scherzo and rondo but the skill and vitality of the writing make this an audience winner.

Following the première Wynne Delacoma in the *Chicago Sun-Times* wrote: 'He [Blackwood] has succeeded in writing a well-crafted graceful work. The finger prints of Sibelius and other late-Romantic era composers are present in Blackwood's Fifth Symphony, in the music's spacious sweep and serene, unhurried melodies.'

The deliberate avoidance of modern trends has cost Blackwood wide acceptance of his music. Another cause of the relative neglect of his music might be attributed to his long-term residence in Chicago, a city which has lacked the focus of attention accorded to New York, Boston and the West Coast.

**William Bolcom** (b. 1938) studied at the University of Washington (Seattle), Stanford University and with Darius Milhaud at Mills College and Aspen, Colorado. On a French Government scholarship he continued as a student of Milhaud in Paris and was a pupil of Jean Rivier and Olivier Messiaen. After attending classes by Pierre Boulez in Darmstadt, Germany in 1960, Bolcom adopted interval-series techniques in his early works. With a one-act 'pop' opera *Dynamite Tonite* performed off Broadway in 1963, his music broadened in scope to take in American idioms with a gradual trend towards a more diatonic language.

Symphony No.1 is a student work written when Bolcom was 19 years old. He spent the summer of that year at the Aspen music school. It was at the suggestion of Darius Milhaud that he composed this four-movement work in just five weeks. The first performance was given on 16 August 1957 by the Aspen Festival student orchestra conducted by Carl Eberl.

The First Symphony is an assured if eclectic work. Bolcom described it as 'a short and sardonic symphony in the classical mold. It even has a repeated exposition in the first movement.' Reiterated intervals of a minor third bind the thematic material of the opening *Molto allegro*; the transparent texture is often reduced to single unison lines or simple two-part writing, reminiscent of Copland's *Short Symphony*. At one point a macabre waltz emerges for a brief appearance, typical of Bolcom's later use of sharply contrasted idioms in close proximity.

The slow movement, such admired by Milhaud, is a solemn procession, again sparsely scored, providing a distant echo of Roy Harris. The *Tempo di Menuetto* which follows is not a dance from the eighteenth century but a grotesque, expressionist movement. Milhaud is the composer brought to mind in the cheerful bustling rondo finale, with a glance towards Charles Ives in a tune that Bolcom admits to 'Sounding vaguely like *The Yellow Rose of Texas*'. This movement does not reach a conclusion; it simply stops.

Symphony No.2 (*Oracles*) composed in 1964, was premièred on 2 May 1965 by the Seattle Symphony Orchestra conducted by Milton Katims. The composer has withdrawn the score for revision.

Symphony No.3 (Symphony for Chamber Orchestra) was commissioned by the St Paul Chamber Orchestra who gave the official first performance under Dennis Russell Davies on 15 September 1979, although a preview had been heard three days earlier. Bolcom provided a brief description of the work:

> While there is nothing directly programmatic about the Symphony, I have several images that I might share about it. One is my own feeling that we are born from the collective unconscious and eventually return to it; thus the opening of the work is like the close. Another is the half-humorous visualization of three spirits (as in Mozart's *The Magic Flute* perhaps) who watch over the process of our birth and death and who are represented here by alto flute, English horn and first bassoon.

The score is prefaced by a Biblical quotation:

> Man, that is born of woman, hath but a short time to live, and is full of misery. He cometh up, and is cut down, like a flower; he fleeth as it were a shadow, and never continueth in one stay.

The first movement, *Aleph*, acknowledges eighteenth-century classical form with a sonata allegro, including a repeated exposition and development. In the slow introduction, against an eerie background of pianissimo muted tremolo violins, the three 'spirits' appear in turn, alto flute, bassoon, English horn, offering short cadenza-like prayers. As the music opens into the allegro, the mood alternates between dramatic and reflective gestures. The incisive rhythms and wide-ranging melodic lines remind one of other chamber symphonies, especially the two by Schoenberg.

Bolcom describes the second movement, *Scherzo Vitale*, as:

> A Seven Ages of Man in miniature, although not with any attempt to fix a program. At the beginning it seems as if many different ideas are propagated, but by the end it becomes clear that all of these ideas reduce to very little material; a dominant seventh, four scale-notes rising and falling – in other words, no more than a handful of musical chromosomes.

This is one of Bolcom's most curious creations; into the melting pot are thrown diverse fragments. Unexpectedly from this mélange there emerges a slow 1930s foxtrot in all its sentimental grandeur, with a catchy tune that looks back with nostalgia to a lost era. This in turn is interrupted by a hectic tarantella which itself is overtaken by a reprise of the dance in exaggerated Palm Court decor, after which the scene dissolves into thin air.

The third movement, *Chiaroscuro*, a short, highly chromatic and lightly scored interlude, balances atonal elements and the key of D flat major which serves as the leading note to the D major finale, *Omega*. This finale is very slow and predominantly quiet; the opening half is restricted to an extended melody for unaccompanied violins, broken at several points by silence. The serene concluding section is based on a sustained chord of D major, with a reappearance in the coda of the three woodwind spirits conferring a benediction on the symphony.

His Fourth Symphony, composed in 1986, differs from the other four in its setting for mezzo-soprano of a poem by Theodore Roethke (1908–1963) as its second movement. The opportunity to set the poem *The Rose* came with a commission from the St Louis Symphony Orchestra who performed the complete symphony under the direction of Leonard Slatkin on 13 March 1987, with the composer's wife Joan Morris as soloist.

Bolcom explained that he 'felt the setting needed a counterbalancing movement, structured musically in its own way as much as Roethke's quadripartite poem is'. The first movement 'Soundscape' for orchestra alone is in binary form, some 12 minutes in duration, half the length of the second movement. The composer described this rugged music as 'less thematic than textural'. He sees the whole symphony as 'like a reverse wedge in that it starts with high energy and progresses in stages towards a deep calm'. The opening bars of dazzling orchestral colour and reiterated rhythmic patters are reminiscent of Messiaen, even to the imitation of birdsong in the second movement. There is a narrative excitement to this volatile score with sufficient ever-changing material for a whole symphony.

Like Matthew Arnold in his poem 'Dover Beach', Roethke stands by the sea, interpreting the images he sees as reflections of his own thoughts. In the orchestral introduction of the second movement, Bolcom creates the stillness of the sea, a timeless atmosphere to prepare for Stanza I, where the poet describes the birds in flight: hawks, eagles, gulls, herons. Stanza II portrays the ships at sea. The rose of the title is observed amid seaweed, an emblem of survival with which the poet identifies himself. In Stanza III many of the lines are spoken by the soloist. Roethke considers birds in the garden, the seasons of the year and times of the day. Stanza IV concerns the rocks on the edge of the tranquil sea. Bird calls, drops of rain and rippling water are all vividly depicted in the orchestral score. The poet is transformed beyond his body:

And I stood outside myself
Beyond becoming and perishing,
A something wholly other.

The syllabic vocal line is by turns treated almost as recitative and lyrical melody closely integrated into the orchestral texture. (Samuel Barber's *Knoxville of Summer 1915* is a forerunner.) At times the orchestra prepares the way for the singer; at other times it reacts to the words. Bolcom moves from introspective gloom to celebratory joy. The glorious climax in Stanza II to the lines:

And I think of roses, roses
White and red...

reaches the sublime, a moment of intense uplifting emotion. The Fourth Symphony is one of the high peaks in Bolcom's impressive output of works.

Symphony No.5 was commissioned by the Philadelphia Orchestra on the instigation of Dennis Russell Davies, and dedicated to their manager Stephen Sell, who died before the score was complete. The work underwent a long period of gestation; several attempts by the composer ended up as other pieces of music. As with the two previous symphonies, Bolcom explored the polarities of tonal and non-tonal music in a manner that he described as 'a two-edged ironic feel, at once sardonic and grieving like certain kinds of satire'.

This is particularly evident in the first movement, *Pensive/Active*, the first mood in free tonality, the second tending towards the key of G minor. After a slow introduction, the movement is a sonata allegro. The combination of a powerful rhythmic impetus and compact development of material produces an opening movement of decisive intention.

There follows *Scherzo Mortale*, a companion piece to the *Scherzo Vitale* of the Third Symphony. The composer explained:

In my 1972 *Satires* for madrigal group I'd discovered that the funeral hymn 'Abide with me' and the Wedding March from *Lohengrin* fit in perfect Irving Berlin-style counterpoint – a funeral marriage, Love with Death; the same idea here, plus quotations from *Tristan* arranged in a big-band foxtrot tempo, adds to *Scherzo Mortale*'s Père-Lachaise cemetery creepiness.

Some clue to the intentions in this movement lies in the dedication to the Austrian composer H.K. Gruber, noted for his wildly anarchic *Frankenstein!* Bolcom conjures up a similar sinister world of pastiche and distortion. He is able to alternate instantly between slow and fast tempi as the snatches of the hymn and march surface. This manipulation of simple melodic fragments in a complex harmonic environment evokes the ghost of Mahler. The fearsome climax created by the jazzing-up of the Tristan motif sounds as if Armageddon has arrived.

Of the slow movement Bolcom writes:

*Hymne a l'Amour*, the same music as the last of my Twelve New Etudes for Piano (written for Paul Jacobs but not completed until after his death), treats the Love-Death axis from another more tragic viewpoint: Death generated by Love. In the Etudes, the *Hymne* feels like the triumph of the *Ewigweibliche*; here it is in ironic contrast to the rest of the work, particularly the concluding *Machine*.

A pervasive 8-note ostinato prevents this movement having a point of rest. The dissonant 'wrong-note' harmony of the brass chorale prepares the huge Messiaen-like colourful close where densely packed chords eventually resolve into a radiant chord of E major.

In the finale, subtitled *Machine*, Bolcom reproduces the mindless motor rhythms that mark the popular music of today. The relentless pounding beat, reminiscent of the *Dies Irae* movement of Honegger's Third Symphony (*Liturgique*) is menacing, most insidious when the music is relatively quiet.

The première of Symphony No.5 was given by the Philadelphia Orchestra under Dennis Russell Davies in Philadelphia on 11 January 1990.

Although the symphonies of William Bolcom reveal different characteristics, they are clearly the work of the same composer. His ambivalent use of tonality is all-pervading, as is the eventual resolution in most instances into a definite key. Unique to him is the ability to incorporate widely differing styles into a single movement without risking complete incongruity. His four extant works in the medium have established him in the forefront of American symphonic creation at the end of the twentieth century.

**John Harbison** (b. 1938) studied at Harvard with Walter Piston and in Berlin with Boris Blacher. The formative influence upon his music was the period from 1961 to 1963 when he was a pupil of Earl Kim and Roger Sessions at Princeton.

Harbison joined the music faculty at Massachusetts Institute of Technology, Cambridge in 1969. As a practical musician he learnt to play the piano, violin, viola and tuba. In addition he studied singing and was in his younger days a formidable jazz pianist. As a conductor of various choirs, orchestras and ensembles he has made a valuable contribution to musical life in and around Boston.

Although possessing complete individuality, Harbison's symphonies have a distinct family resemblance. The First Symphony was commissioned in 1980 by the Boston Symphony Orchestra to mark their centenary in the following year. Seiji Osawa conducted the première in March 1984 and recorded the work seven months later. Harbison began the score at the American Academy in Rome, completing it while living at the family farm in Token Creek, Wisconsin.

The symphony is in the traditional four movements. In principle, Harbison adopts Sessions' process of continuous variations but the language is more diatonic than that of his former teacher. Marked 'Drammatico', the opening movement originated in a dream the composer experienced in which he saw acquaintances, some of them musicians, performing mainly on metal instruments in a room used as a bar in Symphony Hall, Boston.

When I woke up I was haunted by the metallic harmonies, but it took a while to realize that they were in the public domain – that the 'composer' was an inhabitant of my subconscious. As with previous 'dream ideas' I felt able to get very close to what I had heard, and recognized the idea as one I was waiting for. The first idea permeates the whole piece: I thought of it as being like a forge.

Explosive repeated chords on brass and percussion like massive bells frequently interrupt the legato melodic flow. An incipient restless mood is occasionally alleviated by brief moments of more settled emotion. The very short fantastic scherzo is lightly scored and nimble in execution.

In the opening of the third movement, Harbison admitted the influence of songs by Schumann and Gershwin which he had been playing at the time. Beginning in a pastoral vein, there is a powerful but restrained emotion in this deeply moving music. A recurring interval of a low sixth was later identified by the composer as an unconscious reference to the closing bars of Seymour Shifrin's *In Eius Memoriam*, which he had recently conducted; Shifrin had died in 1979. Strong rhythms dominate the finale, an allegro based on a ritornello with varied episodes.

Symphony No.2 was performed by the San Francisco Symphony Orchestra in May 1987 under the direction of Herbert Blomstedt. The inspiration behind the work, which he called his 'theme song' was a poem by the Polish-American writer Czesław Miłosz (b. 1911) entitled 'A Task' which considers personal needs and constraints.

We are permitted to shriek in the tongues of dwarfs and demons,
But pure and generous words are forbidden.

The four movements, played without a break, are entitled Dawn, Daylight, Dusk and Darkness. How these parts of the day relate to the music itself is a mystery unrevealed by the composer.

Dawn breaks with luminous passionate string writing and bird calls on woodwind. Daylight bursts in with relentless energy. Against a *moto perpetuo* on violins, the rest of the orchestra indulge in a wild orgy, reminiscent in the trumpet and horn fanfares of Roussel's ballet *Bacchus et Ariadne*. As daylight merges into Dusk, dense elaborate string textures are accompanied by 'night nature' sounds. The enigmatic Darkness contrasts moments of calm with violent clashes and turmoil as if some giant monster is in its death throes. Mysterious fanfares on muted and open brass echo through the orchestra to herald the coming dawn. The close is equally strange when the music simply ceases. This fascinating symphony does not easily reveal its 'message'. Increased familiarity will bring out the overt musical argument but any intrinsic motivation behind its composition may continue to baffle.

The Third Symphony (1990) was composed for David Zinman and the Baltimore Symphony Orchestra who gave the première. In one extended movement, it develops along lines familiar in the previous two symphonies. Most notable is the bold innovative writing for brass and percussion, especially vibraphone, xylophone and marimba.

Harbison is currently working on his Fourth Symphony.

**John Corigliano** (b. 1933) studied with Otto Luening, Paul Creston and Vittorio Giannini. He established his name in 1964 in the United States with a Piano Concerto, followed by concertos for oboe (1975), clarinet (1977) and flute (1982). A *Thomas Trilogy*, three choral works to poems by Dylan Thomas completed in 1976 for the American Bicentennial added to his reputation. His second opera *The Ghosts of Versailles*, commissioned in 1984 for the centenary of the Metropolitan, New York proved to be one of the most successful contemporary operas in recent times.

Corigliano was over 50 before committing himself to write a symphony. Symphony No.1 was commissioned in honour of the centennial of the Chicago Symphony Orchestra and first performed in Chicago on 15 March 1990 under the baton of Daniel Barenboim.

The scoring is of Mahlerian proportions, 3 flutes *and* 3 piccolos, 3 oboes and English horn, 3 clarinets, E flat clarinet, bass clarinet, contrabass clarinet, etc. The composer instructs the brass to partially encircle the rest of the orchestra. Behind are 5 trumpets, flanked on either side by 3 horns, 2 trombones and tuba on the end of each semicircle. This creates a stereophonic antiphonal effect which is exploited at several points in the score.

Corigliano was driven to compose his Symphony as a response to the devastating AIDS epidemic in the United States. He explained:

> During the past decade I have lost many friends and colleagues to the AIDS epidemic, and the cumulative effect of those losses has, naturally, deeply affected me. My First Symphony was generated by feelings of loss, anger and frustration.
>
> A few years ago, I was extremely moved when I first saw 'The Quilt', an ambitious interweaving of several thousand fabric panels, each memorializing a person who had died of AIDS, and, more importantly, each designed and constructed by his or her loved ones. This made me want to memorialize in music those I have lost, and reflect on those I am losing. I decided to relate the first three movements of the Symphony to three lifelong musician-friends. In the third movement, still other friends are recalled in a quilt-like interweaving of motivic melodies.

Inevitably in a work originating from such deep personal feelings, the emotional and technical content will be closely integrated. Corigliano provided a detailed and comprehensive programme note which it would be pointless to paraphrase.

> Cast in free, large-scale A–B–A form, the first movement (Apologue: Of Rage and Remembrance) is highly charged and alternates between the tension of anger and the bittersweet nostalgia of remembering. It reflects my distress over a concert-pianist friend. The opening (marked 'Ferocious') begins with the nasal open A of the violins and violas. This note, which starts and finishes the symphony, grows in intensity and volume until it is answered by a burst of percussion. A repeat of this angry-sounding note climaxes, this time in the entrance of the full orchestra which is accompanied by a slow timpani beat. This steady pulse – a kind of musical heartbeat – is utilized in this movement as the start of a series of overlapping accelerandos interspersed with antagonistic chatterings of antiphonal brass. A final multiple acceleration reaches a peak climaxed by the violins in their high register, which begins the middle section (B).
>
> As the violins make a gradual diminuendo, a distant (offstage) piano is heard, as if a

memory, playing the Leopold Godowsky transcription of Albeniz's *Tango*, a favorite piece of my pianist-friend. This is the start of an extended lyrical section in which nostalgic themes are mixed with fragmented suggestions of the *Tango*. Little by little, the chattering-brass motives begin to reappear, interrupted by the elements of tension that initiated the work, until the lyrical 'remembrance' theme is accompanied by the relentless pulsing timpani heartbeat. At this point, the lyrical theme continues its slow and even rhythm, but the drumbeat begins simultaneously to accelerate. The tension of a slow, steady melody played against a slow, steady accelerando culminates in a recapitulation of the multiple accelerations heard earlier in the movement, starting the final section A.

By this time the accelerations reach an even bigger climax in which the entire orchestra joins together playing a single dissonant chord in a near-hysterical repeated pattern that begins to slow down and finally stops. Unexpectedly, the volume of this passage remains loud, so that the effect is that of a monstrous machine coming to a halt but still boiling with energy. This energy, however, is finally exhausted, and there is a diminuendo to piano. A recapitulation of the original motives along with a final burst of intensity from the orchestra and offstage piano concludes the movement, which ends on a desolate high A.

The second movement (Tarantella) was written in memory of a friend who was an executive in the music industry. He was also an amateur pianist, and in 1970 I wrote a set of dances (*Gazebo Dances* for piano, four hands) for various friends to play and I dedicated the final, tarantella, movement to him. This was a jaunty little piece whose mood, as in many tarantellas, seems to be at odds with its purpose. For the tarantella, as described in *Grove's Dictionary*, is a 'South Italian dance played at continually increasing speed [and] by means of dancing it a strange kind of insanity (attributed to tarantula bites) could be cured'. The association of madness and my piano piece proved both prophetic and bitterly ironic when my friend, whose wit and intelligence were legendary in the music field, became insane as a result of AIDS dementia. In writing a tarantella movement for this symphony, I tried to picture some of schizophrenic and hallucinatory images that would have accompanied that madness, as well as the moments of lucidity. This movement is formally less organized than the previous one, and intentionally so – but there is a slow and relentless progression toward an accelerated 'madness'. The ending can only be described as a brutal scream.

The third movement (Chaconne: Giulio's Song) recalls a friendship that dated back to my college days. Giulio was an amateur cellist, full of that enthusiasm for music amateurs tend to have and professionals try to keep. After he died several years ago, I found an old tape-recording of the two of us improvising on cello and piano, as we often did. That tape, dated 1962, provided material for the extended cello solo in this movement. Notating Giulio's improvisation, I found a pungent and beautiful motto which when developed, formed the melody played by the solo cello at this point in the symphony. This theme is preceded by a Chaconne, based on 12 tones (and the chords they produce) which runs through the entire movement. The first several minutes of this movement are played by the cellos and double basses alone. The chaconne chords are immediately heard, hazily dissolving into each other, and the cello melody begins over the final chord. Halfway through this melody, a second cello joins the soloist. This is the first of a series of musical rememberances of other friends (the first friend having been a professional cellist who was Giulio's teacher and who also died of AIDS).

At the conclusion of the section, as the cell recapitulates Giulio's theme, the solo trumpet begins to play the note A that began the symphony. This is taken up by the other brass, one by one, so that the note grows to overpower the other orchestral sonorities. The entire string section takes up the A and builds to a restatement of the initial assertive orchestral entrance in the first movement. The relentless drumbeat returns but this time it does not accelerate. Instead it continues its slow and somber beat against the chaconne augmented by two sets of antiphonal chimes tolling the 12 pitches as the intensity increases and the persistent rhythm is revealed to be that of a funeral march.

Finally, the march-rhythm starts to dissolve, as individual choirs and solo instruments accelerate independently, until the entire orchestra climaxes with a sonic explosion. After this, only a solo cello remains, softly playing the A that opened the work, and introducing the final part *Epilogue*.

The entire section is played against a repeated pattern consisting of waves of brass chords. Against this, the piano solo from the first movement (the Albeniz/Godowsky *Tango*) returns, as does the tarantella melody (this time sounding distant and peaceful) and the two solo cellos, interwoven between, recapitulate their dialogue. A slow *diminuendo* leaves the solo cello holding the same perpetual A, finally fading away.

Even without access to the specific references behind the music, it is possible to judge this symphony as an abstract work. The searing note A (A = AIDS?) that pervades the first movement and the pounding drumbeat have structural musical significance. The composer's own emotional reactions have been directed into musical order.

To follow the wild 'madness' of the Tarantella with its John Adams-like frenzied repeated figures, Corigliano produces ten minutes of utter calm in the Chaconne which opens the third movement. Here there are numerous inter-related motifs both conscious and subconscious that weld the four movements together. This is a symphony of considerable strength and integrity. In the five years following the première, the symphony has been taken up by over 60 orchestras.

**Gloria Coates** (b. 1933) studied with Alexander Tcherepnin at De Paul University, Chicago and with Otto Luening and Jack Beeson at Columbia University. In 1969 she settled in Munich where she pursued a varied career as composer, teacher, singer, actress and stage director. From 1971 to 1984 she organized the German American Contemporary Music Series and has been an active promoter of new music throughout Europe. In recent years she divides her time between Munich and New York.

The uniquely personal style of her orchestral works has few antecedents with only Penderecki and Lutoslawski as possible influences. Her compositional techniques are complex but the results for the listener are in essence relatively simple. Although the basic pulse of much of her music is slow, it usually contains a mass of internal activity. The ends can be seen in some respects minimal but the means are intricate and rigidly controlled.

Against repeated melodic patterns with tonal or modal centres, Coates creates dense textures of multi-sonic moving parts incorporating tone clusters, glissandi, microtones, close canons and other devices to produce a haze of sound, the musical equivalent of a painting by Turner or Whistler.

Not until Symphony No.7 (1990–91) did Miss Coates use the term 'symphony', numbering the previous six retrospectively. Symphony No.1 for string orchestra, her best-known work, is subtitled *Music on Open Strings*. It was composed between 1973 and 1974 and first performed on 20 September 1978 at the Warsaw Autumn Festival by the Polish Chamber Orchestra conducted by Jerzy Maksymiuk.

Every kind of string technique is employed, various means of bowing and pizzicato, glissandi, tremolos and striking the instrument. At the outset the strings are tuned to special pitches derived from Chinese scales given to her by her former teacher Alexander Tcherepnin (whose wife was Chinese), to whom the work is dedicated. These pentatonic tunings are B flat, C, D flat, F and G flat.

The first movement 'Themes and Transformation' begins with a simple unison melody in the bass line which builds up through much-repeated sequences to a massive climax of full string forces. The short second movement, Scherzo, mixes elaborate pizzicato effects with tremolos and the striking of the instruments in a percussive display of frenzy.

In the course of the third movement 'Scordatura', the instruments change their tuning to the orthodox western system (A, C, D, E, G) while playing, producing inevitable microtonal inflexions on long sustained notes. The combination of open string fifths creates an ever-evolving modal texture. In the fourth movement, 'Refracted Mirror Canon for Fourteen Lines', close canons with slow microtonal glissandi and fortissimo unco-ordinated across-the-string arpeggios generate sonic effects of an extraordinary richness.

Symphony No.2, doubly subtitled 'Illuminate in Tenebris' and 'Music in Abstract Lines' was commissioned for New Music America in 1989. Dedicated to the memory of the composer's father, it was first performed in New York by the Brooklyn Philharmonic Orchestra conducted by Tania Leon on 21 May 1989.

*Symphony Nocturne* (No.3) for string orchestra was completed in 1977 and first performed in Heidelberg, Germany by the Uppsala Festival Strings conducted by Roland Haroldson on 24 June 1988.

Symphony No.4, 'Chiaroscuro', was composed in 1984 and revised in 1990. Scored for full orchestra with a large percussion section including a flexatone, it was premièred by the Stuttgart Philharmonic Orchestra under Wolf-Dieter Hauschild on 22 June 1990.

The first movement 'Illumination' opens as a slow procession accompanied by moaning and wailing in the upper strings and woodwind. Through the dense foggy texture, there emerges a brass chorale which mutates into repetitions of the Lament from Purcell's opera *Dido and Aeneas*. Against this the rest of the orchestra add not so much counterpoint as simultaneous 'happenings' of chordal clusters of the most opaque kind. The shades of Charles Ives' *Central Park in the Dark* come to mind as the ear is distracted by a plethora of unrelated material.

The solemn tread of a funeral march pervades the central movement 'Mystical plosives', accompanied by ubiquitous glissandi. To some the repeated drum beats will be a reminder of *Mars* from Holst's Suite *The Planets*. It is probably a coincidence that Miss Coates had composed a work entitled *The Planets* in 1975. The funeral atmosphere is continued into the last movement 'Corridors of Time' with drones modified by quarter tones and very slow glissandi.

In Symphony No.5 'Three Mystical Songs' (1985–86), a double chorus vocalizes on texts by Alexandra Coates. The first performance took place on 7 November 1990 during the American Music Week in Berlin with the Spectrum Ensemble and the RIAS Chorus conducted by Marcus Creed.

*Music in Microtones* (Symphony No.6) was commissioned by Theodore Antoniou who conducted the première with the Alea III orchestra on 6 November 1987 during the American Music Week in Boston.

Symphony No.7, the only one of the set without a descriptive subtitle, was composed in 1991 to a commission from South German Radio, Stuttgart. It was first performed by the Stuttgart Philharmonic Orchestra conducted by Georg Schmoehe on 7 January 1992. It is dedicated to 'those who brought down the wall in PEACE'. Although this is not programme music, the composer expresses her strong support for those who achieve political freedom without violence.

The first movement, 'Whirligig of Time', unleashes a frenzied orchestral activity of rapid repeated figuration and canonic imitation in long passages of static harmony. The central movement alternates between free melodic expression and passages of intense collective agitation. In the finale multiple glissandi lead to a slowly accumulating crescendo of irresistable force before sinking to a less assertive conclusion. The effect is like an army of celestial vacuum cleaners supported by a squadron of dive bombers. The composer uses a large orchestra (quadruple woodwind and brass) with a formidable array of percussion including roto tom-toms and the much favoured flexatone.

Symphony No.8 subtitled 'Indian Sounds (Indian Grounds, Indian Mounds, Indian Rounds)' was composed in 1991 and performed in Munich by the Musica Viva Ensemble, Dresden, conducted by Juergan Wirrmann on 27 February 1992. It is scored for small orchestra to which are added exotic percussion including Indian instruments and chanting voices.

**Ellen Taffe Zwilich** (b. 1939) studied piano, trumpet and violin. From 1965 to 1972 she was a professional violinist in Stokowski's American Symphony Orchestra where she gained an invaluable insight into orchestral music. She believes strongly that composers should have practical skills. 'I think performance experience is absolutely critical for a composer.' Her activities as a jazz trumpeter in her youth are reflected in the particularly generous writing for the trumpet in her orchestral pieces.

As a student at Florida State University, Zwilich benefited from attending the conducting classes of the Hungarian composer Ernst von Dohnányi. Later she was a pupil of Elliott Carter and Roger Sessions at the Juilliard School. She is the recipient of numerous prestigious awards and has won popular acclaim without compromising her artistic integrity.

Since the early 1980s, Zwilich's music has moved away from the influences of the Second Viennese School and her former teacher Roger Sessions towards a more direct communication with her audience. Her use of repeated figures, emphatic unison passages and identifiable motifs combined with an overall coherent plan for each work make it possible to follow closely the musical argument.

Of her approach to composition she has said:

> It's the notion of a piece as a voyage that fascinates me. I think the central issue in composition is continuity. It's not just the material you use, it's how it unfolds. The trick is not only to write bar after bar, but to make it inexorable, so a piece grabs you and pulls you through.

Zwilich's Symphony No.1 subtitled 'Three Movements for Orchestra', was first performed by the American Composers' Orchestra, conducted by Gunther Schuller on 5 May 1982. It was awarded the Pulitzer Prize in 1983, the first to be awarded in music to a woman composer. In the preface to the printed score, the composer provided an insight into the music.

> First I have long been interested in the elaboration of large-scale works from the initial material. This 'organic' approach to musical form fascinates me both in the development of the material and in the fashioning of a musical idea that contains the 'seeds' of the work to follow.
>
> Second, in my recent works I have been developing techniques that combine modern principles of continuous variation with older (but still immensely satisfying) principles, such as melodic recurrence and clearly defined areas of contrast.
>
> Finally, Symphony No.1 was written with great affection for the modern orchestra, not only for its indescribable richness and variety of color, but also for the virtuosity and artistry of its players.

The entire work is based on the melodic and harmonic material of the first 15 bars, where the interval of a third predominates, with complex chords built up from multiples of thirds. The same interval pervades the bell-like sonorities which open the song-like second movement. The third movement serves as scherzo and finale, an arresting display of instrumental virtuosity. At a little over 17 minutes, the First Symphony is a compact piece, containing an abundance of material within the three movements.

Symphony No.2 (Cello Symphony) was composed in 1985 to a commission from the San Francisco Symphony Orchestra who performed it under Edo de Waart on 13 November of that year. The subtitle derives from a passage in the work where the entire cello section is given a cadenza.

Symphony No.3 was commissioned by the New York Philharmonic Orchestra for their 150th anniversary in 1992. The première on 25 February 1993 was conducted by Jahja Ling, deputizing at short notice for Kurt Masur. A sense of drama and adventure imbues the opening movement, beginning with a slow majestic recitative that leads to wide-ranging string melodies. Intriguingly Zwilich combines slow moving music on the strings with faster motifs on the wind. The tough and assertive central Vivace makes reference to material from the previous movement, contrasting *tutti* sections with passages of almost chamber music quality.

Mysterious cross-string arpeggios accompany the stately theme of the Largo finale which follows the scherzo without a break. Here there is a sense of a wanderer returning home after an active expedition.

Of the 'younger' generation, **Christopher Rouse** (b. 1949) has established an early reputation as a composer of serious orchestral music. He studied with Richard Hoffmann at the Oberlin College Conservatory and with Karel Husa and Robert Palmer at Cornell. He also took private composition lessons with George Crumb. Since 1981 he has taught composition at the Eastman School, Rochester NY. Subsequently he has also joined the composition faculty at the Juilliard School in New York. His Trombone Concerto of 1991 was awarded the Pulitzer Prize for Music in 1993.

While composer-in-residence with the Baltimore Symphony Orchestra he was commissioned to write a symphony in 1986. It was premièred in the following year. This striking single-movement work lasting half an hour sustains a slow tempo throughout. The dark ominous opening sets a mood of menace and impending doom; the hesitant emergence of melodic fragments, especially phrases on lower brass, echoes Wagner's *Gotterdammerung*. With no express programme, the Symphony could be viewed as a reflection of the troubles of the outside world.

Rouse claims that 'to live one's life now is an act of heroism'. In the symphony he endeavoured 'to express the feelings of those who can never recover from the blows of fate'. After facing overwhelming odds, the tragic hero is destroyed – like *Manfred*. His death serves no high purpose.

In his programme note for the first performance Rouse explained:

> In my Symphony No.1 I have attempted to pay conscious homage to many of those I especially admire as composers of *Adagios*: Shostakovich, Sibelius (4th Symphony), Hartmann (8th Symphony), Pettersson (7th Symphony) and William Schuman, for example. But only one is recognizably quoted (the famous opening from the second movement of Bruckner's Symphony No.7, played both in the original and here by a quartet of Wagner tubas).

The restless ebb and flow gradually builds to a stormy climax of frightening violence, three repeated notes pounding through the orchestra. This nagging figure reminds one of the slow movement of Vaughan Williams' Sixth Symphony, a similarly prophetic utterance. In the coda, an extended passage of relative calm is unexpectedly interrupted by a fierce cry of anguish before the eventual quiet close in a Shostakovich-like bleak musical landscape – sustained strings, celeste, brass and timpani.

Some critics were surprised, even shocked, that an American composer could express despair on such a massive scale. Hitherto only William Schuman and Peter Mennin had encapsulated unrelieved pessimism in a symphony. Richard Dyer of the *Boston Globe* described the First Symphony as 'Probably the most completely successful symphony yet written by an American composer of his rising generation'. The First Symphony has become one of the most frequently performed of American Symphonies, taken up by more than 20 major orchestras. In 1988 Rouse's First Symphony received the Kennedy Center Friedheim Award for the best American orchestral work premièred during the previous two years.

In 1995 the Houston Symphony Orchestra premièred Rouse's Second Symphony under their musical director Christoph Eschenbach, to whom the work is dedicated. There is a close relationship between the thematic material of the three movements. The Adagio is dedicated to the memory of the American composer Stephen Albert, a close friend of Rouse, who died in an automobile accident on 27 December 1992.

In a programme note the composer provided an insight into the form of the work.

> The central adagio functions as a kind of prism through which the music of the first movement is 'refracted', in the process altering the mood and affect. This adagio might be said to act as a tunnel through which the mercurial first allegro passes. At the other end of the tunnel, the allegro emerges recognizable, but with its light temperament darker and more threatening in tone. The arch-like form thus brings the symphony to a close at virtually the same structural point at which it began, but the emotional world of the conclusion is light years away from that of the beginning.

There is little one can add to the composer's comments. The heart of the Second Symphony is the Adagio, a movement almost equal in length to the other two combined. For the most part, it is a slow, almost static lament with an extended melody that begins on high violins, moving in turn to oboe, flute and trumpet, and finally, after a violent outburst of grief, to an unaccompanied bass clarinet which fades into silence. In contrast to the slow calm of the previous movement, the finale unleashes an unrelenting onslaught of anger, culminating in frantic cannonading timpani to release the pent-up emotions.

**Daniel Asia** (b. 1953) was born in Seattle. At Yale he was a pupil of Jacob Druckman and Penderecki. After teaching at the Oberlin Conservatory (1981–86) he joined the music faculty of the University of Arizona, Tucson in 1988 where he is Professor of Composition. His early compositions are dense in texture with complex rhythmic features. After facing practical problems of performance, Asia determined to make his music more accessible and direct for the sake of players and listeners.

Symphony No.1 was commissioned in 1987 jointly by the Seattle Symphony Orchestra and the American Composers Orchestra. The première took place on 19 February 1990 by the Seattle Symphony Orchestra conducted by Christopher Kendall. Asia based this work on five of the seven movements of his *Scherzo Sonata* for piano of 1987.

Symphony No.2 (1988–90) is also partly derived from another composition, *Celebration* (1988) for baritone, chorus, brass quintet and organ written for a Massachusetts synagogue. It was first performed by the Tucson Symphony Orchestra conducted by Robert Bernhardt on 30 April 1992. Asia gave the symphony a double subtitle: *Celebration Symphony: Khagiga In Memoriam Leonard Bernstein*.

The five movements are based on parts of the Jewish Sabbath prayer service. 1. *Ma Tovu* (Your love is great); 2. *Ashrenu* (Therefore it is our duty to thank and praise you); 3. *L'kha Adonai* (Yours, O Lord is the greatness); 4. *Hine El Yeshvati* (Behold God is my deliverance); 5. *Halleluyah*. A mood of strong religious devotion permeates the work, in which Asia succeeds in producing a synthesis of Hasidic tradition and symphonic form. In the finale the sprung rhythms have a Messiaen-like ecstacy including flashes of birdsong.

Symphony No.3 (1992) was written for the Phoenix Symphony Orchestra 'Meet the Composer' program, and premièred under the direction of James Sedares on 6 May 1993. As with the previous two symphonies, Asia incorporated another work into the score, *At the Far Edge*, written in 1992 for the Seattle Youth Orchestra. The opening section of the first movement and the finale between them encapsulate the earlier piece. This 40-minute symphony shows some influence of both Copland and Bernstein.

Symphony No.4 was composed in 1994 to a commission from the Phoenix Symphony Orchestra who premièred it on 27 October 1994 under the composer's direction.

# 21 Symphonic Music for Band

The considerable expansion of the concert band repertoire in the second half of the twentieth century to include large-scale serious compositions has inevitably led composers to write symphonies for such emsembles. Wind ensemble, wind band and concert band are terms almost but not quite synonymous. Wind ensemble implies one instrument to a part. Wind band suggests some multiples of certain instruments, particularly clarinets and brass. Symphonic or concert band by its very name means that the players are seated. Some doubling is often the case and there is the inclusion of non-portable instruments, especially percussion, tuned and untuned, double-basses and sometimes harp and piano. The Anglo-European brass band is rarely found in North America except in the Salvation Army.

The *Theme and Variations* for symphonic band composed by Arnold Schoenberg in 1943 and Hindemith's Symphony in B flat (1951) for concert band bestowed respectability on a medium that to many is still associated with marching bands. The concert band repertoire can be divided into two categories: those works written by composers who specialize in band music and those by composers more accustomed to the symphony orchestra who have broadened their horizons.

Among the former is **Warren Benson** (b. 1924). He studied at the University of Michigan and was for a time timpanist with the Detroit Symphony Orchestra. He has taught composition at Ithaca College, New York (1957–67) and at the Eastman School since 1967. His two symphonies are landmarks in band music.

Symphony for drums and winds orchestra (1962) was commissioned by the American Wind Symphony who premièred the work in Pittsburgh on 4 July 1964. Benson had studied African drumming and its influence is notable especially in the outer movements, although he does not use any African music as such. The scoring includes four sets of timpani, and five solo percussionists who cover a range of different drums and tuned percussion. The instruments are arranged spatially across the back of the platform to produce antiphonal effects.

In the first movement, tension is created by the exchanges between the different sets of drums, like skirmishes in a battle. The wind, which had a secondary role, are brought to the fore in the second movement, an elegiac chorale beginning on woodwind and building to a climax for the whole band. Ghostly percussion opens the finale, a long and gradual crescendo of accumulating excitement created by brilliant jazzy rhythmic figures over extended pedal points, before the music slowly subsides back to the quiet opening and eventual silence. Symphony No.1 represents a *tour de force* of percussion writing that has been imitated by numerous other composers since.

By contrast Symphony No.2 Lost Songs (1982) is a more introverted piece, cast in a single movement of a huge span lasting almost half an hour. At a predominantly slow tempo, Benson builds up a complex dissonant harmonic texture of overlapping sonorities above long sustained pedal points. At the centre of the symphony there is a brief increase in pace but the original tempo is soon restored for a graduated return to the calm of the opening. These two substantial symphonies in their different ways demonstrate the huge potential that is offered by the concert band of today, where performance standards are often on a par with those of leading professional orchestras.

The two symphonies for band of **John Barnes Chance** (1932–1972), No.1 in C (1956) and No.2 (1972), are the work of another expert who handles his forces with consummate skill. The Second Symphony, Chance's last work, is an intense piece obsessively based on a four-note motto, C#, D, F, E, in all three movements. It cannot be a coincidence that these notes are the same as those that represent Shostakovich's 'musical signature' DSCH (D, E flat, C, B) reversed and transposed up a tone. As with Shostakovich, this motto must represent some autobiographical significance.

A slow introduction, quiet and mysterious, announces the motto at various pitches before embarking on the stormy allegro where the four notes occur in almost every bar. In the second movement, the dark mood prevails. Long sustained chords supporting the motto. The finale which follows without a break is a violent dance totally preoccupied with the figure. The Second Symphony is an unremittingly serious work, deeply personal with an added air of tragedy in the light of Chance's early death in the same year as a result of a domestic accident.

Mention should also be made of **H. Owen Reed**'s *La Fiesta Mexicana* of 1948, later given the subtitle 'A Mexican Folk Song Symphony'. Its extensive use of Latin American rhythms and tunes has made it a classic of its kind. Reed, a pupil of Hanson, Harris and Bernard Rogers, travelled extensively abroad studying folk music which influenced his compositions. From 1939 to 1976 he taught at Michigan State University.

A major contribution to symphonic band music has been made by the prolific **Walter S. Hartley** (b. 1927) whose opus numbers exceed 200. Nine of his eleven Sinfonias and three of his four Symphonies are scored for wind instruments, ranging from full symphonic band to ensembles of saxophones and tubas. He studied at the Eastman School with Burrill Phillips, Herbert Elwell, Bernard Rogers and Howard Hanson. In 1995 he was commissioned to write *Centennial Symphony* to mark the 100th birthday of Howard Hanson. Hartley has taught at several universities and is Professor Emeritus and Composer in Residence at the State University of New York, Fredonia.

The similarly industrious **Timothy Broege** (b. 1947) has composed 18 Sinfonias, mostly for symphonic wind band or wind ensembles. He is a graduate of Northwestern University, Evanston, Illinois where he studied composition with William Karlins, Alan Stout and Anthony Donato. Currently he teaches at Monmouth Conservatory in Red Bank, New Jersey.

**Frank Erickson** (b. 1923) has spent a lifetime in the service of band music as a composer and arranger. His three symphonies (1954), (1959), (1984) and Sinfonia (1973) are frequently performed. **Alfred Reed** (b. 1921) has written music in all forms, but is specially known for his band compositions, including an impressive set of five symphonies.

Among the symphonies written by non-band specialists, **Vincent Persichetti**'s Symphony No.6 for band has remained a popular item since its première in St Louis on 16 April 1956. It has received hundreds of performances, being his most frequently heard work. In the classical four-movement form, the symphony is tuneful, exuberant and brilliantly scored for every instrument. The lyrical woodwind writing in the two central movements has touches of folk-song, gratefully distributed among the instruments. It is perhaps the energetic and rhythmic outer movements that make this a band favourite among players.

In a more serious mood, but equally expertly devised is **Vittorio Giannini**'s Third Symphony written in 1959 for the band of Duke University, North Carolina. Giannini (1907–1966), of Italian parentage, is best known as an opera composer. He also taught composition at the Juilliard School from 1939 until his death.

**Morton Gould** (1913–1996) wrote his Symphony No.4 for the West Point Band who performed it under the composer's direction on 13 April 1952. 'Epitaphs', the first of the two movements, begins in a pastoral vein, broadening into a powerful contrapuntal *tutti* of some force before an unexpected transformation into a cheery, humorous march in which the players are required to stamp their feet in imitation of marching soldiers. Fragments of tunes are tossed around the band, reminiscent of a Charles Ives' collage. The music fades into the distance leaving a sole muted trumpet in the closing bars.

The second movement 'Marches' begins in the distance. Spiky rhythms and catchy tunes recall the fife and drum military music of the Civil War where hints of 'Dixie' and other popular melodies pass swiftly by. A full-blooded fugue leads to the more dignified coda and a grand final flourish. As one would expect for a composer of experience and expertise, Gould provides a rewarding piece for his players at West Point, combining wit with more weighty material.

Among the many symphonies by Alan Hovhaness, six are scored for wind band. His approach is similar to that of the orchestral works, making use of Eastern idioms and scales, especially Armenian chant, with strong quasi-religious modal harmony. Symphony No.4 (1959) and Symphony No.20 (*Three Journeys to a Holy Mountain*) (1968) have found favour with bands in search of out-of-the-way works that do not make excessive technical demands upon the players.

Of a more specific kind than traditional band music, are symphonies for brass and percussion by Gunther Schuller and Herbert Haufrecht. Both are scored for the orthodox orchestral brass, not the more extended brass instrumentation of the standard band.

Symphony for Brass and Percussion by **Gunther Schuller** (b. 1925), composed in 1950, is an early work which combines the 12-note system with classical form. First performed under Leon Barzin at an International Society for Contemporary Music concert in New York in 1950, it was later taken up by Dimitri Mitropoulos and the New York Philharmonic Orchestra who gave the European première at the Salzburg Festival in 1957.

In addition to his activities as a composer, **Herbert Haufrecht** (b. 1909) is noted as an editor and arranger of American music who has worked extensively behind the scenes in the music publishing business. Of his Symphony for Brass and Timpani he writes:

> The Symphony was composed between 1953 and 1956. That was a time when, after a long period of wars, all mankind yearned for peace. This theme is reflected in the Symphony in the titles of its movements. Beyond that the work has no program.
>
> It may seem paradoxical that I have chosen an instrumental combination commonly associated with the military and war to plead the cause of peace. An answer to this might be found in the lines of *Isaiah*, 'And they shall beat their swords into plowshares...'. By bringing out the expressive qualities of the brass instruments alongside their somber and clangourous aspect, I have sought to endow them with more human utterance.

In the first movement, 'Dona Nobis Pacem', Haufrecht treats his forces in the manner of a present day Gabrieli with antiphonal exchanges between the instrumental groupings and imitative counterpoint combining homophonic chorales with joyous fanfares. The second movement 'Elegy' is a passacaglia; the finale 'Jubilation' recalls music of the opening, transformed into triumphant peace celebrations.

# Postscript

Throughout the twentieth century, writers on music, many of them practising composers, have between them confirmed and denied that there is a distinctive 'American' music to compare with European models. In 1903 Arthur Farwell was certain that the United States had already produced its own kind.

> A new day of American music is not about to dawn, it had already dawned with the appearance of an appreciable number of persons who no longer demanded solely the product of European art, and the appearance of an appreciable number of composers to supply that demand. And now the number has vastly increased.

> ('The Affirmation of American Music', *The Musical World*, Vol. III, No.1, January 1903)

A decade later Henry F.B. Gilbert was less convinced:

> In a truthful and honest consideration of the art of Musical Composition in America, one is compelled to admit that there are as yet no real American composers. That is, speaking in the same sense in which we consider Beethoven, Wagner and Strauss as German composers; Delibes, Massenet or Saint-Saens as French composers; and Verdi, Rossini and Donizetti as Italian composers.
>
> In the sense of the foregoing we certainly do not have *American* composers. Possibly one reason for this, and perhaps the greatest reason, is that we have hardly as yet developed an American race. The population of America is, as everyone recognizes, a hodge-podge of almost all conceivable racial elements.

> ('The American Composer', *The Musical Quarterly*, Vol. I, No.2, 1915)

Those who had taken up Dvořák's challenge to explore home-grown material soon discovered that folk-song alone was insufficient to create a new nationalism.

> One explanation of the failure of American nationalism through the quotation of folk music lies in the absence of a homogeneous population with a peasant or folk culture that could provide music recognizable by an entire population as American. European composers had a tradition of country dances and folk melodies from which to draw for their compositions.

> (Barbara L. Tischler (1986) *An American Music*, Oxford University Press: New York, p.6)

193

In 1945 the critic and composer Deems Taylor expressed anxiety over the desire for composers to be American. Had he been alive today, much of his disquiet would have been resolved.

> People seem to be worrying almost continuously because they can see no sign of an American 'school' of music. They seem to feel that it is very slow in getting under way, and keep poking at it in an effort to make it move faster. Opinions differ as to what kind of school it ought to be, and just what should be its characteristics. Some think it ought to convey the spirit of American independence and initiative, the spaciousness of the wind-swept prairies and the solitude of the Grand Canyon; the uncurbed spirit of the Boston Tea Party, coupled with a slight hint of the Monroe Doctrine.
>
> There are others who think it should convey the roar of the cities, the mechanical perfection of the airplane engine, and the relentless mechanization of the Ford plant. Still others want it to be expressive of our idealism and international goodwill – the Ku Klux Klan and the brotherhood of man.
>
> But the quest continues, the search for an American musical speech, some characteristic turn of harmony, melody or rhythm that will stamp its creator's nationality beyond the possibility of doubt, the search that has bedevilled American music and musicians for a century. It is a vain one, I think. There is no American School of music, and I doubt that there will ever be one.

> (Deems Taylor (1945) *Music and the Flag: Of Men and Music*, Simon and Schuster: New York, pp. 123, 126)

All of Deems Taylor's references can be found in American music, but in the realm of symphonic music, the strength of personality of the individual has predominated over mere pursuit of American themes to create the body of works which characterize what is recognized as American. Raw nationalism has been sought only by minor figures. Similarly, the leading orchestras in the United States have developed their own particular sound which makes them different from their European colleagues.

Through their environment and culture, Ives, Copland, Harris, Schuman, Barber and Sessions and other major composers were inevitably American, but their achievements were a result of their own innate genius. Their music has a universality beyond nationalism. Virgil Thomson's aphorism that to be an American composer all that one requires is to be an American and to write music may be simplistic but is fundamentally true.

Daniel Gregory Mason has identified this contention as early as 1928:

> But in art no formula can be universal, and it is precisely the pretension of nationalism to universality that is its most injurious trait. Nationalism is excellent as an ingredient, but disastrous as a dogma. The promising way towards a rich and various American music seems much less likely to lie through any system of branding, organizing, and licensing, such as nationalism and all other 'isms' are too apt to foster, than through an elastic eclecticism of individual choice.

> (*The Dilemma of American Music* (1928) Macmillan Co.: New York)

A distinctive 'American' style is easier to recognize than describe. Generalizations are not particularly helpful and it is impossible and unprofitable to place composers in 'schools'. In 1933 Roy Harris identified two tendencies developed by American composers.

1. The avoidance of definite cadences which can be traced to our unsymmetrically balanced melodies (difficult to harmonize with prepared cadences) and to our national aversion to anything final, our hope and search for more satisfying conclusions.
2. the use of modal harmony which probably comes from *ennui* of the worn-out conventions of the major and minor scales and our adventurous love of the exotic.

(Henry Cowell (ed.) (1933) *American Composers on American Music*, Stanford University Press: Stanford)

These observations are true of the music written in America at that time. What remains distinctly American through all the stylistic changes is the unique attitude to rhythmic flexibility, which Harris described in the same article as different from the European approach.

European musicians are trained to think of rhythm in its largest common denominators, while we are born with a feeling for its smallest units.

The current generation of symphonic composers: Bolcom, Corigliano, Harbison, Rouse, Zwillich *et al.*, represent a distinctive American voice without resorting to folk-song or jazz as a stimulus. These composers live and work in cities, their music is performed in concert halls as part of the artistic heritage of cities and broadcast by urban radio stations. The log cabin belongs to the past; we are now in the world of the skyscraper.

In the twenty-first century, American composers can look forward to the future with confidence that they are equal partners with their European contemporaries, no longer a fringe novelty but a significant part of Western musical culture, with an impressive history of which to be proud. As musical life on both sides of the Atlantic develops and changes, composers in the United States will cease to be seen primarily as American (*pace* Thomson), simply as composers.

# Catalogue of Symphonies by American Composers

ADOMIAN, Lan b. 29 April 1905, d. 9 May 1979

Symphony No.1     (Sinfonia Lirica)
Symphony No.2     (Espanola)
Symphony No.3
Symphony No.4     (Une Petite Musique pour Sachenk)
Symphony No.5     (Yaare Hak'Doshim)
Symphony No.6     (Le Cadeau de la Vie)
Symphony No.7
Symphony No.8

AHLSTROM, David C. b. 22 February 1927

Symphony

AHRENDT, Karl b. 7 March 1904

Symphony in three movements (1944)

ALBERT, Stephen b. 6 February 1941, d. 27 December 1992

River Run Symphony (1984)
Symphony No.2 (1992)

ALETTE, Carl b. 31 May 1922

Symphony for chamber orchestra (1954)

ALEXANDER, Josef b. 15 May 1907

Symphony No.1     (Clockwork) for strings (1947)
Symphony No.2     (1954)
Symphony No.3     (1961)
Symphony No.4     (1968)

ALEXANDER, William Peddie b. 8 November 1927

Symphony No.1     (1957)
Symphony No.2     (1982)
Symphony No.3     (1987) withdrawn

ALIFERIS, James b. 1913, d. 22 December 1992

Symphony No.1

ALLANBROOK, Douglas Phillips b. 1 April 1921

Symphony No.1     (1958)
Symphony No.2     in one movement (An Elegy) (1964)
Symphony No.3     (Four Orchestral Landscapes) (1967)
Symphony No.4
Symphony No.5     for brass quintet and orchestra (1977)
Symphony No.6     (Five Heroic Attitudes) (1978)
Symphony No.7     (Music from the Country) (1979)

ALLEN, Paul Hastings b. 28 November 1883, d. 28 September 1952

| | |
|---|---|
| Symphony No.1 | in G minor (Al Mare) |
| Symphony No.2 | in C (Cosmopolitan) |
| Symphony No.3 | in E (Liberty) (1912) |
| Symphony No.4 | in A (Lyra) |
| Symphony No.5 | in E (Phoebus) |
| Symphony No.6 | in D (Pilgrim Symphony) (1937) |
| Symphony No.7 | in E flat (Somerset) |
| Symphony No.8 | in D (Utopia) |

ALMAND, Claude b. 31 May 1915, d. 12 September 1957

Symphony (The Waste Land) (1940)

ALSPACH, Addison b. 1904

Symphony in A minor

AMES, William b. 20 March 1901

| | |
|---|---|
| Symphony No.1 | (1933) |
| Symphony No.2 | (1943) |

AMIRKHANIAN, Charles Benjamin b. 19 January 1945

Symphony No.1 for 4 perc., trumpet trio, clarinet, piano and viola (1965)

ANDERSON, Arthur Olaf b. 30 January 1880, d. 11 January 1958

Symphony in F

ANDERSON, John Maxwell b. 11 August 1948

Symphony No.1

ANDERSON, Michael b. 26 January 1938

| | |
|---|---|
| Chamber Symphony | (1965) |
| Symphony In A | (Commemorating Carl Sandburg) (1967) |
| Symphony No.2 | in three movements (1964) |

ANDERSON, Thomas Jefferson b. 17 August 1928

Classical Symphony (1961)
Symphony in three movements (1963)
Chamber Symphony in one movement (1968)

ANTHEIL, George b. 8 July 1900, d. 12 February 1959

| | |
|---|---|
| Symphony No.1 | (Zingareska) (1920–22, rev. 1923) |
| Jazz Symphony | (1925, rev. 1955) |
| Symphony in F | (1925–26) |
| Symphony No.2 | (1931–38, rev. 1943) |
| Symphony No.3 | (American) (1936–39, rev. 1946) |
| Symphony No.4 | (1942) |
| Symphony No.5 | (Tragic) (1945–46) |

Symphony No. 5      (Joyous) (1947–48)
Symphony No.6       (After Delacroix) (1947–48, rev. 1949–50)
Symphony No.7       (1953–54) incomplete

APPLEBAUM, Edward b. 28 September, 1937

Symphony (1970)

ASENJO, Florencio Gonzalez b. 28 September 1926

Symphony No.1       for strings (1948)
Symphony No.2       (Instrumental Dialogues) (1979)
Symphony No.3       (Crystallizations: a Symphony in the Nascent State) (1989)

ASIA, Daniel (Isaac) b. 27 June, 1953

Symphony No.1       (1987)
Symphony No.2       (Celebration) (1990)
Symphony No.3       (1992)
Symphony No.4       (1993)

AUSTIN, Elizabeth b. 1938

Wilderness Symphony for 2 narrators and orchestra

AVRAM, David b. 30 June 1930

ESRAJ Symphony Op.84 (1971–73)
Symphony of Alleluias Op.103 for chorus and orchestra (1983)

AVSHALOMOV, Aaron b. 12 November 1894, d. 16 April 1965

Symphony No.1       in C minor (1938–39)
Symphony No.2       (Chinese) in E minor (1949)
Symphony No.3       in B minor (1950)
Symphony No.4       (1951)

AVSHALOMOV, Jacob b. 28 March, 1919

Symphony (The Oregon) (1959–61)
Symphony of Songs

## B

BABBITT, Milton b. 10 May 1916

Symphony (1941) incomplete: withdrawn

BACON, Ernst b. 26 May 1898, d. 16 March 1990

Symphony No.1       in D (1931)
Symphony No.2       (1937)
Symphony No.3       (Great River) (1956) with narrator
Symphony No.4       (1962–63)

BAKER, Joseph W. b. 11 September 1937

Symphony in E

BALADA, Leonard b. 22 September 1933

Sinfonia en Negro    (Symphony in Black) (Homenaje a Martin Luther King) (1968)
Steel Symphony    (1973)

BALAZS, Frederic b. 12 December 1919

An American Symphony (1945)
Symphony on a Plain Chant Fragment (1954)

BANFIELD, William b. 1951

Symphony No.1
Symphony No.2
Symphony No.3
Symphony No.4
Symphony No.5
Symphony No.6    (Four Songs for Five American Voices) for two trumpets and orchestra

BARANOVICK, Fred b. 28 June

Symphony for Strings

BARATI, George b. 3 April 1913, d. June 1996

Symphony (1964)

BARBER, Samuel b. 9 March 1910, d. 23 January 1981

Symphony No.1    Op.9 in one movement (1938, rev. 1942)
Symphony No.2    Op.19 (1944, rev. 1947)

BARLOW, Wayne b. 6 September 1912

Sinfonia da Camera (1962)

BARNES, James Charles b. 9 September 1948

Symphony No.1    in D for symphonic wind band
Symphony No.2    in E flat for symphonic wind band
Symphony No.3    in C for symphonic wind band

BARROW, Edward

Symphony (1952)

BARTH, Hans b. 25 June 1897, d. 8 December 1956

Pantomine Symphony    (1937)
Symphony No.2    Op.25 (Prince of Peace) (1948)

BARTLETT, Edwin

Symphony No.1    (1937)

BASSETT, Leslie Raymond b. 22 January 1923

Symphony in B       (No.1) (1949) withdrawn
Symphony No.2       (1955–56) withdrawn

BAUER, Marion Eugenie b. 15 August 1887, d. 9 August 1955

Symphony            (1947–50)

BAUER, Raymond

Symphony No.1       in C (1941)

BAUM, Russell

Symphony (1933)

BAUMAN, John Ward b. 7 June 1939

Little Symphony     (1977)
Symphony            No. 2 (1994)

BAVICCHI, John Alexander b. 25 April 1922

Festival Symphony for band Op.51 (1963–65))
Symphony No.2       for brass Op.70 (1975–76)

BAZELON, Irwin Allen b. 4 June 1922, d. 2 August 1995

Symphony No.1       (1960)
Symphony No.2       (Testament to a Big City) (1962)
Symphony No.3       for brass, percussion, piano and string sextet (1962)
Symphony No.4       (1964–65)
Symphony No.5       (1966)
Symphony No.6       (1969)
Symphony No.7       (Ballet for orchestra) (1980)
Symphony No.8       for strings (1986)
Symphony No.8$^{1}/_{2}$   (1988)
Symphony No.9       (Sunday Silence) (1990)
Symphony No.10      (1992–1995) (incomplete)

BEACH, Amy Marcy Cheney (Mrs H.H.A.) b. 5 September 1867, d. 27 December 1944

Gaelic Symphony in E minor Op.32 (1896)

BEACH. Perry W. b. 24 October 1917

Symphony            (1952) incomplete

BEADELL, Robert Morton b. 18 June 1925

Symphony No.1       (1962–63)
Symphony No.2       for mezzo-soprano, baritone, chorus and orchestra (1987)

BEALE, James b. 20 January 1924

Symphony No.1       for chamber orchestra Op.10 (1950)
Cressay Symphony    (No.2) Op.26 (1961)

BEALL, John Oliver b. 12 June 1942

Symphony No.1

BECK, Johann Heinrich b. 12 September 1856, d. 26 May 1924

Symphony (Sinbad)   (1876–77)

BECKER, John Joseph b. 22 January 1886, d. 21 January 1961

| | | |
|---|---|---|
| Symphony No.1 | (Etude Primitive) | (1912–15) |
| Symphony No.2 | (Fantasia Tragica) | (1920, rev 1937) |
| Symphony No.3 | (Sinfonia Brevis) | (1929–31) |
| Symphony No.4 | (Dramatic Episodes) for speaking chorus and orchestra (1938) | |
| Symphony No.5 | (Homage to Mozart) for chamber orchestra (1942) | |
| Symphony No.6 | (Out of Bondage) narrator, soprano & chorus (1942) | |
| Symphony No.7 | (The Sermon on the Mount) with speaking and singing chorus and soloists (1954) | |

BECKETT, Wheeler Martin Alfred b. 7 May 1898, d. 25 January 1986

Symphony in C minor

BECKHELM, Paul b. 3 July 1906

Symphony in F      (1948)

BEESON, Jack Hamilton b. 15 July 1921

Symphony in A (1959)

BEGLARIAN, Grant b. 1 December 1927

Symphony in two movements (1950)
Sinfonia for orchestra (1961)
Sinfonia for strings   (1974)

BELL, Elizabeth b. 1 December 1929

Symphony No.1 (1971)

BELL, Larry b. 17 January 1952

Sacred Symphonies    (1985)

BENCRISCUTTO, Frank (Peter Anthony) b. 21 September 1928

Symphony No.1
Symphony No.2      (1959)

BENNETT, Robert Russell b. 15 June 1894, d. 18 August 1981

Abraham Lincoln Symphony   (1927)
Symphony in D      (for the Dodgers) (1941)
Symphony No.3      (The Four Freedoms) (1943)
Symphony No.4      (1946)
Symphony No.5      (1963)

BENOIT, Kenneth Roger b. 12 October 1952

Symphony No.1
Symphony No.2      (1988)

BENSON, Warren Frank b. 26 January 1924

Symphony for drums and wind orchestra (1962)
Symphony No.2      (Lost Songs) for symphonic band (1983)

BEREZOWSKY, Nicolai b. 17 May 1900, d. 27 August 1953

Symphony No.1      Op.12 (1925)
Symphony No.2      Op.18 (1933)
Symphony No.3      Op.21 (1936)
Symphony No.4      Op.29 (1943)

BERG, Cherney b. 1922

Symphony No.1

BERGER, Jean b. 27 September 1909

Sinfonia di San Petronio for three trumpets and strings (1951)
Short Symphony      (1952)

BERGSMA, William Laurence b. 1 April 1921, d. 1994

Symphony for chamber orchestra (1942)
Symphony No.1      (1946–49)
Symphony No.2      (Voyages) for soloists, chorus and orchestra (1976)

BERLINSKI, Jacques b. 13 December 1913

Symphony No.1      (Symphony of Glory) (1965)
Symphony No.2      (America 1976) for chorus and orchestra (1976)

BERNSTEIN, Leonard b. 25 August 1918, d. 14 October 1990

Symphony No.1      (Jeremiah) with mezzo-soprano (1942)
Symphony No.2      (The Age of Anxiety) with piano (1948)
Symphony No.3      (Kaddish) with speaker, mezzo-soprano, chorus and orchestra (1961–63, rev. 1977)

BERVERSDORF, (Samuel) Thomas b. 8 August 1924, d. 15 February 1981

Symphony No.1      Op.4 (1946)
Symphony No.2      Op.10 (1950)
Symphony No.3      Op.18 for wind and percussion (1954, rev. for orchestra 1958)
Symphony No.4      Op.29 (1958)

BEVERIDGE, Thomas Gattrell b. 6 April 1938

Symphony of Peace for chorus and orchestra
Symphony No.2      (To the Masters)
Symphony No.3

BEZANSON, Philip (Thomas) b. 6 January 1916, d. 11 March 1975

Symphony No.1     (1946)
Symphony No.2     (1950)

BIGGS, John Joseph b. 18 October 1932

Symphony No.1     (1964)
Symphony No.2     (1992)

BILIK, Jerry H. b. 7 October 1933

Symphony for band (1972)

BINKERD, Gordon Ware b. 22 May 1916

Symphony No.1     (1955)
Symphony No.2     (1957)
Symphony No.3     (1959)
Symphony No.4     (1963) rev. as *Movement for Orchestra*

BIRD, Arthur Homer b. 23 July 1856, d. 22 December 1923

Symphony in A     Op.8 (1885)

BISH, Diane b. 1941

A Symphony of Hymns
A Symphony of Psalms

BLACKWOOD, Easley Rutland b. 2 April, 1933

Chamber Symphony  Op.2 (1954)
Symphony No.1     Op.3 (1955)
Symphony No.2     Op.9 (1960)
Symphony No.3     Op.14 for small orchestra (1963)
Symphony No.4     (1968)
Symphony No.5     (1978)

BLANK, Allan b. 27 December 1925

Symphony (1994)

BLITZSTEIN, Marc b. 2 March 1905, d. 22 January 1964

Symphony (The Airborne) for narrator, baritone, men's chorus and orchestra (1943–44)

BLOCH, Ernest b. 24 July, 1880, d. 15 July 1959

Symphony in C sharp minor (1901)
Israel Symphony     (1912–17)
Sinfonia Breve      (1952)
Symphony for trombone and orchestra (1953–54)
Symphony in E flat  (1954–55)

BLUMENFELD, Harold b. 15 October 1923

Symphony Amphitryon 4 (1962)

BOATWRIGHT, Howard (Leake Jnr) b. 16 March 1918

Symphony (1976)

BODA, John b. 2 August 1922

Symphony No.1
Symphony No.2
Symphony No.3      (1954)

BOHRNSTEDT, Wayne b. 19 January 1923

Symphony No.1      in E (1951)

BOISE, Otis Bardwell b. 13 August 1844, d. 2 December 1912

Symphony

BOLCOM, William Elden b. 26 May 1938

Symphony No.1      (1957)
Symphony No.2      (Oracles) (1964)
Symphony No.3      for chamber orchestra (1979)
Symphony No.4      with soprano (1986)
Symphony No.5      (1990)

BOROWSKI, Felix b. 10 March 1872, d. 6 September 1956

Symphony No.1      in D minor (1932)
Symphony No.2      in E minor (1933)
Symphony No.3      in G (1937)

BOTTJE, Will Gay b. 30 June 1925

Symphony No.1      (1946) withdrawn
Symphony No.2      withdrawn
Symphony No.3      (1953) withdrawn
Symphony No.4      for band (1956)
Symphony No.5      (1958)
Symphony No.6      for brass, organ & percussion (1963)
Symphony No.7      (Tangents) with tape (1970)

BOWDER, Jerry Lee b. 7 July 1928

Symphony No.1      (1956)
Symphony No.2      (1959)
Symphony No.3      (1968)
Symphony No.4      (Celebration Music) (1976)

BOYADJIAN, Hayg b. 15 May 1938

Symphonia for strings (1980–81)

BRANCA, Glenn b. 6 October 1948

Symphony No.1      (Tonal Plexus) (1981)
Symphony No.2      (The Peak of the Sacred) (1982)

Symphony No.3        (Gloria) (1983)
Symphony No.4        (Physics) (1983)
Symphony No.5        (Describing Planes of an Expanding Hypersphere) (1984)
Symphony No.6        'Devil Chorus at the Gates of Heaven' (1986)
Symphony No.7        (1991)
Symphony No.8        (1992)
Symphony No.9        (L'Eve future) for wordless chorus and orchestra (1993)

BRADSHAW, Merrill Kay b. 18 June 1929

Symphony No.1
Symphony No.2
Symphony No.3
Symphony No.4
Symphony No.5        (1979)

BRANCH, Harold

Chamber Symphony Op.5 (1957)

BRANDT, William Edward b. 14 January 1920

Symphony No.1        (1949)

BRANT, Henry Dreyfus b. 15 September 1913

Symphony No.1        in B (1931)
The Promised Land, a Symphony of Palestine (1941)
Symphony in B flat (The Thirties) (1943–46)
Symphony for percussion (1950)

BRICCETTI, Thomas B. b. 14 January 1936

Symphony No.1        (1956–57) withdrawn

BRICKEN, Carl Ernest b. 28 December 1898, d. 25 January 1971

Symphony No.1        in one movement (1935)
Symphony No.2
Symphony No.3

BRICKMAN, Joel Ira b. 6 February 1946

Symphony in three movements (1968, rev. 1984)

BRIGHT, Robert Houston b. 21 January 1916

Symphony in E minor

BRINGS, Allen Stephen b. 24 February 1934

Symphony (1964, rev. 1984)

BRISMAN, Heskel b. 12 May 1923

Sinfonia Breve (1956)

BRISTOW, George F. b. 19 December, 1825, d. 13 December 1898

Symphony No.1    in E flat Op.10 (1843)
Symphony No.2    in D minor (Jullien) Op.24 (1853)
Symphony No.3    in F sharp minor Op.26 (1858)
Symphony No.4    (Arcadian) in E minor Op.49 (1872)
Symphony No.5    (Niagara) for solo voices, chorus and orchestra Op.62 (1893)

BRITAIN, Radie b. 17 March 1899*, d. 23 May 1994

Southern Symphony (1936–37)
Cosmic Mist Symphony (1962)

*Date of birth is variously recorded as 1903, 1904 and 1908. Her daughter confirms 1899
to be correct.*

BROCKWAY, Howard b. 22 November 1870, d. 20 February 1951

Symphony in D Op.12 (1895)

BROEGE, Timothy David b. 6 November 1947

Sinfonia I (Eland) with jazz-rock ensemble (1971)
Sinfonia II for concert band (1972)
Sinfonia III (Quodlibet for 25 players) for wind ensemble with piano (1972)
Sinfonia IV (Suite for winds and percussion) (1972)
Sinfonia V (Symphonia Sacra et Profana) for wind ensemble (1973)
Sinfonia VI for concert band (1974)
Sinfonia VII (The Continental Saxophone) for wind ensemble with solo instruments
    (1976)
Sinfonia VIII (Songs of Walt Whitman) for concert band with treble chorus and piano
    (1977)
Sinfonia IX (A Concert in the Park) for symphonic band (1977)
Sinfonia X    a) for concert band (1980)
              b) Prelude, Dance and Forced March for orchestra (1987)
Sinfonia XI (1982)
Sinfonia XII (Southern Heart/Sacred Harp) for wind ensemble with piano (1983)
Sinfonia XIII (Storm Variations) for symphonic band (1984)
Sinfonia XIV (Tre Canzoni) for wind ensemble and piano (1985)
Sinafonia XV (Ursa Major) for wind ensemble (1988)
Sinfonia XVI (Transcendental Vienna) for concert band (1989)
Sinfonia XVII (Four Winds) for concert band (1989)
Sinfonia XVIII (Aurora) for wind orchestra (1995)

BROEKMAN, David Hendrines b. 13 May 1899, d. 1 April 1958

Symphony No.1
Symphony No.2

BROHN, William David b. 30 March 1933

Symphony in D

BROOKS, Richard b. 26 December 1942

Symphony (1981)

BROWN, Harold b. 31 October 1909

Symphony No.1
Symphony No.2

BROWN, Philip b. 27 July 1933

Symphony No.1
Symphony No.2

BROWN, Rayner b. 23 February 1912

Symphony No.1    (1952)
Symphony No.2    (1957)
Symphony No.3    (1958)
Symphony No.4    (1980)
Symphony No.5    (1982)
Symphony No.6    (1982)

BRUCKER, Howard

Symphony (1961)

BRUNE, Adolf Gerhard b. 21 June, 1870, d. 21 April 1935

Symphony No.1
Symphony No.2    in E minor Op.29 (1929)
Symphony No.3

BRUNSWICK, Mark b. 6 January, 1902, d. 26 May 1971

Choral Symphony (Eros and Death) for mezzo-soprano, chorus and orchestra (1934–37, rev. 1954)
Symphony in B flat (1945)

BRYAN, Charles Faulker b. 26 July 1911, d. 7 July 1955

White Spiritual Symphony

BUCK, Dudley b. 10 March 1839, d. 6 October 1909

Symphony in E flat (Springtime) Op.70 (lost)

BURLEIGH, Cecil b. 17 April 1885, d. 30 July 1980

Symphony No.1    (Creation) (1944)
Symphony No.2    (Prophesy) (1944)
Symphony No.3    (Revelation) (1944)

BURNHAM, Cardon Vern b. 25 February 1927

Symphony No.1    (Bharata) (1961)

BURTON, Stephen Douglas b. 24 February 1943

Symphony No.1    (1968)
Symphony No.2    (Ariel) for voice and orchestra (1976)

BUTLER, Lois b. 25 May 1912

Symphony of the Hills


# C


CADMAN, Charles Wakefield b. 24 December 1881, d. 30 December 1946

Symphony in E minor (Pennsylvania) (1939)

CALABRO, Louis b. 1 November 1926, d. 21 October 1991

Symphony No.1    in one movement (1956)
Symphony No.2    for strings (1957)
Symphony No.3    in one movement (1959–64)

CALLAHAN, James b. 15 January 1942

Symphony No.1
Symphony No.2    (Markings) for baritone, chorus and orchestra

CAMPBELL, Arthur M. b. 4 April 1922

Symphony No.1    (1958)

CAMPBELL, Charles Joseph b. 8 August 1930

Symphony No.1
Symphony No.2

CAMPBELL-WATSON, Frank b. 22 January 1898

Symphony No.1
Symphony No.2

CAMPO, Frank Philip b. 4 February 1927

Symphony for chamber orchestra Op.9 (1952)
Symphony (Seven Dialogues) Op.17 (1958)

CAREY, Mell

Short Symphony (1958)

CARPENTER, Howard Ralph b. 11 October 1919

Symphony in D (1954)

CARPENTER, John Alden b. 28 February 1876, d. 26 April 1951

Symphony No.1    (Sermon in Stones) (1917)
Symphony in C    (1940) based on Symphony No.1
Symphony No.2    (1942, rev. 1947)

CARROLL, J. Robert b. 31 January 1927

Symphony for strings and percussion (1971)

CARTER, Elliott Cook b. 11 December 1908

Symphony          (1937) withdrawn
Symphony no.1     (1942, rev. 1954)
Symphony of Three Orchestras (1976)
Symphonia         (1993–97)

CASSLER, G. Winston b. 3 September 1906

Symphony (De institutione musica) (1949)

CAZDEN, Norman b. 23 September 1914, d. 18 August 1980

Symphony Op.49    (1948)

CERVONE, D. Donald b. 27 July 1932

Sinfonia tuttu claveri for keyboards and orchestra (1973)

CESANA, Otto b. 7 July 1899, d. 9 December 1980

Symphony No.1
Symphony No.2
Symphony No.3
Symphony No.4
Symphony No.5
Symphony No.6

CHADWICK, George Whitefield b. 13 November 1854, d. 4 April 1931

Symphony No.1     in C Op.5 (1881)
Symphony No.2     in B flat Op.21 (1883–85)
Symphony No.3     in F (1893–94)

CHAMBERS, Wendy Mae

Symphony of the Universe (1989) for tape, timpani, organ, chorus and orchestra

CHANCE, John Barnes b. 20 November 1932, d. 16 August 1972

Symphony No.1     in C (1956)
Symphony No.2     for band (1972)

CHANDLER, Hugh Humphrey

Symphony in D (1989)

CHARLES, Elizabeth

Little Symphony (1941)

CHESLOCK, Louis b. 25 September 1898, d. 19 July 1981

Symphony in D minor (1932)

CHIHARA, Paul Seiko b. 9 July 1938

Symphony No.1     (Symphony in Celebration) (Ceremony V) (1975)
Symphony No.2     (Birds of Sorrow) (1981)

CHILDS, Barney b. 13 February 1926

Symphony No.1    (1954)
Symphony No.2    (1956)

CHRISTENSEN, Robert

Symphony (1963)

CIRONE, Anthony J. b. 8 November 1941

Symphony No.1    for percussion
Symphony No.2    for percussion
Symphony No.3    (Sacred) for percussion

CLAFLIN, Avery b. 21 June 1898, d. 9 January 1979

Symphony No.1    in D minor (1936)
Symphony No.2    (1942–44)
Symphony No.3    (Four Pieces for Orchestra) (1955–56)

CLAPP, Philip Greeley b. 4 August 1888, d. 9 April 1954

Symphony No.1     in E (1908, rev. 1932)
Symphony No.2     in E minor (1911)
Symphony No.3     in E flat (1917)
Symphony No.4     in A (1919, rev. 1941)
Symphony No.5     in D (1926, rev. 1941)
Symphony No.6     in B (Golden Gate) (1927–28)
Symphony No.7     in A (1927–29)
Symphony No.8     in C (1930, rev. 1934, 1937, 1947, 1950)
Symphony No.9     in E flat minor (The Pioneers) (1931)
Symphony No.10    in F (Heroic Symphony) (1935, rev. 1943)
Symphony No.11    in C (1942, rev. 1950)
Symphony No.12    in B flat (The Rime of the Ancient Mariner) (1944)

CLARK, Robert Keyes b. 18 Novemer 1925, d. 1981

Symphony No.1    Op.10 (1952)
Symphony No.2    Op.12 (1953)
Symphony No.3    Op.38 (1963)

CLARKE, Laurence G. b. 8 February 1928

Sinfonia for strings

CLOKEY, Joseph Waddel b. 28 August 1890, d. 14 September 1960

Dorian Symphony in E minor (1942)
Canterbury Symphony for chorus and orchestra

COATES, Gloria b. 10 October 1938

Symphony No.1     (Music for Open Strings for string orchestra (1973–74)
Sinfonia Brevis    (Fonti di Rimini) (1976/1984)
Symphony No.2     (Illuminatio in Tenebris: Music in Abstract Lines) (1974/1988)
Symphony No.3     (Symphony Nocturne) for strings (1976–77)

| | |
|---|---|
| Symphony No.4 | (Chiaroscuro) (1984/90) |
| Symphony No.5 | (Three Mystical Songs) for chorus and orchestra (1985–86) |
| Symphony No.6 | (Music in Microtones) (1986) |
| Symphony No.7 | (1990–91) |
| Symphony No.8 | (Indian Sounds) (1991) |

COBB, Schribner

Short Symphony in F (1943)

COHEN, David b. 14 October 1927

| | |
|---|---|
| Symphony No.1 | (1965) |
| Symphony No.2 | (1970) |

COHN, Arthur b. 6 November 1910

Symphony for double orchestra (1937) withdrawn

COHN, James Myron b. 12 January 1928

| | |
|---|---|
| Symphony No.1 | in E flat Op.11 (1947) |
| Symphony No.2 | in F Op.13 (1949) |
| Symphony No.3 | in G Op.27 (1955) |
| Symphony No.4 | in A Op.29 (1958) |
| Symphony No.5 | in B flat Op.32 (1959) |
| Symphony No.6 | in B Op.43 (1965) |
| Symphony No.7 | in D Op.43 (1967) |
| Symphony No.8 | (1978) |

COKER, Wilson b. 26 November 1928

Symphony No.1

CONE, Edward Toner b. 4 May 1917

Symphony (1953)

CONSTANTINIDES, Constantine (Dinos) Demetrios b. 10 May 1929

| | |
|---|---|
| Symphony No.1 | (1967) |
| Symphony No.2 | (Introspections) (1983) |
| Symphony No.3 | for wind ensemble (1988) |
| Symphony No.4 | (Antigone) (1993) |
| Symphony No.5 | (1996) |

CONVERSE, Frederick Shepherd b. 5 January 1871, d. 8 June 1940

| | |
|---|---|
| Symphony in D minor Op.7 (1898) withdrawn | |
| Symphony No.1 | in C minor (1919) |
| Symphony No.2 | in E minor (1921) |
| Symphony No.3 | in F (1934) |
| Symphony No.4 | in F minor Op.107 (1939)* |

*The manuscript score of this work gives it the number 6.

COOK, Richard G. b. 20 October 1929

Symphony No.1
Symphony No.2

COOKSON, Frank

Symphony No.1        in F minor (1945)

COOLIDGE, Richard Ard b. 1 November 1929

Symphony (1963)

COOPER, John Craig b. 14 May 1925

Symphony No.1
Symphony No.2

COOPER, Paul b. 19 May 1926, d. 1996

Symphony No.1        (Concertant) for solo oboe and wind (1954)
Symphony No.2        (Antiphons) (1956)
Symphony No.3        for strings (Lamentations) (1971)
Symphony No.4        (Landscape) (1973)
Symphony No.5        (1983)
Symphony in two movements (1982–83)
Sinfonia for strings    (1952)

COPLAND, Aaron b. 14 November 1900, d. 2 December 1990

Symphony No.1        for organ (1924); version without organ (1928)
Dance Symphony       (1930)
Short Symphony       (No.2) (1932)
Symphony No.3        (1944–46)

COPLEY, R. Evan b. 22 March 1930

Symphony No.1
Symphony No.2
Symphony No.3
Symphony for band

CORDERO, Roque b. 16 August 1917

Symphony No.1        in E flat (1945)
Symphony No.2        in one movement (1956)
Symphony No.3        (1965)
Symphony No.4        (Panamanian) (1986)

CORIGLIANO, John Jnr b. 16 February 1938

Symphony            (1990)

CORNELL, Richard Eugene b. 18 August 1946

'Blanco': a symphony on a poem of Octavio Paz (1989)

CORTES, Ramiro b. 25 November 1933, d. 2 July 1980

| Sinfonia Sacra | (1954) |
| Sinfonia Breve | (1955–58) |

COWELL, Henry Dixon b. 11 March 1897, d. 10 December 1965

| Symphony No.1 | in B minor (1918, rev. 1940) | |
| Symphony No.2 | (Anthropos: Mankind) | (1938–39) |
| Symphony No.3 | (Gaelic) | (1942–43) |
| Symphony No.4 | (Short) | (1945) |
| Symphony No.5 | | (1948) |
| Symphony No.6 | | (1952) |
| Symphony No.7 | | (1952) |
| Symphony No.8 | (Choral) | (1952) |
| Symphony No.9 | | (1953) |
| Symphony No.10 | for chamber orchestra | (1953) |
| Symphony No.11 | (Seven Rituals of Music) | (1953) |
| Symphony No.12 | | (1954) |
| Symphony No.13 | (Madras) for Indian instruments | (1955) |
| Symphony No.14 | | (1956) |
| Symphony No.15 | (Thesis) | (1960) |
| Symphony No.16 | (Icelandic) | (1962) |
| Symphony No.17 | (Lancaster) | (1962) |
| Symphony No.18 | | (1964) |
| Symphony No.19 | | (1964) |
| Symphony No.20 | | (1965) |
| Symphony No.21 | (sketches) | (1965) |
| | completed by Lou Harrison | |

COWLES, Darleen Louise b. 13 November 1942

Chamber Symphony (1965)

CRESTON, Paul (Joseph Guttoveggio) b. 10 October 1906, d. 24 August 1985

| Symphony No.1 | Op.20 | (1940) |
| Symphony No.2 | Op.35 | (1944) |
| Symphony No.3 | Op.48 | (Three Mysteries) (1950) |
| Symphony No.4 | Op.52 | (1951) |
| Symphony No.5 | Op.64 | (1955) |
| Symphony No.6 | (Organ Symphony) Op.118 (1981) | |

CROOM, John Robert b. 27 April 1941

Symphony for brass and percussion

CROSSMAN, Allan b. 12 December 1942

Symphony No.1    (1979–82)

CUNNINGHAM, Michael Gerald b. 5 August 1937

Free Designs (Symphony) Op.45 (1971)
Irish Symphony Op.48 for strings (1972)
Symphonic Arias (Symphony) for solo singers, chorus and orchestra Op.74 (1976)

CURRY, Vicki Lynn

Symphony in two movements (1988)

CUSENZA, Frank Jerome b. 25 December 1899

Symphony for four movements

CUSTER, Arthur b. 21 April 1923

Symphony No.1      (Sinfonia de Madrid) (1961)

CUTLER, Harry Lynn

The Cycle of Life Symphony (1977)

CZERWONKY, Richard Rudolph b. 23 May 1886, d. 16 April 1949

Symphony


**D**

DALLIN, Leon b. 26 March 1918

Symphony in D      (1948–49)
Chamber Symphony (1940–41)

DANA, Walter b. 26 April 1902

Symphony in C minor

DANBURG, Russell L. b. 2 March 1919

Symphony (1934)

DANIELPOUR, Richard b. 28 January 1956

Symphony No.1      (Dona Nobis Pacem) (1985)
Symphony No.2      (Visions) (1986)
Symphony No.3      (Journey Without Distance) (1989)

DANKNER, Stephen b. 5 November 1944

Symphony (1969)

DAUGHERTY, Michael b. 1954

Metropolis Symphony   (1988–93)

DAVID, Avram b. 30 June 1930

Symphony (ESRAS)

DAVIDSON, Jerome

Symphony in one movement (1933)

DAVIS, Jean Reynolds b. 1 November 1927

Symphony No.1      in one movement
Symphony No.2

DAVIS, John S. b. 1 October 1935

Symphony No.1
Symphony No.2

DAVIS, William Dwight b. 6 April 1949

Symphony in two movements (1971)

DAVIS, William Mac Jnr

Symphony in three movements (1981)

DAVISON, John Herbert b. 31 May 1930

Symphony No.1      for small orchestra (1958)
Symphony No.2      (1959)
Symphony No.3      for winds (1964)
Symphony No.4      for strings (1969)
Symphony No.5      (1979)
Symphony No.6      for chamber orchestra (1993)

DAVISON, Peter b. 26 October 1948

Symphony No.1

DAVYE, John Joseph b. 19 October 1929

Symphony in one movement

DAWSON, William Levi b. 23 September 1899, d. 2 May 1990

Negro Symphony      (1932, rev. 1952)

DEBIASE, Joseph R.

Symphony No.1
Symphony No.2      (1962)

DE FILIPPI, Amedeo b. 20 February 1900

Symphony      (1930)

DE GASTYNE, Serge b. 27 July 1930

Symphony No.1      in one movement (1951)
Symphony No.2      (L'Ile Lumière)
Symphony No.3
Symphony No.4      for band
Symphony No.5      (1970)
Symphony No.6      (1973)

DELAMARTER, Eric b. 18 February 1880, d. 17 May 1953

Symphony No.1    in D (1914)
Symphony No.2    in G minor (after Whitman) (1926)
Symphony No.3    in E minor (1931)
Symphony No.4    (1932)

DELANEY, Robert Mills b. 24 July 1903, d. 21 September 1956

Don Quixote Symphony (1927)
Choral Symphony (John Brown's Song) (1931)
Symphony No.2    (1942)

De LEONE, Francesco Bartolomeo b. 28 July 1887, d. 10 December 1948

Symphony in D minor

DELLO JOIO, Norman b. 24 January 1913

Symphony for Voices and Orchestra (Western Star) (1945) withdrawn and revised as Song
  of Affirmation
The Triumph of St Joan Symphony (1951)

DE LONE, Peter

Symphony No.1    (1960)

DEL TREDICI, David Walter b. 16 March 1937

An Alice Symphony for amplified soprano, folk group and orchestra (1969–75, rev. 1991)

DENNY, William Douglas b. 2 July 1910, d. 2 September 1980

Symphony No.1    (1939)
Symphony No.2    (1949)
Symphony No.3    (1955–57)

DERBY, Richard William b. 23 January 1951

Symphony         (1977)

DE SOMARY, Gene David b. 3 March 1948

Chamber Symphony

DETT, Robert Nathaniel b. 11 October 1882, d. 2 October 1943

Symphony in E minor

DEYO, Felix b. 21 April 1888, d. 21 June 1959

A Lyric Symphony    (1949)
An Ancient Symphony
A Primeval Symphoy

DIAMOND, Arline Rhoda b. 17 January 1928

Symphony

DIAMOND, David Leo b. 9 July 1915

Symphony No.1      (1941)
Symphony No.2      (1942)
Symphony No.3      (1945)
Symphony No.4      (1945)
Symphony No.5      (1947–64)
Symphony No.6      (1951–54)
Symphony No.7      (1959)
Symphony No.8      (1958–60)
Choral Symphony 'To Music' for tenor, baritone, chorus and orchestra (1969)
Symphony No.9      (Michaelangelo Buonarroti) for baritone and orchestra (1985)
Symphony No.10    (1992)
Symphony No.11    (1992)
(Two early symphonies (1933, 1935) and a chamber symphony withdrawn)

DIAMOND, Stuart Samuel b. 15 January 1950

Symphony in one movement

DICK, Marcel b. 28 August 1898, d. 13 December 1991

Symphony          (1950)

DICKINSON, Clarence b. 7 May 1873, d. 2 August 1969

Organ Symphony (Storm King) (1921)

DI DOMENICA, Robert Anthony b. 4 March 1927

Symphony          (1961)

DIEMER, Emma Lou b. 24 November 1927

Symphony No.1      (1952–53)
Symphony No.2      on American Indian themes (1959)
Symphony No.3      Symphonie Antique (1961)

DOELLNER, Robert

Symphony for strings (1947)

DONAHUE, Robert L. b. 8 March 1931

Symphony No.1      for strings (1960)
Symphony No.2      (1963)

DONATO, Anthony b. 8 March 1909

Symphony No.1      (1944)
Symphony No.2      (1945)

DONOVAN, Richard Frank b. 29 November 1891, d. 22 August 1970

Symphony for chamber orchestra (1936)
Symphony in D      (1946)

DORAN, Matt H(iggins) b. 1 September 1921

Symphony No.1        (1946)
Symphony No.2        (1959)
Symphony No.3        (1977)
Symphony No.4        (1977)
Chamber Symphony  (1980)

DORATI, Antal b. 9 April 1906, d. 13 November 1988

Symphony No.1        (1957)
Symphony No.2        (Quereia Pacis) (1985)

DORFF, Daniel Jay b. 7 March 1956

Symphony of Delusions for band

DORSAM, Paul b. 25 January 1941

Symphony No.1
Symphony No.2        (1970)
Symphony No.3        (1970)
Symphony No.4        (1971)

DOUGLAS, Samuel Ostler b. 31 March 1943

Sinfonia Ecclesiastica; chorus and chamber orchestra (1970)

DOWNEY, John Wilham b. 5 October 1927

Symphony (Modules 5) (1972)
Symphony No.1        (1993)

DOWNS, Lamont Wayne b. 9 March 1951

Sinfonia for wind band (1969)
Electric Symphony for junior wind ensemble

DREW, James Mulcro b. 9 February 1929

Symphony No.1        for chamber orchestra (1966–68)
Symphonies for chorus orchestra and three conductors (1969)
Symphony No.2        for chorus and orchestra (1971)
Symphony No.3        (1977)

DROSSIN, Julius b. 17 May 1918

Symphony No.1
Symphony No.2
Symphony No.3
Symphony No.4
Symphony No.5

DUBENSKY, Arcady b. 15 October, 1890, d. 14 October 1966

Symphony in G minor (1916)

DUDLEY, Marjorie Eastwood

Symphony in E flat Op.12 (1938)

DUENO COLON, Braulio b. 26 March 1854, d. 4 April 1934

Sinfonia Dramatica (1878)
Noche de otono Symphony   (1886)
Ecos de mi tierra Symphony   (1892)

DUKELSKY, Vladimir (Vernon Duke) b. 10 October 1903, d. 16 January 1969

Symphony No.1    in F (1928)
Symphony No.2    in D flat (1931)
Symphony No.3    in E (1946)

DUNFORD, Benjamin C. b. 2 September 1917

Symphony          (1952)

DUNN, James Philip b. 10 January 1884, d. 24 July 1936

Symphony in C (1929)

DURHAM, Lowell M. b. 4 March 1917

Symphony No.1    Op.4 (1945)

DUTTON, Brenton Price b. 20 March 1950

Symphony No.1    (1966)
Symphony No.2    (1972)
Symphony No.3    for brass and percussion (1974)
Symphony No.4    (Gilgamesh) (1978)
Symphony No.5    (Dark Spirals) for wind ensemble (1984)
Symphony No.6    (Black Moon) (1988)
Symphony No.7    (Cities, Seasons) for string orchestra (1994)


# E

EASTMAN, Julius b. 27 October 1940

Symphony (1969)

EASTON, Jack b. 10 July 1918

Symphony (1951)

EATON, John Charles b. 30 March 1935

Symphony No.1
Symphony No.2    (1980–81)

EDMONDS, Henry

Symphony No.1    (1952)

EFFINGER, Cecil b. 22 July 1914, d. 22 December 1990

Symphony No.1    (1946)

Symphony No.2        (1947)
Symphony No.3        for chorus and orchestra (1952)
Symphony No.4        (1954)
Symphony No.5        (1958)
Little Symphony No.1    (1945)
Little Symphony No.2    (1958)

EHLE, Robert Cannon b. 7 November 1939

A Space Symphony (Symphony No.1) Op.5 (1961)
A Jazz Symphony for stage band (Symphony No.2) Op.11 (1961)
Symphony No.3 (Bay Psalms) Op.31 for chorus and orchestra (1970)
Soundscapes: Electronic Symphony (Symphony No.4) Op.45 (1974)
A Whole Earth Symphony: Seven tone poems for wind and percussion Op.56 (Symphony
   No.5) (1978–79)
Symphony No.6 for synthesizer and orchestra Op.59 (1980)
Symphony No.7; A New Age Symphony; electronic music on tape Op.64 (1981)
Earth Garden Symphony (Symphony No.8) Op.70 (1983–84)

El-DABH, Halim b. 4 March 1921

Symphony No.1        (1951)
Symphony No.2        (1952)
Symphony No.3        (1955)

ENENBACH, Frederic b. 1 December 1945, d. 18 January 1984

Symphony (1973)

ENGEL, Lehman b. 14 September 1910, d. 29 August 1982

Symphony No.1        (1939)
Symphony No.2        (1945)

EPPERT, Carl b. 5 November 1882, d. 1 October 1961

Symphony No.1        (Symphony of the City Traffic) (1932)
Symphony No.2
Symphony No.3
Symphony No.4
Symphony No.5
Symphony No.6
Symphony No.7        (1945)

EPSTEIN, David M. b. 3 October 1930

Symphony No.1        (1958)

ERB, Donald b. 17 January 1927

Symphony of Overtures (1964)
Symphony for winds (1989)

ERICKSON, Frank William b. 1 September 1923

Symphony No.1        for band (1954)

Symphony No.2     for band (1959)
Symphony No.3     for band (1984)
Sinfonia     (1973)

ESCOT, Olga Pozzi b. 1 October 1933

Symphony No.1     (1953) for strings withdrawn
Symphony No.2     (1955) withdrawn
Symphony No.3     (1957) withdrawn

ETLER, Alvin Derald b. 19 February 1913, d. 13 June 1973

Symphony     (1951)

EVETT, Robert b. 30 November 1922, d. 3 February 1975

Symphony No.1     (1960)
Symphony No.2     (Billy Ascends) for voices and orchestra (1965)
Symphony No.3     (1965)


# F

FARAGO, Marcel b. 17 April 1924

Symphony No.1

FARBERMAN, Harold b. 2 November 1929

Symphony for percussion and strings (1956–57)

FARRAND, Noel b. 26 December 1928

Symphony No.1     (1955)
Symphony No.2     (Lamentation of Dr Faustus) (1964)
Symphony No.3     (1973)

FARWELL, Arthur b. 23 April 1872, d. 20 January 1952

Rudolph Gott Symphony (1934)

FAUST, George T. b. 6 June 1937

Symphony for brass and percussion

FENNER, Burt L. b. 12 August 1929

Chamber Symphony (1958)
Symphony No.2     (1961)
Symphony No.3     (1975)

FERRAZANO, Anthony Joseph (Anthony ZANO) b. 4 June 1937

Symphony No.1     (1959)
Symphony No.2     (1960)

FERRIS, William Edward b. 26 February 1937

Symphony     (1968)

FETLER, David

Symphony on Shaker Themes (1952)

FETLER, Paul b. 17 February 1920

| | |
|---|---|
| Symphony No.1 | in D minor (1948) |
| Symphony No.2 | (1951) |
| Symphony No.3 | (1954) |
| Symphony No.4 | (1968) |

de FILIPPI, Amedeo see DE FILIPPI

FINE, Irving Gifford b. 3 December 1914, d. 23 August 1962

| | |
|---|---|
| Symphony | (1961) |

FINKO, David b. 15 May 1936

| | |
|---|---|
| Symphony No.1 | (1969) |
| Symphony No.2 | (1972) |

FINLEY, Lorraine Noel b. 24 December 1899, d. 13 February 1972

Symphony in D

FINNEY, Ross Lee b. 23 December 1906, d. 5 February 1997

| | |
|---|---|
| Symphony No.1 | (Communique) (1943) |
| Symphony No.2 | (1959) |
| Symphony No.3 | (1960) |
| Symphony No.4 | (1972) |

FIORILLO, Dante b. 4 July 1905, d. c. 1970

Symphony No.1
Symphony No.2
Symphony No.3
Symphony No.4
Symphony No.5
Symphony No.6
Symphony No.7
Symphony No.8
Symphony No.9
Symphony No.10
Symphony No.11
Symphony No.12

Fiorillo is known to have passed off as his own compositions by others. It is probable that some of the above symphonies are in fact by Berthold Goldschmidt, Karl Amadeus Hartmann, Heinrich Kaminski and other unidentified composers.

FISCHER, Irwin b. 5 July 1903, d. 7 May 1977

| | |
|---|---|
| Symphony No.1 | (1942) |
| Short Symphony | (1970–71) |

FLAGELLO, Nicolas b. 15 March 1928, d. 1994

Symphony No.1    Op.57 (1967)
Symphony No.2    for wind Op.63 (1971)
Symphony for strings in one movement

FLETCHER, H(orace) Grant b. 25 October 1913

Symphony No.1    (1950)
Symphony No.2    (1970)
Symphony No.3    (1994)

FLORIDIA, Pietro b. 5 May 1860, d. 16 August 1932

Symphony in D minor (1907)

FLORIO, Caryl (William James ROBJOHN) b. 2 November 1843, d. 21 November 1920

Symphony No.1    in G (1887)
Symphony No.2    in C minor (1887)

FLYNN, George b. 21 January 1937

Symphony No.1    (Music for Orchestra) (1966)
Symphony No.2    (1980)

FORST, Rudolf b. 20 October 1900, d. 19 December 1973

Symphonia Brevis (1933)
Symphony (1937)

FORTE, James b. 19 September 1936

Sinfonia for strings (1972)

FOSS, Lukas b. 15 August 1922

Symphony No.1 in G (1944)
A Symphony of Chorales (1955–58)
Symphony No.3    (Symphony of Sorrows) (1991–92)
Symphony No.4    (1994–95)

FRABIZIO, William V. b. 10 October 1929

Symphony No.1
Symphony No.2
Symphony No.3

FRANCHESCHINI, Romulus b. 5 January 1929

Sinfonia for strings, percussion, piano and celeste (1970)

FRACKENPOHL, Arthur b. 23 April 1924

Symphony No.1    (1957)
Symphony No.2    for strings (1960)

FRANCO, Johan Henri Gustav b. 12 July 1908, d. 1988

| | |
|---|---|
| Symphony No.1 | (1933) |
| Symphony No.2 | (George Washington) (1939) |
| Symphony No.3 | for piano and orchestra (1940) |
| Symphony No.4 | for tenor and orchestra (1950) |
| Symphony No.5 | (The Cosmos) (1958) |

FRANK, Guy

Symphony in three movements (1956)

FRANK, Marcel Gustave b. 3 December 1906, d. 16 April 1985

Symphony (Brazil)
Symphony in E flat
Symphony Miniature

FRANK, Robert E. b. 27 November 1943

Symphony

FREED, Isadore b. 26 March 1900, d. 10 November 1960

| | |
|---|---|
| Symphony No.1 | (Horizon) (1947) |
| Symphony No.2 | for brass (1951) |

FRIML, (Charles) Rudolph b. 7 December 1879, d. 12 November 1972

Symphony 'Round the World'

FROHMADER, Jerold C. b. 3 December 1938

Sinfonia for winds

FRUMKER, Linda b. 11 December 1940

Symphony (1964)

FRY, William Henry b. 19 August 1813, d. 21 December 1864

The Breaking Heart Symphony (1852) lost
Santa Claus (Christmas) Symphony (1853)
A Day in the Country Symphony (1853) lost
Child Harold Symphony (1854) lost
Niagara Symphony (1854)
Hagar in the Wilderness (Sacred Symphony) (1854)
The Dying Soldier Symphony (Dramatic)

FUCHS, Charles Emilio b. 27 June 1907

| | |
|---|---|
| Symphony No.1 | |
| Symphony No.2 | |
| Symphony No.3 | (In Memoriam A Frank) |
| Symphony No.4 | for strings |

FULEIHAN, Anis b. 2 April 1900, d. 11 October 1970

Symphony No.1      (1936)
Symphony No.2      (1962)

FULKERSON, James (Orville) b. 2 July 1945

Symphony          (1980)

FULLER, Donald Sanborn b. 1 July 1919

Symphony

FUNK, Eric Douglas b. 28 September 1949

Symphony

FUSSELL, Charles C. b. 14 February 1938

Symphony in one movement (1963)
Symphony No.2      for soprano and orchestra (1967)
Symphony No.3      (Landscapes) for chorus and orchestra (1978–81)
Wilde: Symphony in three movements for baritone and orchestra (1989–90)
Symphony No.5      in one movement (1994)


# G

GAIDELIS, Julius b. 5 April 1909

Symphony No.1
Symphony No.2
Symphony No.3
Symphony No.4
Symphony No.5
Symphony No.6

GANNETT, Kent

Symphony in A minor (1939)

GANZ, Rudolph b. 24 February 1877, d. 2 August 1972

Symphony in E (1900)

GARLAND, Antony b. 9 December 1927

Symphony No.1
Symphony No.2
Symphony No.3
Symphony No.4
Symphony No.5

GARCIA, Russell E. b. 12 April 1916

New Era Symphony

GAROFALO, Carlo Giorgio b. 5 August 1886, d. 6 April 1962

Romantic Symphony of St Louis
Symphony No.2

GATES, B. Cecil b. 7 August 1877, d. 31 August 1941

Symphony in E minor

GATES, Crawford (Marion) b. 29 December 1921

Symphony No.1      Op.25 (1950–53)
Symphony No.2      (Music to the Hill Cumorah Pageant) Op.29 for narrator (optional),
   chorus and orchestra (1953–57)
Symphony No.3      (War Terrors) Op.38 in one movement (1962–64)
Symphony No.4      (A New Morning) Op.50 for chorus and orchestra (1975–76)
Symphony No.5      (Perelandra) Op.55 for narrator, 4 soloists, mixed chorus, 2 small
   women's choruses and orchestra (1978–79)

GAULDIN, Robert b. 30 October 1931

Symphony No.1      (1957)

GELT, Andrew Lloyd b. 2 February 1951

Symphony No.1      Op.34 (The Art of Eclecticism) (1977)

GEPPORT, David

Symphony No.1      (1954)

GERSCHEFSKI, Edwin b. 10 June 1909, d. 1992

Classic Symphony Op.4 (1931)

GESENSWAY, Louis b. 19 February 1906, d. 11 March 1976

Commemoration Symphony (1966–68)

GIANNINI, Vittorio b. 19 October 1903, d. 28 November 1966

Symphony            (In Memoriam Theodore Roosevelt) in one movement (1935)
Symphony            (IBM) (1939)
Symphony No.1      for wind and percussion (1951)
Symphony No.2      (1956)
Symphony No.3      for band (1958)
Symphony No.4      (1960)

GIBBS, Geoffrey David b. 29 March 1940

Symphony No.1      (1961)
Symphony No.2      (1973)

GIDEON, Miriam b. 23 October 1906, d. 1996

Symphonia Brevis (1953)

GILBERT, Steven Edward b. 20 April 1943

Symphony (1964–65)

GILCHRIST, William Wallace b. 8 January 1846, d. 20 December 1916

| | |
|---|---|
| Symphony No.1 | in C (1891) |
| Symphony No.2 | in D (unfinished) |

GILDERSLEEVE, Charles jnr b. 19 August 1893, d. 19 October 1962

Carolinian Symphony

GILLETTE, James Robert b. 30 May 1886, d. 26 November 1963

Pagan Symphony

GILLIS, Don b. 17 June 1912, d. 10 January 1978

| | |
|---|---|
| Symphony No.1 | (American) (1941) |
| Symphony No.2 | (Symphony of Faith) (1940) |
| Symphony No.3 | (Symphony of Free Men) (1940–41) |
| Symphony No.4 | (1943) |
| Symphony No.5 | (1944–45) |
| Symphony No.5½ | (Symphony for Fun) (1945) |
| Symphony No.6 | (Midcentury USA) (1947) |
| Symphony No.7 | (Saga of a Prairie School) (1948) |
| Symphony No.8 | (Dance Symphony) (1949) |
| Symphony No.9 | (1956) |
| Symphony No.10 | (Big D) (1967) |
| Star Spangled Symphony for strings | |

GIOMPPER, David Karl

| | |
|---|---|
| Symphony No.1 | |
| Symphony No.2 | (1988) |

GIORNI, Aurelio b. 15 September 1895, d. 23 September 1938

Symphony in D minor (1936)

GIOVANNINI, Caesar b. 26 February 1925

Symphony in one movement for band

GLANVILLE-HICKS, Peggy b. 29 December 1912, d. 25 June 1990

Sinfonia da Pacifica (1952)

GLASS, Paul b. 1 March 1910

Symphony

GLASS, Paul Eugene b. 19 November 1934

| | |
|---|---|
| Symphony No.1 | (1959) |
| Symphony No.2 | |
| Symphony No.3 | (1983) |
| Symphony No.4 | |

GLASS, Philip b. 31 January 1937

The 'Low' Symphony (1992)
Symphony No.2 (Heroes Symphony) (1994)

GLASSER, Albert b. 25 January 1916

Symphony No.1      in B flat minor

GOEB, Roger b. 9 October 1914, d. 1997

Symphony No.1      (1941) withdrawn
Symphony No.2      (1945)
Symphony No.3      (1901)
Symphony No.4      (1956)
Symphony No.5      (1981)
Symphony No.6      (1987)

GOLD, Ernest b. 13 July 1921

Pan American Symphony (1941)
Symphony No.2      (1947)

GOODMAN, Alfred b. 1 March 1920

Symphony No.1
Symphony No.2

GOODMAN, Jerome David b. 1933

Symphony No.1
Symphony No.2      (1994)

GOOSSEN, (Jacob) Frederic b. 30 July 1927

Symphony No.1      (1954)
Symphony No.2      (1961, rev. 1977)
Symphony No.3      (1983)
Symphony No.4      (Sinfonia Druidica) (1985)
Symphony No.5      for winds (1992)

GORDON, David A.

Symphony No.1      (1960)

GORTON, Thomas

Symphony No.1      (1947)

GOTTSCHALK, Louis Moreau b. 8 May 1829, d. 18 December 1869

Symphony No.1      (Night in the Tropics) (1859)
Symphony No.2      (A Montevideo) (1869)

GOULD, Morton b. 10 December 1913, d. 21 February 1996

Little Symphony      (1936)
Symphony No.1      (1943)

Symphony No.2      (On Marching Tunes) (1944)
Symphony No.3      (1947, rev. 1948)
Symphony No.4      for band (1952)
Symphony of Spirituals (1976)
Centennial Symphony for band (1983)

GOWER, Albert E. Jnr b. 4 June 1935

Symphony for band

GRANT, Allan b. 2 July 1892, d. 12 November 1969

Symphony

GRANT, William Parks b. 4 January 1910

Symphony No.1      in D minor Op.6 (1930–36)
Symphony No.2      (1947)
Symphony No.3      in one movement Op.54 (1961)

GRASSE, Edwin b. 13 August 1884, d. 8 April 1954

Symphony No.1      in G
Symphony No.2      in D

GREEN, Bernard b. 14 Septemer 1908, d. 8 August 1975

Symphony

GREEN, Ray Burns b. 13 September 1909

Symphony No.1      (Country Dance)
Symphony No.2      (1943)
Sunday Sing Song Symphony (1946)
Short Symphony in A (1946–53)
Short Symphony in F (1970)
Short Symphony in C (1974–80)

GREGORIAN, Rouben b. 23 September 1915, d. 28 March 1991

Symphony No.1      (1964)
Symphony No.2

GRIFFIS, Elliot      b. 28 January 1893, d. 8 June 1967

Symphony (1931)

GRIMM, Carl Hugo b. 31 October 1890, d. 25 October 1978

Symphony in F minor (1950)

GROFÉ, Ferde (Ferdinand Rudolph von) b. 27 March 1892, d. 3 April 1972

Symphony in Steel      (1937)

GRUENBERG, Louis b. 3 August 1884, d. 9 June 1964

Symphony No.1      Op.17 (1919, rev. 1928)

Symphony No.2    Op.43 (1941, rev. 1959, 1963)
Symphony No.3    Op.44 (1942, rev. 1964)
Symphony No.4    Op.50 (1947, rev. 1964)
Symphony No.5    (1948)

GUTCHË, Gene b. 3 July 1907

Symphony No.1    Op.7 (1950)
Symphony No.2    Op.14 (1950)
Symphony No.3    Op.19 (1952)
Symphony No.4    in one movement Op.30 (1960)
Symphony No.5    for strings Op.34 (1962)
Symphony No.6    Op.45 (1970)

# H

HADLEY, Henry Kimball b. 20 December 1871, d. 6 September 1937

Symphony No.1    in D minor (Youth and Life) (1897)
Symphony No.2    in F minor (Four Seasons) Op.30 (1901)
Symphony No.3    in B minor Op.60 (1906–07)
Symphony No.4    in D minor (North, East, South, West) Op.64 (1911)
Symphony No.5    in C minor (Connecticut) Op.140 (1935)

HAESCHE, William Edwin b. 11 April 1867, d. 26 January 1929

Symphony

HAIEFF, Alexei (Vasilievich) b. 25 August 1914, d. 1 March 1994

Symphony No.1    (1942)
Symphony No.2    (1958)
Symphony No.3    (1961)

HAILSTORK, Adolphus (Cunningham) b. 17 April 1941

Symphony No.1    (1988)

HAINES, Edmund b. 15 December 1914, d. 5 July 1974

Symphony in Miniature (1939)
Symphony No.1    Op. 8 (1941)

HALEN, Walter John b. 17 March 1930

Sinfonia Sonore (1957)

HALLSTROM, Henry b. 12 July 1906

Symphony No.1    (1949)
Symphony No.2    in G (1950)

HALPIN, Brooke

Symphony No.1    (1982)

HAMMEL, William Carl Jnr b. 4 December 1944

Symphony             (1977–79)

HANEY, Gerald Ray b. 15 March 1921

Symphony No.1

HANNA, James Ray b. 15 October 1922

| | |
|---|---|
| Symphony No.1 | (1948, rev. 1949, 1956, 1957) |
| Symphony No.2 | (1956, rev. 1967) |
| Symphony No.3 | (1965) |
| Symphony No.4 | for strings (1985) |

HANNAY, Roger (Durham) b. 22 September 1930

| | |
|---|---|
| Symphony No.1 | (1953, rev. 1973) |
| Symphony No.2 | (1956) |
| Symphony for band | (1963) |
| Symphony No.3 | (The Great American Novel) with optional chorus (1977–78) |
| Symphony No.4 | (American Classic) for solo vocal quartet, optional tape and orchestra (1977) |
| Symphony No.5 | (1987–88) |
| Symphony No.6 | for large string orchestra (1992) |
| Symphony No.7 | in one movement (1996) |

HANSEN, Theodore Carl b. 5 February 1935

(Three Movements for Orchestra) (1975)
Symphony No.1      (1976)

HANSON, Howard b. 28 October 1896, d. 26 February 1981

| | |
|---|---|
| Symphony | (1914) unpublished |
| Symphony No.1 | (Nordic) in E minor Op.21 (1922) |
| Symphony No.2 | (Romantic) Op.30 (1930) |
| Symphony No.3 | in A minor Op.33 (1936) |
| Symphony No.4 | (Requiem) Op.34 (1943) |
| Symphony No.5 | (Sinfonia Sacra) Op.43 (1955) |
| Symphony No.6 | (1967) |
| Symphony No.7 | (Sea Symphony) for chorus and orchestra (1977) |

HARBISON, John b. 20 December 1938

Sinfonia for violin and double orchestra (1963)
| | |
|---|---|
| Symphony No.1 | (1981) |
| Symphony No.2 | (1987) |
| Symphony No.3 | (1990) |
| Symphony No.4 | (in progress) |

HARRIS, Donald b. 7 April 1931

Symphony in two movements (1959–63)

HARRIS, Roy (Leroy) Ellsworth b. 12 February 1898, d. 1 October 1979

Symphony (American Portrait) (1929) unpublished
Symphony No.1      (1933)
Symphony No.2      (1934)
Symphony No.3      (1938)
Symphony No.4      (Folk Song) for chorus and orchestra (1940)
Symphony No.5      (1942, rev. 1945)
Symphony No.6      (Gettysburg) (1944)
Symphony No.7      (1951, rev. 1955)
Symphony No.8      (San Francisco) (1962)
Symphony No.9      (1962)
Symphony No.10     (Abraham Lincoln) for chorus, brass and two amplified pianos and
     percussion (1965)
Symphony No.11     (1967)
Symphony No.12     (Pere Marquette) for tenor, speaker and orchestra (1968)
Symphony No.13     (1969)
Symphony No.14     (Bicentennial) for chorus and orchestra (1976)
Symphony No.15     (1978)
Symphony for Band (West Point) (1952)


HARRISON, Lou (Silver) b. 14 May 1917

Symphony on G      (1947–64, rev. 1966)
Sinfony in Free Style
Elegiac Symphony   (1942–75)
Symphony No.3      (1937–81)
Symphony No.4      (Last Symphony) (1990, rev. 1991, 1993, 1995)


HART, Weldon b. 19 September 1911, d. 20 November 1957

Symphony            (1945)


HARTKE, Paul Stephen b. 6 July 1952

Symphony No.1      (1974–76)
Symphony No.2


HARTLEY, Walter Sinclair b. 21 February 1927

Chamber Symphony for small orchestra (1954)
Sinfonia No.1      for wind ensemble (1961)
Sinfonia No.2      for orchestra (1962)
Sinfonia No.3      for brass choir (1963)
Sinfonia No.4      for wind ensemble (1965)
Symphony No.1      for wind orchestra (1970)
Sinfonia No.5      for band (1977)
Symphony No.2      for large wind ensemble (1978)
Symphony No.3      for orchestra (1983)
Sinfonia No.6      for saxophone ensemble (1985)
Sinfonia No.7      for orchestra (1986)
Sinfonia No.8      for tuned percussion (1987)
Sinfonia No.9      for band (1991)
Lyric Symphony     for band (1993)
Sinfonia No.10     for tuba-euphonium ensemble (1994)

Centennial Symphony for wind ensemble (1995)
Sinfonia No.11      for orchestra (1996)

HARTMANN, Thomas de b. 21 September 1885, d. 25 March 1956

Symphony No.1
Symphony No.2      (The Legend of the Sun) Op.68 (1944)

HASKINS, Robert James b. 27 December 1937

Symphony in one movement
Symphony No.2      for soli, chorus and orchestra
Symphony No.3      (And Man Created God in his Own Image)
Symphony No.4      (Sinfonia Requiem) for soprano, baritone and orchestra

HASLAM, Herbert b. 23 April 1928

Symphony in one movement

HASTINGS, Ross Ray b. 26 February 1915, d. 5 July 1991

Sinfonia Brevis

HAUBIEL, Charles b. 30 January 1892, d. 26 August 1978

Symphony No.1      in Variation Form (1937)

HAUFRECHT, Herbert b. 3 November 1909

Symphony for brass and timpani (1956)

HAUPT, Thomas Edward

Symphony (Origins) (1989)

HAUSSERMANN, John William Jnr b. 21 August 1909

Symphony No.1      Op.16 (1938)
Symphony No.2      Op.22 (1941)
Symphony No.3      Op.34 (1947)

HAXTON, R. Kenneth b. 20 October 1919

Symphony            'The Sound and the Fury' for contralto and orchestra (1966)
Symphony No.1      (1982)
Symphony            (Welty Women) (1985)
Symphony No.2      (1990)

HAYES, Joseph b. 5 December 1920

Symphony (Sunday 3.00 p.m.) for wind, piano, percussion and strings

HAYS, Robert D. b. 31 January 1923

Symphony            (1965)

HEDGES, Roy Warner

Symphony No.1      (1948)

HEDWALL, Paul D. b. 18 April 1939

Symphony: Psalm 128 for soloists, chorus and orchestra (1972)

HEFTI, John

Symphony in F minor for small orchestra (1941)

HEIDEN, Bernhard b. 24 August 1910

Symphony No.1      (1938)
Symphony No.2      (1954)

HEIFETZ, Vladimir b. 28 March 1893, d. 3 May 1970

Symphony (New Era) Op.75 for soloists and orchestra (1939)

HEILNER, Irwin b. 14 May 1908

Swing Symphony      (1942)

HEINRICH, Anton Philipp b. 11 March 1781, d. 3 May 1861

Schiller: grande sinfonia dramatica (1830, rev. 1847)
Gran Sinfonia Eroica (c 1835)
The Columbiad: a Grand American Chivalrous Symphony (1837)
Manitou Mysteries: The Voice of the Forest Spirit (before 1845)
Gran Sinfonia Misteriosa Indiana (1845)
Grand Symphony: The Ornithological Combat of Kings (The Battle of the Cordilleras)
    (1847, rev. 1856)
Sinfonia Sacra: The Tomb of Genius to the Memory of Mendelssohn Bartholdy (1847?)
The Indian Carnival or Indian Festival of Dreams (sinfonia erotico fantachino) (c 1849)
Bohemia: sinfonia romantica (before 1854)
Homage à la Boheme (1855)
The Mastadon: a Grand Symphony (1857)
National Memories: a Grand British Symphony
Grande Sinfonia Dramatica
The Empress Queen and the Magyars: Sinfonia patriotica
To the Spirit of Beethoven: monumental symphony for grand orchestra

HELFER, Walter b. 30 September 1896, d. 16 April 1959

Symphony on Canadian Airs (1937)

HELLER, Alfred E. b. 8 December 1931

Symphony No.1
Symphony No.2
Symphony No.3

HELLER, John Henry Jnr b. 22 February 1945

Symphony Concerto for bass clarinet and orchestra (1966)

HELM, Everett b. 17 July 1913

Symphony for String Orchestra (1955)
Sinfonia da Camera    (1962)

HELPS, Robert Eugene b. 23 September 1928

Symphony No.1 (1955)

HENDRICKS, W. Newell b. 23 February 1943

Symphony in B        (1968)

HENNE, David Waterbury

Symphony            (1979)

HENRY, George

Symphony No.1 in one movement (1945)

HENSLER, Bernice

Symphony in three movements (1945)

HERMAN, Harry Martin

Hawthorne Symphony (1990)

HERRIED, Henry

Symphony            (1938)

HERMANN, Bernard b. 29 January 1911, d. 24 December 1975

Symphony            (1940)

HERVIG, Richard Bilderbeck b. 24 November 1917

Symphony No.1
Symphony No.2

HEUSSENSTAMM, George b. 24 July 1926

Chamber Symphony Op.16 (1964)

HEWITT, Harry D(onald) b. 4 March 1921

| | | |
|---|---|---|
| Symphony No.1 | Op.15 | (1938–39) |
| Symphony No.2 | Op.38 | (1940) |
| Symphony No.3 | Op.43 | (1941, rev. 1951) |
| Symphony No.4 | Op.59 | (1941, rev. 1951) |
| Symphony No.5 | Op.74 | (1944–46) |
| Symphony No.6 | Op.82 | (1952, rev. 1976) |
| Symphony No.7 | Op.91 | (1946–50) |
| Symphony No.8 | in C Op.103 | (1948, rev. 1952) |
| Symphony No.9 | Op.112 | (1945–50) |
| Symphony No.10 | Op.121 | (1946–49) |

Symphony No.11    Op.133  (1946–50)
Symphony No.12    Op.140  (1946)
Symphony No.13    Op.150  (1946–50)
Symphony No.14    Op.162  (1946–50)
Symphony No.15    Op.171  (1949–51)
Symphony No.16    Op.180  (1955, rev. 1977)
Symphony No.17    Op.193  (1955)
Symphony No.18    Op.200  (1952–56, rev. 1978)
Symphony No.19    Op.212  (1953–55)
Symphony No.20    Op.293
Symphony No.21    Op.408  (1970–75)
Symphony No.22    Op.446  (1974–75)
Symphony No.23    Op.450  (1978–81)
Symphony No.24    Op.462  (1955, rev. 1982)
Symphony No.25    Op.464  (1977, rev. 1983)
Symphony No.26    Op.466  (1978, rev. 1982)
Symphony No.27    Op.469  (1981–82)
Symphony No.28    Op.470  (1984, rev. 1988)
Symphony No.29    Op.472
Symphony No.30    Op.474  (1982, rev. 1988)
Symphony No.31    Op.476  (1982, rev. 1986)
Symphony No.32    Op.478  (1983–84)
Symphony No.33    Op.485  (1988, rev. 1994)

HICKEN, Stephen Dyal

Choral Symphony    (1989)

HILL, Edward Burlingame b. 9 September 1872, d. 9 July 1960

Symphony No.1    in B flat Op.34 (1928)
Symphony No.2    in C (1930)
Symphony No.3    in G Op.41 (1937)

HILLER, Lejaren Arthur b. 23 February 1924, d. 1994

Symphony No.1    Op.15 (1953)
Symphony No.2    Op.27 (1959)

HILLERT, Richard b. 14 March 1923

Symphony in three movements (1955)

HILLIARD, John Stanley b. 29 October 1947

Chamber Symphony (Appearance – Disappearance) (1984)

HOAG, Charles K. b. 14 November 1931

Symphony (1970)

HODKINSON, Sydney Phillip b. 17 January 1934

Symphony No.1    (Fresco) (1968)
Symphony No.2    (The Celestial Omnibus) (1975)
Symphony No.3    (Sonata Quasi una Fantasia) (1982)

Symphony No.4     (Hora Canonica) for soprano, baritone, SATB chorus, male chorus, cello obbligato and orchestra (1977–83)
Symphony No.5     (Sinfone Concertante) (1980)
Symphony No.6     for violin and large orchestra (1990)
Symphony No.7     (The Vanishing Hand) for wind ensemble (1992)
Symphony No.8     (1994– )
Symphony No.9     (Epiphanies) for orchestral winds (1994)
Symphony No.10    (1994– )

HOFFMAN, Joel Harvey b. 27 September 1953

Chamber Symphony

HOFFMAN, Adolf G. b. 30 May 1890

Symphony in E

HOFFMANN, Newton b. 16 July 1921

Symphony No.1     (1951)

HOFREITER, Paul b. 9 September 1952

Symphony No.1
Symphony No.2
Symphony No.3     Op.47 (1973–74)

HOLDEN, David Justin b. 16 December 1911

Symphony
Choral Symphony

HOLLIDAY, Kent Alfred b. 9 March 1940

Symphony
Symphonia Brevis

HOLLOWAY, Elizabeth

Symphony No.1     (1954)

HOLMES, Markwood b. 18 August 1899

Sinfonia

HOMMANN, Charles b. *c.* 1800 d. after 1862

Symphony in E flat

HOOKER, Adelaide

Symphony in E     (1930)

HOOSE, Alfred b. 17 September 1918

Symphony No.1     (1981)
Symphony No.2     'Winter Sunshine' for piano and orchestra (1994)

HOPKINS, Harry Paterson b. 25 May 1873, d. 21 September 1954

Symphony

HOPKINS, James Frederick b. 8 April 1939

Symphony No.1        (1964)
Symphony No.2

HOPKINS, Kenyon b. 1932

Symphony in two movements

HOPKINS, (Charles) Jerome b. 4 April 1936, d. 4 November 1997

Symphony

HOVDESVEN, Elmer Archibald b. 4 May 1893

Symphony in A minor

HOVHANESS, Alan b. 8 March 1911

| | |
|---|---|
| Symphony No.1 | (Exile Symphony) Op.17 (1936) |
| Symphony No.2 | (Mysterious Mountain) Op.132 (1955) |
| Symphony No.3 | Op.148 (1956) |
| Symphony No.4 | Op.165 for wind orchestra (1959) |
| Symphony No.5 | Op.165 (1953, rev. 1963) |
| Symphony No.6 | (Celestial Gate) in one movement for small orchestra Op.173 (1959) |
| Symphony No.7 | (Nanga Parvat) for wind orchestra Op.178 (1959) |
| Symphony No.8 | (Arjuna) Op.179 (1947) |
| Symphony No.9 | (Saint Vartan) Op.180 (1949–50) |
| Symphony No.10 | (Vahaken) Op.184 (1959) |
| Symphony No.11 | (All Men Are Brothers) Op.186 (1960, rev. 1969) |
| Symphony No.12 | (Choral: Psalm 23) for chorus and orchestra Op.188 (1960) |
| Symphony No.13 | in one movement (1944, rev. 1953) |
| Symphony No.14 | (Ararat for wind orchestra Op.194 (1960) |
| Symphony No.15 | (Silver Pilgrimage) Op.199 (1962) |
| Symphony No.16 | for Eastern instruments Op.202 (1962) |
| Symphony No.17 | (Symphony for Metal Orchestra) Op.203 (1963) |
| Symphony No.18 | (Circe) Op.204a (1963) |
| Symphony No.19 | (Vishnu) Op.217 (1966) |
| Symphony No.20 (1968) | (Three Journeys to a Holy Mountain) for concert band Op.223 |
| Symphony No.21 | (Etchmiadzin) for brass, percussion and strings Op.234 (1968) |
| Symphony No.22 | (City of Light) Op.236 (1970) |
| Symphony No.23 | (Ani) for large band and brass choir Op.249 (1972) |
| Symphony No.24 (1973) | (Majnun) for tenor, chorus, trumpet, violin and strings Op.273 |
| Symphony No.25 | (Odysseus) Op.275 (1973) |
| Symphony No.26 | Op.280 (1975) |
| Symphony No.27 | Op.285 (1976) |
| Symphony No.28 | Op.286 (1976) |
| Symphony No.29 | for baritone horn and orchestra Op.289 (1976) |
| Symphony No.30 | Op.293 (1957–77) |

| | |
|---|---|
| Symphony No.31 | for string orchestra Op.294 (1976–77) |
| Symphony No.32 | (The Broken Wings) Op.296 (1977) |
| Symphony No.33 | Op.307 (1977) |
| Symphony No.34 | for bass trombone and strings Op.310 (1977) |
| Symphony No.35 | for two orchestras Op.311 (1978) |
| Symphony No.36 | for flute and orchestra Op.312 (1978) |
| Symphony No.37 | Op.313 (1978) |
| Symphony No.38 | for high soprano, flute, trumpet and strings Op.314 (1978) |
| Symphony No.39 | for guitar and orchestra Op.321 (1978) |
| Symphony No.40 | Op.324 (1979) |
| Symphony No.41 | Op.330 (1979) |
| Symphony No.42 | Op.332 (1979) |
| Symphony No.43 | for oboe, trumpet, timpani and strings Op.334 (1979) |
| Symphony No.44 | Op.339 (1980) |
| Symphony No.45 | Op.342 (1954) |
| Symphony No.46 | (To the Green Mountains) Op.347 (1980) |
| Symphony No.47 | (Walla Walla, land of many waters) for coloratura soprano and orchestra Op.348 (1980) |
| Symphony No.48 | (Vision of Andromeda) Op.355 (1981) |
| Symphony No.49 | (Christmas Symphony) for string orchestra Op.356 (1981) |
| Symphony No.50 | (Mount St. Helens) Op.360 (1982) |
| Symphony No.51 | for trumpet and strings Op.364 (1982) |
| Symphony No.52 | (Journey to Vega) Op.372 (1982) |
| Symphony No.53 | (Star Dawn) for wind band Op.378 (1982) |
| Symphony No.54 | Op.379 (1982) |
| Symphony No.55 | Op.380 (1982) |
| Symphony No.56 | (Cold Mountain) for tenor (or soprano), clarinet and strings Op.381 (1982) |
| Symphony No.57 | |
| Symphony No.58 | |
| Symphony No.59 | |
| Symphony No.60 | |
| Symphony No.61 | |
| Symphony No.62 | |
| Symphony No.63 | |
| Symphony No.64 | |
| Symphony No.65 | (1991) |
| Symphony No.66 | |
| Symphony No.67 | |

HOWARD, Dean Clinton b. 17 November 1918

An Illinois Symphony (1967)

HUFFMANN, Walter Spencer

| | |
|---|---|
| Symphony No.1 | (1951) |
| Symphony No.2 | |
| Symphony No.3 | |
| Symphony No.4 | |
| Symphony No.5 | |
| Symphony No.6 | |
| Symphony No.7 | (1955) |

HUGGLER, John b. 30 August 1928, d. 1993

Symphony for strings
Symphony for 13 instruments
Symphony in three movements (1974)

HUGO, John Adam b. 5 January 1873, d. 29 December 1945

Symphony

HUMEL, Gerald b. 7 November 1931

Symphony              (1967–69)

HUMEZ, Nicholas D. b. 11 March 1948

Symphony No.1      Op. 15 (1967)

HUNT, Frederick b. 3 December 1906, d. 11 June 1967

Symphony in E flat   (1940)
Symphony in G minor (1964)

HUSA, Karel b. 7 August 1921

Symphony No.1      (1953)
Symphony No.2      (Reflections) (1983)

HUSTON, (Thomas) Scott Jnr b. 10 October 1916

Symphony No.1      in A minor (1941) withdrawn
Symphony No.2      withdrawn
Symphony No.3      (Phantasms) (1968)
Symphony No.4      for strings (1972)
Symphony No.5      (1975)
Symphony No.6      (The Human Condition) (1981)

HUTCHESON, Ernest b. 20 July 1871, d. 29 December 1945

Symphony

HUTCHESON, Jere Trent b. 16 September 1938

Symphony              (1966)
Earth God's Symphony for solo wind quintet and band (1977)
Symphony (Dance of Time) for large orchestra (1994)


I


IANNACCONNE, Anthony J. b. 14 October 1943

Symphony No.1      (1965)
Symphony No.2      (1966)
Symphony No.3      (Night Rivers) in one movement (1992)

IATAURO, Michael Anthony b. 26 February 1943

Symphony No.1     for band

IDE, Chester Edward b. 13 June 1878 d. 18 March 1944

Symphony in A minor (1932)

IHRKE, Walter R. b. 21 May 1908

Symphony No.1     (1946)

IMBRIE, Andrew Welsh b. 6 April 1921

Symphony No.1     (1965)
Chamber Symphony  (1968)
Symphony No.2     (1969)
Symphony No.3     (1970)

INCE, Kamran b. 1960

Symphony No.1
Symphony No.2     'Fall of Constantinople'

INCH, Herbert Reynolds b. 25 November 1904, d. 14 April 1988

Symphony        (1932, rev. 1937–38)

ISRAEL, Brian M. b. 5 February 1951

Symphony No.1     (1974)

IVES, Charles b. 20 October 1874, d. 19 May 1954

Symphony No.1     (1897–98)
Symphony No.2     (1897–1902)
Symphony No.3     (1904)
Symphony No.4     (1910–16)
Holidays Symphony  (1909–13)
Universe Symphony  (The Earth and the Firmament) (1915–1928) incomplete, many
    sketches lost

IVEY, Jean Eichelberger b. 3 July 1923

Little Symphony     (1948)
Festive Symphony     (1955)
Symphony 'Forms and Motion' (1972)

# J

JACKSON, John Calvin b. 26 May 1919

Carl Sandburg Symphony

JACOBI, Frederick b. 4 May 1891, d. 24 December 1952

Symphony No.1    in C (Assyrian) (1922)
Symphony No.2    (1947)

JAGER, Robert Edward b. 25 August 1939

Symphony for band
Symphony No.2    for band

JAMES, Philip b. 17 May 1890, d. 1 November 1975

Kammersymphonie   (1926)
A Sea Symphony for baritone and orchestra (1928)
Symphony No.1    (1943, rev. 1961)
Symphony No.2    in one movement (1946)

JAMESON, Robert b. 29 March 1947

Symphony No.1    in A minor (Yerevan)

JAMGOCHIAN, Robert see JAMESON, Robert

JARECKI, Tadeusz b. 31 December 1888, d. 29 April 1955
Sinfonia Breve    (1932)

JARRETT, Jack Marius b. 17 March 1934

Choral Symphony on American Poems for chorus and orchestra or band

JENKINS, Joseph Willcox b. 15 February 1928

Symphony No.1
Symphony No.2
Sinfonia de la frontera

JENSEN, James A. b. 29 December 1944

Symphony    (1968)

JOHNS, Paul Emile b. *c.* 1798, d. 10 August 1860

A Warlike Symphony (1824) lost

JOHNSON, A. Paul b. 27 January 1955

Noche Oscura Del Alma: Choral Symphony

JOHNSON, Harold Victor b. 16 May 1918

Symphony No.1
Symphony No.2
Symphony No.3
Chorale Symphony

JOHNSON, Hunter b. 14 April 1906

Symphony (1931)

JOHNSON, James P(rice) b. 1 February 1891, d. 17 November 1955

Harlem Symphony    (1932)
Symphony in Brown  (1935)

JOHNSON, Lockrem b. 15 March 1924

Symphony No.1     in C Op.46 (1966)

JOHNSTON, Donald O. b. 6 February 1929

Symphony No.1   '   Op.7 (1954)
Symphony No.2       Op.13 (1958–59)
Symphony No.3       Op.16 (1960)
Symphony No.4       for band Op.17a (1961–62)
Symphony No.5       (Time and Space Studies) Op.42 (1977)
Symphony No.6       (Celebration Symphony) (1992)
Symphony No.7       The Final Cosmic Oratorio: The Revelation to John for narrator,
   soloists, chorus and orchestra (1997– )

JOHNSTON, Jack

Symphony          Op.38 (1959)

JOHNSTON, Richard

Symphony No.1     (1946)

JONES, Charles William b. 21 June 1910

Symphony No.1     (1939)
Symphony No.2     (1957)
Symphony No.3     (1962)
Symphony No.4     (1965)
Little Symphony for the New Year (1953)

JONES, George Thaddeus b. 6 November 1917

Symphony No.1     (1949)
Symphony No.2

JONES, J. Randolph b. 1910

Symphony in D flat (Southern Scenes)

JONES, Roger Parks b. 7 August 1944

Symphony for band

JONES, Samuel b. 2 June 1935

Symphony No.1     (1960)
Symphony No.2     (Canticles of Time) (1990)
Symphony No.3     (Palo Duro Canyon) (1992)

JOSEPH, Don Verne b. 8 June 1926

Symphony
Symphony for band

JOSEPHSON, Harry D.

Symphony

JOSTEN, Werner b. 12 June 1885, d. 6 February 1963

Symphony for strings (1935)
Symphony in F      (1936)

JULSTROM, Clifford Arthur b. 22 July 1907, d. March 1991

Symphony in C      (1948)

# K

KAHN, Erich Itor b. 23 July 1905, d. 5 March 1956

Symphonies bretonnes (1955)

KAIL, Robert

Bicentennial Symphony (1975)

KALMANOFF, Martin b. 24 May 1920

Symphony in D

KANITZ, Ernst (Ernest) b. 9 April 1894, d. 7 April 1978

Symphony No1      (Sinfonia Breve) (1963)
Sinfonia Seria      (No.2) (1965)
Symphony No.3      (Sinfonia Concertante) for violin, cello and orchestra (1967)

KANNER, Jerome Herbert b. 17 November 1903

Symphony No.1
Symphony No.2

KARLINS, M(artin) William b. 25 February 1932

Symphony No.1      (with speaker) (1979–80)

KARRICK, Cecil b. 1919

Symphony No.1      (1956)
Symphony No.2      (1957)

KAUDER, Hugo b. 9 June 1888, d. 22 July 1972

Symphony No.1      (1928)
Symphony No.2      (1939)
Symphony No.3
Symphony No.4      (1956)
Symphony No.5

KAUFMAN, Frederick b. 24 March 1936

Symphony No.1     for strings (1966)
Symphony No.2     for wind (1971)
Symphony No.3     for strings and percussion (1974)
Symphony No.4
Symphony No.5     (American) (1986)

KAUN, Bernhard b. 5 April 1899

Romantic Symphony (1969)

KAY, Hershy b. 17 November 1919, d. 2 December 1981

Western Symphony (ballet) (1954)

KAY, Ulysses b. 7 January 1917, d. 1995

Sinfonia in E        (1950)
Symphony          (1967)

KEATS, Donald b. 27 May 1929

Symphony No.1     (1955–57)
An Elegiac Symphony (Symphony No.2) (1960–62)

KECHLEY, Gerald b. 18 March 1919

Symphony          (1956)

KELLER, Homer T. b. 17 February 1915

Symphony No.1     in A minor (1939)
Symphony No.2     (1948)
Symphony No.3     (1954)
Chamber Symphony  (1941)

KELLEY, Edgar Stillman b. 14 April 1857, d. 12 November 1944

Symphony No.2     in B flat (New England) Op.33 (1913, rev. 1922)
Symphony no.1     in F (Gulliver) (1914–35)

KELLY, Peter b. 1965

Symphony No.1     (1988)

KELLY, Robert b. 26 September 1916

Symphony No.1     in A (Minature Symphony) (1950)
Symphony No.2     (1958)
Symphony No.3     (Emancipation) (1961) also for band

KENNAN, Kent Wheeler b. 18 April 1913

Symphony          (1938) withdrawn

KENNEDY, Gurney

Symphony No.1     (1953)

KERNIS, Aaron Jay b. 15 January 1960

Symphony in Waves  (1989)
Symphony No.2    (1995)

KERR, Harrison b. 13 October 1897, d. 15 August 1978

Symphony No.1    in C minor in one movement (1928–29, rev. 1938)
Symphony No.2    (1939) withdrawn
Symphony No.2    in E minor (1943–45)
Symphony No.3    in D minor (1953)
Symphony No.4    (unfinished)

KIEVMAN, Carson b. 1949

Symphony No.1
Symphony No.2    (1991)

KILPATRICK, Jack Frederick b. 23 September 1915, d. 22 February 1967

Symphony No.1    in F minor
Symphony No.2
Symphony No.3    in C minor
Symphony No.4    for voices and orchestra (1950)
Symphony No.5    in F sharp minor
Symphony No.6    (1956)
Symphony No.7    (The Republic of Texas) (1957)
Symphony No.8    (Oklahoma) for narrator, dancers and orchestra (1957)

KIM, Byong-Kon b. 28 May 1929

Symphony         (1967)
Symphony of Three Metaphors (1983)
Festival Symphony    (1984)

KINGMAN, Daniel C. b. 16 August 1924

Symphony in one movement Op.15 (1965)

KIRCHNER, Leon b. 24 January 1919

Sinfonia in two parts (1950)

KIRK, Theron Wilford b. 28 September 1919

Symphony No.1
Symphony No.2    in D (Saga of the Plains) (1960)

KISS, Janos b. 20 March 1921

Sinfonia Atlantis

KLAUS, Kenneth Blanchard b. 11 November 1923, d. 4 August 1980

Symphony No.1
Symphony No.2
Symphony No.3

Symphony No.4
Symphony No.5
Symphony No.6

KLAUSS, Noah b. 14 October 1901, d. 15 December 1977

Symphony in one movement (1969)

KLEIN, John M. b. 21 February 1915

Symphony for the Dance (1941)

KLEIN, Lothar b. 27 January 1932

Symphony No.1      (1955)
Symphony No.2      (1959)

KLEINMAN, Stephen Robert b. 18 August 1943

Fargo-Moorhead Symphony (1974)

KLEINSINGER, George b. 13 February 1914, d. 1982

Symphony            (1942)
Symphony for narrator and winds

KLETZSKY, Charles

Symphony

KNIGHT, Eric W. b. 24 October 1932

Symphony No.1
Symphony No.2
Symphony No.3
Symphony No.4      (American Idioms)

KNIGHT, Morris b. 25 December 1933

Symphony No.1      (1956)
Symphony No.2      (Concise Symphony) (1961)
Symphony No.3      (Crucial Symphony) (1963)
Symphony No.4      (Summer Symphony) (1966)

KNOX, Charles b. 19 April 1929

Symphony for brass and percussion (1965)

KOCH, Frederick b. 4 April 1924

Short Symphony

KOCH, John Gordon b. 1928

Symphony            (1961)

KOELLING, Eloise b. 3 March 1908

Symphony

KOHS, Ellis Bonoff b. 12 May 1916

Symphony No.1     in A for small orchestra (1950)
Symphony No.2     for chorus and orchestra (1956)

KOLAR, Victor b. 12 February 1888, d. 16 June 1957

Symphony in D     (1916)

KOPP, Frederick Edward b. 21 March 1914

Symphony No.1     in A in one movement
Symphony No.2     in A (A Symphony for Young Children)

KORF, Anthony b. 14 December 1951

Symphony No.1     (In Twilight) (1985)
Symphony No.2     (Blue Note) (1987)
Symphony No.3     in progress

KORN, Peter Jona b. 30 March 1922

Symphony No.1     in C Op.3 (1940, rev. 1957, 1977)
Symphony No.2     Op.13 (1952)
Symphony No.3     Op.30 in one movement (1956, rev. 1973)

KORNGOLD, Erich Wolfgang b. 29 May 1987, d. 29 November 1957

Symphony in F sharp Op.40 (1950)

KORTE, Karl b. 23 June 1928

Symphony No.1
Symphony No.2     in one movement (1961)
Symphony No.3     (1968)

KOSTECK, Gregory William b. 2 September 1937

Symphony          (1971)

KOUTZEN, Boris b. 1 April 1901, d. 10 December 1966

Symphony in C     (1939)

KOYKKAR, Joseph Noel b. 11 December 1951

Chamber Symphony

KOZINSKI, David B. b. 29 July 1917

Sinfonia for Easter

KRAFT, Leo b. 24 July 1922

Symphony in one movement

KRAFT, William b. 9 June 1923

Symphony for strings and percussion (1960)
Symphony            (1981)

KRAMER, Arthur Walter b. 23 September 1890, d. 8 April 1969

Symphony No.1
Symphony No.2

? KRAMER, Mark

Symphony No.1      (American) (1939)

KRANCE, John Paul Jnr b. 25 June 1934

Sinfonia in one movement

KREMEN, Israel b. 26 September 1949

Peace Symphony for tenor and orchestra (1989)

KREMENLIEV, Boris b. 23 May 1911, d. 1988

Symphony No.1      in A (Song Symphony) for contralto and orchestra (1940–41)
Symphony No.2

KRENEK, Ernest b. 23 August 1900, d. 23 December 1991

Symphony for wind and percussion Op.34 (1924–25)
Symphony No.1      Op.7 (1921)
Symphony No.2      Op.12 (1922)
Symphony No.3      Op.16 (1922)
Little Symphony Op.58 (1928)
Symphony No.4      Op.113 (1947)
Symphony No.5      Op.119 (1949)
Symphony (Pallas Athene) Op.137 (1955)

KRETER, Leo b. 29 August 1933

Symphony

KREUTZ, Arthur b. 25 July 1906

Symphony No.1      (Music for Orchestra) (1940)
Symphony No.2      (1943)

KRIENS, Christiaan Pieter Wilhelm b. 29 April 1881, d. 17 December 1934

Symphony No.1
Symphony No.2

KROEGER, Alfred C. b. 14 March 1890

Symphony in E flat    (1931)

KUBIK, Gail b. 5 September 1914, d. 20 July 1984

| Symphony No.1 | in E flat (1947–49) |
|---|---|
| Symphony No.2 | in F (1955) |
| Symphony No.3 | (1956) |

KUPFERMAN, Meyer b. 3 July 1926

| Symphony No.1 | (1950) |
|---|---|
| Symphony No.2 | (Chamber Symphony) (1950) |
| Symphony No.3 | (Little Symphony) |
| Symphony No.4 | (1956) |
| Symphony No.5 | (Lyric Symphony) |
| Symphony No.6 | (Ying Yang) (1972) |
| Symphony No.7 | Twilight (1974) |
| Symphony No.8 | (Sinfonia Brevis) (1975) |
| Symphony No.9 | (1980) |
| Symphony No.10 | (FDR) (1981) |
| Symphony No.11 | (1983) |
| Symphony for 12 | (1974) |
| Symphony for Six | (1984) |

Jazz Symphony for mezzo-soprano, alto saxophone and orchestra (1988)

KURKA, Robert b. 22 December 1921, d. 12 December 1957

| Symphony No.1 | Op.17 (1951) |
|---|---|
| Symphony No.2 | Op.24 (1953) |

Chamber Symphony Op.3
Symphony for brass and strings Op.7

KURTZ, Edward Frampton b. 31 July 1881, d. 8 June 1965

| Symphony No.1 | in A minor (1932, rev. 1949) |
|---|---|
| Symphony No.2 | in C (1939) |
| Symphony No.3 | in C minor (1939) |
| Symphony No.4 | in D (1942) |
| Symphony No.5 | in G (1943–49) |

KURTZ, Eugene Allen b. 27 December 1923

Symphony for strings (1956)
Chamber Symphony for the 4th of July (1958–59)

KYNASTON, Trent P. b. 7 December 1946

| Symphony | (1969) |
|---|---|

KYR, Robert Harry b. 20 April 1952

| Symphony No.1 | |
|---|---|
| Symphony No.2 | |
| Symphony No.3 | (The Fifth Season) (1989) |

# L

LABUNSKI, Felix b. 27 December 1892, d. 28 April 1979

Symphony No.1     in G minor (1937)
Symphony No.2     in D (1954)

LABUNSKI, Wiktor b. 14 April 1895, d. 26 January 1974

Symphony     in G minor Op.14 (1936)

LADERMAN, Ezra b. 29 June 1924

Leipzig Symphony     (1945)
Sinfonia     (1956)
Symphony No.1     (1963–64)
Symphony No.2     (Luther) (1968)
Symphony No.3     (Jerusalem) (1973)
Symphony No.4     for brass and orchestra (1980)
Symphony No.5     (Isaiah) (1982)
Symphony No.6     for soprano and orchestra (1983)
Symphony No.7     (1984)
Symphony No.8     (1993)

La MONTAINE, John b. 17 March 1920

Symphony No.1     Op.28 (1957)

La MOTTE, Diether de

Symphony in two movements (1964)

LANG, Henry Albert b. 9 October 1854, d. 27 May 1930

Symphony No.1
Symphony No.2

LANGE, Arthur b. 16 April 1889, d. 7 December 1956

Symphony No.1     (Lyric American) (1948)

LANGLEY, Allen Lincoln b. 1892

Symphony No.1
Symphony No.2

LANIER, Sidney b. 3 February 1842, d. 7 September 1881

Symphony of the Plantations (unfinished)

LANO, Stephen

Sinfonia Eikasia (1989)

La PORTA, Louis F. b. 23 September 1944

Symphony in one movement

LARGENT, Edward J. Jnr b. 8 February 1936

Symphony for brass  (1966)

LARSEN, Libby (Elizabeth) b. 24 December 1950

Symphony No.1      (Water Music) (1985)
Symphony No.2
Symphony No.3      (Lyric) (1991–92)

LATHAM, William Peters b. 4 January 1917

Symphony No.1      (1950)
Symphony No.2      (Sinfonietta) (1953)

LAUER, John David b. 21 May 1945

Symphony 1980      (1980)

LAUFER, Beatrice b. 27 April 1923

Symphony No.1      (1944)
Symphony No.2      (1961)

LAURIDSEN, Morten Johannes b. 27 February 1943

Symphony No.1

LAVALLÉE, Calixa b. 28 December 1842, d. 21 January 1891

Symphony

La VIOLETTE, Wesley b. 4 January 1894, d. 29 July 1978

Symphony No.1      (1936)
Symphony No.2      (Tom Thumb) in B flat (1940)
Symphony No.3      (1942)
Symphony for band  (1942)

LAZAROF, Henri b. 12 April 1932

Chamber Symphony  (1977)
Symphony No.1      (1978)
Symphony No.2      (1990)
Symphony No.3      (Choral Symphony) (1993)

LEAHY, Mary Weldon b. 20 August 1926

Symphony in one movement
Symphony for strings

LEE, Dai-Keong b. 2 September 1915

Symphony No.1      in one movement (1942, rev. 1947)
Symphony No.2      (1952)
Symphony with a Tahitian Happening for Tahitian dancer and orchestra

LEEF, Yinam Arie b. 21 December 1953

Symphony No.1

LEES, Benjamin b. 8 January 1924

| | |
|---|---|
| Symphony No.1 | (1953) withdrawn |
| Symphony No.2 | (1958) |
| Symphony No.3 | (1969) |
| Symphony No.4 | (Memorial Candles) for mezzo soprano, violin and orchestra (1989) |
| Symphony No.5 | (Kalmar Nyckel) (1988) |

LEFTWICH, Vernon b. 19 June 1881, d. 8 March 1977

Symphony No.1

LEHRMAN, Leonard Jordan b. 20 August 1949

Chamber Symphony

LEICHTENTRITT, Hugo b. 1 January 1874, d. 13 November 1951

Symphony

LEICHTLING, Alan Robert b. 16 April 1947

| | |
|---|---|
| Symphony No.1 | |
| Symphony No.2 | (1966) |
| Symphony No.3 | |

LEIDZEN, Erik b. 25 March 1894, d. 20 December 1962

| | |
|---|---|
| Irish Symphony | (1939) |
| Symphony No.2 | (Symphony in the Sky) |

LEMIEUX, Glenn Claude

Sacred Symphony     (1989)

LEPLIN, Emanuel b. 3 October 1917, d. 1 December 1972

Symphony of the 12th century (1961)
Symphony No.2     (1965)
Symphony No.3

LESEMANN, Frederick b. 12 October 1936

Symphony in three movements (1971)

LEVENSON, Boris b. 10 March 1884, d. 11 March 1947

Symphony     (1909)

LEVITCH, Leon b. 9 July 1927

| | |
|---|---|
| Symphony No.1 | Op.15 (1967) |
| Symphony No.2 | (The Taos) Op.18 (1983) |

LEVY, Ellis b. 23 October 1887

Symphony No.1
Symphony No.2
Symphony No.3
Symphony No.4
Symphony No.5
Symphony No.6
Symphony No.7
Symphony No.8
Symphony No.9
Symphony No.10
Symphony No.11
Symphony No.12
Symphony No.13
Symphony No.14      (1964)

LEVY, Frank Ezra b. 15 October 1930

Symphony No.1      for small orchestra (1968)
Symphony No.2      for brass and percussion (1972)
Symphony No.3
Symphony No.4      (Structures of the Mind)

LEVY, Marvin David b. 2 August 1932

Symphony            (1960)

LEWIS, Gordon

Symphony No.1      (1960)

LEWIS, H. Merrills b. 1 October 1908, d. 14 May 1979

Symphony in A      (1936)
Symphony in one movement

LEWIS, John Leo b. 11 May 1911

Symphony in A

LEWIS, Robert Hall b. 22 April 1926

Symphony No.1      (1964)
Symphony No.2      (1971)
Symphony No.3      (1982–85)
Symphony No.4      (1990)

LIEBERSON, Goddard b. 5 April 1911, d. 29 May 1977

Symphony            (1937)

LINDENFELD, Harris Nelson b. 15 May 1945

Sinfonia for concert band (1971)

LINN, Robert b. 11 August 1925

Symphony in one movement (1956, rev. 1961)
Sinfonia for strings   (1967, rev. 1972)

LIST, Kurt b. 21 June 1913, d. 16 November 1970

Symphony No.1      for voices and orchestra

LOCKWOOD, Larry Paul b. 18 June 1943

Symphony            (1969)

LOCKWOOD, Normand b. 19 March 1906

Symphony in E       (1928–29) withdrawn
Symphony            (A Year's Chronicle) (1934)
Symphony            (1941)
Symphony for strings (1975)
Symphony for large orchestra (1978–79)
Symphony in four movements and coda (1993)

LOEB, David b. 11 May 1939

Symphony for chamber orchestra of Japanese instruments

LOEFFLER, Charles Martin Turnow b. 30 January 1861, d. 19 May 1935

Symphony: Hora Mystica (1916) with men's chorus

LONG, Newell Hillis b. 12 February 1905

Symphony for band

LOOS, Armin b. 20 February 1909, d. 23 March 1971

Symphony in memoriam Ferrucio Busoni (1940)
Symphony for strings (1940)
Symphony in Canon Form (1941)
Symphony: View, approach, goodbye

LOPATNIKOFF, Nicolai b. 16 March 1903, d. 7 October 1976

Symphony No.1       Op.12 (1929)
Symphony No.2       in F minor Op.24 (1939) (withdrawn)
Symphony No.3       Op.35 (1954)
Symphony No.4       Op.46 (1971)

LO PRESTI, Ronald b. 28 October 1933, d. 25 October 1985

Symphony No.1       (1968)
Symphony No.2       (1970)

LORA, Antonio b. 2 December 1900, d. 19 October 1965

Symphony No.1
Symphony No.2       (1955)

LOSH, Werner J.

| | |
|---|---|
| Symphony No.1 | (1959) |
| Symphony No.2 | (1962) |

LOVALLO, Lee

| | |
|---|---|
| Symphony | (1980) |

LUCKMAN, Phillis b. 13 September 1927

Symphony for massed cellos

LUEDEKE, Raymond b. 1 November 1944

Chamber Symphony No.1 (1971)

LUENING, Otto b. 15 June 1900, d. 2 September 1996

Short Symphony for chamber orchestra (1929, rev. 1980)
A Wisconsin Symphony (1975)

LUKE, Ray b. 30 May 1928

| | |
|---|---|
| Symphony No.1 | (1958–59) |
| Symphony No.2 | (1961) |
| Symphony No.3 | (1963) |
| Symphony No.4 | (1970) |

LYNN, George b. 5 October 1915

| | |
|---|---|
| Symphony No.1 | (1962–63) |
| Symphony No.2 | |
| Symphony No.3 | |

# M

McAFEE, Don b. 3 June 1935

Choral Symphony
Short Symphony

McBETH, William Francis b. 9 March 1933

| | |
|---|---|
| Symphony No.1 | (1955) |
| Symphony No.2 | (1957) |
| Symphony No.3 | (1963) |
| Symphony No.4 | (1970) |

McBRIDE, Robert b. 20 February 1911

Hill-Country Symphony for band (1962)

McCOY, William J. b. 15 March 1848, d. 15 October 1926

Symphony in F

McCULLOUGH, James b. 1939

Call Me Ishmael Symphony (1980)

McCULLOH, Byron B. b. 1 March 1927

Sinfonia for wind and percussion (1974)
Symphony            (1975)

McDONALD, Harl b. 27 July 1899, d. 30 March 1955

Symphony No.1      (The Santa Fé Trail) (1933)
Symphony No.2      (Rhumba) (1934)
Symphony No.3      (Tragic Circle: The Lament of Fu Hsuan) for soprano, chorus and
  orchestra (1936)
Symphony No.4      (Festival of Workers) (1938)
Symphony No.5      (Children's Symphony on Familiar Themes) (1948)

McGRATH, Joseph J. b. 1889, d. 1968

Symphony

McHUGH, Charles Russell b. 5 August 1940

Symphony No.1      (1965)
Symphony No.2      (1968)
Symphony No.3

McKAY, George Frederick b. 11 June 1899, d. 4 October 1970

Short Symphony (From the Black Hills) Op.5 (1925)
Symphonie Miniature Op.40
Symphony (Evocation) Op.133c (1951)
Symphony Miniature No.2 (1967)
Symphony No.5      (For Seattle) (1950)

McKAY, Harper b. 13 October 1921

Symphony No.1      (1955–56)

McKAY, (Roderick) Neil b. 16 June 1924

Symphony            (1955–56)

McKINLEY, William Thomas b. 9 December 1938

Symphony No.1      (1977)
Symphony No.2      (1978)
Symphony No.3      (1983)
A Short Symphony for brass ensemble (1983)
Symphony No.4      (1985)
Symphony No.5      (Irish) (1988)

McKUEN, Rod Marvin b. 29 April 1933

Symphony No.1      (All Men Love Something) Op.7.
Symphony No.2

Symphony No.3    (A Piece of the Continent, a Part of the Main) Op.45 (1973)
Symphony No.4    (Birch Trees) Op.53

MacLEAN, John Torry b. 12 April 1933

Symphony: In Memoriam (1966–67)

McMAHON, John E. b. 1889

Symphony in Syncopation in B flat minor Op.6 (1939–40)

McPHEE, Colin Carhart b. 15 March 1901, d. 7 January 1964

Symphony No.1    in one movement (1930) lost
Symphony No.2    (Pastoral) (1957)
Symphony No.3    (1962) (incomplete)

MACE, Richard Arthur b. 3 September 1913

Symphony to Normandy '44

MACY, Carleton b. 10 September 1933

Chamber Symphony

MADDEN, Edward J.

Sinfonia on Jewish Folk Songs for band (1962)

MAESCH, LaVahn K. b. 15 October 1904

Symphony in E    (1941)

MAGANINI, Quinto b. 30 November 1897, d. 10 March 1974

Symphony No.1    in C minor (1932)
Sylvan Symphony Op.29 for 13 instruments (1932)

MAILMAN, Martin b. 30 June 1932

Symphony No.1    Op.46 (1969)
Symphony No.2    Op.63 (1980)
Symphony No.3    (1983)

MAINENTE, Anton Eugene b. 5 November 1889, d. 18 August 1963

Symphony    (America)

MAMLOK, Ursula b. 1 February 1928

Symphony No.1    in E flat (1956) withdrawn

MANDEL, Alan b. 17 July 1935

Symphony    (1961)

MANDEL, David

Symphony No.1    (1950)

MANSON, Eddy Lawrence b. 9 May 1919
Symphony

MARAFFI, Lewis Frederick
Symphony No.1

MARCELLI, Nino b. 21 January 1890, d. 16 August 1967
Symphony

MARCUS, Adabelle Gross b. 8 July 1929
Symphony to the Spheres

MARET, Stanley b. 25 June 1926
Symphony No.1      (1956)

MARGOLIS, Jerome N. b. 30 October 1941
Symphony

MARRA, James Richard
Symphony         (1977)

MARTIN, Paul A. b. 12 December 1919
Symphony No.1 for chamber orchestra

MARTINO, Donald James b. 16 May 1931
Sinfonia           (1953) withdrawn

MARVEL, Robert b. 1918
Symphony No.1      (1947)

MASLANKA, David Henry b. 30 August 1943
Shibui Symphony     (1970)
Symphony No.2
Symphony No.3

MASON, Daniel Gregory b. 20 November 1873, d. 4 December 1953
Symphony No.1      in C minor Op.11 (1913–14, rev. 1924)
Symphony No.2      in A Op.30 (1929–30)
Symphony No.3      (Lincoln) Op.35 (1935–36)

MATSON, Siegfred C. b. 17 February 1917
Symphony No.1      (1945)

MATTHEWS, Holon b. 17 July 1904, d. 1993
Symphony No.1      (1947)

Symphony No.2
Symphony No.3
Symphony No.4

MATTILA, Edward Charles b. 30 November 1927

Symphony No.1

MAURICE-JACQUET, H. b. 18 March 1886, d. 29 June 1954

American Symphony

MAVES, David W(alter) b. 3 April 1937

Symphony No.1      for student orchestra (1970)
Symphony No.2      (1975)
Symphony No.3      (1977)
Symphony No.4      for student orchestra (1980)
Symphony No.5      (1983) unfinished
Symphony No.6      (1984) unfinished

MAYNARD, George

Symphony in G      (1939)

MAXFIELD, Richard Vance b. 2 February 1927, d. 27 June 1969

Symphony for strings (1951)

MAXWELL, Charles b. 25 October 1892, d. 20 August 1962

Symphony (Congo Spirituale)

MAY, David W. b. 28 September 1931

Symphony No.1
Symphony No.2      (1973)

MAY, Walter Bruce b. 28 September 1931

Symphony No.1
Symphony No.2

MECHEM, Kirke Lewis b. 16 August 1925

Symphony No.1      Op.16 (1958–59)
Symphony No.2      Op.29 (1966, rev. 1968)

MEIGNEN, Leopold b. 1793, d. 4 June 1873

Grand Military Symphony

MENNIN, Peter b. 17 May 1923, d. 17 June 1983

Symphony No.1      (1941) withdrawn
Symphony No.2      (1944)
Symphony No.3      (1946)
Symphony No.4      (The Cycle) for chorus and orchestra (1948)

Symphony No.5      (1950)
Symphony No.6      (1953)
Symphony No.7      (Variations) (1963)
Symphony No.8      (1973)
Symphony No.9      (1981)
Sinfonia for chamber orchestra (1946)
Sinfonia           (1971) withdrawn

MENNINI, Louis b. 18 November 1920

Symphony No.1      (Da Chiesa) (1960)
Symphony No.2      (Da Festa) (1963)

MENOTTI, Gian Carlo b. 7 July 1911

Symphony           (The Halcyon) (1976)

MERRYFIELD, Norman L. b. 19 November 1906

Symphony

MERRIMAN, Margarita Leonor b. 29 November 1927

Symphony No.1      (1958)
Symphony No.2      (1981)

MEYEROWITZ, Jan b. 23 April 1913

Symphony Midrash Esther (1955)
Silesian Symphony  (1957)
Sinfonia Brevissima (1965)

MEYERS, Emerson b. 27 October 1910

Symphony for small orchestra

MICHALSKY, Donal b. 13 July 1928, d. 31 December 1975

Little Symphony for band (1959)
Choral Symphony (No.1) (Wheels of Time) (1967)
Symphony No.2      (Sinfonia Concertante) (1969)
Symphony No.3      (1975)

MIDDLETON, Owen b. 8 August 1928

Symphony in one movement (1965)

MIDDLETON, Robert b. 18 November 1920

Sinfonia filofonica (1969)

MIDGLEY, Charles William b. 17 December 1899, d. 2 April 1985

Symphony No.1      in C (Peace)
Symphony No.2      (Teacher-Pupil)
Symphony No.3      in G (For the Children)

MILLER, Charles b. 1 January 1899
Symphony

MILLER, Ralph Dale b. 17 March 1909, d. 1 July 1989
Symphony for band   (1974)

MILLS, Alvin Marvin b. 2 February 1922
Symphony No.1      (The Big Mountain) (1960)

MILLS, Charles b. 8 January 1914, d. 7 March 1982
Symphony No.1      in E minor (1939)
Symphony No.2      in C (1942)
Symphony No.3      in D minor (1952)
Symphony No.4      (Crazy Horse) (1957)
Symphony No.5      for strings (1980)
Symphony No.6      (1981)

MINEO, Attilio b. 28 August 1918
Symphony No.1
Symphony No.2
Symphony No.3
Symphony No.4
Symphony No.5

MIRANTE, Thomas b. 11 October 1911
Symphony No.1      (1968)

MISSAL, Joshua M. b. 12 April 1915
Symphony No.1      (1939)

MOEVS, Robert Walter b. 2 December 1920
Symphony in three movements (1954–56)
Symphonic Pieces Nos 4–6 (1973–86)

MOHAUPT, Richard Ernest Edward b. 14 September 1904, d. 3 July 1957
Symphony (Rhythm and Variations) (1942)

MOLLER, John Christopher b. 1755, d. 21 September 1803
Sinfonia           (1793)

MOLS, Robert
Symphony No.1      (1961)

MONELLO, Spartaco Vindice b. 29 June 1909
Symphony No.1      Op.9 (1946)
Symphony No.2      Op.11 for strings (1947)

Symphony No.3     Op.22
Symphony No.4     Op.30

MOORE, Dorothy Rudd b. 4 June 1940

Symphony No.1     (1963)

MOORE, Douglas Stuart b. 10 August 1893, d. 25 July 1969

A Symphony of Autumn (1928)
Symphony No.2     in A (1945)

MORGAN, Robert P. b. 28 July 1934

Symphony          (1967)

MORILL, Dexter G. b. 17 June 1938

Symphony          (1971)

MORITZ, Edvard b. 23 June 1891, d. 30 September 1974

Symphony No.1     in C minor
Symphony No.2     in D minor Op.108
Symphony No.3     in A minor Op.115
Symphony No.4     Op.127

MOROSS, Jerome b. 1 August 1913, d. 25 July 1983

Symphony          (1940–42)

MORRIS, Franklin E. b. 1920

Symphony

MORRIS, Harold b. 17 March 1890, d. 6 May 1964

Symphony No.1     (Prospice) (1923)
Symphony No.2     (Victory) (1936)
Symphony No.3     (Amaranth) (1946)
Symphony No.4     (1952)

MORSE, Richard

Symphony No.1     (1951)

MOSS, Lawrence K(enneth) b. 18 November 1927

Symphonies for brass quintet and chamber orchestra (1977)

MOURANT, Stanley

Symphony          (1930)

MOYER, J. Harold b. 6 May 1927

Symphony No.1     (1957)

MUCZYNSKI, Robert b. 19 March 1929

Symphony Op.5    (1953)

MUELLER, Frederick A. b. 3 March 1921

Symphony No.1    (1957)

MULLER, Gerald Frank b. 25 July 1932

Symphony No.1    (1980)

MUMMA, Gordon b. 30 March 1935

Sinfonia for 12 instruments and tape (1958–60)

MURADIAN, Vazgen b. 17 October 1921

| | |
|---|---|
| Symphony No.1 | in G minor Op.56 (1957) |
| Symphony No.2 | in D major Op.62 (1958) |
| Symphony No.3 | in B minor Op.65 (1959) |
| Symphony No.4 | in E minor Op.96 (1963) |
| Symphony No.5 | in C major Op.114 (1963) |
| Symphony No.6 | in A minor Op.115 (1964) |
| Symphony No.7 | in C minor Op.131 (1967) |
| Symphony No.8 | in D minor Op.132 (1968) |
| Symphony No.9 | in D minor Op.137 (1972) |
| Symphony No.10 | in F major Op.138 (1973) |
| Symphony No.11 | in C minor Op.139 (1973) |
| Symphony No.12 | in G major Op.140 (1974) |
| Symphony No.13 | in D major Op.143 (1975) |
| Symphony No.14 | in A minor Op.144 (1977) |
| Symphony No.15 | in A major Op.145 (1978) |
| Symphony No.16 | in D major Op.146 (1979) |
| Symphony No.17 | in A minor Op.149 (1981) |
| Symphony No.18 | in C major Op.150 (1983) |
| Symphony No.19 | in G minor Op.151 (1984) |
| Symphony No.20 | in E minor Op.152 (1986) |
| Symphony No.21 | in A major Op.153 (1988) |
| Symphony No.22 | in A minor Op.156 (1989) |
| Symphony No.23 | in C major Op.157 for strings (1990) |
| Symphony No.24 | in A minor Op.158 (1991) |
| Symphony No.25 | in D minor Op.159 (1992) |
| Symphony No.26 | in G minor Op.162 for strings (1993) |
| Symphony No.27 | in E minor Op.163 for strings (1993) |
| Symphony No.28 | in C minor Op.164 (1994) |
| Symphony No.29 | in D minor Op.165 for strings (1994) |
| Symphony No.30 | in A minor Op.166 (1994) |
| Symphony No.31 | in C minor (1995) |
| Symphony No.32 | in A minor (1995) |
| Symphony No.33 | in E minor (1996) |
| Symphony No.34 | in D major (1996) |
| Symphony No.35 | in D minor (1996) |
| Symphony No.36 | in G major (1996) |

MYERS, Theldon b. 4 February 1927

Symphony          (1969)

MYROW, Frederic b. 16 July 1939

Chamber Symphony (1963)
Sand Mountain Symphony for banjo, singer and orchestra

# N

NABOKOV, Nicholas b. 17 April 1903, d. 6 April 1978

Symphony No.1     (Lyrical) (1930)
Symphony No.2     (Sinfonia Biblica) (1941)
Symphony No.3     (A Prayer) (1967)

NAGINSKI, Charles b. 29 May 1909, d. 4 August 1940

Symphony No.1     (1935)
Symphony No.2     (1937)

NANES, Richard b. 1941

Symphony No.1     in B flat (1984)
Symphony for strings (1986)
Symphony No.2     in B (1986)
Symphony No.3     (1984–86)
Symphony No.4     (1987–88)

NAYLOR, William

Symphony in Miniature (1941)

NEAL, Charles Taylor b. 4 July 1946

Symphony No.1     for band
Symphony No.2     for band

NEDELSON, Andrew

A Symphony of Praise (1988)

NEIKRUG, Marc (Edward) b. 24 September 1946

Symphony No.1     (1991)

NELHYBEL, Vaclav b. 24 September 1919, d. 1996

Symphony          (1942)

NEWLIN, Dika b. 22 November 1923

Chamber Symphony for 12 instruments (1949)
Sinfonia          (1947)
Symphony for chorus and orchestra

NEWMAN Anthony b. 12 May 1941

Sinfonia No.1        (Of Fallen Heroes) (1991)

NEWMAN, Theodore Spencer b. 18 June 1933, d. 16 February 1975

Symphony No.1        in F sharp

NEWMAN, William Stein b. 6 April 1912

Little Symphony        (1940)

NIBLOCK, James F. b. 1 November 1917

Symphony            (1954)
Chamber Symphony    (1959)

NICHOLL, Horace Wadham b. 17 March 1848, d. 10 March 1922

Symphony No.1        in G minor (The Nation's Mourning) Op.8
Symphony No.2        in C Op.12 (1878–89)

NIX, Theo M. b. 1 December 1910

Symphony

NORDEN, Hugo b. 31 December 1909

Symphony            (1948)

NORDOFF, Paul b. 4 June 1909, d. 18 January 1977

Symphony No.1        (Winter) (1954)
Symphony No.2        (Spring) (1956)
Tranquil Symphony    (1955)
Little Symphony

NORMAN, Theodore b. 14 March 1912

Symphony            (1951)

NORTH, Alex b. 4 December 1910, d. 8 September 1991

Symphony No.1        (1947)
Symphony No.2        (Africa) (1968)
Symphony No.3        (1971)

NOTT, Douglas Duane b. 27 February 1944

Symphony No.1        (Places I) (1979)
Symphony No.2        (Places II) (The Kalama)

# O

OBRECHT, Eldon b. 9 June 1920

Symphony No.1        (1950) with soprano solo

Symphony No.2      (1955)
Symphony No.3      (1972)

OʼBRIEN, Eugene b. 24 April 1945

Symphony            (1969)

OHLEY, Maxwell

Symphony in A minor (1941)
Symphony in Time of War (1943)

OLAN, David b. 1949

Symphony            (1984)

OLDBERG, Arne b. 12 July 1874, d. 17 February 1962

Symphony No.1
Symphony No.2
Symphony No.3      in F minor Op.41 (1927)
Symphony No.4      in B minor Op.50 (1942)
Symphony No.5      in E minor Op.54 (1950)

OLDS, Gerry b. 26 February 1933

Short Symphony     (1956)

ORLAND, Henry b. 23 April 1918

Symphony No.1
Symphony No.2      (Song of Songs)
Symphony No.3      (Ode, epitaph and dithyramb) Op.19
Symphony No.4      (Ariadne episode and Psyché) for narrator, soprano and string
  orchestra

ORLOB, Harold F. b. 3 June 1883, d. 25 June 1982

Symphony (Recreation) with optional chorus

ORNSTEIN, Leo b. 11 December 1892

Symphony            (1930)

OROWAN, Thomas F. b. 15 November 1940

Symphony No.1      (A New England Symphony) (1967)

OSENTOWSKI, Francis Eugene

Symphony for band  (1977)

OSTERLING, Eric Alfred b. 21 March 1926

Symphony No.1      for band

OTEY, Orlando b. 1 February 1925

Sinfonia Breve      (1956)

OTT, David b. 1947

Symphony No.1
Symphony No.2      (1991)
Symphony No.3      (1992)

OVANIN, Nikola Leonard b. 25 November 1911, d. 5 February 1992

Symphony No.1      (Mars) in one movement (1939)
Symphony No.2      (1946)
Symphony No.3      (Toys Symphony) (1969)

OVERTON, Hall b. 23 February 1920, d. 24 November 1972

Symphony No.1      for strings (1955)
Symphony No.2      in one movement (1962)

OWEN, Blythe b. 8 February 1900

Symphony            (1947)

OWEN, Jerry Michael b. 6 June 1944

Symphon [sic]       (1967)


P

PADWA, Vladimir b. 8 February 1906

Symphony in D
Symphony for strings

PAINE, John Knowles b. 9 January 1839, d. 25 April, 1906

Symphony No.1      in C minor Op.23 (1876)
Symphony No.2      in A (In the Spring) Op.34 (1880)

PALANGE, Louis Salvador b. 17 December 1917, d. 8 June 1979

Symphony No.1      (Invasion) (1946)
Symphony No.2      in E minor (1950)
Symphony in Steel for band (1940)

PALMER, Robert Moffat b. 2 June 1915

Symphony No.1      (1953, rev. 1979)
Symphony No.2      (1966)

PARCHMAN, Gen Louis b. 2 May 1929

Symphony No.1      for strings (1960)
Symphony No.2      for strings (1962)
Symphony No.3      (1962)
Symphony No.4      (Spring) for chorus and orchestra (1968)
Symphony No.5      for chorus and orchestra (1968)

PARK, Stephen b. 23 September 1911

Symphony No.1
Symphony No.2
Symphony No.3

PARKER, Horatio William b. 15 September 1863, d. 18 December 1919

Symphony in C      Op.7 (1884)

PARKS, Gordon b. 30 November 1912

Tree Symphony

PARMENTIER, Francis Gordon b. 24 April 1923

Symphony No.1      (1957)
Symphony No.2      (1965)
Symphony No.3      (1976)
Symphony No.4      (1993)

PARRIS, Herman M. b. 30 October 1903, d. 14 January 1973

Symphony No.1      (1946)
Symphony No.2      (1947)
Symphony No.3      (1949)
Symphony No.4      (1952)

PARRIS, Robert b. 21 May 1924

Symphony for chamber orchestra (1952)

PATTERSON, Andy James b. 20 February 1929

Symphony           (1969)

PAULUS, Stephen Harrison b. 24 August 1949

Symphony in three movements (Soliloquys) (1986)
Symphony for Strings (1989)

PELOQUIN, Alexander b. 16 June 1918

Symphony of Praise (Psalm 150) for men's chorus, congregation and orchestra (1963)

PENN, William Albert b. 11 January 1943

Symphony           (1971)

PERKINS, Charles Callahan b. 1 March 1823, d. 25 August 1886

Grand Symphony      (1850)

PERKINS, William b. 28 April 1941

Chamber Symphony (1971)

PERLE, George b. 6 May 1915

Symphony No.1      (1948)
Symphony No.2      Op.26 (1950) withdrawn
Symphony No.3      Op.31 (1952) withdrawn
Symphony for band Op.38 (1959) withdrawn
A Short Symphony    (1980)

PERPESSA, Hariolaos b. 13 September 1900

Symphony              (The Seventh Seal)

PERRY, Julie b. 25 March 1924, d. 29 April 1979

Symphony No.1      for violas and string basses (1959)
Symphony No.2      (1960)
Symphony No.3      (1962)
Symphony No.4      (1964)
Symphony No.5      (1965)
Symphony No.6      (1966) for band
Symphony No.7      (Symphony U.S.A.) for chorus and small orchestra (1967)
Symphony No.8      (1968–69)
Symphony No.9      (1965–70)
Symphony No.10     (1971)
Symphony No.11     (Soul Symphony) (1972)
Symphony No.12     (1972)
A Simple Symphony in one movement (1973)

PERSICHETTI, Vincent b. 6 June 1915, d.14 August 1987

Symphony No.1      Op.18 (1941)
Symphony No.2      Op.19 (1942)
Symphony No.3      Op.30 (1946)
Symphony No.4      Op.51 (1951)
Symphony No.5      for strings Op.61 (1953)
Symphony No.6      for band (1956)
Symphony No.7      (Liturgical) Op.80 (1958)
Symphony No.8      Op.106 (1967)
Symphony No.9      Op.113 (Sinfonia Janiculum) (1970)

PETERS, William Cumming b. 10 March 1805, d. 20 April 1866

Symphony in D       (1831)

PHELPS, Ellsworth C. b. 11 August 1827, d. 29 November 1913

Symphony              (Hiawatha) (1880)

PHELPS, Norman F. b. 27 April 1911

Symphony              (1949)

PICKER, Tobias b. 18 July 1954

Symphony              (1982)
Symphony No.2      (Aussöhnung: Goethe) for soprano and orchestra (1986)
Symphony No.3      for string orchestra (1989)

PIERCE, Alexandra b. 21 February 1934

Symphony No.1
Symphony No.2        (Dances on the Face of the Deep) Op.74 (1988)

PIKET, Frederick b. 6 January 1903, d. 28 February 1974

Symphony in B (with tenor in finale)

PILLIN, Boris William b. 31 May 1940

Symphony            (1964)

PIMSLEUR, Solomon b. 19 September 1900, d. 22 April 1962

Symphony to Disillusionment in one movement Op.25 (1928–29)
Symphony to Terror and Despair Op.55
Symphony to the Struggle for Existence

PINKHAM, Daniel Rogers b. 5 June 1923

Symphony No.1        (1960)
Symphony No.2        (1963)
Symphony No.3        (1985)
Symphony No.4        (1990)

PISTON, Walter Hamor b. 20 January 1894, d. 12 November 1976

Symphony No.1        (1937)
Symphony No.2        (1943)
Symphony No.3        (1947)
Symphony No.4        (1949–50)
Symphony No.5        (1954)
Symphony No.6        (1955)
Symphony No.7        (1960)
Symphony No.8        (1964)

PLAYMAN, Gordon b. 29 January 1922

Symphony No.1        (1947)
Symphony No.2        (After Camus' Myth of Sisyphus) (1971)
Symphony No.3        (Celebration Symphony) (1974)

PLETTNER, Arthur (Rudolph) b. 15 November 1904

Symphony in G        (1950–51)

POLIN, Claire b. 1 January 1926

Symphony No.1        (1961) withdrawn
Symphony No.2        (Korean) with optional narrator (1976)

POLLAK, William Thomas b. 22 December 1900

Symphony

POPE, Conrad b. 21 November 1951

Symphony              (1973)

PORTER, (William) Quincy b. 7 February 1897, d. 12 November 1966

Symphony No.1        (1934)
Symphony No.2        (1962)

POWELL, John b. 6 September 1882, d. 15 August 1963

Symphony in A (Virginian) (1945)

POWELL, Laurence b. 13 January 1899, d. 29 January 1990

Symphony No.1        (1928–30)
Symphony No.2        (1943)

POZDRO, John Walter b. 14 August 1923

Symphony No.1        (1949)
Symphony No.2        (1957)
Symphony No.3        (1960)

PRATT, Silas Gamaliel b. 4 August 1846, d. 30 October 1916

Symphony No.1        (1871)
Symphony No.2        (Prodigal Son) (1875)
Symphony No.3        (Lincoln Symphony)

PRESSER, William Henry b. 19 April 1916

Symphony No.1        for band (1962) withdrawn
Symphony No.2        for band (1968)

PREVIN, André b. 6 April 1929

Symphony for Strings (1962)

PRICE, Florence Beatrice b. 9 April 1888, d. 3 June 1953

Symphony No.1        in E minor (1925)
Symphony No.2        (Mississippi River) in D minor (1934)
Symphony No.3        in C minor (1940)
Symphony No.4        in G minor

PRIESING, Dorothy M. b. 31 July 1910

Symphony No.1        in one movement

PROCTOR, Leland H. b. 26 March 1914

Symphony No.1        (1948)
Symphony No.2        (Moby Dick)

PURSELL, William b. 1926

Symphony No.1        (1953)

PURSWELL, Patrick W. b. 1 July 1939

Symphony          (1959)

PUTSCHE, Thomas b. 29 June 1929

Symphony          (1963)

PYLE, Francis Johnson b. 13 September 1903, d. 31 December 1983

Symphony No.1      for symphonic band (1940)
Symphony in D minor


# Q

QUEENER, Charles Conant b. 27 July 1921

Symphony No.1      (1967)
Symphony No.2
Symphony No.3
Symphony No.4

QUILLING, Howard Lee b. 16 December 1935

Symphony for wind and percussion (1973)


# R

RACKLEY, Lawrence b. 10 September 1932

Symphony in G      (1957)

RAGLAND, Robert Oliver b. 3 July 1933

Symphony No.1
Symphony No.2
Symphony No.3
Symphony No.4
Symphony No.5
Symphony No.6
Symphony No.7
Symphony No.8
Symphony No.9
Symphony No.10
Symphony No.11
Symphony No.12

RAKOWSKI, David b. 1958

Symphony No.1 for soprano and orchestra

RAPHLING, Sam b. 19 March 1910

Symphony No.1      (1946)

Symphony No.2      (1947)
Symphony No.3      (1960)
Symphony No.4      (1960)
Symphony for chamber orchestra
Symphony for brass

RAPTAKIS, Kleon b. 25 May 1905, d. 9 November 1980

Symphony No.1
Symphony No.2
Symphony No.3

RATHAUS, Karol b. 16 September 1895, d. 21 November 1954

Symphony No.1      (1922)
Symphony No.2      (1923)
Symphony No.3      Op.50 (1942)

RATNER, Leonard Gilbert b. 30 July 1916

Symphony

READ, Gardner b. 2 January 1913

Symphony No.1      in A minor Op.30 (1934–36)
Symphony No.2      in E flat minor Op.45 (1940–42)
The Temptation of St Anthony: Dance Symphony Op.56 (1940–47)
Symphony No.3      Op.75 (1946–48)
Symphony No.4      Op.92 (1951–58)

READ, Thomas L. b. 3 July 1938

Symphony (with piano obbligato) (1986)

REED, Alfred b. 25 January 1921

Symphony No.1      for brass and percussion (1968)
Symphony No.2      for concert band (1979)
Symphony No.3      for concert band (1988)
Symphony No.4      for concert band (1993)
Symphony No.5      for concert band (1994–95)

REED, Herbert Owen b. 17 June 1910

Symphony No.1      (1939)
La Fiesta Mexicana (A Mexican Folksong Symphony)
   a)   for concert band (1948)
   b)   for orchestra (1965)

REID, Sarah Johnston b. 30 January 1948

Wasatch Symphony for band (1970)

REILLY, Jack b. 1 January 1932

Chamber Symphony No.1

RETI, Rudolf b. 27 November 1885, d. 7 February 1957

Symphonia Mystica   (1951)

REYNOLDS, Roger b. 18 July 1934

Symphony (Vertigo) for orchestra and tape (1986)

RICCI, Robert J. b. 25 April 1938

Symphony

RICHARDSON, Darrell Ervin b. 17 September 1911

Symphony in D minor (1965)

RIEGGER, Constantin Wallingford b. 29 April 1885, d. 2 April 1961

| | |
|---|---|
| Symphony No.1 | Op.37 (1944) withdrawn |
| Symphony No.2 | Op.41 (1945) withdrawn |
| Symphony No.3 | Op.42 (1946–47) |
| Symphony No.4 | Op.63 (1956) |

RIETI, Vittorio b. 28 January 1898, d. 19 February 1994

| | |
|---|---|
| Symphony No.1 | (1929) |
| Symphony No.2 | (1930) |
| Symphony No.3 | (Sinfonietta) (1932) |
| Symphony No.4 | (Sinfonia Tripartita) (1942) |
| Symphony No.5 | (1945) |
| Symphony No.6 | (1973) |
| Symphony No.7 | (1977) |
| Symphony No.8 | (1980–81) |
| Symphony No.9 | (1983–84) |

RILEY, Dennis (Daniel) b. 28 May 1943

Symphony for large orchestra (1983)

RITTER, Frédéric Louis b. 22 June 1824, d. 4 July 1891

| | |
|---|---|
| Symphony No.1 | |
| Symphony No.2 | (1881) |
| Symphony No.3 | |

ROBB, John Donald b. 12 June 1892

| | |
|---|---|
| Symphony No.1 | for strings Op.9 (1947) |
| Symphony No.2 | in C Op.23 (1952) |
| Symphony No.3 | in one movement Op.34 (1962) |
| Symphony No.4 | (Scenes from a New Mexican Mountain Village) |

ROBERTSON, Hugh Sterling II b. 19 June 1940, d. 15 November 1973

Symphony

ROBYN, Alfred George b. 29 April 1860, d. 18 October 1935

Symphony in D

ROCHBERG, George b. 5 July 1918

| | |
|---|---|
| Symphony No.1 | (1948–57, rev. 1971–77) |
| Symphony No.2 | (1955–56) in one movement |
| Symphony No.3 | for soloists, chorus and orchestra (1966–69) |
| Symphony No.4 | (1976) |
| Symphony No.5 | (1984–85) |
| Symphony No.6 | (1986) |
| Chamber Symphony | (1953) |

ROGERS, Bernard b. 4 February 1893, d. 24 May 1968

| | |
|---|---|
| Symphony No.1 | (Adonais) (1925) |
| Symphony No.2 | in A flat in one movement (1928) |
| Symphony No.3 | in C (On a Thanksgiving Song) (1936) |
| Symphony No.4 | in G minor (To Soldiers) (1945) |
| Symphony No.5 | (Africa) (1958) |

ROREM, Neb b. 23 October 1923

| | |
|---|---|
| Symphony No.1 | (1949) |
| Symphony No.2 | (1955) |
| Symphony No.3 | (1957–58) |
| Symphony for strings (1985) | |
| Sinfonia for wind and percussion (1957) | |

ROSNER, Arnold b. 8 November 1945

| | |
|---|---|
| Symphony No.1 | Op.3 (1961) |
| Symphony No.2 | Op.8 (1961) |
| Symphony No.3 | Op.20 (1963) |
| Symphony No.4 | Op.29 (1964) |
| Symphony No.5 | Op.57 (1973) |
| Symphony No.6 | Op.64 (1976) |

ROSS, Walter Beghtol b. 3 October 1936

A Jefferson Symphony for tenor, chorus and orchestra (1976)

ROUSE, Christopher (Chapman) b. 15 February 1949

| | |
|---|---|
| Symphony | (1986) |
| Symphony No.2 | (1994) |

RÓZSA, Béla b. 14 February 1905, d. 8 October 1977

Symphony (Ibis)

RÓZSA, Miklós b. 18 April 1907, d. 27 July 1995

Symphony Op.6 (1930, rev. 1990 as Op.6a)

RUBENSTEIN, William

Sinfonia          (1960)

RUDNĬTSKY, Antin b. 7 February 1902, d. 30 November 1975

Symphony No.1    (1936)
Symphony No.2    (1941)
Symphony No.3    (1942)

RUSSELL, Armand b. 23 June 1932

Balletic Symphony    (1957)

RUSSO, William b. 25 June 1928

Symphony No.1    (1957)
Symphony No.2    (The Titans) (1958)

RZEWSKI, Frederic Anthony b. 13 April 1938

Symphony for Several Performers (1968)


S

SACCO, P(atrick) Peter b. 25 October 1928

Symphony No.1    Op.18 (1955)
Symphony No.2    (Of Thanksgiving) (1965–76)
Symphony No.3    (The Convocation Symphony) (1968)

SAFRAN, Arno M. b. 27 August 1932

Symphony          (1954)

SAHL, Michael b. 2 September 1934

Symphony No.1    (1972)
Symphony No.2    for big band (1973)
Symphony No.3    (1978)
Symphony No.4    (1982)
Symphony No.5    (1983)

SAMINSKY, Lazare b. 27 October 1882, d. 1 July 1959

Symphony No.1    (Of the Great Rivers) Op.10 (1914)
Symphony No.2    (Of the Summits) Op.19 (1918)
Symphony No.3    (Of the Seas) (1924)
Symphony No.4    Op.35 (1926)
Symphony No.5    (Jerusalem: City of Solomon and Christ) Op.38 for chorus and
    orchestra (1932)
Symphony No.6    (1948)

SAMUEL, Gerhard b. 20 April 1924

A Short Symphony (Out of Time) (1978)

SAMUEL, Virginia Elizabeth

Symphony              (1988)

SANDBERG, Mordecai b. 4 February 1897, d. 28 December 1943

Symphony No.1
Symphony No.2

SANDERS, Robert L. b. 2 July 1906, d. 26 December 1974

Little Symphony No.1 in G (1937)
Symphony in B flat for band (1943)
Little Symphony No.2 in B flat (1953)
Symphony in A        (1954–55)
Little Symphony No.3 in D (1963)

SAPIEYEVSKY, Jerzy b. 20 March 1945

Symphony (Morpheus) for wind (1973)

SARACENI, Raymond b. 19 February 1932

Symphony No.1      in A flat

SAVINO, Domenico b. 13 January 1882, d. 8 August 1973

Symphony No.1

SAYLOR, Richard b. 6 August 1926

Symphony              (1966)

SCARMOLIN, Anthony Louis b. 30 July 1890, d. 13 July 1969

Symphony No.1      in E minor in one movement Op.154 (1937)
Symphony No.2      Op.200 (1946)
Symphony No.3      (Sinfonia Brevis) (1952)
Miniature Symphony No.1 in C Op.171 (1939)
Miniature Symphony No.2 in D minor (1942)

SCHAPHORST, Kenneth William

Symphony in E flat   (1990)

SCHELLING, Ernest b. 26 July 1876, d. 8 December 1939

Symphony in C sharp minor

SCHEVE, Edward Benjamin b. 13 February 1865, d. 19 June 1924

Symphony

SCHIFFMAN, Harold (Anthony) b. 4 August 1928

Symphony              (1961)

SCHILLINGER, Joseph b. 31 August 1885, d. 23 March 1943

North Russian Symphony for accordian and orchestra (1931)

SCHLEIN, Irving b. 18 August 1905, d. 11 July 1986

Symphony No.1
Symphony No.2
Symphony No.3
Symphony No.4
Symphony No.5
Symphony No.6
Symphony No.7
Symphony No.8
Symphony No.9
Symphony No.10

SCHOENEFELD, Henry b. 4 October 1857, d. 4 August 1936

Symphony No.1     in G (Rural) (1893)
Symphony No.2     (Spring)

SCHREIBER, Frederick Charles b. 13 January 1895

Symphony No.1     in D minor Op.42 (1927)
Symphony No.2     Op.63
Symphony No.3     Op.67
Symphony No.4     (Fate and Farewell)
Symphony No.5
Symphony No.6
Symphony No.7     (Death and Eternity) for soli, chorus and orchestra (1957)
Symphony No.8
Symphony No.9

SCHRYOCK, Buren b. 13 December 1881, d. 20 June 1974

Symphony

SCHULLER, Gunther b. 22 November 1925

Symphony for brass and percussion (1949–50, rev. 1964)
Symphony          (1964)

SCHUMAN, William b. 4 August 1910, d. 14 February 1992

Symphony No.1     for 18 instruments (1935) withdrawn
Symphony No.2     in one movement (1937) withdrawn
Symphony No.3     (1941)
Symphony No.4     (1941)
Symphony No.5     for strings (1943)
Symphony No.6     in one movement (1948)
Symphony No.7     (1960)
Symphony No.8     (1961–62)
Symphony No.9     (Le Fosse Ardeatine) (1968)
Symphony No.10    (American Muse) (1975)

SCHUYTEN, Ernest Eugene Emile b. 7 November 1881, d. 13 November 1974

Symphony

SCHWAB, Harold

Symphony No.1    (1950)

SCHWANTNER, Joseph C. b. 22 March 1943

Sinfonia Brevis    (1963)
Evening Land: Symphony for chorus and orchestra (1992)

SCHWARTZ, Elliott b. 19 January 1936

Symphony in two movements  (1965)

SCIANNI, Joseph b. 6 October 1928

Sinfonia Breve    (1958)

SCLATER, James Stanley b. 24 October 1943

Symphony    (1975)

SCOTT, Tom (Thomas Jefferson) b. 28 May 1912, d. 12 August 1961

Symphony No.1    Op.2 (1946)

SEAGRAVE, Michael

Sinfonia    (1951)
Symphony No.1    (1960)

SEAR, Walter E. b. 27 April 1930

Symphony No.1
Symphony No.2    (1953)

SEARCH, Frederick Preston b. 22 July 1889, d. 1 November 1959

Symphony No.1    (1913)
Symphony No.2    (1931)
Symphony No.3    (1938)
Symphony No.4    in B flat (Roan Stallion) (1941)

SEARCH, Sara Opal (Heron PIANTIKOWSKI) b. 1890, d. 3 September 1961

Symphony in C minor for strings (1940)
Symphony No.2 in C minor (1941)

SELBST, George b. 21 February 1917

Symphony

SELIG, Robert b. 29 January 1939

Symphony No.1    (1962)
Symphony No.2    (1969)

SELLARS, James Edward b. 8 October 1943

Symphony    (1965)

SENDREY, Albert Richard b. 26 December 1900, d. 3 March 1976

Symphony No.1
Symphony No.2·          (Into America)
Symphony No.3

SEREBRIER, Jose b. 3 December 1938

Symphony No.1          in one movement (1956)
Symphony No.2          (Partita) (1960)
Symphony for percussion (1964)

SERLY, Tibor b. 25 November 1900, d. 8 October 1978

Symphony No.1          in B minor (1931)
Symphony No.2          for wind and percussion (1932)
Symphony for Strings (1956–58)
Symphony for Four Cycles for strings (1960)

SESSIONS, Roger b. 28 December 1896, d. 16 March 1985

Symphony in D          (1917) unpublished
Symphony No.1          in E minor (1926–27)
Symphony               (1934–35) lost
Symphony No.2          (1944–46)
Symphony No.3          (1955–57)
Symphony No.4          (1958)
Symphony No.5          (1964)
Symphony No.6          (1966)
Symphony No.7          (1967)
Symphony No.8          (1968)
Symphony No.9          (1978)

SEYFRIT, Michael Eugene b. 16 December 1947

Symphony No.1          for wind (Windfest) (1968)
Symphony No.2          for wind (Peace) (1969)
Symphony No.3          (Dichroism) for chamber orchestra (1970)

SHAHAN, Paul W. b. 2 January 1923

Symphony No.1          (1955)

SHAPERO, Harold Samuel b. 29 April 1920

Symphony for Classical Orchestra (1948)
Sinfonia in C minor

SHAPEY, Ralph b. 12 March 1921

Symphony               (1951)
Chamber Symphony  (1962)

SHAPLEIGH, Bertram b. 15 January 1871, d. 2 July 1940

Symphony No.1          in B minor Op.62
Symphony No.2          in A Op.68

SHELLEY, Harry Rowe b. 8 June 1858, d. 12 September 1947

Symphony No.1      in E flat (1897)
Symphony No.2

SHEPHERD, Arthur b. 19 February 1880, d. 12 January 1958

Symphony No.1      (Horizons) (1927)
Symphony No.2      in D minor (1938)

SHERMAN, Robert William b. 17 January 1921

Symphony in A      (1953)

SHIFRIN, Seymour b. 28 February 1926, d. 26 September 1979

Chamber Symphony  (1952–53)

SHORT, Gregory Norman b. 14 August 1938

Symphony No.1      (1968)
Symphony No.2      for brass choir and percussion (1973)

SHORTALL, Harrington b. 1895

Symphonia Breve    (1937)

SHULMAN, Alan M. b. 4 June 1915, d. 1993

Symphony No.1
Symphony No.2

SHURE, R(alph) Deane b. 31 May 1885

Symphony No.1
Symphony No.2
Symphony No.3
Symphony No.4
Symphony No.5

SHURTLEFF, Lynn Richard b. 3 November 1939

Symphony No.1
Symphony No.2

SIEGEL, Paul b. 8 December 1914, d. 2 April 1976

One World Symphony

SIEGMEISTER, Elie b. 15 January 1909, d. 10 March 1991

Symphony No.1      (1947, rev. 1971)
Symphony No.2      (1950, rev. 1971)
Symphony No.3      (1957)
Symphony No.4      (1967–70)
Symphony No.5      (Visions of Time) (1971–75)
Symphony No.6      (1983)
Symphony No.7      (1983)
Symphony No.8      (1984)

SIMUN, Francis George b. 3 July 1944
Symphony No.1      in D

SINGLETON, Alvin (Elliott) b. 28 December 1940
Sinfonia Diaspora (1991)

SLY, Allan B. b. 1907
Minature Symphony in one movement (1935)

SLATER, Philip b. 24 September 1924, d. 1966
Symphony          (1947)

SMIT, Johannes b. 1913
Symphony No.1      (1950)

SMIT, Leo b. 12 January 1921
Symphony No.1      in E flat (1955)
Symphony No.2      (1965)
Symphony No.3      (Symphony of Songs and Dances) (1981)

SMITH, Claude Thomas b. 14 March 1932
Symphony No.1      for band

SMITH, DAVID Stanley b. 6 July 1877, d. 17 December 1949
Symphony No.1      in F minor Op.28 (1910)
Symphony No.2      in D Op.42 (1917)
Symphony No.3      in C minor Op.60 (1928)
Symphony No.4      in D minor Op.78 (1937)

SMITH, Julia Frances b. 25 January 1911, d. 1989
Folkways Symphony (1947–48)

SMITH, Laurance
Symphony in G      (1956)

SMITH, Leland C(layton) b. 6 August 1925
Symphony          (1951)

SMITH, N(athaniel) Clark b. 31 July 1877, d. 8 October 1933
Negro Choral Symphony for chorus and orchestra (1933)

SMITH, Russell b. 23 April 1927
Symphony for alto and large orchestra (1977)
Symphony No.2      in C major for large orchestra (1982)
Symphony No.3      in G major for small orchestra (1994)

SNOECK, Kenneth Maurice b. 11 January 1946

Symphony No.1
Symphony No.2
Symphony No.3      for wind and percussion

SNYDER, Theodore b. 27 November 1924

Symphony

SODERLUND, Gustave Frederic b. 25 January 1881, d. 28 November 1972

Symphony No.1      (Festival Symphony) (1942)

SONGER, Lewis A. 4 September 1935

Symphony No.1
Symphony No.2

SORRENTINO, Charles b. 23 August 1906, d. 6 November 1972

Symphony in C minor

SOWERBY, Leo b. 1 May 1895, d. 7 July 1968

Symphony No.1      (1921)
Symphony No.2      in B minor (1926–27)
Symphony No.3      in F sharp minor (1939–40)
Symphony No.4      in B (1944–47)
Symphony No.5      (1964)

SPEARS, Jared Tozier b. 15 August 1936

Symphony No.1      for band

SPELMAN, Timothy Matthew b. 21 January 1891, d. 21 August 1970

Symphony in G minor (1934)

SPENCER, James Houston b. 28 July 1895, d. 3 September 1967

Symphony No.1      (American Dance Fanstasy)
Symphony No.2      (American Folk Symphony)

SPERRY, Don J. b. 17 February 1947

Symphony No.1      (1972)
Symphony No.2      (1973)

SPINO, Pasquale J. b. 7 July 1942

Symphony No.1

SPRING, Glenn E. Jnr b. 19 April 1939

Short Symphony      (Shapes) (1974)

STAHL, Willy b. 1896, d. 11 April 1963

Symphony No.1      (1934)

STAHLBERG, Fritz b. 7 June 1877, d. 23 July 1937

Symphony No.1
Symphony No.2

STANLEY, Helen Camille b. 6 April 1930

Symphony No.1      (1954)

STARER, Robert b. 8 January 1924

Symphony No.1      (1948)
Symphony No.2      in one movement (1951)
Symphony No.3      (1969)

STAROBIN, Michael Abram b. 19 May 1956

Symphony          (1978)

STEARNS, Peter Pindar b. 7 June 1931

Little Symphony No.1 (1952)
Symphony No.2
Symphony No.3
Symphony No.4
Symphony No.5      (1961)
Symphony No.6      (Concertato) (1966)
Symphony No.7      (1983)

STEG, Oskar b. 24 August 1919

Symphony for chamber orchestra (1961)

STEIN, Leon b. 18 September 1910

Symphony No.1      in C (1940)
Symphony No.2      in E minor (1942)
Symphony No.3      in A (1950–51)
Symphony No.4      (1975)

STEINBERG, Carolyn b. 17 May 1956

Chamber Symphony  (1990)

STEINER, Max b. 10 May 1888, d. 28 December 1971

Symphonie Moderne (1940)

STERN, Max b. 31 March 1947

Symphony

STERN, Robert Lewis b. 1 February 1934

Symphony          (1961)

STEVENS, Halsey b. 3 December 1908, d. 20 January 1989

Symphony No.1      in one movement (1941–45, rev. 1950)
Symphony No.2      (1947) withdrawn
Symphony No.3      (Sinfonia Breve) (1957)

STILL, William Grant b. 11 May 1895, d. 3 December 1978

Afro-American Symphony (1930, rev. 1939)
Symphony No.2      in G minor (Song of a New Race) (1937)
Symphony No.3      (Sunday Symphony) (1958)
Symphony No.4      (Autochthonous) (1947)
Symphony No.5      (Western Hemisphere) (1945)

STINE, Robert Everett b. 24 December 1951

Symphony in one movement
Symphony No.2

STOCK, David Frederick b. 3 June 1939

Symphony in one movement (1963)

STOCK, Frederick b. 11 November 1872, d. 20 October 1942

Symphony No.1 in C minor Op.18 (1910)

STÖHR, Richard b. 11 June 1874, d. 11 December 1967

Symphony No.1
Symphony No.2
Symphony No.3
Symphony No.4

STOKES, Eric Norman b. 14 July 1930

Symphonys I        (1979)
Symphonys II       (1981)
Symphonys III      (Captions on the War Against Earth) (1989)
Symphonys IV       (The Ghost Bus to Eldorado) (1991)
Symphonys V        (Nature Dancer) (1991)

STOKES, Harvey

Lyric Symphony

STOKOWSKI, Leopold b. 18 April 1882, d. 13 September 1977

Symphony

STOLTZE, Robert H. b. 21 January 1910

Melodic Symphony for band (1970)

STOUT, Alan b. 26 November 1932

Symphony No.1      (1959)
Symphony No.2      (1951–66)

Symphony No.3      (with soprano and male chorus (1959–62)
Symphony No.4      for chorus and orchestra (1970)

STRANG, Gerald b. 13 February 1908, d. 2 November 1983

Symphony No.1      (1938–42)
Symphony No.2      (1946–47)

STRAUSS, George R. b. 19 November 1951

Symphony No.1      (1973)
Symphony No.2      (1974)

STRINGHAM, Edwin John b. 11 July 1890, d. 1 July 1974

Symphony No.1      in B minor (Italian) (1929)

STRONG, George Templeton b. 26 May 1856, d. 27 June 1948

Symphony No.1      in F (In the Mountains) (1887)
Symphony No.2      in G minor Op.50 (Sintram, after Fouqué) (1887–1889)
Symphony No.3      (By the Lake)

STRUBE, Gustav b. 3 March 1867, d. 2 February 1953

Symphony          in C minor Op.11 (1896)
Symphony No.1      in B minor (1910)
Symphony No.2      in G (1921–22)
Little Symphony No.1 (1922)
Symphony (Lanier)  (1925)

STUCKY, Steven Edward b. 7 November 1949

Symphony No.1      withdrawn
Symphony No.2      withdrawn
Symphony No.3      (1972)
Symphony No.4      (Kenningar) (1977–78)

SUESSE, Dana b. 3 December 1911, d. 16 October 1987

Antique Symphony   (1946)

SUMERLIN, Macon Dee b. 24 October 1919

Symphony No.1
Symphony No.2
Symphony No.3
Symphony No.4
Symphony No.5      (Destiny) for chorus and orchestra

SURINACH, Carlos b. 4 March 1915

Symphony No.1      (Passacaglia) (1945)
Symphony No.2      (1949)
Sinfonia Chica     (1957)

SVOBOBA, Tomáš b. 6 December 1939

| | |
|---|---|
| Symphony No.1 | (Of Nature) Op.20 (1957) |
| Symphony No.2 | Op.61 (1962) |
| Symphony No.3 | in one movement with organ Op.43 (1965) |
| Symphony No.4 | (Apocalyptic) Op.69 (1974) |
| Symphony No.5 | Op.92 (In Unison) (1978) |
| Symphony No.6 | Op.137 for clarinet and orchestra (1992) |

SWACK, Irwin b. 8 November 1919

| | |
|---|---|
| Symphony No.1 | |
| Symphony No.2 | in one movement |

SWANN, Jeffrey b. 24 November 1951

Symphony No.1

SWANSON, Howard b. 18 August 1907, d. 12 November 1978

| | |
|---|---|
| Symphony No.1 | (1945) |
| Symphony No.2 | (1948, rev. 1965) |
| Symphony No.3 | (1970) |

SWIFT, Richard G. b. 24 September 1927

| | |
|---|---|
| Symphony | (1970) |

T

TAFFS, Anthony b. 15 January 1916

| | |
|---|---|
| Symphony in B flat | (1951) |

TAMBLYN, John

| | |
|---|---|
| Symphony in A | (1955) |

TANENBAUM, Elias b. 20 August 1924

| | |
|---|---|
| Symphony No.1 | in one movement (1955) |

TANG, Jordan Cho-Tung b. 27 January 1948

| | |
|---|---|
| Symphony No.1 | |
| Symphony No.2 | (1979) |
| Sinfonia Brevissima | (1973) |

TAYLOR, Clifford Oliver b. 20 October 1923

| | |
|---|---|
| Symphony No.1 | Op.17 (1958) |
| Symphony No.2 | Sinfonia seria for band (1965) |
| Symphony No.3 | (1978) |

TAYLOR, Laurence

| | |
|---|---|
| Symphony | (1963) |

TCHEREPNIN, Alexander Nikolayevitch b. 21 January 1899, d. 29 September 1977

| | |
|---|---|
| Symphony No.1 | in E Op.42 (1927) |
| Symphony No.2 | in E flat Op.77 (1945–51) |
| Symphony No.3 | Op.83 (1951) |
| Symphony No.4 | Op.91 (1957) |
| Symphony No.5 | (1968) |
| Symphony No.6 | (1977) incomplete |

TEPPER, Albert b. 1 June 1921

Symphony for strings (1951)

TESSIER, Albert Denis b. 8 April 1900

Celesta Symphony for organ and orchestra

THATCHER, Harry Jnr b. 6 July 1905, d. 1937

Symphony in E minor (1933)

THOMPSON, Randall b. 21 April 1899, d. 9 July 1984

| | |
|---|---|
| Symphony No.1 | (originally with chorus) (1929) |
| Symphony No.2 | in E minor (1930–31) |
| Symphony No.3 | in A minor (1947–49) |

THOMSON, Virgil b. 25 November 1896, d. 30 September 1989

| | |
|---|---|
| Symphony (No.1) | on a Hymn Tune (1928) |
| Symphony No.2 | (1931, rev. 1941) |
| Symphony No.3 | (1972) |

THORNE, Francis Burrett Jnr b. 23 June 1922

| | |
|---|---|
| Symphony No.1 | (1960) |
| Symphony No.2 | (1964) |
| Symphony No.3 | in one movement for percussion and strings (1969) |
| Symphony No.4 | (Waterloo Bridge) (1977) |
| Symphony No.5 | (1984) |
| Symphony No.6 | for strings (1992) |
| Symphony No.7 | (The Hudson River) for chorus and orchestra (1994) |

THORNE, Nicholas C.K. b. 7 November 1953

| | |
|---|---|
| Symphony No.1 | |
| Symphony No.2 | (A Symphony of Light) |

THORNTON, William b. 31 July 1919

Symphony No.1

THREATTE, Charles b. 15 February 1940

Symphony of Carols (1971)

TILLIS, Frederick C. b. 5 January 1930

Niger Symphony for chamber orchestra (1975)
In the Spirit and the Flesh: Choral symphony for solo voices, chorus and orchestra (1985)
A Festive Journey: Symphony/concerto for orchestra with solo percussion (1992)

TIRRO, Frank Pacale b. 20 September 1935

Symphony            (1973)

TOCH, Ernst b. 7 December 1887, d. 1 October 1964

| | |
|---|---|
| Symphony No.1 | Op.72 (1950) |
| Symphony No.2 | Op.73 (1951) |
| Symphony No.3 | Op.75 (1955) |
| Symphony No.4 | Op.80 (1957) |
| Symphony No.5 | (Jeptha) Op.89 (1963) |
| Symphony No.6 | Op.93 (1963) |
| Symphony No.7 | Op.95 (1964) |

TORKE, Michael b. 21 September 1961

Brick Symphony       (1997)

TOWNSEND, Douglas b. 8 November 1921

Symphony for strings (1958)
Symphony No.2       for strings (1983)
Chamber Symphony No.1 (1958)
Chamber Symphony No.2 (1961)

TREMBLAY, George Amedée b. 14 January 1911, d. 14 July 1982

Chaparral Symphony (1938)
Symphony No.1       in one movement (1949)
Symphony No.2       (1952)
Symphony No.3       (1970)
A Dance Symphony    (1982)

TRIMBLE, Lester b. 29 August 1923, d. 31 December 1986

Symphony in Two Movements (1951)
Symphony No.2       (1966–68)
Symphony No.3       (The Tricentennial) (1985–86)

TRINKAUS, George J. b. 13 April 1878, d. 19 May 1960

Symphony No.1       in F
Symphony No.2

TRUBITT, Allen Ray b. 24 August 1931

Symphony No.1       (1964)
Symphony No.2       (1978)

TRUGLIO, Mario Thomas b. 26 May 1942

Symphony for band

TRYTHALL, Gilbert b. 28 October 1930

Symphony No.1      Op.2 (1958, rev. 1961)

TRYTHALL, Richard Aaker b. 25 July 1939

Symphony      (1961)

TUCKER, Tui St. George b. 25 November 1924

Symphony      (1961)

TULL, Fisher Aubrey b. 24 September 1934, d. 1994

Liturgical Symphony for brass and percussion

TURNER, Thomas Sample b. 21 April 1941

Symphony No.1
Symphony No.2

TUROK, Paul Harris b. 3 December 1929

Symphony in two movements (1955)

TURRIN, Joseph Egidio b. 4 January 1947

Symphony in two movements (1975)

TUTHILL, Burnet Corwin b. 16 November 1888, d. 18 January 1982

Symphony in C      Op.21 (1940)


U

UBER, David Albert b. 5 August 1921

Minature Symphony

ULTAN, Lloyd 12 June 1929

Symphony No.1      for symphonic band (1954)
Symphony No.2      (1971)

UNDERWOOD, William L. b. 9 March 1940

Symphony No.1      (1966)
Symphony No.2      (1971)


V

VAN APPELDORN, Mary Jeanne b. 2 October 1927

Symphony No.1
Symphony No.2

Symphony No.3
Symphony No.4       (Prayer) for mezzo-soprano, trumpet, piano and tam tam (1985–87)

VAN NOSTRAND, Burr b. 1945

Symphony (Nos Feratu) for chorus and orchestra (1969–71)

VAN VACTOR, David b. 8 May 1906, d. 1994

Symphony No.1       in D minor (1936)
Symphony No.2       (Music for the Marines) (1943)
Symphony No.3       in C (1958)
Symphony No.4       (Walden) for chorus and orchestra (1969)
Symphony No.5       (1975)
Symphony No.6       for band or orchestra (1980)
Sinfonia Breve for small orchestra (1964)

VARDELL, Charles G. Jnr b. 19 August 1893, d. 19 October 1962

Symphony No.1       (Folk Symphony from the Carolina Hills) (1938)

VARS, Henry b. 29 December 1902, d. 1 September 1977

Symphony No.1

VAUCLAIN, Constant b. 5 August 1908

Symphony No.1       in one movement (1947)
Symphony for strings and piano (1948)
Symphony No.3       in G minor
Symphony No.4
Symphony No.5

VAUGHAN, Clifford b. 23 September 1893, d. 23 November 1987

Symphony No.1
Symphony No.2
Symphony No.3
Symphony No.4

VAUGHAN, Rodger Dale b. 2 February 1932

Centennial Symphony

VAYO, David Joseph

Symphony: Blossoms and Awakenings (1990)

VAZZANA, Anthony (Eugene) b. 4 November 1922

Symphony       (1963)

VEENEMAN, Curt H. b. 1953

Symphony No.1
Symphony No.2       (Alcuin's Riddle) (1989)

VEGA, Aurilio de la b. 28 November 1925

Symphony in 4 parts (1960)

VERRALL, John Weedon b. 17 June 1908

Symphony No.1      (1939)
Symphony No.2      in E (For Young Orchestras) (1943)
Sinfonia Festiva for band (1954)
Symphony No.3      for chamber orchestra (1966)

VINCENT, John b. 17 May 1902, d. 21 January 1977

A Folk Song Symphony (1931) lost
Symphony in D      in one movement (1954, rev. 1956)
Symphony No.2      (1966)


# W

WAGENAAR, Bernard b. 18 July 1894, d. 19 May 1971

Symphony No.1      (1926)
Symphony No.2      (1930)
Symphony No.3      (1936)
Symphony No.4      (1946)

WAGNER, Joseph Frederick b. 9 January 1900, d. 12 October 1972

Symphony No.1      (1934)
Symphony No.2      (1945)
Symphony No.3      (1951)
Symphony No.4      (1976)

WALDROP, Gideon William, Jnr b. 2 September 1919

Symphony No.1      (1952)

WALENSKY, Dana Grant b. 24 July 1948

Symphony          (1975)

WALKER, George Theophilus b. 27 June 1922

Symphony          (1961) withdrawn
Sinfonia No.1      (1984)
Sinfonia No.2      (1990)
Sinfonia No.3      (1994)

WALKER, Robert S. b. 12 October 1937

Symphony

WALTERS, Ingram

Symphony in one movement   (1945)

WARD, Frank Edwin b. 7 October 1872, d. 15 September 1953

Symphony

WARD, Robert Eugene b. 13 September 1917

| | |
|---|---|
| Symphony No.1 | (1941) |
| Symphony No.2 | (1947) |
| Symphony No.3 | (1950, rev. 1953) |
| Symphony No.4 | (1958, rev. 1978) |
| Symphony No.5 | (Canticles of America) for soprano, baritone, narrator, chorus and orchestra (1976) |
| Symphony No.6 | (1988) |

WARD, William Reed b. 20 May 1918

| | |
|---|---|
| Symphony No.1 | (1938) |
| Symphony No.2 | in one movement (1947) |
| Symphony No.3 | (1954) |

WARD-STEINMAN, David b. 6 November 1936

Symphony          (1959)

WARE, Harriet b. 26 August 1877, d. 9 February 1962

New York Symphony (1910)

WARREN, Elinor Remick b. 23 February 1900, d. 27 April 1991

Symphony in one movement (1970)

WASHBURN, Robert Brooks b. 11 July 1928

Symphony No.1     (1958)
Symphony for band   (1963)
Sinfonia for voices and orchestra (1977)
Symphony (In Praise of Music) for chorus and orchestra (1986)

WEBER, Ben Brian b. 23 July 1916, d. 9 May 1979

Sinfonia for cello and orchestra Op.21 (1945)
Symphony on Poems of William Blake for baritone and 12 instruments Op.33 (1950)
Sinfonia Clarion for small orchestra Op.62 (1973)

WEBER, Joseph b. 31 July 1937

Symphony

WEED, Maurice James b. 16 October 1912

Symphony          (1955)
Symphonia Breve

WEIDIG, Adolf b. 28 November 1876, d. 23 September 1931

Symphony No.1
Symphony No.2

WEIGEL, Eugene Herbert b. 11 October 1910

Prairie Symphony     (1953)

WEIGL, Karl b. 6 February 1881, d. 11 August 1949

| | |
|---|---|
| Symphony No.1 | in E Op.6 (1908) |
| Symphony No.2 | in D minor Op.19 (1912) |
| Symphony No.3 | in B flat (1931) |
| Symphony No.4 | in F minor (1936) |
| Symphony No.5 | in C minor (Apocalyptic) (1945) |
| Symphony No.6 | in A minor (1947) |

WEILLE, F. Blair b. 9 November 1930

Short Symphony     (1957)

WEINER, Eric b. 1 August 1900

Symphony Requiem

WEINER, Lawrence b. 22 June 1932

Symphony No.1     (1956)
Daedalic Symphony (Symphony No.2) for band (1966)
Symphoy No.3     for band (1972)

WEISGARBER, Elliot b. 5 December 1919

Symphony     (1947)
Sinfonia Pastorale     (1961)

WEISS, Adolph A. b. 12 September 1891, d. 20 February 1971

Chamber Symphony for 10 instruments (1927)

WELCHER, Dan Edward b. 2 March 1948

Symphony No.1     (1992)

WELLMAN, Samuel Edison

Symphony of the Apocalypse (1990)

WENDELBURG, Norma Ruth b. 26 March 1918

Symphony No.1     (1967)

WERLE, Floyd Edwards b. 8 May 1929

Symphony No.1     (Sinfonia Sacra) for rock combo and band
Symphony No.2     (Sinfonia di Chiesa) for winds

WERNER, Eric b. 1 August 1901, d. 28 July 1988

Symphony Requiem

WERNICK, Richard (Frank) b.19 January 1934

Symphony No.1      (1988–89)

WESSEL, Mark E. b. 26 March 1894, d. 2 May 1973

Symphony            (1932)

WHALEY, George Boyd b. 9 March 1929

Symphony for band

WHEAR, Paul William b. 13 November 1925

Symphony No.1      (Stonehenge) for band (1970)
Symphony No.2      (The Bridge) (1971)
Symphony No.3      (The Galleries) (1975)
Symphony No.4      for band (1979)

WHITCOMB, Robert B. b. 7 December 1921

Symphony No.1      (1958)

WHITE, Clarence Cameron b. 10 August 1880, d. 30 June 1960

Symphony in D minor (1928)

WHITE, Gary C. b. 27 May 1937

Symphony            (1969)

WHITE, John (David) b. 28 November 1931

Symphony No.1      (1954)
Symphony No.2      (1960)
Symphony (No.3)    for Wind Band (1985)
Symphony (No.4)    for a Saint for solo voices and orchestra (1986–87)
But God's Own Descent: a Symphony (No.5) for chorus and winds (1991)
Symphony No.6. (Colors of Earth and Sky) (1996)

WHITE, Paul Taylor b. 22 August 1895, d. 3 May 1973

Symphony in E minor (1932)

WHITE, Ruth S. b. 1 September 1925

Shofar Symphony    (1965)

WHITHORNE, Emerson b. 6 September 1884, d. 25 March 1958

Symphony No.1      Op.49 (1929)
Symphony No.2      Op.56 (1935)
Symphony No.3      Op.57 (1937)

WHITING, George E(lbridge) b. 14 September 1842, d. 14 October 1923

Symphony            in C minor

WHITNEY, Robert Sutton b. 6 July 1904, d. 22 November 1986

Symphony          in E minor (1936)

WHITTINGHAM, W.H. d. 1852

Symphony          (1828) incomplete

WIENER, Ivan Harvey b. 15 June 1933

Symphony

WIGGLESWORTH, Frank b. 3 March 1918, d. 1996

Symphony No.1     (1953)
Symphony No.2     for strings (1958)
Symphony No.3     (Three Portraits) for strings (1967–69)
Symphony No.4     (1994)

WILLIAMS, David Russell b. 21 October 1932

Sinfonia in E      Op.14 (1956)
Sinfonia in B flat   Op.26 for band (1957)

WILLIAMS, Ernest S. b. 1881, d. 8 February 1947

Symphony in C minor for band (1938) for orchestra (1940)

WILLIAMS, James Clifton b. 26 March 1923, d. 12 February 1976

Symphony for Young People

WILLIAMS, James Kimo b. 1950

Symphony for the Sons of Nam

WILLIAMS, John T. b. 8 February 1932

Symphony          (1966)
Symphony No.2
Sinfonia for band

WILLIS, Mickie Denver

Symphony No.1     (1989)

WILLIS, Richard Murat b. 21 April 1929

Symphony No.1     (1953)
Symphony No.2     (1964, rev. 1965)

WILLMAN, Regina Hansen b. 5 October 1914, d. 28 October 1965

Symphony

WILLSON, Meredith b. 18 May 1902, d. 15 June 1984

Symphony No.1     in F minor (San Francisco) (1934–36)
Symphony No.2     in E minor (Missions of California) (1963–64)

WILSON, Mortimer b. 6 August 1876, d. 27 January 1932

Symphony No.1
Symphony No.2
Symphony No.3      (The Quaker) Op.18
Symphony No.4
Symphony No.5

WILSON, Olly Woodrow b. 7 September 1937

Sinfonia          (1983–84)

WILSON, Richard b. 15 May 1941

Symphony No.1      (1984)

WINDINGSTAD, Ole b. 18 May 1886, d. 3 June 1959

Symphony          (1913)

WINKLER, Peter (Kenton) b. 26 January 1943

Symphony          (1976–78)

WINSTIN, Robert Ian b.

Symphony No.1
Symphony No.2      (Symphony for Strings)
Symphony No.3
Symphony No.4      (The Circus)

WIRTH, Carl Anton b. 24 January 1912

Symphony No.1      (1940)

WOLFE, Stanley Andrew b. 7 February 1924

Symphony No.1      Op.6 (1954)
Symphony No.2      Op.8 (1966)
Symphony No.3      Op.14 (1959)
Symphony No.4      (1965)
Symphony No.5      (1970)

WOLPE, Stefan b. 25 August 1902, d. 4 April 1972

Symphony No.1      (Concerto for 16 instruments)
Symphony          (1956, rev. 1964)

WOLTMANN, Frederick b. 13 May 1908

Symphony (Songs for Autumn) for soprano, baritone and orchestra (1937)
Symphony for voice and orchestra on poems of Walt Whitman (1946)

WOOD, Joseph (Roberts) b. 12 May 1915

Symphony No.1      (1939)
Symphony No.2      in one movement (1949)
Symphony No.3      (1956)

WOOD, William Frank b. 3 August 1935

Symphony in three movements (1962)

WOOLLEN, Charles Russell b. 7 January 1923

Symphony No.1    Op.37 (1957–61)
Symphony No.2    Op.86 (1977–78)

WRIGHT, James

Symphony No.1    (1950)

WRIGHTSON, Herbert James b. 20 December 1869, d. 24 December 1949

Symphony        in E minor    (1901)

WUORINEN, Charles b. 9 June 1938

Symphony No.1    (1958)
Symphony No.2    (1959)
Symphony No.3    (1959)
Sinfonia Sacra for men's voices and chamber orchestra (1961)
Percussion Symphony for 24 players (1976)
Two-part Symphony (1978)
Ecclesiastical Symphonies (1980)
Microsymphony    (1991–92)

WYKES, Robert Arthur b. 19 May 1926

A Lyric Symphony    (1980)
Symphony No.2    (Pairs) (1981 – in progress)

WYLIE, Ruth Shaw b. 24 January 1916, d. 30 January 1989

Symphony No.1    (Archaic) Op.6 (1943)
Symphony No.2    Op.11 (1948)

WYRICK, Jerold Jay

Revelations: Choral Symphony of Praise (1990)


# Y

YARDUMIAN, Richard b. 5 April 1917, d. 15 August 1985

Symphony No.1    (1950)
Symphony No.2    (Book of Psalms) for contralto and orchestra (1947/1964)
Symphony No.3    (1981)

YORK, Walter Wynn b. 6 August 1914

Symphony in A minor    (1948)

# Z

ZÁDOR, Eugene b. 5 November 1894, d. 4 April 1977

Romantic Symphony (1922)
Sinfonia Technica    (1931)
Symphony No.3      (Dance Symphony) (1936)
Symphony No.4      (Children's Symphony) (1941)

ZECH, Frederick, Jnr b. 10 May 1858, d. 25 October 1926

Symphony No.1      (1883)
Symphony No.2
Symphony No.3
Symphony No.4
Symphony No.5      (1895)

ZEISL, Eric b. 18 May 1905, d. 18 February 1959

Little Symphony     (1937)

ZUR, Menachem b. 6 March 1942

Short Symphony      (No.1) for chamber orchestra (1981)
Symphony No.2      (Letters) (1988–94)
Symphony No.3      (1994)

ZWILICH, Ellen Taaffe b. 30 April 1939

Chamber Symphony (1979)
Symphony No.1      (Three Movements for Orchestra) (1982)
Symphony No.2      (1985)
Symphony No.3      (1992)

# Discography

Only compact discs are listed below since 33rpm long-playing records have become obsolete, and audio cassettes have been generally superseded. For the latest CD issues, *The Schwann Opus Reference Guide* in the United States and *The Gramophone Classical Catalogue* in Great Britain should be consulted.

ADAMS, John
Chamber Symphony (1992)
    Ensemble Moderne: Sian Edwards            RCA 09026 68674.2
    London Sinfonietta: John Adams      ELEKTRA NONESUCH 79219.2

ALBERT, Stephen
RiverRun Symphony (1984)
    Washington National Symphony: Mstislav Rostropovich     DELOS DE 1016

ANTHEIL, George
A Jazz Symphony (1925, rev. 1955)
    New Palais Royale Orchestra: Maurice Peress     MUSIC MASTERS 67094.2
    Ensemble Moderne            BMG 69026.68066.2
Symphony No.4 (1945)
    London Symphony Orchestra: Sir Eugene Goossens     BAY CITIES BCD 1016
             EVEREST EVC 9039
Symphony No.5 (Joyous) (1947–48)
    Slovak Symphony Orchestra: Barry Kolman     CENTAUR CRC 2293

ASIA, Daniel
Symphony No.2 (1990)
    Phoenix Symphony: James Sedares     NEW WORLD NW 80447.2
Symphony No.3 (1991)
    Phoenix Symphony: James Sedares     NEW WORLD NW 80447.2

AVSHALOMOV, Jacob
Symphony of Songs
    Portland Youth Philharmonic: Jacob Avshalomov     ALBANY TROY 160.2

AUSTIN, Elizabeth
Wilderness Symphony
    Cracow RTV: Meinda Liebormann: Anthony King     CAPSTONE CPS 8625

BANFIELD, William
Symphony No.6 (Four Songs for American Voices)
    John English: Jack Schantz: Akron Symphony: Alan Balter　　　TELARC CD 80409

BARBER, Samuel
Symphony No.1 (1938/1942) Op.9
| | |
|---|---|
| Baltimore Symphony: David Zinman | ARGO 436.288.2ZH |
| Detroit Symphony: Neemi Järvi | CHANDOS CHAN 8958 |
| London Symphony: David Measham | UNICORN KANCHANA UKCD 2046 |
| Ljublana Symphony: C. Nice | STRADIVARI SCD 6048 |
| | VOX CDX 5091 |
| New York Philharmonic: Bruno Walter | SONY SMK 64466 |
| | MAGIC TALENT CD 48018 |
| St Louis Symphony: Leonard Slatkin | RCA RD60732.2 |

Symphony No.2 (1944/1947) Op.19
| | |
|---|---|
| Boston Symphony: Sergei Koussevitzky | AS DISC 563 |
| Detroit Symphony: Neeme Järvi | CHANDOS CHAN 9169 |
| New Zealand Symphony: Andrew Schenck | STRADIVARI SCD 8012 |
| | VOX CDX 5091 |

BAZELON, Irwin
Symphony No.5 (1967)
    Indianapolis Symphony: Izler Solomon　　　CRI CD 623
Symphony No.7 (1980)
    Bournemouth Symphony　　　ALBANY TROY 174.2
Symphony No.8 for strings (1986)
    London Philharmonic: Harold Farberman　　　LEONARDO LE 331
Symphony No.9 (Sunday Silence) (1990)
    Bournemouth Symphony　　　ALBANY TROY 174.2

BEACH, Amy
Symphony in E minor (Gaelic) Op.32 (1898)
    Detroit Symphony: Neemi Järvi　　　CHANDOS CHAN 8958
    Royal Philharmonic: Karl Krueger　　　LIBRARY OF CONGRESS OMP 105

BECKER, John
Symphonia Breve (Symphony No.3) (1929)
    Louisville Orchestra: Jorge Mester　　　ALBANY TROY 027.2

BEESON, Jack
Symphony No.1 in A (1959)
    Polish National Radio: William Strickland　　　BAY CITIES BCD 1034

BELL, Larry
Sacred Symphonies for orchestra (1985)
    Slovak Radio Symphony: Szymon Kawalla
        VIENNA MODERN MASTERWORKS VMM 3016

BERNSTEIN, Leonard
Symphony No.1 (Jeremiah) (1943)
| | |
|---|---|
| Arnhem Symphony: Jard van Nes: Elyakum Shapirra | OTTAVO OTRC 58920 |
| Israel Philharmonic: Christa Ludwig: Leonard Bernstein | DG 445.245.2 GC2 |
| | DG 431.028.2GBE |
| | DG 415.964.2GH |
| | DG 447.953.2 |

| | |
|---|---|
| New York Philharmonic: Jennie Tourel: Leonard Bernstein | SONY SM3K 47162 |
| St Louis Symphony: Nan Merriman: Leonard Bernstein | RCA 09026.61581.2 |
| Symphony No.2 (The Age of Anxiety) (1948) | PEARL GEM 50005 |
| Arnhem Symphony: Christina Ortiz: Elyakum Shapirra | OTTAVO OTRC 58920 |
| Bournemouth Symphony: Jeffrey Kahane: Andrew Litton | VIRGIN CUV5 61119.2 |
| | VIRGIN CDC 59038 |
| Israel Philharmonic: Lukas Foss: Leonard Bernstein | DG 445.245.2.GC2 |
| | DG 415.964.2GH |
| | DG 447.953.2 |
| New York Philharmonic: Philippe Entremont: Leonard Bernstein | SONY SM3K 47162 |
| Symphony No.3 (Kaddish) (1961–63, 1977) | |
| Israel Philharmonic: Montserrat Cabale: Vienna Boys Choir: | |
| Vienna Jeunesse Choir: Leonard Bernstein | DG 445.245.2.GC2 |
| | DG 423.582.2.GH |
| | DG 447.953.2 |
| New York Philharmonic: Felicia Montealegre: Jennie Tourel | |
| Camerata Singers: Leonard Bernstein | SONY SM3K 47162 |
| Royal Philharmonic: Richard Dreyfuss: Gilbert Levine | JUSTICE JR 1803 |

BILIK, Jerry
Symphony for band (1972)
Dutch Royal Military Band: Pierre Kuijpers — OTTAVO OTRC 18924

BINKERD, Gordon
Symphony No.2 (1960)
Oslo Philharmonic: George Barati — CRI C 139 (cassette)

BISH, Diane
A Symphony of Hymns: A Symphony of Psalms
Coral Ridge Chamber Choir and Orchestra: Sung Sook Lee:
R. McMurrin — VCPR QR 1041

BLACKWOOD, Easley
Symphony No.1 Op.3 (1954–55)
Boston Symphony: Charles Munch — CEDILLE CDR 90000.016
Symphony No.5 Op.34 (1978)
Chicago Symphony: James de Priest — CEDILLE CDR 90000.016

BLITZSTEIN, Mark
Airborne Symphony (1943–44)
New York City Symphony: Charles Holland: Walter Scheff:
Victor Chorus: Leonard Bernstein — RCA 09026.62568.2

BLOCH, Ernest
Symphony in C# minor (1901–03)
Malmo Symphony: Lev Markiz — BIS BISCD 576
Slovak Philharmonic: Stephen Gunzenhauser — MARCO POLO 8.223103
Israel Symphony (1912–17)
Utah Symphony: Maurice Abravanel — VANGUARD 08 4047 71
Sinfonia Breve (1952)
Minneapolis Symphony: Antal Dorati — MERCURY 434.329.2MM
New Zealand Symphony: James Sedares — KOCH KIC CD 7237

Symphony for Trombone (1954)
    Berlin Sinfonia: Branimir Slokar: Lior Shambadal            CLAVES 50.9606
    Berlin Radio Symphony: Uros Lajovic: Armin Rosin  KOCH SCHWANN CD 311.086
    New Zealand Symphony: Mark Taddei: James Sedares      KOCH KIC CD 7237
    Portland Youth Symphony: H. Prince: Jacob Avshalomov        CRI CR 634
    Swedish Radio Symphony: Christian Lindberg: Leif Segerstam     BIS CD 538
    USSR Symphony: Grigory Khersonsky: Vladimir Kozhurkar   CONSONANCE 81002
Symphony in E flat (1954–55)
    New Zealand Symphony: James Sedares              KOCH KIC CD 7329
    Royal Philharmonic: Dalia Atlas Sternberg          ASV CDDA 1019

BOLCOM, William
Symphony No.1 (1957)
    Louisville Orchestra: Lawrence Leighton Smith
                     FIRST EDITION RECORDINGS LCD 007

Symphony No.3 (1979)
    Louisville Orchestra: Lawrence Leighton Smith
                     FIRST EDITION RECORDINGS LCD 007
Symphony No.4 (Soundscape) (1987)
    St Louis Symphony: Joan Morris: Leonard Slatkin    NEW WORLD NW 356.2
Symphony No.5 (1990)
    American Composers Orchestra: Dennis Russell Davies     ARGO 433.077.2

BRANCA, Glenn
Symphony No.9 (L'Eve Future) (1993)
    Polish National Radio Symphony: Camerata Silesia Singers:
      Christian von Borries               PHILIPS 446.505.2PH

BRISTOW, George
Symphony No.2 in F# minor Op.26
    Detroit Symphony: Neemi Järvi            CHANDOS CHAN 9169

CARTER, Elliott
Symphony No.1 (1942)
    American Composers Orchestra: Paul Dunkel         CRI CD 552

Symphony of Three Orchestras (1976)
    New York Philharmonic: Pierre Boulez         SONY SK 68334

CHADWICK, George
Symphony No.2 in B flat Op.21 (1883–86)
    Albany Symphony: Ildiko Hegyi         NEW WORLD NW 339.2
    Detroit Symphony: Neemi Järvi        CHANDOS CHAN 9334

Symphony No.3 in F (1893)
    Detroit Symphony: Neemi Järvi        CHANDOS CHAN 9253
    Royal Philharmonic: Karl Krueger    LIBRARY OF CONGRESS OMP 107

CHAMBERS, Wendy Mae
Symphony of the Universe (1989)
    Mixed ensembles           NEWPORT CLASSIC NPD 85552

COATES, Gloria
Symphony No.1 (Music on Open Strings) (1973–74)
    Bavarian Radio Symphony Orchestra; Elgar Howarth           CPO 999.392.2
Symphony No.4 (Chiaroscuro) (1984/1990)
    Stuttgart Philharmonic Orchestra: Wolf-Dieter Hauschild      CPO 999.392.2
Symphony No.7 (1990–91)
    Stuttgart Philharmonic Orchestra: Georg Schmohe         CPO 999.392.2

CONSTANTINIDES, Dinos
Symphony No.2 (1983)
    Bohuslav Martinu Orch.: M.A. Machek  VIENNA MODERN MASTERS VMM 3007
Symphony No.5 (1996)
    Ruse Harmonic: T. Delibozov      VIENNA MUSIC MASTERS VMM 3035

COOPER, Paul
Symphony No.4 (Landscape) (1975)
    Houston Symphony: S. Jones               CRI CD 579

COPLAND, Aaron
Dallas Symphony: Wayne Marshall: Andrew Litton        DELOS DE 3221
Symphony No.1 (Organ Symphony) (1924)
    New York Philharmonic: E. Power Biggs: Leonard Bernstein    SONY SM2K 47232
                                    SMK 63085
    St. Louis Symphony: Simon Preston: Leonard Slatkin     RCA 09026.68292.2
Symphony No.1 (1924/1928)
    Orchestre Nationale: Aaron Copland         ECETERA KTC 1098
Dance Symphony (1930)
    Detroit Symphony: Antal Dorati          LONDON 414273.2LH
                                      448.261.21
                              DECCA 430.705.2DM
                                448.261.2DF2
    London Symphony: Aaron Copland           SONY SM2K 47232
    Mexico City Philharmonic: Enrique Batiz   EMI EMINENCE CD EMX 2147
    MIT Symphony: David Epstein       TURNABOUT CD 30371.00112
    St Louis Symphony: Leonard Slatkin         RCA 09026.68292.2
Short Symphony (No.2)
    London Symphony: Aaron Copland           SONY SM2K 47232
    Orchestra of St Luke's: Dennis Russell Davies  MUSIC MASTERS 01612.67101.2
    Orpheus Chamber Orchestra           DG 427.335GH
    St Louis Symphony: Leonard Slatkin         RCA 09026.68292.2
    St Paul Chamber: Dennis Russell Davies       PRO ARTE CDD 140
    San Francisco Symphony: Michael Tilson Thomas     RCA 09026.68541.2
Symphony No.3 (1944–46)
    Atlanta Symphony: Yoel Levi           TELARC CD 80201
    Dallas Symphony: Eduardo Mata       ANGEL/EMI CDM 64304
                                      CDC 54282
    Detroit Symphony: Neemi Järvi        CHANDOS CHAN 9474
    London Symphony: Aaron Copland        PHILIPS 422307.2PM
    London Symphony: Aaron Copland        EVEREST EVC 9040
    New Philharmonica: Aaron Copland       SONY SM3K 46559
                                    SMK 63085
    New York Philharmonic: Leonard Bernstein       DG 419170.2
    St Louis Symphony: Leonard Slatkin        RCA RD 60149.2RC

CORIGLIANO, John
Symphony No.1 (1990)
   Chicago Symphony: Daniel Barenboim               ERATO 2292.45601.2
   National Symphony of Washington: Leonard Slatkin     RCA 09026.68450

COWELL, Henry
Symphony No.5 (1948)
   Vienna Symphony: Dean Dixon              BAY CITIES BCD 1017
Symphony No.7 (1952)
   Vienna Symphony: William Strickland            CRI CD 740
Symphony No.16 (Icelandic) (1962)
   Icelandic Symphony: William Strickland           CRI CD 740

CRESTON, Paul
Symphony No.2 Op.35 (1944)
   Detroit Symphony: Neemi Järvi           CHANDOS CHAN 9390
   Krakow Philharmonic: David Amos     KOCH INTERNATIONAL 3.7036.2
Symphony No.3 (Three Mysteries) Op.48 (1950)
   Seattle Symphony: Gerard Schwartz           DELOS DE 3114
Symphony No.5 Op.64 (1956)
   Seattle Symphony: Gerard Schwartz           DELOS DE 3127

DANIELPOUR, Richard
Symphony No.3 (Journey Without Distance) (1989)
   Seattle Symphony: Faith Esham: Gerard Schwartz     DELOS DE 3118

DAUGHERTY, Michael
Metropolis Symphony (1988–93)
   Baltimore Symphony: David Zinman          ARGO 452.103.2

DAWSON, William
Negro Folk Symphony (1930)
   Detroit Symphony: Neemi Järvi          CHANDOS CHAN 9226

DELLO JOIO, Norman
Triumph of St Joan Symphony (1951)
   New Zealand Symphony: James Sedares         KOCH KIC 7243

DEL TREDICI, David
An Alice Symphony (1969/1975)
   Tanglewood Center Orch: Phyllis Bryn-Julson: Oliver Knussen    CRI 688

DIAMOND, David
Symphony No.1 (1940–41)
   Seattle Symphony: Gerard Schwartz           DELOS DE 3119
Symphony No.2 (1944)
   Seattle Symphony: Gerard Schwartz           DELOS DE 3093
Symphony No.3 (1946)
   Seattle Symphony: Gerard Schwartz           DELOS DE 3103
Symphony No.4 (1948)
   Seattle Symphony: Gerard Schwartz           DELOS DE 3093
Symphony No.5 (1961–64)
   Juilliard Orchestra: Christopher Keane        NEW WORLD 80396.2

Symphony No.8 (1960)
    Seattle Symphony: Gerard Schwartz            DELOS DE 3141
Symphony No.11 (1992) (Adagio only)
    Seattle Symphony: Gerard Schwartz            DELOS DE 3189

DORATI, Antal
Symphony No.1 (1957)
    Stockholm Philharmonic: Antal Dorati            BIS CD 408
Symphony No.2 (Queria Pacis) (1985)
    Stockholm Philharmonic: Antal Dorati            BIS CD 408

ERB, Donald
Symphony for winds (1989)
    University Circle Wind Ensemble: G. Ciepluch            NEW WORLD 80457.2

FINE, Irving
Symphony (1962)
    Boston Symphony: Irvin Fine            PHOENIX PHCD 106
    Moscow Radio Symphony: Joel Spiegelman            DELOS DE 3139

FLAGELLO, Nicholas
Symphony No.2 Op.63 (Symphony of the Winds) (1971)
    Rome Chamber Orchestra: Nicholas Flagello            CITADEL CTD 88115

GIANNINI, Vittorio
Symphony No.3 (1959)
    Dallas Wind Symphony: Frederick Fennell            REFERENCE RR 52CD
    Eastman Wind Ensemble: A Clyde Roller            MERCURY 434.320.2
    Northwestern University Symphonic Winds: John P. Paynter
           NORTHWESTERN UNIVERSITY 6704

GIDEON, Miriam
Symphonia Brevis (1953)
    Unknown orchestra: Robert Black            MASTER MUSICIANS MMC 2008

GILLIS, Don
Symphony No.5½ (1947)
    BBC Philharmonic: Vernon Handley            CHANDOS CHAN 7025

GLANVILLE-HICKS, Peggy
Sinfonia de Pacifica (1952)
    Tasmanian Symphony: Robert Mills            VOX AUSTRALIS VAST 013

GLASS, Philip
Low Symphony (1992)
    Brooklyn Philharmonic: Dennis Russell Davies            POINT MUSIC 438.150.2PTH
Heroes Symphony
    American Composers Orchestra: Dennis Russell Davies            POINT MUSIC 452.8522

GOEB, Roger
Symphony No.4 (1956)
    Japan Philharmonic Symphony: Akao Watanabe           CITADEL CTD 88121

GOODMAN, David Jerome
Symphony No.2 (1994)
    Warsaw National Philharmonic: Jerzy Swoboda          MMC 2027

GOTTSCHALK, Louis Moreau
Symphony No.1 (La Nuit des Tropiques) (1859)
    Utah Symphony: Maurice Abravanel           VANGUARD OVC 4051
                                        SVC 9
    Vienna State Opera: Samuel Adler            VOX 1154842
                        TURNABOUT 30371.00077
Symphony No.2 (A Montevideo) (1869)
    Vienna Symphony: Samuel Adler             VOX 1154842

GOULD, Morton
West Point Symphony (1952)
    Eastman Wind Ensemble: Frederick Fennell     MERCURY 434.320.2
Symphony of Spirituals (1975)
    London Philharmonic: Kenneth Klein         ANGEL CDC 49462
    Louisville Orchestra: Lawrence Leighton Smith   ALBANY TROY 013.1

HAILSTORK, Adolphus
Symphony No.1 (1988)
    Bohuslav Martinu Philharmonic: Julius Williams   ALBANY TROY 104

HANSON, Howard
Symphonies Nos 1 to 7 complete
    Seattle Symphony: Gerard Schwartz         DELOS DE 3150
Symphony No.1 (Nordic) in E minor Op.21
    Eastman-Rochester Orchestra: Howard Hanson   MERCURY 432008.2MM
                        BIDDULPH WHL 038
    Seattle Symphony: Gerard Schwartz         DELOS DE 3073
Symphony No.2. (Romantic) Op.30 (1930)
    Eastman-Rochester Orchestra: Howard Hanson   MERCURY 432008.MM
                        BIDDULPH WHL 038
    Jena Symphony: David Montgomery       ARTA NOVA 74321.433062
    Mormon Youth Symphony: Howard Hanson     CITADEL CTD 88110
    San Remo Symphony: Walter Proost         GALLO CD 890
    Seattle Symphony: Gerard Schwartz         DELOS DE 3073
    St Louis Symphony: Leonard Slatkin        ANGEL/EMI CDC 47860
                        CDM 64304
Symphony No.3 in A minor Op.33 (1936–38)
    Boston Symphony: Sergei Koussevitzky      BIDDULPH WHL 044
    Eastman-Rochester Orchestra: Howard Hanson   MERCURY 434302.2
    Seattle Symphony: Gerard Schwartz         DELOS DE 3092
Symphony No.4 (Requiem) Op.34 (1943)
    Jena Philharmonic: David Montgomery      ARTA NOVA 74321.433062
    Seattle Symphony: Gerard Schwartz         DELOS DE 3105
Symphony No.5 (Sinfonia Sacra) Op.43 (1955)

| | |
|---|---|
| Seattle Symphony: Gerard Schwartz | DELOS DE 3130 |
| Symphony No.6 (1967) | |
| Seattle Symphony: Gerard Schwartz | DELOS DE 3092 |
| Westchester Symphony: Siegfried Landau | VOX 116021.2 |
| Symphony No.7 (Sea Symphony) (1977) | |
| Seattle Chorale & Symphony: Gerard Schwartz | DELOS DE 3130 |
| World Youth Orchestra: Howard Hanson | BAY CITIES BCD 1009 |
| | CITADEL CTD 88110 |

HARBISON, John
Symphony No.1 (1984)

| | |
|---|---|
| Boston Symphony: Seiji Osawa | NEW WORLD NW 80331.2 |

Symphony No.2 (1987)

| | |
|---|---|
| San Francisco Symphony: Herbert Blomstedt | DECCA 443.376.2DH |

HARRIS, Roy
Symphony No.1 (1933)

| | |
|---|---|
| Boston Symphony: Sergei Koussevitzky | PEARL GEMM CD 9492 |
| Louisville Orchestra: Jorge Mester | ALBANY AR 012 |

Symphony No.3 (1938)

| | |
|---|---|
| Boston Symphony: Sergei Koussevitzky | PEARL GEMM CD 9492 |
| Dallas Symphony: Eduardo Mata | DORIAN DOR 90170 |
| Detroit Symphony: Neemi Järvi | CHANDOS CHAN 9474 |
| NBC Symphony: Arturo Toscanini | Del ARTE CD DA 9020 |
| New York Philharmonic: Leonard Bernstein | DG 419780.2 |

Symphony No.4 (Folksong) (1940)

| | |
|---|---|
| American Festival Choir & Orchestra: Vladimir Golschmann | |
| | VANGUARD OVC 4076 |

Symphony No.5 (1943/1945)

| | |
|---|---|
| Louisville Orchestra: Robert Whitney | ALBANY AR 012 |

Symphony No.6 (Gettysburg Address) (1944)

| | |
|---|---|
| Pacific Symphony: Keith Clark | ALBANY AR 012.2 |
| Boston Symphony: Serge Koussevitzky | AS DISC 563 |

Symphony No.7 (1951 rev. 1955)

| | |
|---|---|
| Philadelphia Orchestra: Eugene Ormandy | ALBANY TROY 256 |

Symphony No.10 (1968)

| | |
|---|---|
| Dallas Symphony: Eduardo Mata | DORIAN 90170 |

Symphony for band (West Point) (1952)

| | |
|---|---|
| UCLA Wind Ensemble: James Westebrook | BAY CITIES BCD 1008 |

HARRISON, Lou
Symphony on G (1948–61)

| | |
|---|---|
| Royal Philharmonic: Gerhard Samuel | CRI CD 715 |

Symphony No.2 (Elegiac) (1975)

| | |
|---|---|
| American Composers Orchestra: Dennis Russell Davies | MUSIC MASTERS 7021.2 |

Symphony No.3 (1982)

| | |
|---|---|
| Cabrillo Music Festival: Dennis Russell Davies | MUSIC MASTERS 7073.2 |

Last Symphony (Symphony No.4) (1990)

| | |
|---|---|
| California Symphony: B. Jekowsky | DECCA/ARGO |

HARTKE, Stephen
Symphony No.2

| | |
|---|---|
| Riverside Symphony: Rothman | NEW WORLD 80533.2 |

312    *The American Symphony*

HEINRICH, Anthony Philip
Ornithological Combat of Kings Symphony (1847/1856)
   Syracuse Symphony: Christopher Keene      NEW WORLD 80208.2

HELPS, Robert
Symphony (1955)
   Columbia Symphony: Zoltan Roznai      CRI CRI 711

HERRMANN, Bernard
Symphony No.1 (1941)
   National Philharmonic: Bernard Herrmann
      UNICORN KANCHANA UKCD 2063
   Phoenix Symphony: James Sedares      KOCH 3.7135.2HI

HOVHANESS, Alan
Symphony No.1 (Exile) Op.17/2 (1936)
   Seattle Symphony: Gerard Schwartz      DELOS DE 3168
      DE 3700
Symphony No.2 (Mysterious Mountain) Op.132 (1955)
   American Composers Orchestra: Dennis Russell Davies
      MUSIC MASTERS 7021.2C
   Chicago Symphony: Fritz Reiner      RCA 5733.2RC
   Cincinatti Symphony: Jesus Lopez Corbos      TELARC CD 80462
   Dallas Symphony: Andrew Litton      DORIAN DOR 90224
   London Symphony: John Williams      SONY SK 62729
   Seattle Symphony: Gerard Schwartz      DELOS 3157
Symphony No.3 Op.148 (1956)
   Korean Broadcasting System
   Symphony: Vakhtang Jordania      SOUNDSET SR 1004
Symphony No.4 Op.165 (1958)
   Eastman Wind Ensemble: A. Clyde Roller      MERCURY 434.320.2
Symphony No.6 (The Celestial Gate) Op.113 (1959–60)
   I. Fiammighi: Rudolf Werthen      TELARC CD 80392
   London Polyphonia: Alan Hovhaness      CRYSTAL CD 807
   Manhattan Chamber: Richard Auldon Clark      KOCH 37221.2
Symphony No.9 (St Vartan) Op.80 (180) (1960)
   National Philharmonic: Alan Hovhaness      CRYSTAL CD 802
Symphony No.11 (All Men Are Brothers) Op.186 (1960)
   Royal Philharmonic: Alan Hovhaness      CRYSTAL CD 801
Symphony No.17 (Symphony for Metal Instruments) Op.203 (1963)
   Manhattan Chamber: Richard Auldon Clark      KOCH 37289.2
Symphony No.19 (Vishnu) Op.217 (1966)
   Sevan Philharmonic: Alan Hovhaness      CRYSTAL CD 805
Symphony No.20 (Three Journeys to the Holy Mountain) Op.223 (1968)
   excerpt: Ohio State Concert Band: Keith Brion      DELOS DE 3158
Symphony No.21 (Symphony Etchmiadzin) Op.234 (1970)
   Royal Philharmonic: Alan Hovhaness      CRYSTAL CD 804
Symphony No.22 (City of Light) Op.236 (1971)
   Seattle Symphony: Alan Hovhaness      DELOS DE 3137
      DE 3700

Symphony No.24 (Manjun) Op.273 (1973)
   National Philharmonic of London: Alan Hovhaness      CRYSTAL CD 803
Symphony No.25 (Odysseus) Op.275 (1973)

| | |
|---|---|
| London Polyphonia: Alan Hovhaness | CRYSTAL CD 807 |
| Symphony No.29 for wind band Op.289 (1976–77) | |
| Ohio State Concert Band: Christian Lindberg: Keith Brion | DELOS DE 3158 |
| Symphony No.31 Op.294 (1976–77) | |
| North West Sinfonia: Gerard Schwartz | CRYSTAL CD 811 |
| Symphony No.38 Op.314 (1978) | |
| Seattle Symphony: Alan Hovhaness | KOCH 374222 |
| Symphony No.39 Op.321 (1978) | |
| KBS Symphony: Michael Long: Vakhtang Jordania | KOCH 37208.2 |
| Symphony No.46 (To the Green Mountains) Op.347 (1980) | |
| KBS Symphony: Vakhtang Jordania | KOCH 37208.2 |
| Symphony No.49 (Christmas Symphony) Op.356 (1981) | |
| North West Sinfonia: Alan Hovhaness | CRYSTAL CD 811 |
| Symphony No.50 (Mount St Helens) Op.360 (1982) | |
| Seattle Symphony: Gerard Schwartz | |
| Symphony No.53 (Star Dawn) Op.377 (1983) | |
| Ohio State Concert Band: Keith Brion | DELOS DE 3158 |

HUSA, Karel
Symphony No.1 (1963)

| | |
|---|---|
| Prague Symphony: Karel Husa | CRI CD 592 |
| Symphony No.2 (Reflections) (1982–83) | |
| Slovak Radio Symphony: Barry Kolman | MARCO POLO 8.223640 |

IMBRIE, Andrew
Symphony No.3 (1970)

| | |
|---|---|
| London Symphony: Harold Farberman | CRI CD 632 |

INCE, KAMRAN
Symphony No.2 (Fall of Constantinople)

| | |
|---|---|
| Albany Symphony: David Alan Miller | ARGO 455.151.2 |

IVES, Charles
Symphony No.1 (1898)

| | |
|---|---|
| Chicago Symphony: Morton Gould | RCA 74321.292.462 |
| Chicago Symphony: Michael Tilson Thomas | SONY SK 44939 |
| Detroit Symphony: Neemi Järvi | CHANDOS CHAN 9053 |
| New Philharmonia: Harold Farberman | VANGUARD 8615371 |
| Symphony No.2 (1897–1902) | |
| Detroit Symphony: Neemi Järvi | CHANDOS CHAN 9390 |
| New Philharmonia: Harold Farberman | VANGUARD 8615371 |
| New York Philharmonic: Leonard Bernstein | DG 429220.2GH |
| New York Philharmonic: Leonard Bernstein | CBS MK 42407 |
| | SONY SMK 47568 |
| Nuremburg Symphony: Johannes Somary | CLAVES CD 50.9806 |
| Royal Concertgebouw: Michael Tilson Thomas | SONY SK 46440 |
| Symphony No.3 (1901–04) | |
| Academy of St Martins: Neville Marriner | ARGO 417818.2ZH |
| Eastman-Rochester Orchestra: Howard Hanson | MERCURY 432.755.2 |
| New Philharmonia: Harold Farberman | VANGUARD 8615471 |
| New York Philharmonic: Leonard Bernstein | CBS MK 42407 |

|                                                          |                              |
|----------------------------------------------------------|------------------------------|
|                                                          | SMK 47568                    |
| Orpheus Chamber Orchestra                                | DG 439.869.2GH               |
| Royal Concertgebouw: Michael Tilson Thomas               | SONY SK 46440                |
|                                                          | CBS MK 42407                 |
| St Louis Symphony: Leonard Slatkin                       | RCA 09026.61222.2            |
| St Paul Chamber: Dennis Russell Davies                   | PRO ARTE CDD 140             |
|                                                          | PRO ARTE CDS 3429            |

Symphony No.4 (1910–16)
  American Symphony: Leopold Stokowski     SONY MKP 46726
  Boston Symphony: Seiji Osawa     DG 423243.2
  Chicago Symphony: Michael Tilson Thomas     SONY SK 46726
      CBS SK 44939
  Cleveland: Christoph von Dohnanyí     DECCA 443.172.2DH
  London Philharmonic: Jose Serebrier     CHAN ABR 1118*
  New Philharmonia: Harold Farberman     VANGUARD 8615471
Holidays Symphony (1904–13)
  Baltimore Symphony: David Zinman     ARGO 444.860.2
  Chicago Symphony: Michael Tilson Thomas     CBS MK 42381
  Dallas Symphony: Donald Johanos     VOX CDX 5035
      115844.2
      TURNABOUT CD 30371.0012
      ANALOGUE PRODUCTIONS CAPC004
  Leipzig Radio Symphony: Wolf Dieter Hauschild     BERLIN CLASSICS BER 90082BC
  New York Philharmonic: Leonard Bernstein     SONY SMK 60203
Universe Symphony
  Cincinnati Philharmonic: Gerhard Samuel     CENTAUR CRC 2205

JOHNSON, James P.
Harlem Symphony (1932)
  Concordia Orchestra: Marin Alsop     MUSIC MASTERS MM 67140

JONES, Samuel
Symphony No.3 (Palo Duro Canyon) (1992)
  Amarillo Symphony: James Setapen     AMARILLO SYMPHONY No number

JOSTEN, Werner
Symphony in F (1936)
  Polish National Radio: Willian Strickland     CRI CD 597

KELLER, Homer
Symphony No.3 (1956)
  Japan Philharmonic: William Strickland     BAY CITIES BCD1004
      CITADEL CTD 88121

KELLY, Peter
Symphony No.1 (1988)
  Warsaw National Philharmonic: Robert Black
      VIENNA MUSIC MASTERS VMM 3005

KERNIS, Aaron Jay
Symphony in Waves (1989)
  New York Chamber Symphony: Gerard Schwartz           ARGO 436.267.2ZH
Symphony No.2 (1995)
  City of Birmingham Symphony: Hugh Wolff           DECCA 448.900.2

KIEVMAN, Carson
Symphony No.2 (1991)
  Polish National Radio Symphony: Delta David Gier    NEW ALBION NA 081CD

KORF, Anthony
Symphony No.2 (Blue Note) (1987)
  Riverside Symphony: G. Rothman           NEW WORLD NW 383.2

KORN, Peter Jona
Symphony No.1
  Bamberg Symphony: Rudolf Albert           PREMIER PRCD 1058

KORNGOLD, Erich
Symphony in F sharp Op.40 (1950)
  BBC Philharmonic: Sir Edward Downes          CHANDOS CHAN 9171
  London Symphony: André Previn           DG 453436.2
  Munich Philharmonic: Rudolf Kempe     VARESE SARABANDE VSD 5346
  Northwest German Philharmonic: Werner Andreas Albert     CPO 999.146.2
  Philadelphia Orchestra: Franz Welser-Most         EMI CDCS 56169.2

KORTE, Karl
Symphony No.3 (1969)
  Louisville Orchestra; Lawrence Leighton Smith      LOUISVILLE LCD 001

KRENEK, Ernst
Symphony No.1 Op.7 (1921)
  Hannover Radio Philharmonic: Takeo Ukigaya         CPO 999.359.2
Symphony No.2 Op.12 (1922)
  Hannover Orchestra: Takeo Ukigaya          CPO 999.255.2
  Leipzig Gewandhaus: Lothar Zagrosek         DECCA 452.479.2
Symphony No.3 Op.16 (1922)
  Radio Philharmonic Hannover: Takeo Ukigaya         CPO 999.236.2
Symphony No.5 Op.119 (1949)
  Hannover Radio Philharmonic: Takeo Ukigaya         CPO 999.359.2
Symphony for winds and percussion Op.34 (1924–25)
  Berlin Radio: Vinko Globokar          THOROFON CTH 2043

KUPFERMAN, Meyer
Symphony No.2 (Chamber Symphony) (1950)
  Prisma Chamber Players: Harold Farberman        SOUNDSPELLS SP 112
Little Symphony (1952)
  Vienna State Opera: Franz Litschauer        SOUNDSPELLS CD 121
Symphony No.4 (1955)
  Louisville Orchestra: Robert Whitney        SOUNDSPELLS CD 121
Twilight Symphony (No.7) (1974)
  Baja California Orchestra: Eduardo Garcia Barrios    SOUNDSPELLS CD 117
Jazz Symphony (1988)
  Lithuanian Philharmonic: L. Holkmann: R. Fink: J. Domarka SOUNDSPELLS SP 104

LARSEN, Libby
Symphony No.1 (Water Music) (1985)
   Minnesota Orchestra: Sir Neville Marriner     ELEKTRA NONESUCH 79147.2
   London Symphony: Joel Revzen     KOCH
Symphony No.3 (Lyric) (1991–93)
   London Symphony: Joel Revzen     KOCH

LAZAROF, Henri
Symphony No.2 (1990)
   Seattle Symphony: Gerard Schwartz     DELOS DE 3133

LEVY, Frank Ezra
Symphony No.4
   Slovak Radio Symphony: Robert Stankovsky     MASTER MUSICIANS MMC 2021

LEWIS, Robert Hall
Symphony No.2 (1971)
   Royal Philharmonic: Robert Hall Lewis     CRI CD 596
Symphony No.4 (1990)
   Philharmonia: Robert Hall Lewis     NEW WORLD 80444.2

McDONALD, Harl
Symphony No.2 (Rumba) (1934) Rumba movt. only
   Philadelphia: Leopold Stokowski     CALA CACD 0501

McKAY, George
Symphony No.5 (for Seattle) (1950)
   Northwest Symphony: Anthony Spain     ALBANY TROY 184

McKINLEY, William Thomas
Symphony No.3 (1984)
   Warsaw National Philharmonic: Robert Black     MUSIC MASTERS MMC 2003
Symphony No.4 (1985)
   Slovak Radio Symphony: Robert Stankovsky     MASTER MUSICIANS 2034
Symphony No.5 (Irish) (1988)
   Warsaw National Philharmonic: Robert Black
     VIENNA MUSIC MASTERS VMM 3005

McPHEE, Colin
Symphony No.2 (Pastoral) (1957)
   Brooklyn Philharmonic: Dennis Russell Davies
     MUSIC MASTERS MM 01612.67159.2
   Espiriz Orchestra     PAUK CBC

MECHEM, Kirke
Symphony No.1 Op.16 (1959)
   USSR TV and Radio Orchestra: Corrick Brown     RUSSIAN DISCS RDCD 10005
Symphony No.2 Op.29 (1969)
   USSR TV and Radio Orchestra: Corrick Brown     RUSSIAN DISCS RDCD 10005

MENNIN, Peter
Symphony No.3 (1946)
   Seattle Symphony: Gerard Schwartz     DELOS 3164

Symphony No.4 (The Cycle) (1948)
    Camarata Singers and Orchestra: Abraham Kaplan      PHOENIX PCHD 107
Symphony No.5 (1950)
    Albany Symphony: David Allan Miller      ALBANY TROY 260
    Eastman-Rochester Orchestra: Howard Hanson      MERCURY 432755.2
Symphony No.6
    Albany Symphony: David Allan Miller      ALBANY TROY 260
Symphony No.7 (Variations) (1963)
    Chicago Symphony: Jean Martinou      CRI 741
    Seattle Symphony: Gerard Schwartz      DELOS 3164
Symphony No.8 (1973)
    Columbus Symphony: Christian Badea      NEW WORLD NW 371.2
Symphony No.9 (1981)
    Adelaide Symphony: Jose Serebrier      FINNADER 90937.4
    Columbus Symphony: Christian Badea      NEW WORLD NW 371.2

MOORE, Douglas
Symphony in A (1945)
    Japan Philharmonic Symphony: William Strickland      CRI CD 714

MOROSS, Jerome
Symphony No.1 (1942)
    London Symphony: JoAnn Falletta      KOCH 37.188.2

MOSS, Lawrence
Symphonies for brass quintet and chamber orchestra (1977)
    American Camarata: Annapolis Brass Quintet: J. Stephens      AmCam ACR 10305CD

MYERS, Theldon
Symphony (1969)
    Polish Radio Krakov: J.M. Florencio Jnr VIENNA MODERN MASTERS VMM 3019

NANES, Richard
Symphony No.1 in B flat (1984)
    London Philharmonic: Keith Clark      DELFON CDR 1211
Symphony No.2 in B (1984)
    London Philharmonic: Keith Clark      DELFON CDR 1211
Symphony No.3 (1984–85)
    London Philharmonic: Thomas Sanderling      DELFON CDR 4050
Symphony No.4 (1987–88)
    London Philharmonic: Thomas Sanderling      DELFON CDR 4050

NEWMAN, Anthony
Sinfonia No.1 (Of Fallen Heroes) (1991)
    New York Arts Orchestra: Anthony Newman      NEWPORT CLASSICS NCD 60140

OTT, David
Symphony No.2 (1991)
    Grand Rapids Symphony: Catherine Comet      KOSS CLASSICS KC 3301
Symphony No.3 (1992)
    Grand Rapids Symphony: Catherine Comet      KOSS CLASSICS KC 3301

PAINE, John Knowles
Symphony No.1 in C minor Op.23 (1876)
   New York Philharmonic: Zubin Mehta     NEW WORLD NW 374.2
Symphony No.2 in A (In the Spring) Op.34 (1880)
   New York Philharmonic: Zubin Mehta     NEW WORLD NW 350.2

PAULUS, Stephen
Symphony in three movements (Soliloquies) (1986)
   Minnesota Orchestra: Sir Neville Marriner   ELEKTRA NONESUCH 79147.2
Symphony for Strings (1989)
   Atlanta Symphony: Yoel Levi     NEW WORLD NW 363.2

PERSICHETTI, Vincent
Symphony No.5 (Symphony for Strings) Op.61 (1953)
   Philadelphia Orchestra: Riccardo Muti    NEW WORLD NW 370.2
Symphony No.6 for wind ensemble Op.69 (1956)
   Cincinnati College of Music Wind Symphony: Eugene Corporon
             KLAVIER KCD 11047
   Eastman Wind Ensemble: Frederick Fennell   MERCURY 432754.2
Symphony No.8 Op.106 (1967)
   Louisville Orchestra: Jorge Mester    ALBANY TROY 024.2

PICKER, Tobias
Symphony No.2 'Aüssohnüng' (Goethe) (1986)
   Houston Symphony: Leona Mitchell: Sergiu Comissiona
             ELEKTRA NONESUCH 79246.2
PIERCE, Alexandra
Symphony No.2 (Dances on the Face of the Deep) Op.74 (1988)
   Koszalin State Philharmonic: Szymon Kawalla
          VIENNA MUSIC MASTERS VMM 3029

PINKHAM, Daniel
Symphony No.3 (1985)
   London Symphony: James Sedares     KOCH 371.792
Symphony No.4 (1990)
   London Symphony: James Sedares     KOCH 371.792

PISTON, Walter
Symphony No.1 (1937)
   Louisville Orchestra: Jorge Mester    ALBANY TROY 044
Symphony No.2 (1944)
   Boston Symphony: Michael Tilson Thomas   DG 429860.2GC
   Seattle Symphony: Gerard Schwartz    DELOS DE 3074
Symphony No.4 (1950)
   Philadelphia Orchestra: Eugene Ormandy   ALBANY TROY 256
   Seattle Symphony: Gerard Schwartz    DELOS DE 3106
Symphony No.5 (1954)
   Louisville Orchestra: Robert Whitney    ALBANY AR 011
Symphony No.6 (1955)
   St Louis Symphony: Leonard Slatkin    RCA 60798.2RC
   Seattle Symphony: Gerard Schwartz    DELOS DE 3074
Symphony No.7 (1961)
   Louisville Orchestra: Jorge Mester    ALBANY AR 011

Symphony No.8 (1965)
    Louisville Orchestra: Jorge Mester               ALBANY AR 011

READ, Gardner
Sinfonia di Chiesa Op.61b (1969)
    Atlantic Brass Quintet: Leonard Raver       NORTHEASTERN NR 239.CD

REED, Alfred
Symphony No.2 (1978)
    Artistica Bunol: Henrie Adams        WORLD WIND WWM 500.008
Symphony No.3 (1988)
    Artistica Bunol: Henrie Adams        WORLD WIND WWM 500.008
Symphony No.4 (1992)
    Artistica Bunol: Henrie Adams        WORLD WIND WWM 500.008
Symphony No.5 (1995)
    Senzoku Gakuen Symphonic Winds       WALKING FROG WFR 140

REED, H. Owen
La Fiesta Mexicana: Folk song symphony (1948)
    Cincinnati Wind Symphony: Eugene Corporon     KLAVIER KCD 11048
    Dallas Symphonic Winds: Howard Dunn      REFERENCE RRCD 38

RIEGGER, Wallingford
Symphony No.3 Op.42 (1948)
    Eastman-Rochester Orchestra: Howard Hanson     CRI CD 572

RIETI, Vittorio
Symphony No.4 (Sinfonia Tripartita) (1944)
    NBC Symphony: Arturo Toscanini     TOSCANINI SOCIETY ATCD 100

ROREM, Ned
Symphony No.3 (1957–58)
    Utah Symphony: Maurice Abravanel        VOX 116021.2
String Symphony (1985)
    Atlanta Symphony: Robert Shaw        NEW WORLD 353.2

ROUSE, Christopher
Symphony No.1 (1986)
    Baltimore Symphony: David Zinman   MEET THE COMPOSER 79230.2
Symphony No.2 (1994)
    Houston Symphony: Christoph Eschenbach     TELARC 80452

RÓZSA, Miklós
Symphony Op.6a (1930, rev. 1990)
    New Zealand Symphony: James Sedares       KOCH 37244.2

SCARMOLIN, Anthony Louis
Symphony No.1 in E minor Op.154 (1937)
    Slovak Radio Symphony: Joel Eric Suben     NEW WORLD 80502.2
Symphony No.2 Op.200 (1946)
    Slovak Radio Symphony: Joel Eric Suben     NEW WORLD 80502.2

Symphony No.3 (Sinfonia Brevis) (1952)
Polish National Radio: Joel Eric Suben                     NEW WORLD 80502.2

SCHULLER, Gunther
Symphony for brass and percussion (1950)
Summit Brass                                               SUMMIT DCD 127

SCHUMAN, William
Symphony No.3 (1941)
New York Philharmonic: Leonard Bernstein                   DG 419780.2GH
New York Philharmonic: Leonard Bernstein                   SONY SMK 63163
Symphony No.4 (1941)
Louisville Orchestra: Jorge Mester                         ALBANY TROY 027.2
Symphony No.5 (Symphony for Strings) (1943)
Seattle Symphony: Gerard Schwartz                          DELOS DE 3115
New York Philharmonic: Leonard Bernstein                   SONY SMK 63163
Symphony No.6
Philadelphia Orchestra: Eugene Ormandy                     ALBANY TROY 256
Symphony No.7 (1960)
Pittsburgh Symphony: Lorin Maazel                          NEW WORLD NW 348.2
Utah Symphony: Maurice Abravanel                           VOX 116021.2
Symphony No.8 (1961–62)
New York Philharmonic: Leonard Bernstein                   SONY SMK 63163
Symphony No.10 (American Muse) (1975)
St Louis Symphony: Leonard Slatkin                         RCA 09026. 61282.2

SESSIONS, Roger
Symphony No.1 (1927)
Japan Philharmonic: Akeo Watanabe                          CRI CD 573
Symphony No.2 (1946)
New York Philharmonic: Dmitri Mitropoulos                  CRI CD 573
San Francisco Symphony: Herbert Blomstedt                  DECCA 443.376.2DH
Symphony No.3 (1957)
Royal Philharmonic: Igor Buketoff                          CRI CD 573
Symphony No.4 (1958)
Columbus Symphony: Christian Badea                         NEW WORLD NW 345.2
Symphony No.5 (1964)
Columbus Symphony: Christian Badea                         NEW WORLD NW 345.2
Symphony No.6 (1966)
ACO: Dennis Russell Davies                                 ARGO 444.519.2
Symphony No.7 (1967)
ACO: Dennis Russell Davies                                 ARGO 444.519.2
Symphony No.9 (1978)
ACO: Dennis Russell Davies                                 ARGO 444.519.2

SHAPERO, Harold
Symphony for Classical Orchestra (1947)
Los Angeles Philharmonic: André Previn                     NEW WORLD NW 372.2

SIEGMEISTER, Elie
Symphony No.3 (1956–57)
Olso Philharmonic: Elie Siegmeister                        CITADEL CTD 88121

STILL, William Grant
Symphony No.1 (Afro American) (1930)
  Cincinatti Philharmonic: Jindong Cai            CENTAUR CRC 2331
  Detroit Symphony: Neemi Järvi            CHANDOS CHAN 9154
  Royal Philharmonic: Karl Krueger     LIBRARY OF CONGRESS OMP 106
Symphony No.2 (Song of a New Race) (1937)
  Detroit Symphony: Neemi Järvi (1937)        CHANDOS CHAN 9226
Symphony No.3 (Sunday Symphony) (1958)
  North Arkansas Symphony: Carleton R. Woods      CAMBRIA CD 1060

SWACK, Irwin
Symphony No.2 in one movement
  Polish National Radio: David Amos
          CONTEMPORARY RECORD SOCIETY CRS CD 9459


TCHEREPNIN, Alexander
Symphony No.3 (Chinese Symphony) Op.83 (1952–56)
  Rheinland-Pfalz State Philharmonic: P. Gulke     THOROPHON CTH 2021
Symphony No.4 Op.91 (1957)
  Czech-Slovak Philharmonic: Wing-Sie Yip       MARCO POLO 8.223380

THOMPSON, Randall
Symphony No.1 (1931)
  New Zealand Symphony: James Sedares          KOCH 37181.2
                                        73413.2

Symphony No.2 (1930–31)
  Detroit Symphony: Neemi Järvi            CHANDOS CHAN 9439
  New Zealand Symphony: Andrew Schenck          KOCH 3.7074.2
                                        374132
  Vienna Symphony: Dean Dixon           BAY CITIES BCD 1007
Symphony No.3 (1947–49)
  New Zealand Symphony: Andrew Schenck          KOCH 3.7074.2
                                        374132

THOMSON, Virgil
Symphony on a Hymn Tune (1926–28)
  Eastman-Rochester Orchestra: Howard Hanson       MERCURY 434310.2
  Monednock Festival Orchestra: James Bolle         ALBANY ARO 017.2
Symphony No.2 (1930, rev. 1941)
  Monednock Festival Orchestra: James Bolle         ALBANY ARO 017.2
Symphony No.3 (1972)
  New Hampshire Symphony: James Bolle       BAY CITIES BCD 1003

THORNE, Francis
Symphony No.5 (1984)
  American Composers Orchestra: Dennis Russell Davies       CRI CD 552
Symphony No.6 for strings (1992)
  Cleveland Chamber: Edwin London           ALBANY TROY 208
Symphony No.7 (1994)
  Albany Symphony: David Allan Miller          ALBANY TROY 244

TILLIS, Frederick
Niger Symphony (1975)
  Royal Philharmonic: Paul Freeman       MASTERSOUND DFCD.1.015

TOCH, Ernest
Symphony No.3 Op.75 (1955)
   Stokowski Orchestra: Leopold Stokowski               EMI CDMS 65868.2
Symphony No.5 (1963)
   Berlin Symphony: Alun Francis                       CPO 999389.2
   Louisville Orchestra: Robert Whitney           ALBANY TROY 021.2
Symphony No.6 (1963)
   Berlin Symphony: Alun Francis                       CPO 999389.2
Symphony No.7 (1964)
   Berlin Symphony: Alun Francis                       CPO 999389.2

TRIMBLE, Lester
Symphony in two movements (1951)
   Japanese Philharmonic: Akeo Watanabe           CRI CD 187
Symphony No.3 (Tricentennial) (1985–86)
   Albany Symphony: Ildiko Hegyi                      CRI CD 555

VAN APPELDORN, Mary Jeanne
Symphony No.4 (Prayer) (1985–87)
   The Barton Workshop                     ETCETERA KTC 1170

VAN VACTOR, David
Symphony No.1 in D (1937)
   Hessian Radio Symphony: David Van Vactor        CRI CD 702
Symphony No.3 (1958)
   Hessian Radio Symphony: David Van Vactor        CRI CD 702

VINCENT, John
Symphony in D (1954 rev. 1956)
   Philadelphia Orchestra: Eugene Ormandy      ALBANY TROY 250

WALDROP, Gideon
Symphony No.1 (1951)
   Sofia Philharmonic: R. Georgescu               GEGA GD 155

WARD, Robert
Symphony No.2 (1947)
   Japanese Philharmonic: William Strickland     BAY CITIES BCD 1001
Symphony No.3 (1956)
   Iceland Symphony: Igor Buketoff            BAY CITIES BCD 1001
Symphony No.4 (1958)
   North Carolina Symphony: Gerhardt Zimmermann    ALBANY AR 001
Symphony No.6 (1988)
   St Stephen's Chamber; Lorenzo Muti        BAY CITIES BCD 1015

WARREN, Elinor Remick
Symphony in one movement (1971)
   Krakow Radio and Television Symphony: Szymon Kawalla    CAMBRIA CD 1042

WASHBURN, Robert
Symphony for band (1963)
   Keystone Wind Ensemble: Jack Stamp          CITADEL CTD 88108

WAYNE, Hayden
Symphony No.4 (Funk)
   Brno State Philharmonic: Leos Swarowsky        NEW MILLENIUM 61596

WIGGLESWORTH, Frank
Symphony No.1 (1957)
   Vienna Orchestra: Kurt Adler             CRI CD 733

WILLIAMS, James Kimo
Symphony for the Sons of Nam
   Chicago Sinfonietta: Paul Freeman          INTERSOUND 3534

WILSON, Olly
Sinfonia (1983–84)
   Boston Symphony: Seija Osawa           NEW WORLD 80331.2

WINSTIN, Robert Ian
Symphony No.2 (Symphony for Strings)
   Illinois Chamber: S.E. Squires            ERM CCC 6659
Symphony No.4 (The Circus)
   Virtual Orchestra: Robert Ian Winstin         ERM CCC 6660

WOLPE, Stefan
Symphony for orchestra (1956, rev. 1964)
   Orchestra of the 20th Century; Anton Weisberg       CRI CD 676
Symphony No.1 (1956 rev. 1964)
   North German Radio Symphony: Johannes Kalitzke
               ARTE NOVA CLASSICS 74321.46508.2


YARDUMIAN, Richard
Symphony No.2 (Book of Psalms) (1947/1964)
   Utah Symphony: Lili Chookasian: Varujan Kojian     PHOENIX PHCD 112

ZWILICH, Ellen Taafe
Chamber Symphony (1979)
   Boston Musica Viva: Richard Pittman           CRI CRI 621
Symphony No.1 (Three Movements for Orchestra) (1982)
   Indianapolis Symphony: John Nelson         NEW WORLD 336.2
Symphony No.2 (Cello) (1985)
   Louisville Orchestra: Lawrence Leighton Smith
          FIRST EDITION RECORDINGS LCD 002
Symphony No.3 (1992)
   Louisville Orchestra: James Sedares           KOCH 37278.2

# Bibliography

## General

E. Ruth Anderson (1976) *Contemporary American Composers: A Biographical Dictionary*, G.K. Hall: Boston, MA.

William Austin (1966) *Music in the 20th Century*, W.W. Norton: New York.

Neil Butterworth (1984) *A Dictionary of American Composers*, Garland Publishing: NY.

Gilbert Chase (1966) *America's Music*, McGraw Hill: NY.

Gilbert Chase (ed.) (1969) *The American Composer Speaks*, Louisiana State University Press: Baton Rouge.

Aaron Copland (1960) *On Music*, Andre Deutsch: London.

Aaron Copland (1968) *The New Music 1900–1960*, MacDonald: London.

Henry Cowell (ed.) (1933) *American Composers on American Music*, Stanford University Press: Stanford University Press: Stanford, CA.

Louis C. Elson (1904: rev. 1915) *The History of Music in America*, Macmillan: NY.

David Ewen (1942) *Music Comes to America*, Thomas Crowell: NY.

David Ewen (1982) *American Composers*, Robert Hale: London.

*Edwin A. Fleisher Collection; A Cumulative Catalog*, G.K. Hall: Boston, MA. (1979).

*Grove's Dictionary of American Music* (1986), Macmillan: London and NY.

H. Wiley Hitchcock (1974) *Music in the United States*, 2nd ed., Prentice Hall: Englewood Cliffs, NJ.

H. Wiley Hitchcock and Stanley Sadie (eds) (1986) *The New Grove Dictionary of American Music*, Macmillan: London and NY.

John Tasker Howard (1954) *Our American Music*, 3rd ed., Thomas Crowell: NY.

Robert Hughes (1900) *Contemporary American Composers*, L.C. Page: Boston.

Henry Charles Lehee (1922, repr. 1970) *Annals of Music in America*, Books for Libraries Press: Freeport, NY.

Alan Howard Levy (1983) *Musical Nationalism: American Composers' Search for Identity*, Greenwood Press: Westport, CT.

Wilfred Mellers (1964) *Music in a New Found Land*, Barrie and Rockcliff: London; 2nd ed. 1982, Faber: London.

W.T. Marrocco and H. Gleason (1964) *Music in America*, W.W. Norton: NY.

Jogn Rockwell (ed.) (1983) *All American Music*, Alfred A Knopf: NY.

Lazare Saminsky (1949) *Living Music of the Americas*, Howell, Soskin and Crown Publishers: NY.

Robert Simpson (ed.) (1967) *The Symphony*, Volume 2, Penguin Books: Harmondsworth.

Barbara L. Tischler (1986) *An American Music: a Search for an American Musical Identity*, Oxford University Press: NY.

Taylor, Deems (1945) *Of Men and Music*, Simon & Schuster: NY.

Virgil Thomson (1971) *American Music Since 1900*, Weidenfeld and Nicholson: London.

John Vinton (ed.) (1974) *Dictionary of 20th Century Music*, Thames and Hudson: London.

Barbara Zuck (1980) *A History of Musical Americanism*, UMI Research Press: Ann Arbor: MI.

## Composers

### George Antheil

George Antheil (1945) *Bad Boy of Music*, Doubleday: Garden City, NY.

L. Whitesitt (1983) *The Life and Music of George Antheil 1900–1959*, Ann Arbor: MI.

### Samuel Barber

Russell Edward Friedewald (1957) A Formal and Stylistic Analysis of the Published Music of Samuel Barber, PhD Thesis: Iowa State University.

'The Composing Composer: Samuel Barber', *ASCAP Today*, Autumn 1968, pp.4–7.

D.A. Hennessee (1985) *Samuel Barber: A Bibliography*, Greenwood Press: Westport, CT.

Barbara Heyman (1992) *Samuel Barber: American Composer and His Music*, OUP: NY.

### Leonard Bernstein

Humphrey Burton (1994) *Leonard Bernstein*, Faber & Faber: London.

### Gordon Binkerd

R. Schalkelford (1975) 'The Music of Gordon Binkerd', *Tempo* No. 114, September, pp.2–3.

### George W. Chadwick

Victor Fell Yellin (1990) *Chadwick, Yankee Composer*, Washington DC.

### Aaron Copland

Vivian Perlis and Aaron Copland (1984) *Copland 1900 Through 1942*, Faber: London.

Vivian Perlis (1989) *Copland Since 1943*, St Martin's Press: NY.

**Paul Creston**

Henry Cowell (1951) 'Creston's Symphony No.3', *Music Quarterly*, XXXVII.

W. Simmons, (1976) 'Paul Creston: Maintaining a Middle Course', *Musical Journal*, XXXIV/10.

**Antonín Dvořák**

John C. Tibbetts (ed.) (1993), *Dvořák in America*, Amadeus Press: Portland, OR.

**Howard Hanson**

H. Gleason and W. Becker (1981) *Howard Hanson: 20th Century American Composers: Music Literature Outlines*, Bloomington: IN.

Ruth Watanabe (1984) *The Music of Howard Hanson*, Rochester: NY.

**Roy Harris**

D. Stehman (1973) 'The Symphonies of Roy Harris: An Analysis of Linear Materials and of Related Works', Dissertation, University of Southern California.

D. Stehman (1984) *Roy Harris: An American Musical Pioneer*, Boston.

**Lou Harrison**

V. Rathbun (1976) Lou Harrison and his Music, Thesis, San José State University.

**Anthony Philip Heinrich**

W.T. Upton (1939, rev. 1967) *Anthony Philip Heinrich: a 19th Century Composer in America*, Columbia University Press: NY.

W.R. Maunt (1973) The Symphonies of Anthony Philip Heinrich on American Themes, Dissertation, Indiana University.

**Charles Ives**

Bernard Herrmann (1944/5) 'Four Symphonies of Charles Ives', *Modern Music*, XXII.

Charles Ives, ed. John Kilpatrick (1972) *Memos*, W.W. Norton: NY.

J.V. Badolato 'The Four Symphonies of Charles Ives: A Critical, Analytical Study of the Musical Style of Charles Ives', Dissertation, Catholic University of America.

**John Knowles Paine**

J.C. Schmidt (1980) *The Life and Works of John Knowles Paine*, University of Michigan Press, Ann Arbor: MI.

**Walter Piston**

H.N. Lindenfield (1975) 'Three Symphonies of Walter Piston: an Analysis', Dissertation, Cornell University.

H. Gleason and W. Becker (1981) *Walter Piston: 20th Century American Composers: Music Literature Outlines*, Bloomington: IN.

H. Pollack (1981) *Walter Piston*, Ann Arbor: MI.

**Wallingford Riegger**

H. Gleason and W. Becker (1981) *Wallingford Riegger: 20th Century American Composers*, Bloomington: IN.

**William Schuman**

Flora Rheta Schreiber and Vincent Persichetti (1954) *William Schuman*, G. Schirmer: NY.

Christopher Rouse (1980) *William Schuman Documentary*, Theodore Presser & G. Schirmer: NY.

H. Gleason and W. Becker (1981) *William Schuman: 20th Century American Composers: Music Literature Outlines*, Bloomington: IN.

**Roger Sessions**

Roger Sessions (1940) 'On the American Future', *Modern Music*, XVII/2, Jan/Feb, p.73.

Andrew Imbrie (1972) 'The Symphonies of Roger Sessions', *Tempo*, No.103.

Edward Cone (ed.) (1979) *Roger Sessions on Music*, Princeton University Press.

H. Gleason and W. Becker (1981) *Roger Sessions: 20th Century American Composers: Music Literature Outlines*, Bloomington: IN.

Andrea Olmstead (1984) 'Roger Sessions' Ninth Symphony', *Tempo*, No.133.

**Virgil Thomson**

Virgil Thomson (1966) *Virgil Thomson*, Alfred Knopf: NY.

# Index